Policing the European Union

CLARENDON STUDIES IN CRIMINOLOGY

Published under the auspices of the Institute of Criminology, University of Cambridge, the Mannheim Centre, London School of Economics, and the Centre for Criminological Research, University of Oxford

GENERAL EDITOR: ROGER HOOD (University of Oxford)

EDITORS: ANTHONY BOTTOMS and TREVOR BENNETT
(University of Cambridge)

DAVID DOWNES and PAUL ROCK
(London School of Economics)

NICOLA LACEY and ANDREW SANDERS
(University of Oxford)

Other titles in this series:

Policing the European Union

Malcolm Anderson
Monica den Boer
Peter Cullen
William Gilmore
Charles Raab
Neil Walker

CLARENDON PRESS · OXFORD

*This book has been printed digitally and produced in a standard specification
in order to ensure its continuing availability*

OXFORD
UNIVERSITY PRESS

Great Clarendon Street, Oxford OX2 6DP

Oxford University Press is a department of the University of Oxford.
It furthers the University's objective of excellence in research, scholarship,
and education by publishing worldwide in

Oxford New York

Auckland Bangkok Buenos Aires Cape Town Chennai
Dar es Salaam Delhi Hong Kong Istanbul Karachi Kolkata
Kuala Lumpur Madrid Melbourne Mexico City Mumbai Nairobi
São Paulo Shanghai Taipei Tokyo Toronto

Oxford is a registered trade mark of Oxford University Press
in the UK and in certain other countries

Published in the United States
by Oxford University Press Inc., New York

Malcolm Anderson, Monica den Boer, Peter Cullen, William Gilmore, Charles Raab and Neil
Walker 1995

The moral rights of the author have been asserted
Database right Oxford University Press (maker)

Reprinted 2003

ISBN 0-19-825965-4

General Editor's Introduction

Clarendon Studies in Criminology, the successor to Cambridge Studies in Criminology, which was founded by Leon Radzinowicz and J.W.C. Turner more than fifty years ago, aims to provide a forum for outstanding work in criminology, criminal justice, penology and the wider field of deviant behaviour. It is edited under the auspices of three criminological centres: the Cambridge Institute of Criminology, the Mannheim Centre for Criminology and Criminal Justice at the London School of Economics, and the Oxford Centre for Criminological Research.

Policing the European Union is the sixth volume to appear in this new series, and the second to deal with aspects of policing. It breaks new ground in a number of ways, most notably by approaching its subject matter from the perspective of political science. Economic and political co-operation between Member States of the European Union and the development of a 'border-less Europe' has naturally fueled fears that crime (especially organised crime) will spread across national boundaries and become increasingly immune to efforts of the police and other law enforcement agencies to control it. This is not only because countries are policed in different ways but also because each have, to some degree, their own definitions of crime and the 'crime problem', separate criminal laws and procedures, systems of criminal justice, and forms of political accountability. Professor Anderson and his colleagues thoroughly explore the ramifications of this diversity—conceptual, theoretical, political, administrative, and practical—for the development of an effective system of European police co-operation.

What makes their inquiry and discussion particularly valuable is that it is based on a wide range of sources drawn from many member states of the European Union: legal texts, parliamentary and governmental debates and inquiries, documents produced by the main organisations and pressure groups, newspapers and journals. All this is supplemented in a subtle way by insights gained from interviews with over a hundred senior officials from all States of the Union.

The authors begin, wisely, by defining the nature of the problem which police co-operation is intended to address—namely the concept of 'Euro-crime', its dimensions and various manifestations. They then proceed to offer a wealth of information about, and analyses of, European police institutions and the political, legal (including national and international law), and organisational contexts within which they operate. The complexity of the picture is evident, the prospects daunting. In bringing together, in such a thorough, yet sufficiently concise, way a wealth of scattered materials and opinions, and in identifying the emerging patterns and problems, the authors will have opened up a new field of study to many readers.

In welcoming this work to the *Series*, the editors are confident that it will be widely read and referred to not only in this country and throughout Europe, but in many other parts of the world where finding an appropriate response to criminal activity which crosses national boundaries has become a matter of great concern.

Roger Hood
Oxford, September 1995

Contents

Glossary

ACPO	Association of Chief Police Officers
AMSS	Automated Message Switch System
ASF	Automated Search Facility
ASS	Automated Switch System
BGS	*BundesGrundgesetz*
BKA	*Bundeskriminalamt*
BND	*Bundesnachrichtendienst* (German State Security Service)
BRD	*Bundesrepublik Deutschland*
BvD	*Binnenlandse Veiligheidsdienst* (Dutch State Security Service)
CAP	Common Agricultural Policy
CCE	Continuing Criminal Enterprise
CFSP	Common Foreign and Security Policy
CIPC	Commission Internationale de Police Criminelle
CIREA	Centre for Information, Discussion and Exchange on Asylum
CIREFI	Centre for Information, Discussion and Exchange on the Crossing of Borders and Immigration
CIS	Customs Information System
CMLR	Common Market Law Review
CoE	Council of Europe
COREPER	Committee of Permanent Representatives
COT	Computer Organic Tracer
CRI	*Divisie Centrale Recherche Informatie* (Dutch Central Criminal Intelligence Service)
DEA	Drug Enforcement Administration
DIA	*Direzione Investigazione Anti-mafia* (Anti-Mafia Investigation Directorate)
DICILEC	*Direction Centrale de la Lutte contre l'Immigration et le Travail Clandestin* (Central Directorate for the Fight against Illegal Immigration and Employment)
DNA	Deoxyribonucleic Acid
EC	European Community

ECHR	European Convention of Human Rights
ECR	European Court Reports
ECHR	European Convention for the Protection of Human Rights and Fundamental Freedoms
ECJ	European Court of Justice
ECPR	European Consortium for Political Research
ECSA	European Communities Studies Association
ECU	European Currency Unit
EDIU	European Drugs Intelligence Unit
EDU	European Drugs Unit
EEA	European Economic Area
EEC	European Economic Community
EFTA	Economic Free Trade Association
EHRR	European Human Rights Reports
EIS	European Information System
EP	European Parliament
EPC	European Political Co-operation
ETA	*Euskadi Ta Askatasuna* (Basque Separatist Movement)
EU	European Union
Europol	European Police Office
FBI	Federal Bureau of Investigation
GDR	German Democratic Republic
GERN	*Groupe Européen de Recherche sur les Normatives*
GCHQ	Government Communications Headquarters
HED	Hydrogenous Explosive Detector
HM	Her Majesty's
IAPC	International Association of Chiefs of Police
ICPC	International Criminal Police Commission
ICPO	International Criminal Police Organization
ID	Identity
IHESI	*Institut des Hautes Etudes de la Sécurité Intérieure*
INCB	International Narcotics Control Board
INS	Immigration and Naturalization Service
Interpol	International Criminal Police Organization
IRCA	Immigration and Refugee Control Act
IRS	Inland Revenue Service
JCMS	Journal of Common Market Studies
JCWG	Judicial Co-operation Working Group
JHA	Justice and Home Affairs
KGB	'State Security Police of the USSR'

KLPD	*Korps Landelijke Politie Dienst* (National Dutch Police Service)
LSD	Lysergic Acid Diethylamide
MAG	Mutual Assistance Group (for Customs Co-operation)
MEP	Member of the European Parliament
MI5	Military Intelligence [Unit 5]
MI6	Military Intelligence [Unit 6]
MP	Member of Parliament
NATO	North Atlantic Treaty Organization
NCB	National Central Bureau
NCIS	National Criminal Intelligence Service
NDIU	National Drugs Intelligence Unit
NJW	*Neue Juristische Wochenschrift*
NRC	*Nieuwe Rotterdamse Courant*
OCRGDF	*Office Central de Répression contre la Grande Délinquance Financière*
OECD	Organization for Economic Co-operation and Development
OJ(E)C	Official Journal of the European Communities
OrgKG	*Gesetz zur Bekämpfung des illegalen Rauschgifthandels und anderer Erscheinungsformen der Organisierten Kriminalität* (Drug Trafficking and Organized Crime Control Act)
PAF	*Police de l'Air et des Frontières*
PIRA	Provisional Irish Republican Army
PWGOT	Police Working Group on Terrorism
SEA	Single European Act
SEM	Single European Market
SIRENE	Supplementary Information Request at the National Entry
SIS	Schengen Information System
TEU	Treaty on European Union ('Maastricht Treaty')
TNA	Thermal Neutron Activation
Trevi	Anti-terrorist group of EPC
UCLAF	*Unité de la Coordination de la Lutte Anti-Fraude* (Co-ordination Unit for the Fight against Fraud)
UN	United Nations
UNICRI	United Nations Interregional Crime and Justice Research Institute
VAT	Value Added Tax

VIP	Very Important Person
WEU	West European Union
WG	Working Group
XTC	Ecstasy Drug

Acknowledgements

The authors are grateful to the Economic and Social Research Council (Grant No. R000 23 2639) for providing us with financial support for a three-year research project entitled 'A System of European Police Co-operation after 1992', supplemented by the Jean Monnet Project of the European Community and the Nuffield Foundation.

The University of Edinburgh and the Netherlands Institute for the Study of Criminality and Law Enforcement (NISCALE) in Leiden offered us invaluable support in terms of time and facilities. We are grateful to those secretaries, librarians and computing officers who helped us out whenever we needed their assistance.

Interviews with senior police officers and public officials in the former twelve (prior to the 1995 expansion) Member States of the European Union (EU), Austria, Hungary, Norway, Sweden and the United States have been crucial in developing our understanding of European law enforcement co-operation. Our interviewees gave us a wealth of information and personal judgments, and provided us with key references and documents. Access to persons and papers would not have been possible without the co-operation of a large number of institutions. We would like to thank the following organizations and institutions.

In the UK, the Home Office, HM Customs and Excise, the National Criminal Intelligence Service, the London Metropolitan Police, Kent County Constabulary, Sussex Constabulary, the Association of Chief Police Officers, the Association of Chief Police Officers (Scotland), the Scottish Crime Squad, the Scottish Police College, Lothian and Borders Police, Strathclyde Police, Grampian Police, HM Inspectorate of Constabulary, and the Office of the Data Protection Registrar.

In France, the Ministry of Interior (*Police Judiciaire*), the *Service Technique de Coopération Internationale de Police*, the *Unité de Coordination de la Lutte Anti-Terroriste*, OCRGDF, and the *Institut des Hautes Études de la Securité Intérieure*.

In the Federal Republic of Germany, the Federal Ministry of

Interior, the *Bundeskriminalamt*, the *Landeskriminalämter* in Saarbrücken and Stuttgart, and the *Polizeiführungsakademie*.

In the Netherlands, the Ministry of Justice, the Ministry of Interior, the *Centrale Recherche Informatiedienst* (CRI), the *Koninklijke Marechaussee*, the *Nederlandse Politie Academie* (NPA), the *Politiestudiecentrum*, Police Headquarters at Maastricht, the *Fiscale Inlichtingen en Informatiedienst* (FIOD), the *Registratiekamer*, Eurocard, and the Europol Drugs Unit.

In Belgium, the *Gendarmerie* Headquarters of West and East Flanders and the National Gendarmerie Headquarters in Brussels.

In Denmark, the Ministry of Interior and Interpol National Central Bureau.

In Ireland, the Garda Headquarters and the Department of Justice.

In Italy, the *Dipartimento di Pubblica Sicurezza* (Interpol National Central Bureau, Central Anti-Drugs Directorate, Central Anti-Terrorist Directorate, Road, Rail, Border and Postal Police) the Ministry of Foreign Affairs and the *Scuola di perfezionamento di polizia*.

In Luxembourg, the *Service de Police Judiciaire*.

In Portugal, the Ministry of the Interior (Foreigners and Frontiers Service, the Immigration Service, the Judicial Police, Press and Public Relations, and the Inspectorate).

In Spain, the Ministry of Interior, the *Guardia Civil* and the *Policia Nacional*.

In Greece, the Ministry of Public Order (International Relations Division, Anti-terrorist Unit, Public Security Division) and the Ministry of Transport (Maritime Police).

The United States Information Agency (London and Washington, DC) and the Consulate-General of the United States in Edinburgh, who generously arranged for Peter Cullen to visit seven cities in the United States and the Detroit-Canada Tunnel on the Canadian border under the auspices of the Agency's International Visitor Programme. Interviews and visits were conducted with the Department of Justice, the US Customs Service, the US Congress (House Committee on the Judiciary's sub-committee on international law, immigration and refugees), the Immigration and Naturalization Service, the Federal Bureau of Investigation, the Drug Enforcement Administration, the US Border Patrol, various police forces and organizations, federal prosecutors' offices and academic and research institutions with an interest in police matters. Thanks go to the organizers, sponsors and hosts as well as all interviewees.

In Sweden, the Foreign Office and the Swedish National Police College (*Polishögskolan*); in Hungary, the Judicial Police; in Norway, the Ministry of Justice.

In Brussels, the *Unité de la Coordination de la Lutte Anti-Fraude,* the European Commission, the Civil Liberties and Internal Affairs Committee of the European Parliament, the Schengen Secretariat and the Customs Cooperation Council; in Lyon, the General Secretariat and the European Secretariat of Interpol; in Strasbourg, the Directorate of Legal Affairs of the Council of Europe; in Vienna, the United Nations International Drug Control Programme; and in London, the Legal and Constitutional Affairs Division of the Commonwealth Secretariat.

International conferences and networks have been invaluable in the development and criticism of our research. We have benefited greatly from the intellectual exchanges with many academic colleagues, particularly those at the University of Southampton, the Centre for the Study of Public Order at the University of Leicester, the Europa Institute of the University of Edinburgh, the Institute of Political Sciences in Paris, the European University Institute in Florence, the Free University of Berlin, the Max Planck Institute in Freiburg i. Breisgau, the Catholic University of Louvain, the Norwegian School of Management in Oslo, the Free University of Amsterdam and the College of Europe in Bruges. The European Consortium of Political Research twice provided the opportunity for in-depth discussion with academic colleagues. Similarly, we have developed significant insights from our discussions with policy-makers and law enforcement officials at a number of gatherings including the annual Oxford Conference on International White Collar Crime.

Our respective partners, families and friends have had to endure our absence when we were travelling and writing; we are grateful for their warm encouragement and support. Finally, the authors would like to thank each other for the exchange of information and ideas, and for a stimulating and enjoyable collaboration. We have learnt a great deal from each other's expertise in a challenging interdisciplinary enterprise.

Edinburgh/Leiden
March 1995

Introduction

Co-operation over law enforcement in Europe has been on the international agenda for more than a century. The problems addressed at first were of a relatively small scale, as they concerned smugglers, itinerants and political anarchists. But improved means of transport and communication significantly widened the scope of criminal activities and of law enforcement initiatives. Although public concern about international terrorism has weakened somewhat since the 1980s, general alarm about organized crime, drug-trafficking and illegal immigration now pervades sections of all West European societies. The governments of the West European states have been under increasing pressure to design an international co-operative machinery through which (organized) cross-border crime could be combated effectively and efficiently. The European Community (EC) came to be thought of as a suitable vehicle for the various international law enforcement initiatives. This perception was reinforced by the prospect of abolition of internal border controls.

This book analyses the development of a police facility for the European Union (EU) and the establishment of new forms of law enforcement co-operation for a 'borderless Europe'. Although the problems associated with this development appear at first sight to be technical and administrative, closer examination shows that it lies at the very heart of the process of European integration and concerns crucial dimensions of state sovereignty. The permanent alliance and the integrated command structure of NATO, established in the post-1945 period, represented a remarkable shift away from the unfettered independence of state action in the military realm. Stable and institutionalized police co-operation, which is now emerging, offers the medium-to-long-term prospect of an equivalent change in the authority of the state in the domain of internal security. Important issues concerning the harmonization of criminal law and criminal law procedure, law enforcement strategy, police organization and discipline, and the politics of immigration and civil liberties (to mention only the most obvious) are raised by it. When a political decision is taken to go beyond the discretionary exchange of information about criminal matters towards an institutionalized police co-operation which includes operational criminal investigations across borders, a Pandora's box of issues and problems is opened.

There is, however, a broad agreement that improved police co-operation is desirable, with some politicians, police officials and civil liberties activists dissenting. However, this consensus is fragile and contains scope for mutual conflict and misunderstanding. But the debate is also a crucially important one, the outcome of which will have a profound effect on all citizens (and non-citizens) of the European Union Member States and beyond. This book aims to make the debate more comprehensible and to highlight the underlying dynamics. It also aims at elucidating what is at stake in the proposals and at analysing views about ways to improve co-operation.

The debate on law enforcement co-operation is a difficult one. A basic conceptual difficulty is that the term 'police' has different meanings in different organizations and especially in different countries. The criminal justice discourse in Europe comprises a variety of perspectives and concerns. No cohesive international policy community exists in the field of police co-operation. Different participants in the discussion, coming from various professional and political backgrounds seem to speak different languages. A modicum of agreement has emerged about the threat posed to all EU Member States by international organized and serious crime, and the need to take measures to 'immobilize' criminals. But the wider policy debate is characterized less by the engagement of conflicting positions than by participants failing to address the points which others are making. In a sense, this is inevitable because political considerations are bound to differ from practical-operational police concerns.

Political leaders talk in terms of objectives using the language of broad generalities. President Mitterrand has said 'Since terrorism is international—investigation, prevention, repression and sanctions should be international', and Chancellor Kohl has talked of the desirability of a European FBI, but those professionally concerned with criminal law and law enforcement do not often address, at least in public, the difficulties and obstacles in the way of such broad ambitions. Police officers regard the necessity of standardizing, simplifying, and even abolishing extradition procedures within the European Union as a self-evident truth; defence lawyers and courts ignore this view and are more concerned with safeguarding the rights of the accused. Politicians, senior police officers and national police agencies talk generally of new criminal and security threats, requiring the planning of effective strategies to counter them; by contrast, criminal investigators who work on specific cases emphasize the need to get information quickly and without difficulty from foreign jurisdictions. Interpretations of what is at stake in police co-operation therefore vary considerably between and within countries.

Points of Departure

A number of points of departure are used in this book in establishing an analysis of the emerging system of European police co-operation. Each is concerned with an aspect of the relationship between policing and the broader domain of politics. The first point of departure is that particular forms of police co-operation may be given very high priority as a result of specific criminal events, such as the killing of Israeli athletes at the 1972 Munich Olympics. These events create an overwhelming pressure for action on the part of governments. This has been aptly described as the 'politics of the latest outrage'. But when the general international security context undergoes a radical change, as it did when Soviet Communism collapsed after 1989, the 'pressure of events' is crucial, but less clearly focused and more difficult to interpret. Political pressures on European policing are constantly changing. This makes the creation of institutions of co-operation and the formulation of long-term strategies difficult.

The second point concerns the relationship between the nature of the criminal acts and the purposes of European police co-operation. Most criminal acts do not have a 'European dimension'. Some of the most hideous crimes—rape, child abuse, kidnapping, serial murder—often have strictly local ramifications and only in a small minority of cases is European co-operation relevant. For other categories of crimes such as traffic in stolen works of art and money laundering, criminal inquiries are not necessarily limited to the territory of the EU. Therefore, the geographical scope of European police co-operation does not reflect neatly the pattern of criminal activity. An additional complicating 'geographical' factor is that the criminalization of certain behaviour is still predominantly a matter of national criminal laws.

The third point is that criminality and repression of criminality are two partially interdependent semi-autonomous fields. There is no straightforward relationship between, on the one hand, crime and repression of crime, and, on the other hand, the exercise of political and economic power in a society. In law enforcement, even in centralized political systems such as France, where there is a direct hierarchical relationship between minister, government and police, policing takes forms which go beyond explicit government instructions. The calculations of the police and the criminals are specific to these milieus and are not fully shared by other categories of the population. There is also a symbiotic relationship between the police (and the state more generally) and the criminals; between the upperworld and the underworld. Conspiracies between the two may be rare in the EU Member States, although they occasionally come to light. But changes in the general social and economic policy of the state or weaknesses in the organization of policing provide incentives and openings for criminal activity, while new forms of criminal activity encourage new police tactics, sometimes even leading to reorganizations of the police, the establishment of new police institutions, or the promulgation of new laws.

The fourth point is that there are strict limits to the professional authority of the police, as there are many decisions which the police forces cannot take. Actions and decisions often lie outside their power. For example, they cannot set up new police institutions and decide on the level of the human and financial resources which they command. These decisions are outside their autonomous control and are formulated in a policy community in which senior police officers participate, alongside civil servants, members of parliament and ministers, with lawyers, academics and journalists as sporadic players.

The fifth point of departure is that the level and form of law enforcement co-operation is never a strictly functional choice—political and ideological factors intervene. Particular initiatives are never a self-evident response to the 'needs' of international law enforcement. The setting up of a European police facility separate from Interpol and the protracted controversy over the role of the Schengen initiative in a borderless Europe are obvious examples of political and ideological concerns entering into policy-making.

Studying European Police Cooperation

Academic contributions to recent developments have concerned attempts to map out 'international criminality', which was first restricted to terrorism, and later also included drug-trafficking, money laundering and international fraud. Terrorism has been the subject of a vast amount of writing which often uncritically accepts the official definitions and ways of categorizing the problem. The literature on the drug problem often mirrors the differences in policy preferences within the official policy-making community, which varies from harm reduction and a health-care approach to drug addiction, to a concentration on repression of the trade in illegal substances and heavy penalties for the addict. The writing on fraud and money laundering has a different character. Some of it is path breaking, such as the work of Michael Levi on the problems of generating and linking information about transfrontier crime (see e.g. Gold and Levi 1994), while the bulk of it is closely argued legal analysis. This is not the place to review these extensive writings, although they have a bearing on international police co-operation and have been useful in the preparation of this book.

Studies on the phenomenon of European or transfrontier crime and on European police co-operation have been very uneven in the EU Member States. Research in these fields has been concentrated in Germany, the Netherlands and Belgium, and, to a lesser extent in the United Kingdom. Empirical studies are rare. In Belgium and the Netherlands a few reports have analysed crime and policing in border regions (Ghent, Maastricht, Louvain). One of the first studies into European policing was *Police Cooperation in the European Community* (Fijnaut and Hermans 1987), which adopted a critical attitude to Interpol. The next general contribution to the literature on international police co-operation (Anderson 1989) emphasized the effort which had been made within Interpol both to create an effective European regional structure and to modernize its equipment and practices. The Leicester University-based Centre for the Study of Public Order has published a report on police co-operation which is a useful work of reference for practitioners (Benyon *et al.* 1993). The literature should be enriched by new contributions in the near future. Since 1990 a number of projects on police co-operation or on topics closely related to it have commenced, among others, at the *Institut d'Etudes Politiques* in Paris, the Free University of Amsterdam, the European University Institute in Florence, the Norwegian School of Management in Oslo and the University of Ghent.

In this contribution to the literature we seek to provide a comprehensive analysis of the issues arising from police co-operation from a theoretically-informed standpoint. We take the view that the success of co-operation will depend on the legal and political framework in which it is set. A robust legal–political framework means several things. Crucially, it requires the drafting of a convention for Europol so that the EU Member States undertake reciprocal obligations to one another which go beyond the voluntary exchange of police information and intelligence, practised within Interpol, or even the binding but vague commitments contained in the Justice and Home Affairs (JHA) Title of the TEU. But it means many other things, such as a broadly consistent treaty framework between the EU and the rest of the world, legal agreements which allow easy extradition and transfer of evidence between the EU Member States, some harmonization of the criminal law (or at least of criminal law procedure) of the Member States in areas where co-operation is frequently sought, the adoption of compatible rules concerning the relationship between police and judicial authorities and a system of accountability for European police institutions. Some progress has been made in some of these areas but from the legal point of view there is still a long road to travel before there is a European Union in criminal law enforcement (see chapters 6–8).

Our approach is informed by the recent revival of neo-functionalist theory which was stimulated by the quickening pace of European integration after the Single European Act (SEA). We see improved police co-operation as a functional demand associated with the Single Market, a 'spillover' from the decisions to move a further stage in economic integration. The form of police co-operation is, however, a matter for negotiation at both ministerial and senior official level. This process is also influenced by professional groups and external pressures (such as those exercised by libertarian groups and the European Parliament). But we recognize that the neo-functional approach has severe intellectual shortcomings, which are explained in our chapter on the political theory of police co-operation (chapter 3). The attempt to reconcile functional determinism (in which action is an automatic result of circumstances) with an area of free choice for politicians (in which institutions and forms of co-operation are the result of political decision) cannot, in the final resort produce an entirely satisfactory account of EU policing. But, as chapter 3 demonstrates, we can gain a number of important insights from a critical appraisal of neo-functionalism.

We have sought a balance between the historical, political and legal dimensions of the subject. Historically, we are concerned with the developments of the last twenty years; from the proposal in 1974 to establish the Trevi Group to the official inauguration of Europol Drugs Unit Headquarters in The Hague in February 1994 and the subsequent tentative efforts to move towards agreement on a Europol Convention. In these intervening years, a series of international agreements was adopted. These included the 1977 Council of Europe (CoE) Convention on the Suppression of Terrorism, the 1979 EC Agreement on the application of this Convention, the 1982 Headquarters Agreement of Interpol (which came in force in 1984), the 1985 and 1990 Schengen Agreements, the 1990 Council of Europe Convention on Laundering, Search, Seizure and Confiscation of the Proceeds from Crime, and the 1992 Treaty on European Union, Title VI of which introduces co-operation in justice and home affairs and which provides the legal basis for Europol. As well as the negotiation of new agreements, there was the ratification of old ones. In the early 1990s, the United Kingdom ratified the European Conventions on Mutual Legal Assistance in Criminal Matters and on Extradition, thirty years after they had been negotiated, and France waited ten years before ratifying the European Convention on the Suppression of Terrorism. In the context of the EU, significant new agreements were negotiated (or are in the process of being negotiated) in the fields of the external frontier, data protection, immigration and asylum, but they have not been brought into force by the Member States. Some global agreements have also been reached—for example, the 1988 UN Vienna Convention on Drugs Trafficking—which have direct implications for European law enforcement co-operation.

Politically, we have made a rough distinction between 'internal' and 'external' politics, or between the 'micro' and 'macro' politics of European police co-operation. The level of micro-politics relates to the dynamics of the policy-making community which is involved in laying out projects and making decisions in the field of international law enforcement. Macro-politics, on the other hand, relates to the exogenous factors which have an influence on these projects and decisions, such as the enlargement of the EU, global trends in drug trafficking operations, and the dynamics of external security threats. The level of micro-politics can thus be associated with the individual and organizational dynamics of decision-making, whereas the level of macro-politics can be translated as the influence of contextual factors and variables.

In terms of law, we have attempted to take account of legal norms operating at various levels. The most significant level in the field of criminal justice is still that of the state, but it is noteworthy that much of recent domestic law on money laundering, fraud, and corruption has been introduced in the wake of international agreements. At the international and supranational levels, progress has been particularly related to the work of the United Nations, the Council of Europe and the European Union. Agreements reached at these levels are characterized by different degrees of intrusiveness into domestic legal systems and have attracted varying levels of participation by states.

The Political Prerequisites of European Police Co-operation

One of the important current objectives for the EU is to specify a political framework for European police co-operation. Agreement on the aims and objectives of police co-operation is a basic requirement for establishing this framework. The difficulty of defining exactly what the objectives of this co-operation are is a recurrent theme in this book. The ability to call European policing to account and to ensure that nothing improper is done in a good cause is essential for public acceptance. In the absence of transparent systems of monitoring and control for Europol and Schengen, their legitimacy is not ensured (see chapter 8). This is *a fortiori* the case because of the still widespread distrust of foreign police systems. Another political requirement is an extension of the notion of European citizenship beyond the limited reciprocal recognition of voting rights envisaged in the TEU. A positive commitment on the part of individuals to assist law enforcement throughout the EU is essential before a European operational law enforcement unit is set up (see chapter 3).

Political agreement and commitment at the level of heads of state and government are necessary in order to introduce any ambitious scheme of law enforcement co-operation. At the time of writing, the omens are not good. Commitment to the idea of a EU, expressed by President Mitterrand and Chancellor Kohl on many occasions, and by the latter in support of Europol, is not sufficient. It has to be supplemented by support from groups most concerned with serious problems of law enforcement, including determined co-ordinated initiatives by political and administrative coalitions. In the period immediately preceding the planned date of the completion of the 1992 programme (1 January 1993), influential sections of the law enforcement community were clearly expressing the wish to move quickly towards improved systems of co-operation. Since then, political enthusiasm has waned. The electoral situation in leading Member States partly explains this, but practical security issues have also played a role. The uncertain security implications of enlargement of the EU, the hesitant and uneven abolition of frontier controls on citizens of other EU Member States, the frequent postponement of the implementation of the Schengen Agreements, and the difficulty of assigning a clearly defined operational role to Europol all reflect and contribute to a lack of enthusiasm for European integration in law enforcement initiatives.

Research Procedures

We have based this enquiry on a combination of interviews and documentary sources. More than a hundred interviews were conducted with senior officials in all twelve EU Member States (as it was prior to the 1995 expansion), in Vienna, Budapest, Stockholm, Oslo and in various cities in the United States. Most of our informants must remain anonymous. The circumstances surrounding these interviews varied from country to country, as there were different levels of access to information and as it was not always practical to interview equivalent people in the countries we visited, sometimes because the 'opposite number' simply does not exist. The approach to each person was tailored to circumstances, the time available, the seniority of the person concerned, and the topics that individuals were most ready or likely to discuss. We took account of the 'legitimation-effect' of interviews, namely the tendency of interviewers to interpret positively their own role and the importance of their organization.

We have used several kinds of documentary sources. Legal texts are a primary source and are readily available, as too are parliamentary and official governmental papers for the EU and the Member States. The newspaper press of the United Kingdom, the Netherlands, France and Germany has been utilized. Material has been acquired from police professional associations and presssure groups. 'Grey' material—semi-confidential reports, background papers, agendas—made available to us has been essential to the understanding of policy processes. The writings and advice of academic colleagues have been a most valuable secondary source. But, without talking to participants, it is difficult to establish a coherent account of the development of policing. The future historian, piecing together the course of European police co-operation from scattered references in the archives, will not have an easy task.

The Structure of this Book

The themes of the chapters highlight what we view as the most important dimensions and aspects of the development of European police co-operation. In chapter 1 we review the symbiotic relationship between policing and crime in an international perspective; we describe the contours of 'Euro-crime' and 'Euro-policing', investigate the availability of statistics on transfrontier crime in Europe, and discuss the now routinized categories of international crime (terrorism, organized crime and drug-trafficking). The chapter concludes with an overview of the possible dimensions along which the field of European police co-operation can be analysed. Chapter 2 analyses the third pillar of the TEU (Co-operation in Justice and Home Affairs) as a catalyst assisting the transition from old systems of European police co-operation to new systems. We give an account of 'old' systems, such as Interpol and Trevi, and of 'new' systems, such as Schengen and Europol. Drawing extensively on the interviews, it also analyses the politics of transformation from old to new as seen from the perspective, and as enacted through the strategies, of senior police officers and policy-makers. Chapter 3 discusses the dynamic relationship between 'micro' and 'macro'-politics of European police co-operation, and sets out to develop a political theory of police co-operation. The question of borders, so crucial to both law enforcement policy and wider political interests, is situated at the intersection between micro-politics and macro-politics. Through a review of European frontier control policy, particularly in the light of the Schengen Agreements, the Palma

Document and the External Borders Convention, Chapter 4 deals with the changing significance of borders and repercussions on the Member States.

Chapter 5 takes the macro-political issues one step further by analysing the changing conceptualization of internal and external security in Europe. It highlights the merging of internal and external security, the narrowing gap between ordinary policing and undercover or pro-active policing, and the prospects for the EU of becoming a regional security community. Chapters 6 and 7 contain a discussion of the existing and future legal framework for criminal justice and law enforcement co-operation. The first of these focuses on the competence of the EC in criminal matters, the respective roles of the European Court of Human Rights and the European Court of Justice (ECJ), and the way in which the provisions of Title VI could lift law enforcement co-operation into the main institutional core of the European Union. The second of these analyses the already existent body of agreements created by the United Nations, the Council of Europe, and between members of the EU. It also pays particular attention to an examination of the critical Council of Europe Conventions on Extradition and Mutual Assistance. Chapter 8 brings to the fore an issue which has become pre-eminent in the creation of 'new' systems of European police co-operation—accountability.

The selection of these subject areas for analysis imposes its own constraints. We regret that we cannot do full justice to a number of important topics. These include informal and regional frameworks of international police co-operation; the essential relationship between the police and other law enforcement organizations such as the customs services; the detailed policy implications of the internationalization of policing at the national level, such as the institution of new central intelligence services and the creation of regional criminal investigation teams on organized crime; the network of liaison officers, the range of bilateral and multilateral agreements on police and criminal justice co-operation; proposals such as the creation of a European Police Institute, a European Police Council, a European Commissioner for Police and Internal Security and special task forces attached to Europol; and the involvement of private security firms in international law enforcement. Some of these interesting and relevant issues are discussed in the light of future developments (chapter 9).

1

Euro-Crime and Euro-Policing

Introduction

The creation of Europe-wide policing structures and organizations presupposes a problem: the existence of European criminality. Public anxieties about the new criminal threat within the EU and from the East have increased as a consequence of intensive political and media attention devoted to 'Euro-crime' and international crime (Den Boer 1994b). This chapter offers a critical analysis of the main issues in the policy-making debate on the relationship between transfrontier crime and international policing. The first of these issues is the general presupposition that 'national' and 'international' crime are increasing, partly as a consequence of relaxed border controls. This relates to a second issue, which is the doubtful reliability of comparative crime statistics and the lack of hard evidence about the relationship between border controls and crime levels. A clear definition of what constitutes international crime is usually not given in the annual reports of the national intelligence services and is absent in most discussions. Yet, certain crimes tend to be automatically associated with international or transnational potential, in particular, organized crime.

This chapter views criminal activities in two ways. First, crimes are the exploitation of socio-economic opportunities and of weaknesses in crime prevention and law enforcement regimes. Second, crimes are activities defined as such by positive law. Hence, society exercises control over the definition of crime. In this chapter we analyse how crimes, while sometimes having transfrontier ramifications, may be defined differently in the individual European criminal justice systems. Also, certain 'international crimes' are slowly losing priority status in anti-crime programmes, while other categories—in particular organized crime—have become far more prominent. International crime is a multifaceted concept, its scope and emphasis influenced by political, legal, socio-economic and geographical factors. The complexity of the concept 'international crime' is mirrored in the multi-level character of European law enforcement initiatives. Parallel difficulties exist in analysing police response to international crime. The relatively unstructured character of European police co-operation and the uncertainty over its scope and its targets forms a major obstacle in the design of a theoretical model capable of making sense of it in its entirety. Nevertheless, the first attempts at modelling cross-border policing in Europe are referred to in the final part of this chapter.

The Definition of 'Euro-Crime'

Various concepts of international crime should be discussed before we describe the aims and purposes of international law enforcement initiatives. These concepts tend to vary considerably. Partly as a result of this, there are also variations in the predictions about the rise of international crime as a consequence of the abolition of border controls. Statistics about the magnitude of international crime have only recently become available, and crime indicators are notoriously unreliable as indicators of underlying trends.

The term 'Euro-crime' covers a diverse range of criminal activities that have transnational characteristics and tendencies, but that are still defined within the term of national criminal laws. In fact, it has been argued that the loopholes caused by this diversity are exploited widely by criminals (Den Boer 1994b: 189; Calvi 1993: 155; Killias 1993: 9; Levi 1993a: 185). But despite detailed differences between national systems of regulations, there is a broad consensus among law enforcement agencies that international crime includes terrorism, organized crime, drug-trafficking, money-laundering, serious fraud, computer crime, traffic in persons, and certain forms of theft (valuable works of art, high value cars).[1] Further, the high-profile character of these crimes sometimes obscures numerous other cross-border criminal offences over which there is little international disagreement, such as smuggling and drug-tourism.

Two general distinctions of a preliminary nature ought to be made: border crimes do not always coincide with cross-border crimes (De Ruyver et al. 1992:93); and cross-border crimes are not

---

[1] An extended version of this list is included in the Annex to the draft Europol Convention. Terrorism was included for the first time in the German draft Convention of Oct. 1994.

necessarily identical with 'Euro-crime'. Border crimes, such as selling drugs in border villages, take place in locations along the borders but do not involve transporting the illegal goods or services across the borders. Cross-border crimes, in contrast to crimes along the borders, involve transportation of the illegal goods or services across the border of a national jurisdiction: some involve one border crossing, others involve several crossings, embracing the external frontiers of the EU as well as its internal frontiers.

The category of 'Euro-crimes' can be applied to a series of individual criminal incidents or transactions, which in aggregate, have a European dimension. But the term seems to be most applicable to those criminal offences which have a high-profile character, may involve more than two countries, and usually have a systemic quality (such as co-operative networks which turn into durable trading communities). Van Duyne (1993) uses the term 'European crime regions', which are related areas of criminal trade in which one can discern an interlocking of personnel and economic cohesion and which have developed from regular working connections. Martin and Romano (1992: 5) define this group of crimes as 'multinational systemic crimes': crimes perpetrated by groups and organizations moving across the various national jurisdictions in which they are defined as a violation of the criminal code. Van Duyne (1993: 104–5) demonstrates this link in the flows of drug money into legitimate industries, such as real estate and the transport industry. A consequence is that both politicians and police officers see a strong link between the 'organized' and 'international' constituents of crime. This link is also emphasized in some annual reports of the national intelligence services of EU Member States: for example, according to the 1993 Annual Report of the CRI in the Netherlands, almost all organized crime has an international character (Divisie Centrale Recherche Informatie 1994: 47).

But not all observers see a rising tide of international organized crime. Martin and Romano (1992: 22) add that multinational crime is a 'statistically infrequent' phenomenon. Crime spreading inexorably across the European continent is, according to Martin and Romano, an overdrawn perspective: they argue that the concept of 'Euro-crime' tends to underestimate the distinctions between crime phenomena. While some forms of international criminal practices are peculiar to particular borders or regions within the EU, others spread beyond the boundaries of the EU. Indeed, a substantial part of transfrontier criminal activity is not restricted to the territorial boundaries of the wider European continent. Many criminal activities, in particular those in the sphere of international organized crime, have a supra-European or global dimension (Martin and Romano 1992: 4; Savona and Defeo 1994: 90).[2] Examples are the Pizza-connection and the mafia-activities in St Maarten and Surinam (Calvi 1993: 23; Minc 1993). On the other hand, criminal organizations sometimes expand across EU borders. Fears have been expressed that Cosa Nostra, the Camorra, 'Ndrangheta, and Sacra Corona Unita have started to co-operate and centralize their activities with a view to expanding these activities north of the Alps. Alleged signs of this expansion are increased Mafia activity along the French Côte d'Azur, the Spanish Costa del Sol, Lake Geneva, and the City of London (Calvi 1993: 21).

The fragility of the idea of 'Euro-crime' is underscored by the legal faultlines between Member States. 'Crime' and 'illegality' are essentially the alter-egos of legality (Nadelmann 1993). Activities are illegal by virtue of law. Almost all crimes and misdemeanours are the product of national criminal legislation supplemented in common law jurisdictions such as England by case law and judicial precedent. The term 'Euro-crime', occasionally used in law-enforcement circles,[3] is not yet matured as a juridical concept, because it suggests there is a genuine European criminal justice system (see chapters 6 and 7). The only appropriate application of the term 'Euro-crime' is to crimes committed against the EU itself, such as agricultural fraud and budgetary fraud. This should not, however, be dismissed as modest in scale or narrow in the interests it involves. As EU subsidies to non-agricultural funds increase, an estimate for the Netherlands suggests that fraud against the EU will increase by 25 per cent over the next few years (Ministerie van Justitie, Ministerie van Binnenlandse Zaken 1992: 3).[4] In relation to fraud against the financial interests of the Community, Passas

---

[2] Savona and Defeo claim that despite globalization tendencies, it would be a mistake to assume that criminal organizations 'can become "global" in the sense that they can take flight, detach themselves from their base of operations, and become free–floating opportunists who could operate on the world market or criminal activities with no need for a fixed home–basing arrangement. Criminal organizations do not allow themselves to be cut off from their roots.' (at p. 90)

[3] E.g. 'Furcht vor Euro–Kriminalität', in Focus 44, 1993, pp. 22–3.

[4] See also: Annual Report from the Commission on the Fight against Fraud, Background Report ISEC/B17/93, 7 June 1993, European Communities, COM (93) 141 final, Brussels 20 April 1993.

and Nelken (1993) argue in favour of abandoning the distinction between white collar crime and organized crime, and would like to see it replaced by the term 'enterprise model of crime'.

The Incidence of International Crime

The general expectation in law enforcement circles is that a border-free Europe will make crime control more difficult, and that crime in general will rise (Clutterbuck 1990; Latter 1991; Zachert 1992b). The official German police criminal statistical analysis for 1993, for instance, relates the increase in criminality—amongst other factors—to the increased permeability of Europe's internal borders.[5] One of the reasons cited for the expected increase in transfrontier drug tourism is that, with the eradication of physical controls, borders lose their symbolic and practical significance for drug consumers and drug traffickers (Driessen and Jansen 1991: 34). Indeed, in some respects the symbolic dimension may be more significant than the practical dimension, the perception more important than the reality (see chapter 4). In the United Kingdom, for example, despite efforts to keep some of the natural protection afforded by its sea borders, senior police officers such as Chief Constable Roger Birch, have expressed concern about the expanding ambitions of transnational criminals simply because these criminals believe that the system of border controls has been extensively liberalized since 1992.

There are conflicting views on whether borders are useful against crime. Ziegenaus (1992) insists that borders provide an essential filter function when he observes that 60 per cent of drug hauls are made at the borders of the German Federal Republic, accounting for 80 per cent of all illegal drugs seized within the country. Kühne (1991: 49) argues the contrary case—again on the basis of statistics—that the contribution of borders to the preservation of internal security is 'exceptionally limited in both qualitative and quantitative terms'.

Predictions about crime trends in a Europe without internal borders also vary from country to country. In Belgium, Germany and the Netherlands, and specifically within the 'Euregio' Meuse-Rhine, drug-tourism and car-smuggling are expected to increase

---

[5] 'Die Kriminalität in der Bundesrepublik Deutschland', *Bulletin des Presse und Informationsamts der Bundesregierung*, Nr. 50, 30 May 1994, at p. 464.

(Brammertz *et al.* 1993: 17, 61). In the Netherlands, there is generally less pessimism about the increase in crime than in Germany (Hofstede *et al.* 1993: 16). Germany's proximity to East Europe and associated feelings of insecurity may provide a partial explanation. In the United Kingdom, there is a strong view that its sea borders provide substantially greater protection than the porous land borders of continental Europe. For example, it remains the considered opinion of the British police that sea borders provide the first opportunity for prevention and the last chance of detection (Home Affairs Committee 1990: 95). The British Government holds a similar view, and it has consistently resisted efforts to remove border controls entirely under the '1992' Single European Market programme.[6] Furthermore, expectations about the development of transfrontier crime also vary between police ranks: the higher the position of a police officer in the hierarchy of the police organization, the more sceptical he is likely to be about the expected rise in transfrontier crime (Hofstede *et al.* 1993: 16). This may be because senior officers are more exposed than their junior colleagues to the sharp division of political opinion on this matter and more aware of the flimsiness of the evidence supporting these opinions. Indeed, some police officers, as well as drug traffickers, do not believe that the abolition of internal border controls produces any increase in international drug trafficking operations. The disappearance of internal border controls may thus not make a significant difference, especially as these were already lax over much of the continental core of the EU in the decade prior to the completion of the '1992' programme (Van Duyne 1993: 101).

By the same token, while the reinforced external frontiers may provide some difficulties for criminals, this too, may have little impact on the overall level of international crime. Speculating about the future, criminal entrepreneurs indicate an interest in investing in new methods of penetration of the reinforced external frontiers of the EU, which demonstrates a continuing confidence in the ability of sophisticated criminal enterprises to evade even the most comprehensive border controls (Driessen and Jansen 1991: 33–4; see chapter 4). Again, depending on their position within law enforcement organizations, police officers will be more or less

---

[6] See *e.g.* the written answer by Home Office Minister, Charles Wardle, to a Parliamentary Question in House of Commons Report, 9 July 1993.

exposed to such arguments and more or less sceptical about the value of creating a hard 'outer shell' around the EU.

The disproportionate media attention for high-profile international crimes distracts attention from more mundane issues such as the absence of reliable statistical comparisons between the incidence of international crime and the incidence of local crimes, like burglary and pickpocketing. The trend common to crime statistics in nearly every European country is that crime in general—both reported and unreported—is still on the increase (*i.e.* Van Dijk and Mayhew 1993: 28). But these statistics, including those on crime enterprises, seldom look beyond the national level (Van Duyne 1991) and do not differentiate 'ordinary' or 'conventional' crime from 'international' crime. Furthermore, they tend to exclude 'white collar' crime, and they fail to mention the criteria according to which these forms of crime can be distinguished, such as their socio-economic impact, the motives and strategies of those who commit them, the security threat they generate or the instruments most appropriate to combat them. Not only the public, but police officers also seem susceptible to conventional opinion about the increasing incidence of international and organized crime. As noted above, perspectives of police officers are often associated with their role; officers situated in rural communities tend to give priority to community policing and local crime, while officers based in large urban communities or who have a position in a national criminal intelligence service are more likely to argue that removing the incentives for organized and international crime will benefit the investigation and repression of local crime.

The basic reason for this contrast in perspectives may be that much international crime flows through major urban centres. An added reason may be that national policy agendas often pay disproportionate attention to the concerns of the 'centre' (Shils 1982: chapter 4), the immediate social milieu of the opinion-formers and the policy-makers. In the British context, for instance, debates about the problems of London and a few other major urban centres tend to become debates about 'national' problems. If international crime is affecting key national centres, it is likely to be taken more seriously than if, for example, it is confined to remote border areas. Professionals working in semi-urban and rural communities may feel that they are being forced to address issues and adopt priorities which are of no immediate relevance or concern to them.

Police officers, therefore, do not have privileged access to information about the scale and scope of international crime or any special competence to decide what priority should be given to its prevention and repression. Their professional expertise cannot overcome the limitations of the objective knowledge base. As already mentioned, it is hard to obtain an empirical impression of the scale of transfrontier criminality in the EU Member States (Levi 1993b: 57, 60, 75)[7], and even harder to quantify the contribution of border controls to law enforcement, through arrests, seizures of illegitimate goods, and even more problematically, deterrence (Collier 1992). Deriving conclusions from crime statistics about drug seizures is complicated because they are seldom concerned with transit and export and they tend to focus on import. Also, financial estimates of trafficking seem arbitrary, such as impressions of the 'value' of drugs seized (Clark and Sanctuary 1992). Moreover, crime statistics tend to obscure the role of intelligence and the way locations for search-operations are selected (Levi 1993b: 61), which are essential data in any assessment of the quality and effectiveness of border controls. Often, there is no distinction between *flagrante delicto* and intelligence-related arrests and seizures, no measurement of the relative status of suspects apprehended (major *versus* minor offenders, first offenders *versus* re-offenders), and no specification of the type of crimes to which seizures and arrests relate. With regard to organized crime statistics, Levi (1993b: 61) notes that: 'whether international or domestic, [they] tend to take on a life of their own and there is seldom any serious attempt to deconstruct the method by which they are compiled . . .'

In any event, compared with the available national crime statistics, statistics about the incidence of transfrontier crime are still rare. Studies are beginning to appear on the incidence of organized crime, which often has an international dimension. A co-ordinated, pan-European attempt at threat assessment has not yet been made, although this will be one of Europol's tasks. The first authoritative analyses have merely underlined the paucity of empirical data (Heidensohn and Farrell 1993; Levi 1993b; Robert and van Outrive

---

[7] Levi (1993b) claims that the best and most systematic data for his analysis was information from the private sector and credit card companies, who gathered hard data on patterns of victimization in order to try to cut down their commercial losses. See also Hoogenboom (1994: 395, 401–6).

1993). The rudimentary character of international comparative statistics can be explained by the fact that national categorizations of crime prevail (Levi and Maguire 1992: 169):[8] there is a lack of cooperation to overcome this conceptual difficulty, as in so many other aspects of international law enforcement. Furthermore, it is hard to compare crime statistics without a detailed knowledge of the criminal justice system in which they are compiled. There are differences between laws and law enforcement systems, between reporting procedures and techniques, as well as between definitions of crime: in one country crimes confessed to by persons already imprisoned for other crimes may be taken into account in the crime statistics, while in the other they may not; in one country euthanasia and abortion may be included in the categories of murder and manslaughter, while in another they may be classified under a separate legal heading. The final difficulty of comparing statistics relates to the variety of methods according to which police performance is rated (Meijer 1994: 10–11). In so far as the police are judged by quantifiable results they may be tempted to present the figures in the manner which reflects most favourably upon their efficiency and effectiveness. Quantification obscures the fact that crime figures are social constructs which are susceptible to the fluctuations of reporting rates and detection rates and changes in recording procedures, and dependent on variation of the interpretation of certain crimes (Hall *et al.* 1978, chapters 1 and 2; Maguire 1994: 236; Matka 1990; Van Dijk 1993: 30).

Neither national nor international statistics have the capacity to reveal the link between the one criminal activity and the other. The occurrence of a particular form of crime is often accompanied by other deviant phenomena. Examples in the realm of international crime are the money laundering of profits obtained through illegal drug- and arms-trafficking (Cooney 1992: 57), and the (relatively rare) use by terrorists of drug-trafficking profits for the acquisition of weapons (see chapter 3). On a lower level, drug use is frequently accompanied by an increase in stolen goods and prostitu-

---

[8] The Helsinki *ad hoc* Expert Group on a cross-national study on trends in crime and information sources on criminal justice and crime prevention in Europe noted for instance that there were 'considerable differences' in the offences of bribery, corruption, drugs, crime, fraud and embezzlement. Some countries include tax fraud, cheque fraud and the use of false pretences while others only include commercial fraud (Helsinki Institute 1985: 18).

tion.[9] De Ruyver *et al.* (1992: 97) provide evidence that these are forms of instrumental crime, through which drug addicts provide themselves with means to finance their habit. Cigarettes and drink stolen from shops and supermarkets are often sold directly in pubs, below their market value. Drug addiction and drug use is also frequently accompanied by an increase in the number of stolen cars (De Ruyver *et al.* 1992: 98). In addition to instrumental crimes, there are forms of consensual transfrontier crimes, such as drug users driving a car or playing courier when they accompany others to another country to buy drugs in exchange for a portion of drugs (De Ruyver *et al.* 1992: 97). Another phenomenon associated with drug use is the resale or fencing of illegally obtained goods across the border: drug users who have stolen goods exchange them directly for drugs. Crime statistics, however, remain blind to these associations, and so are poor instruments for revealing general trends in deviant behaviour.

Crime and Opportunity Structures

In conventional psychological approaches to criminology, criminal offences are often explained in terms of deviant individual behaviour (Martin and Romano 1992: 88; Taylor, Walton and Young 1974). Within the many sociological variants of criminology, by contrast, criminal behaviour is explained in terms of how society is organized and the way in which people acquire social attributes. Criminal activities are often present when certain opportunities exist or arise (Van Duyne 1993: 100). Geographical and economic factors affect the distribution of crime and the mobility of criminals (Helsinki Institute 1985: 4). As far as geographic factors are concerned, the 'adjacency of opportunities', such as the availability of drugs in a neighbouring area and the non-availability of drugs

---

[9] The causal relationship between drug use and property crime was questioned in a Dutch study (Korf 1990). Although many drug users have a criminal record, not all commit property crimes, especially not women; the majority of drug users purchase drugs from their salaries, social security benefits, sale of drugs or prostitution. Much abuse and crime seem to be products of the same factor, namely socio-economic deprivation. Dorn and South (1993: 77) argue that there are competing hypotheses about the relationship between drugs and crime ('drug use leads to crime'; 'involvement in crime leads to drug use'; 'both crime and drug use are results of some other factors') and claim that 'the conventionally assumed direction of causality linking drugs to crime is questionable'.

in one's own area, or the relative economic prosperity[10] is of crucial significance. As regards patterns of drug trafficking and drug
consumption in Belgium for instance, the proximity of the
Netherlands is a decisive factor: most drugs for personal consumption are bought in the Netherlands from a dealer or intermediary
(*e.g.* Paasch 1987). This is specifically the case for cannabis, heroin,
cocaine, LSD and to a lesser extent XTC (De Ruyver *et al.* 1992:
47, 264). Economic inequality and relative social deprivation also
seem to be important factors behind international crime. For
instance, cross-border crime between Belgium and its neighbours
has been shown to be promoted by the juxtaposition of 'totally different lifestyles' (De Ruyver, Bruggeman and Zanders 1993: 88).
The contrast in affluence, as well as domestic law enforcement
regimes, between East and West also helps to explain the
significance of the external frontiers separating the EU from its
post-communist neighbours. Drug consumption and drug production are expected to soar in East European countries, as the law-
enforcement structure is weak and socio-economic factors may
encourage the use of drugs (Driessen and Jansen 1991: 36f); in
turn, this may be subsidized by trafficking in the more lucrative
markets of bordering EU Member states, which may have substantial repercussions for the internal security of these States.

The availability of illegal goods and the pricing of these goods in
different countries or regions determine transfrontier drug-
trafficking patterns. Drugs are relatively expensive in the periphery
of Europe (*e.g.* Dublin, Hamburg), and relatively cheap in transit
towns (*e.g.* Amsterdam) (Driessen and Jansen 1991: 18).[11]
According to a recent study of the Council of Europe's Pompidou
Group (1994: 139-40), the average price of one tenth gramme
heroin packets in Amsterdam was quoted at 35–60 ecu (in 1991),
while in Helsinki this was 1,000 ecu (in 1990). Hence, the price of
illegal goods such as drugs is linked to geographical factors (such
as the presence of seaports), the availability of drugs, and develop-

[10] The availability of targets to steal, for example in countries where vehicles are
common, raises the level of cross–border supply and demand. Relatively high rates
of car theft were found in North America, Australia, New Zealand, the
Netherlands, England and Sweden (Van Dijk and Mayhew 1993: 46). See also the
German police criminal statistics of 1993 at p. 464.

[11] Driessen and Jansen (1991: 18) based their assessment of street-prices on data
from the Pompidou Group (1987, U. Avico *et al.*, *Multi-city study of drug misuse*,
Strasbourg).

ments in the global drugs market (Pompidou Group 1994: 133–6). Furthermore, saturation of the North American drugs market has encouraged Colombian drug cartels to switch to European markets, which has resulted in a fall in prices by almost 50 per cent (De Ruyver *et al*. 1992: 48). This illustrates the interdependence of global and local developments in crime.

Another example of the adjacency of opportunities concept emerges from 'jurisdiction shopping'—committing a crime in a country where the judicial sanctions tend to be more favourable than in one's own country (De Ruyver *et al*. 1992:311).[12] Organized crime groups undertaking money laundering activities and operating on a global scale have the capacity to avoid unfavourable jurisdictions. They can also minimize the impact of improved crime control policies and take 'advantage of weak links in the global regulatory and enforcement chain, by shifting transactions, communications or assets to the country which has the weakest or most corruptible regulatory or police and prosecution authorities, the most restrictive bank and professional bank secrecy, or extradition, or asset seizure law, the most ineffective bank supervision, etc.' (Savona and Defeo 1994: 93).

The concept of the adjacency of opportunities highlights the rather limited nature of transfrontier crime: the majority of cross-border criminal activities are motivated by the lack of drugs or other illegal commodities in certain locations, influenced by the repressiveness of law enforcement and criminal justice policy, and remoteness from trading routes and networks. Referring to crime in general, Levi (1993b: 59) notes that: 'In most European countries, almost all crime is local in character, and is not highly organized in the sense of being conducted under the aegis of a crime syndicate.'

The concept of adjacency of opportunities can also refer to more

---

[12] Belgian drug users note that operations undertaken by Belgian police officers are notoriously tough and focused on small users rather than big drug dealers; in their view, the situation in the Netherlands is much better for drug users, in particular in terms of legal rights and health care. The mild penal climate in the Netherlands is also emphasized by Hofstede *et al*. (1993: 15). This perspective differs from that of the large drug dealers: they note that criminal sanctions in the Netherlands have become tougher and that methods of criminal investigation have intensified (Driessen and Jansen 1991: 31). Harmonization of criminal justice legislation may resolve the inequalities between countries in terms of rights and sanctions. A concern about these inequalities has already been expressed by the European Parliament (Salisch and Speroni 1994; see also ch. 6).

complex opportunity structures operating within and across societies. From this perspective, the significance of organized crime lies in its capacity to create new opportunity structures, rather than simply exploit existing ones. Gambetta (1993: 9) shows that the Sicilian Mafia acts predominantly as a facilitator for the trade in illegal goods and services: 'Mafiosi deal with no other good (*sic*) than protection.' Gambetta's underlying claim is that the main market for mafia services can be found in unstable transactions where trust is 'scarce and fragile' (Gambetta 1993: 17); for example, when there are economic conflicts over the management or buying of land and related resources, or when there is mobile wealth and numerous transactions, or when there are political conflicts among local factions (Gambetta 1993: 83). These are the typical components of the opportunity structure for organized crime in some Central and East European societies (Killias 1993: 8). As Gambetta points out, societal transition has challenged the claim of the state and its police to a monopoly of force, and has caused a massive increase in demand for protection services (Gambetta 1993: 252): the skills of ex-KGB officers and athletes have become a marketable product in the protection market.

Arguably, there is a broader symbiosis between social upheaval in East European states and the activities of criminal organizations. Not only can organized crime provide an alternative regime of social security, but the weakened state apparatus and deregulated economies of the early post-socialist phase also provide new opportunities for illicit trade. In West European law enforcement circles, there is serious concern about destabilized East European societies developing a supportive environment for criminal enterprises. One of the problems is that the old Balkan route, traditionally used for the purposes of heroin trafficking from Turkey to West Europe, has now been re-routed to the north due to the war in the former Yugoslavia (Van Doorn 1993: 99). Furthermore, cases of trafficking in radioactive substances have been reported and it is widely claimed that international trafficking in stolen motor vehicles has also thrived in East Europe (Cameron-Waller 1994: 104; Cooney 1992: 42).[13]

---

[13] The 1993 Annual Report of the CRI notes however that as more than half of all thefts of motor vehicles in the Netherlands, Belgium, Denmark, Germany, France, England and Wales were perpetrated in England and Wales, and given the difficulty of exporting stolen cars from the British Isles to East Europe (with the

Social instability makes easier the forging of links between the 'under' and the 'upper' worlds. The forms of penetration of the 'upper' world involve the hiring by criminals of financial, fiscal and legal experts, investment in legitimate companies (such as banks, construction firms and trade firms), and corrupting police officers and key civil servants (Van Duyne 1991; Huberts 1992; Ministerie van Justitie/Ministerie van Binnenlandse Zaken 1992: 2; Pijl 1991). Criminal laws and criminal justice policies can create opportunities for profit and the development of lucrative illegal businesses, providing illegitimate goods or services for which a demand exists (such as drugs, pornography and firearms). This is a dynamic process, with new patterns of criminalization and sanctioning creating new opportunities and increasing illicit profit margins. For example, a perfect niche in the illegal services market has been created by the criminalization of chemical waste dumping (Van Duyne 1993; Ministerie van Justitie, Ministerie van Binnenlandse Zaken 1992: 8).

More research is required to establish the relationship between the detailed regulation of the financial sector within the EU and the growth of white collar crime. But the most controversial question is whether and to what extent the decriminalization of illegal goods and substances would remove the basis of criminal organizations.[14] Even Raymond Kendall, Interpol's Secretary-General, has argued that drug-use (as opposed to drug-trafficking) ought to be decriminalized,[15] which, set alongside the recent expression of similar sentiments by domestic police élites in the United Kingdom and other Member States, may signal a changing appreciation of the problem in law enforcement circles.

steering wheel on the right side), it is 'not very likely' that the developments in East Europe have yet had a significant impact on the rise of motor vehicle thefts in West Europe. Less than one per cent of the criminal organizations in the Netherlands specializing in car theft are of East European origin (Divisie Centrale Recherche Informatie 1994: 17–18).

[14] For a discussion of the general implications of decriminalization, see Council of Europe (1980). The authors of this report distinguish between *de facto* decriminalization (discretion exercised by police officers or public prosecutors to refrain from arrest or prosecution) and *de jure* decriminalization (the withdrawal of penal sanctions for certain types of behaviour, commodities or transactions).

[15] Interview in *Le nouvel observateur*, Dec. 1993. In an interview with us, he claimed to have held this view for a long time.

Divergent Classifications of Crime

The classifications of crime used by law enforcement agencies in the European countries fail consistently to identify important similarities and differences in deviant practices. The two most contentious classifications from a conceptual and political point of view are those given prominence in official statements and in the press: international terrorism and international organized crime. But even a crime category such as drug trafficking, the repression of which is a less controversial area of international co-operation, lacks consistency of definition across national boundaries (Levi 1993a: 176). The important implication is that different classifications of crime reflect divergent official perspectives and priorities, and may result in different policy responses.

Some optimism about the standardization of classifications of crime is expressed by Heidensohn (1993: 8). She identifies three trends. First, the international spread of certain crimes, such as terrorism, fraud and drug-trafficking, has increased the pressure on states to arrive at a common appreciation of these crimes. Second, West European states are increasingly part of a global economic system and as such are subject to common influences and problems. Third, there is the diffusion of a new set of perceptions: a similar criminal justice agenda has emerged in various countries as a result, for example, of growing concern for victims of crime and the proliferation of 'private' systems of security and risk-management (see chapter 5). As discussed below, there is an increasing call for common definitions of crime within the EU, and law enforcement agencies have started to use each other's classifications of organized crime.

Terrorism

The definitional problems associated with the concept of terrorism are notorious. One set of difficulties concerns the differentiation of political terrorism from other forms of activity which may attract the terrorist label. Wilkinson, for example, seeks to distinguish political terrorism from criminal, psychic and war terrorism (Wilkinson 1974, chapter 1). In principle, this is a worthwhile attempt at sub-categorization, since most political theorists and some politicians would agree that the manner in which terrorist acts or threats ought to be evaluated and tackled may differ depending upon whether such behaviour is politically motivated. In practice, however, the various sub-categories shade into one another. Criminal terrorism, defined as the systematic use of terror for material ends, may be linked to political terrorism; for example, where the proceeds of the terrorist act are used in support of a wider political struggle. Psychic terrorism has mystical, religious or magical objectives, but who is to say where these categories end and the category of politics begins? If anything, the distinction between war terrorism and political terrorism is even more difficult to sustain. War terrorism may be defined in terms of a commitment to destroy the enemy through a military campaign, but this focuses on means rather than ends. Groups who use the methods of war may do so in pursuit of objectives which are just as 'political' as those sought by other groups using less intensive methods of armed struggle; indeed, in many cases the objectives of rival 'terrorist' groups may be very similar, their main disagreement being over means.[16]

Not only is the definition of political terrorism fuzzy at the edges, but some of its basic constitutive elements are also controversial. Most legal definitions venture little beyond the stock epigrammatic formula of 'the use of violence for political ends',[17] but this leaves a number of questions hanging. These are well illustrated by examining attempts to tease out a fuller definition. For example, following a rigorous analysis of the shortcomings of earlier efforts, Wardlaw settles upon the following well-quoted conceptualization: 'political terrorism is the use, or threat of use, of violence by an individual or group, whether acting for or in opposition to established authority, when such action is designed to create extreme anxiety and/or fear-inducing effects in a target group larger than the immediate victims with the purpose of coercing that group into acceding to the political demands of the perpetrators' (Wardlaw 1989: 16). Some would object to Wardlaw's inclusion of isolated individuals, insisting that terrorism presupposes the existence of a terrorist *organization*. Others would ponder the use of words such as 'design' and 'purpose', debating the extent to which

---

[16] For example, in the struggle against the apartheid system in South Africa, two of the main participants, the African National Congress and the Pan Africanist Congress, often disagreed more about strategy than ends. See Mandela (1994).

[17] As consistently used in the British Prevention of Terrorism Acts, 1974–89. See Finnie (1990: 2).

terrorism need involve the pursuit of a systematic and internally coherent strategy. However, perhaps the most intractable issue raised by this definition concerns the circumstances under which actions either 'for or in opposition to' the 'established authority' of the state fall within the ambit of terrorism.

In the final analysis, the answer to this question rests upon a value judgement which seeks to distinguish legitimate violence from the illegitimate violence of the terrorist. The legitimacy of the state's use of force cannot depend merely upon the lawfulness of its activities, as this would entail the unacceptable consequence that if the police or armed forces stray beyond their legal powers they then automatically become terrorists (Finnie 1990: 3). The justification for official violence must, therefore, rest upon the broader legitimacy of the incumbent regimes, measured by tests such as commitment to democratic values, a minimum framework of individual and minority rights, and the general adherence of state authorities to the rule of law.[18] In turn, this raises the converse question of the justification of violence perpetrated by insurgents against an illegitimate régime, however defined. From this wider perspective, the ethical boundary between state and non-state violence becomes extremely hazy. Hence, the moral relativism implicit in Yasser Arafat's limpid aphorism delivered to the General Assembly of the United Nations, 'one man's terrorist is another man's freedom fighter.'

Faced with a conceptual and normative quagmire, international attempts to co-operate against terrorism have developed slowly and hesistantly. For example, international terrorism has posed difficult problems for Interpol. Its 1956 statutes excluded the communication of information on cases of a political, religious or ethnic character. This ban was dropped at the 1984 Interpol General Assembly, when policy on 'acts of violence commonly called terrorism' was debated and the doctrine of 'preponderance' adopted. According to this doctrine, actions may be more or less criminal and more or less political, and have to be preponderantly criminal for Interpol to transmit messages about them. This approach has

---

[18] Some commentators have argued for a wider definition of state terrorism than that flowing from failure to adhere to basic democratic and rule–of–law standards. For an imaginative attempt to develop a broader approach concentrating on the themes of 'systems terror' and 'terror as effacement', see Christodoulidis and Veitch (1994).

ended the controversy caused by Interpol's previously non-interventionist stance, while retaining an awareness of the complexity of the problem. With a world-wide membership, Interpol is bound to proceed cautiously, and could not adopt a definition of terrorism favoured by the Western democracies, or, indeed, by any other regional bloc.

In western government appreciations of terrorism six characteristics are commonly found (Herman and O'Sullivan 1991: 43–4). First, the West, which stands for decency and the rule of law, is an innocent target and victim of terrorism. Secondly, the West responds only to other people's use of force. Thirdly, in contrast to the West, terrorists do not adhere to 'civilized norms of conduct'. Fourthly, in those cases where the West supports insurgents who use force, this is done on behalf of democracy against repressive régimes. Fifthly, democracies are hated by and vulnerable to terrorists, and the aim of terrorists is to undermine democratic institutions. Sixthly, during the Cold War, the efforts to undermine democracies had Soviet support. The link between international socialism and international terrorism was seen as not simply fortuitous.

A number of overlapping mechanisms have been created through which European governments co-operate to combat terrorism, including the Club of Berne, the Club of Vienna, the Trevi Group and the European Convention on the Suppression of Terrorism (Anderson 1989: 127–47; Riley 1993). Despite their common perception of the general nature of the terrorist problem, the use made of these co-operative fora has remained limited. West European governments have often been unwilling to give unequivocal backing to one another because of different analyses of the specific problem and different political interests (Clutterbuck 1990: 119–23; Martin and Romano 1992: 30ff). This has been apparent in cases such as the *Brigate Rosse,* the ETA and the PIRA. The general desire to co-operate has not always been sufficient to overcome reservations in particular cases, and the open-textured quality of the concept of terrorism has provided ample scope for divergent positions to be articulated. Striking examples exist of reticence and non-co-operation between West European governments on terrorist issues.

Until 1985, the French authorities were reluctant to extradite Basque terrorists; between 1986 and 1988, they seemed willing to bargain with Middle Eastern terrorist groups in return for the release of hostages, but in January 1994 they refused to extradite Iranians wanted for murder in Switzerland on grounds of national interest despite the vigorous protest of Swiss authorities. In 1988, Belgium and Ireland refused to co-operate with the United Kingdom in extraditing Father Ryan suspected of arms trafficking for the PIRA. In August 1994, Charles Pasqua, as French Minister of the Interior, critized the United Kingdom and other West European states for their tolerant attitude to Islamic fundamentalism in the wake of concern that violence would spread from Algeria to France.

Hence, even in West Europe, 'international terrorism' is not a homogeneous criminal threat which governments invariably have a common interest in repressing. This lack of homogeneity may be the product of divergent colonial histories and divergent regional problems with the struggle for autonomy, seldom reaching the surface of public or political discourse (Bourdieu 1992: 132). It may also have to do with calculations of interest of international relations or *raison d'état* which alleges that there are more important national interests at stake than the imprisonment of individual terrorists. Ultimately, the lack of homogeneity also reflects and reinforces the various unresolved tensions in the very definition of terrorism.

Organized Crime

Organized crime, a topic which has recently enjoyed media attention in many EU Member States, is also defined in different ways (Levi 1993b: 58, 62). In law enforcement circles as well as in popular belief it is commonly supposed that organized crime can be described in terms of certain defining characteristics. These characteristics are, first, that crime syndicates monopolize or attempt to monopolize activities such as prostitution, drug-trafficking or unauthorized dumping of chemical waste. Secondly, violence is used systematically against the challengers of these monopolies or against those who break the discipline of the criminal organization, or those who give evidence to police or courts about the crime syndicates (*e.g. pentiti* in Italy). Thirdly, criminal groups or families are deeply embedded in certain societies which makes ordinary measures of crime control ineffective—the police can only occasionally catch individuals without being able to suppress the organizations as such. Fourthly, organized crime tends to have a hierarchical and bureaucratic structure: there are a number of specialized functions within the organization, including the functions of intelligence-gathering and analysis as well as violence. Fifthly, criminal organizations have access to expertise, such as legal, financial and accounting services, normally associated with legitimate commercial activity. Sixthly, the organizations can exercise influence over political, administrative and judicial processes.

The objective of international co-operation against organized crime may appear unproblematic because the term conjures up similar negative associations across a range of societies. However, there is a variety of perspectives on organized crime; different laws, international agreements and law enforcement strategies attempt to address problems associated with it.[19] This prompted the European Parliament to call for all EU Member States to 'incorporate in their legal systems definitions of certain types of offence which will be the same throughout the European Union', and it requested 'that membership of a "mafia-style" association should be considered as a criminal offence in all Member States', in accordance with the current Italian legislation on this subject.[20]

But a survey of Britain, Germany and France shows the problems of arriving at a common approach to organized crime (Bovenkerk 1992: 11–31). This is partly because few criminal organizations share all of the defining characteristics listed above, and because the characteristics themselves are open-ended. Some argue in favour of abandoning the concept of organized crime altogether in favour of the notion of crime enterprises which are a response to market opportunities presented by the criminalization of commodities and services (Van Duyne 1993; Passas and Nelken 1993; Saltmarsh 1993).

Despite these sceptical views, European law enforcement co-operation has recently given high priority to repression of organized crime and it is frequently endorsed as an aim in declaratory statements. The objective of combating organized crime has been

---

[19] The lack of a common system for the analysis and definition of organized crime was also an obstacle in an organized crime survey in the EU Member States by the Drugs and Organized Crime Group of the K4 Committee (doc. 10166/3/94 ENFOPOL 144 REV 3, Brussels, 23 January 1995 (confidential)).

[20] See the debate by the European Parliament on the Report on Criminal Activities in Europe (11/2/94, OCJ 61, 28.2.94, pp. 235 and 237). The report was prepared by the Committee of Civil Liberties and Internal Affairs; Salisch and Speroni (1994).

adopted by summits of the European Council, and it has been an important consideration underlying article 10 of the Draft Convention of the Member States of the European Communities on the crossing of their external borders (see chapter 4).[21] A Ministerial Agreement in September 1992 led to the creation of an anti-mafia group under the then existing Trevi structure to study forms of co-operation in the field of organized crime.[22] The Ministerial Agreement of 2 June 1993 on Europol defines its first task as coordinating the exchange and analysis of intelligence in relation to illegal drug trafficking—an area in which extensive criminal conspiracies are present—and the agreement stated that this was the first step towards tackling all forms of organized crime.[23] In addition, there is considerable discussion both in EU ministerial meetings and in the law enforcement community about the increased threat of organized crime in a Europe 'without frontiers', strengthened by the realization that there are numerous horizontal relations between multinational crime systems (Martin and Romano 1992: 80-1).[24]

Organized Crime in Britain

In Britain, 'organized crime' is a frequently used term in ordinary language but there is no legal concept of organized crime in English or Scots law (Hobbes 1994). British law is predominantly concerned with individual responsibility for criminal acts, although under the Prevention of Terrorism Act 1974–89, there are various offences associated with membership of or support for a terrorist organization (Finnie 1990). People can also be prosecuted as

[21] SN 2528/91 WGI 82.

[22] Council of the European Communities, General Secretariat, Press Release, Interior and Justice Ministers meeting, Brussels, 18/9/92 (159 (8633/92)). See also *Financial Times,* 4 Sept. 1992 and 18 Sept. 1992; *Guardian* 19 Sept. 1992; *Le Monde* 20-21 Sept. 1992. The French Minister of Justice Michel Vauzelle described this decision as 'without precedent and as a strong political signal for all the peoples of Europe, as well as showing our solidarity with Italy.' (*Le Monde,* 22 Sept. 1992). It was widely interpreted as a move to help President Mitterrand in a very closely fought campaign to win the referendum in France on the TEU (internal security was one of several issues highlighted by opponents of the Treaty).

[23] Press Release, Trevi Ministerial Meeting Copenhagen, Denmark, 2 June 1993.

[24] Martin and Romano (1992) mention precedents such as the relation between drugs and terrorism (Bolivia, Colombia), between illegal drug–production and illegal arms trade (Africa, India, Pakistan, Afghanistan, Iran, Burma and Thailand), and between money laundering, illegal trade in arms and drugs and espionage (Panama).

accomplices, as accessories, as participants in a conspiracy or, under Scottish law, for 'art and part guilt', but they cannot be prosecuted, save in exceptional circumstances, for being members of an organization. In other words, the criminal law is essentially 'event-based'; in the absence of a specific criminal event there is no responsibility. Except in the suppression of terrorism legislation, there is no equivalent in ordinary British law of the French concept of an *association de malfaiteurs*,[25] or the Italian anti-mafia legislation, or any special legislation, such as the United States Organized Crime Control Act (1970) directed towards the repression of criminal organizations as such. The concept of organized crime has nonetheless found its way into British law enforcement circles. The National Criminal Intelligence Service has made the gathering of intelligence on organized crime one of its priorities (National Criminal Intelligence Service 1994: 8-9); and a parliamentary committee is currently looking into the incidence and definition of organized crime in Great Britain (Home Affairs Committee 1994).

Organized Crime in Germany

In Germany, the debate about organized crime began in the 1970s as part of a wider public discussion of rising crime rates. While it was generally agreed that criminal organizations did not exist on the scale of American-style mafiosi syndicates (Busch 1991), there was a growing concern about the continued increase in crime rates, corruption scandals and mafia investment. Authoritative criminal lawyers, law enforcement officers and academic experts forecast a significant increase in the impact of organized crime on politics, administration and economic life by the end of the century. Scenarios like these have encouraged the intelligence services, the Constitutional Guard and the Federal Intelligence Agency BKA to take an interest in combating organized crime (Diederichs 1991a).

The German legislation is in advance of that found in other European countries and could help to avoid conceptual problems in using the term organized crime, because it lists the specific activities which come under the heading of organized crime.[26] It also

---

[25] The recent French penal code (law no. 92683 of 22 July 1992) imposes heavier sanctions for criminal acts if they are committed by a member of *une bande organisée* (Art. 222–34 for drug trafficking; Art. 225–8 for living off immoral earnings).

[26] *Gesetz zur Bekämpfung des illegalen Rauschgifthandels und anderer Erscheinungsformen der organisierten Kriminalität* (OrgKG, 15 July 1992; NJW 1993, Heft 4, at p. 234).

recognizes, for example, drug trafficking as a form of organized crime. The new law for fighting organized crime has *inter alia* strengthened the witness protection programme (Diederichs 1991b), has given a legal basis to undercover activities (*i.e.* infiltration by police officers into criminal conspiracies with their possible involvement in criminal acts) and has criminalized the organization of meetings, preparatory activities and the planning of illegal activities (Busch and Funk 1995; Weßlau 1991). Furthermore, the legislative definition is sufficiently wide to include financial fraud and economic crime.

Organized Crime in France

French thinking about organized crime is not expressed in the same terms as the German, partly because, until recently, there has been a relative lack of relevant criminological studies. This does however not mean that France does not have her own rich history of criminal conspiracies. There have been well-established links between criminality and some extremist political groups in Corsica, and, as in Nice, between municipal politicians and criminal organizations.[27] In recent years, following a long established pattern, there have been numerous assassinations as a consequence of competition between criminal factions in the Côte d'Azur. Marseilles was at the centre of the international drugs trade before Cosa Nostra supplanted it in the 1970s. A 1971 bilateral agreement between France and the United States was reached to combat Marseilles' position. During the same period, a specialized 'antigang' police unit was formed within the National Police to investigate criminal gangs, particularly those involved in armed robbery and extortion.

French official opinion has recently tended to analyze the problem of organized crime in terms of foreign intrusion (Giot-Mikkelsen 1993). One example is the 'Aubert report' which took as its starting point the danger represented by 'the Mafia' for the whole of Europe, demonstrated by the assassinations of the Italian judges Falcone and Borsellino in 1992 (Aubert 1993). The report found that although France was not the victim of the highest level of mafia criminality, the mafia had established footholds especially through the investment of funds in casinos, golf courses and prop-

---

[27] *Guardian* 11 Jan. 1991; *Guardian* 21 Aug. 1992.

erty in scattered areas of France. It argued in favour of better national and international co-ordination, new criminal legislation, strengthened police powers and a better system of supervision of the movement of funds. A related theme frequently expressed in public and official opinion is the emphasis on the high incidence of organized criminality in immigrant groups, and their presence in the *banlieux chaudes* (deprived and troubled urban areas). These themes converge in a highly coloured representation in Minc's (1993) recent depiction of France leading the rest of Europe into the 'new Middle Ages', with regional alliances of legitimate business and criminal organization challenging the hegemony of the sovereign state.

The Wider Debate on Organized Crime

Increased public and political attention to the phenomenon of organized crime has to a degree been caused by an 'Americanization' of the European debate on crime (Anderson 1994: 7; Pitts 1993: 109). In the United States, there has been a long standing preoccupation with the relationship between organized crime, drug-trafficking and immigrant communities (Goldstock 1991; Martin and Romano 1992: 85), and this has led a number of influential United States law enforcement agencies to seek international co-operation to combat the crime problem as viewed through this lens (Nadelmann 1993).

Apart from the transatlantic influence, four factors have encouraged the adoption of the objective of fighting organized crime in Europe. The first of these was the growing awareness that the 'war against drugs' was going to be lost: drug-trafficking has 'continued to resist effective control' (Martin and Romano 1992: 19). Judged by the size of drug seizures and the retail price of preferred drugs, the law enforcement problems posed by the consumption of illegal substances have apparently become worse during the past two decades. Numerous characteristics of drug-trafficking conspiracies coincide with those of organized crime, in particular maximizing profit, hierarchy, division of labour, and, sometimes, extortion and assassination. Secondly, as mentioned earlier, the collapse of communist regimes in Eastern and Central Europe has created openings for various criminal channels resulting from the relative absence of regulation and control. This situation has brought into being criminal enterprises and networks which can be conveniently described as organized crime. Thirdly, the relentless increase of reported crime in deprived West European urban areas has contributed to widespread feelings of insecurity among European electorates and fears that problems will increase when frontier controls are dismantled. Governments have to demonstrate that they are taking action (see chapter 4) and 'organized crime' provides a convenient label through which to declare their seriousness of purpose. Finally, the creation of Europol has highlighted the issue of organized crime. In the thinking of its promoters, Europol should—like the FBI—tackle serious cross-border crime (see chapter 2).

In EU Member States, particularly the northern members, two associations are made with organized crime—its transnational tendency and its ethnic basis. In Britain, organized crime is often perceived as a foreign import, such as United States gambling syndicates which attempted a take-over of United Kingdom gambling operations (Albini 1986), Mafiosi engaging in drug-trafficking and money-laundering, Triads pursuing similar activities to the Mafia supplemented by extortion rackets against the Chinese community (Black 1991; Posner 1988), and Jamaican Yardies also primarily involved in the drugs (Ramm 1990). In the Netherlands, Germany and Italy, Turkish clans have been active (Cooney 1992: 35-6). Polish groups have been present particularly in Germany and Italy, and criminal gangs are an increasing problem in East and Central European countries (Joutsen 1993); the deeply entrenched and long established Japanese Yakusas almost took over the French banking group Parisbas in 1986-87 (Choiseul-Praslin 1991; Kaplan and Dubro 1990). Pakistani heroin networks have been identified operating internationally in France, Spain and the United Kingdom. While evidence exists to substantiate these allegations, the depiction of organized crime as alien and imported helps to mobilize public opinion behind efforts to combat it. The way in which crime and criminals are categorized may serve political ends and sometimes expresses a dominant ideology rather than a sober assessment of evidence (Martin and Romano 1992: 100).

Drug Offences

Strategies to combat international crime, such as terrorism and organized crime, are often vague because of lack of clear and unambiguous definitions of what the problem is. Even in relatively straightforward matters such as drug-abuse definitions vary between the European countries, a point illustrated by a number of comparative studies on drug legislation in the CoE and EU Member States (Cervello 1990: 539-40; Leroy 1991). The definition of drug-related crime refers to different stages in drug production, marketing and consumption, such as cultivation, production, fabrication, transformation, distribution, exportation, importation, offer, sale, acquisition and transport (Cervello 1990: 540). The variation in levels of prosecutorial discretion, the distinction between 'soft' and 'hard' drugs, and the overall framework of public policy (varying from health-oriented to repressive) make a crucial difference in the domestic repression of drug abuse.

A certain degree of harmonization in the drugs field is achieved through common participation in a number of international agreements. The most important of these is the 1988 UN Convention Against Illicit Traffic in Narcotic Drugs and Psychotropic Substances, Article 3(1) of which requires signatory states to introduce legislation repressing a range of activities including cultivation, production, transportation and the organization, management and financing of drugs. Influenced by the 1988 UN Convention and the 1991 EC Directive on Prevention of Use of the Financial System for the Purpose of Money Laundering, among other initiatives, EU Member States have put in place legislation procedures designed to tackle the financial basis of drug-trafficking networks. These measures include the confiscation of proceeds from drug-trafficking and the imposition of reporting obligations on financial institutions designed to facilitate the detection and investigation of transactions suspected of being drug-related. Increasingly, similar innovations are being applied to other forms of serious crime (Gilmore 1991; Keyser-Ringnalda 1994, see chapter 7).[28]

Euro-Policing

The variation of classification of crime in Europe has an analogy in the field of 'Euro-policing'. In making an inventory of the current practices of cross-border policing in Europe (Benyon *et al.* 1993; Van der Wel and Bruggeman 1993), we concentrate on more or less institutionalized and formalized practices (see chapter 2). Sometimes an image is presented of European policing taking

---

[28] See Keyser–Ringnalda (1994) for a comparison of money laundering and confiscation laws in the US, the UK, France, Italy, Germany and the Netherlands.

clearly defined institutional forms. In reality however, cross-border policing is a rich mosaic of activities involving numerous bodies and organizations. These activities spill over borders, regions, institutions, and the uncertain line between private and public sectors. The term 'Euro-policing' is only properly used for forms of policing which have been developed within or coincide with the framework of the EU, such as Trevi and Europol. It is, in principle, possible to tackle crimes with global ramifications at the level of the EU. An example of regional law enforcement intervention in the chain of global organized crime was the dismantling of a European cocaine-distribution network in 1992 (Calvi 1993: 15). But, given the complex pattern of international criminal activity, neither the advantage of law enforcement co-operation through the institutions of the EU, nor the EU as an appropriate jurisdiction for criminal law, are self-evident (see chapter 6). In addition, there are practical considerations which weigh against these innovations. Among law enforcement services in the EU Member States there are numerous inter-agency conflicts and rivalries; the interests of the different national police forces tend to diverge, and the criminal justice systems differ in matters of procedure as well as substantive criminal law. This can lead to tensions when different agencies claim an interest in the same investigation (Calvi 1993: 245-50; see chapter 2).

There are, of course, arguments in favour of more co-operation in the EU to resolve the lack of co-ordination between national law enforcement agencies, and reconcile divergent national interests and laws. Some would argue there exists a background of common cultural practices and material interests, political consensus, similar professional experience and a cost-benefit calculation that more co-operation means more effective and cheaper criminal investigations and prosecutions. An important example of the law enforcement implication of a common culture and common interests is in respect of drug-trafficking: given their relative wealth, EU Member States together are an important market for drugs and provide an infrastructure for money laundering. In combination, these factors establish an opportunity structure within the international drugs trade. Although EU Member States are mostly at the 'receiving end' of the narcotics trade,[29] much can be done by law enforce-

---

[29] There are two exceptions to this observation. First, Europe is a major exporter of psychotropics to other regions of the world including Africa. A Joint Conference

ment agencies to disrupt or intercept the financial benefits of both the psychotropic and the narcotic drugs trade.

The evolution of the EU and the wide-ranging criminal justice activities of the Council of Europe have been crucial vehicles for developing a political consensus about the approach to aspects of international crime. The idea of a European Judicial Space, promoted in the seventies by Valérie Giscard d'Estaing and in the eighties by Felipe Gonzalez,[30] was a landmark proposal, but it has given way to a more pragmatic approach which bypasses concerns about sovereignty and practicality. In addition, there has been an increasing tendency to look at law enforcement activities that take place outside the traditional realm of state-sanctioned policing. This shift of focus implies the inclusion of law enforcement activities of customs and immigration authorities, administrative activities of supranational institutions such as the European Commission, criminal investigation activities of private security companies and special departments in multinational companies (insurance companies, credit card companies, banks, etc.). Also the number of international contacts between police organizations and the private sector has to be taken into account (Hoogenboom 1994: 415-21; Johnston 1992; Van Reenen 1989).

From this broad picture, we can derive three important and linked trends. First, the state is losing its monopoly of law enforcement. Supranational and intergovernmental structures are now beginning to take a share in law enforcement, perhaps leading to a

---

of the Pompidou Group and the INCB, held in Strasbourg in March 1993, concluded that the diversion of such substances from legal manufacture and trade in Europe into illicit traffic elsewhere 'has reached dimensions which merit an urgent and effective response by European Governments.' One of the factors contributing to this problem was identified as 'the abolition of customs controls at the internal frontiers of the European Community'. Second, the EU is also the largest producer and exporter of the precursor and other chemicals needed in the manufacture of a number of illicit drugs, including heroin and cocaine. A kind of 'reverse Balkan route' has for long operated whereby European exports are obtained for use in producer countries. EU Member States have been actively seeking to deal with this problem since 1988. This process has been facilitated by virtue of a legislative competence in this area—a competence specifically invoked in the EU ratification of the 1988 UN Convention.

[30] The idea of a European Judicial Space or Area is still being promoted in the nineties. Luciano Violante (1993: 415–16), President of the Anti–Mafia Commission of the Italian Parliament, has argued that a common jurisdiction should be created for some forms of crime, and that it should allow law enforcement agencies to operate with a certain freedom in confronting organized crime.

gradual erosion of state sovereignty (see chapter 3). States have realized that complete and absolute control in terms of law enforcement is now impossible, and have therefore been encouraged to hive off parts of this responsibility to other levels of political authority as well as to the private sector (Johnston 1992). Secondly, most transnational law enforcement co-operation is case-driven and concerned with achieving specific practical results. Companies with international links have important interests in transboundary law enforcement, namely preventing the loss of profit through fraud, corruption and counterfeiting, and they have come to share responsibility for it with the public policing sector. Thirdly, although a tendency of globalization in law enforcement circles is apparent, most cross-border policing contacts remain bilateral and informal, which may have repercussions for accountability and legitimacy (see chapter 8).

These are the trends which account for the absence of a neatly ordered arrangement of co-operative policing institutions in the European arena. The challenge to national sovereignty implies that the traditional system for the organization of criminal justice policy—the system of individual states—no longer suffices to deal with new problems of international crime. However, the case-oriented and predominantly bilateral character of the emerging demand for law enforcement co-operation militates against the development of a coherent alternative. European policing may be moving beyond the sovereign state, but the source and nature of its new regulatory framework remains contested and uncertain. The chapters which follow are predominantly concerned with exploring the implications of this uncertainty.

Dimensions of Analysis

There are several reasons why a theory of European police co-operation does not exist. First, the study of policing has almost always had a national focus, which is a reflection of the practice of policing itself. Most law enforcement problems are local, rather than regional or international. Secondly, the practice of cross-border policing is very difficult to access. The boundaries of this subject are hard to define, as cross-border police co-operation takes place in so many domains and at so many different levels. This problem is aggravated by the practical difficulties faced by researchers required to cover large territories and confronted by the reticence typical of individuals within the law enforcement community (Van Maanen 1978; Punch 1989). Thirdly, there is a problem of method and theoretical approach of whether police co-operation should be analysed in terms of comparative policing or in terms of international relations. Even within these choices, methodological and conceptual problems are extremely difficult. If an international relations approach is preferred, the choice of, for example, a neo-functionalist or a realist approach has to be made (see chapter 3 for a discussion). Implicit in making a choice of theoretical approach is that any theory limits the field of enquiry and may exclude important aspects of the subject.

But the main observation which may be made about the steadily growing literature is that it is predominantly descriptive, rather than analytical. Overviews, organization charts and tables of the various systems of European police co-operation are presented without an in-depth analysis of the internal and external dynamics of these systems. The literature concentrates on the high-profile and 'formalized' systems of European police co-operation, neglecting the grey, spontaneous and informal practices of co-operation. The present study cannot pretend to resolve these problems, but nonetheless attempts to go beyond the level of mere description. Certain 'variables' are identified—political, legal and societal— along which the dynamics of European police co-operation are analysed and an attempt is made to explore the interrelationship between these variables.

Theoretical approaches to European police co-operation may be categorized as *comparative, dimensional, organizational,* and *discursive* approaches. These are ideal types and individual researchers or research groups cannot be neatly assigned to these categories. *Comparative* policing studies is the best developed field of research, and is represented in most EU Member States.[31] The Trevi II group gave considerable attention to the comparative policing dimension in summer courses organized under its auspices. This literature concentrates on the systemic similarities and differences between national police organizations, such as historical development, mandate, the command structure, audit, police powers, and so on (IHESI 1992; Gleizal *et al.* 1993; Mawby 1990; Monet 1993; Roach and Thomaneck 1985; Scandone and Atzori 1990).

[31] Representatives include Albrecht Funk (Berlin), Cyrille Fijnaut (Leuven, Rotterdam), Jean–Claude Monjardet (Paris) and Rob Mawby (Plymouth).

Comparative policing studies are essential for a systematic analysis of cross-border policing. They make students at police academies aware of the legal, organizational and political context in which foreign colleagues operate. They also show the considerable obstacles in establishing effective and efficient cross-border police co-operation for reasons to do with policing and political culture, criminal justice procedures, and different organizational frameworks.

The *dimensional* approach incorporates comparative policing analysis, particularly because it focuses on the territorial and hierarchical organization of policing. European police co-operation may be represented in dimensional terms as a series of concentric circles or hierarchical layers. The Centre for the Study of Public Order (Leicester), for instance, conceptualizes police co-operation as divided in three distinct layers, the macro-, meso- and micro-level.[32] The macro-level is concerned with 'constitutional and international legal agreements' and the 'harmonization of national laws and regulations'; the meso-level is concerned with 'police (and other law enforcement) operational structures, practices, procedures and technology'; and the micro-level is concerned with 'the prevention and detection of particular offences and crime problems' (Benyon *et al.* 1993: 11–13). These levels, although suggestive, are ambiguous because it remains uncertain to what extent each level refers to legal texts and other formal structures, to the policy-making process or operational practice. In the absence of a more detailed attempt to address these matters, it becomes difficult to form a clear understanding of the relationship between the levels on the basis of which an explanatory model of police co-operation might be developed. The model that describes European police co-operation in terms of concentric circles is more modest in scope and far less problematic, because it is based exclusively on the scope of agreements which regulate law enforcement co-operation (King 1994). The scope of the Schengen Conventions is for instance smaller than that of the justice and home affairs co-operation in the TEU, which in turn is more limited than wider regional structures such as the Council of Europe and global structures such as Interpol and the UN.

---

[32] It should be noted that this distinction differs from the distinction between 'micro' and 'macro'–politics used in the introduction.

The *organizational* approach to European police co-operation is likely to be more frequently adopted as systems of co-operation become more mature. Some authors view the development of European police co-operation as a competitive or bargaining process between different bureaucratic interests and professional groups (Johnston 1992; Van Reenen 1989). Associated with this organizational approach is the conceptualization of European police co-operation as a policy-making process which aims at establishing a more or less co-ordinated system of regulatory régimes (Ahnfelt and From 1994; Den Boer 1993b).

The problem with this approach and that of the closely related *discursive* approach (Bigo and Leveau 1992; Bigo 1994b; Den Boer 1994b)—in which enunciations of policy-makers, senior officials and police officers are analysed to arrive at an understanding of power relationships and of changes in the objectives of policy-makers—is the relatively limited access to empirical material, such as the minutes of meetings, necessary to the investigator to achieve an insight into negotiation and bargaining processes. An analysis of European police co-operation in discursive terms requires classified documents and the expression of the opinions of well-placed participants. This methodological obstacle is less serious in the analysis of the discourse of the leading political actors (public speeches, media interviews) than in that of professional law enforcement and civil service discourse (official negotiations, lobbying processes, telephone conversations). But an essential weakness in the discursive approach is that although it may help to unravel the evolution of European police co-operation in terms of processes, it lacks a standpoint from which discursive performances can be analysed or criticized.

Against this backdrop, we attempt to develop a new *dynamic* approach which seeks to incorporate the best of each approach. We acknowledge the importance of the comparative emphasis on divergent national arrangements and attitudes, the dimensional emphasis on formal structures and their interrelationship, the organizational emphasis on the relationship between different levels of structure and action, and the discursive emphasis upon the macropolitical themes which frame general debate on the proper course of European police co-operation. By combining these within a single perspective, we hope to achieve a new balance and comprehensiveness in the treatment of European police co-operation.

Conclusion

The aim of European police co-operation—the prevention and repression of international crime—is hard to define. In policy statements and academic literature it is usually associated with systemic or 'organized' multinational crime. Other forms of international crime, such as small cross-border crime, are usually regarded as a matter for bilateral co-operation. The lack of a clear definition of international crime affects the formulation of strategies to combat it: there are differences in national approaches and there is a lack of effective legal instruments to tackle international crime. Another difficulty is that it is hard to chart the relationships which exist between the one form of (international) crime and another, even though fragmentary evidence exists of some relationships.

The failure to quantify the problem of international crime is due to the lack of reliable comparative criminal statistics. But even if a satisfactory method for the compilation of numerical data was found, an understanding would be required of the background and causes of criminal phenomena. Some mapping of the location of different forms of crime, highlighting attractive opportunities for criminals, such as weak social, economic and political infrastructure, would be a useful beginning. This form of strategic analysis—or threat assessment—could be part of Europol's remit. Our understanding of the nature and significance of European crime is also complicated by the fact that transfrontier crime does not stop at Europe's external frontiers. Hence, European police co-operation does not strictly provide a law enforcement panacea, but should rather be seen as the evolution of a more extensive common anti-crime strategy.

The academic models of European police co-operation, developed thus far, are to a large extent complementary. As European police co-operation is new, diffuse and international, it is hard to impose a fully developed theoretical model. Rather we must combine, and build upon, existing approaches. In the next chapter, we begin to develop our dynamic perspective by taking an historical approach and analysing the evolution of European police co-operation over time. We will also look at the most important views of those involved in the policy-making process, revealing stability and change in their positions. This analysis makes clear that the development of cross-border policing in Europe is very much the result of a sequence of initiatives in which decisions have not been arrived at in accordance with some kind of structural determinism, but only after long and hard negotiations in a fluctuating political environment.

2
Old Systems — New Systems

Introduction

This chapter sets out a framework for the analysis of European police co-operation. The approach in this chapter is to contrast old and new systems of European police co-operation, and the TEU is viewed as a catalyst for the transformation from old into new. The most prominent systems of European police co-operation—Interpol, Trevi, Schengen and Europol—will be discussed, not as static, but as dynamic entities. Trends for the immediate future can be identified, such as formalization, centralization and generalization. But those involved in the policy-making process on European police co-operation have differing views on the desirability of these trends. Opposing views exist concerning informal or formal structures of co-operation, a supranational or intergovernmental framework for institutional development, the role of politics as opposed to the impact of practitioners in the policy-making process, the importance of differences between national policies, legal systems, organizations and cultures, and the preference for a Europol with or without executive powers.

Historical Background of European Policing

The earliest proposals for establishing supranational forms of police co-operation were made at the end of the 19th century, when an awareness about the scope and importance of international crime became a concern for practitioners and academics alike. One of the first to address the problem of international crime was Professor Franz von Liszt of the University of Berlin (Bresler 1992: 17), for whom the growth of international crime was partly a function of the increased mobility of criminals, which in turn was encouraged by improved means of transport and technology. In legal terms, the term 'international crime' designated forms of deviance that transcended national jurisdiction (Nadelmann 1993), whereas in practical-operational terms 'international crime' meant illegal behaviour which required police authorities to look beyond the frontiers of the sovereign state. Controlling fugitives, smugglers, bandits and itinerants was a problem long before the first concerted action to create an organization of international police co-operation. Cross-border policing was then targeted at two distinct groups: law enforcement authorities co-operated informally against ordinary criminals, undesirable aliens, itinerants and fugitives; and, in the era of radical socialist and anarchist agitation, police authorities laid the basis for 'political police' co-operation in the 1898 anti-anarchist Rome conference. They continued a practice initiated by the Austrian police under Metternich and the Tzarist political police, the Okhrana, in shadowing suspects and using informants abroad (Fijnaut 1979; Jensen 1981; Van der Wel and Bruggeman 1993: 12).

In 1914, Prince Albert I of Monaco convened a conference in Monaco in which three hundred participants from fifteen different countries gathered in the first major attempt to create an international police organization to combat ordinary criminality (Anderson 1989: 38). Among the conclusions of the conference, proposals were made to standardize extradition procedures and to create an organization which would be in charge of the international collection and exchange of criminal information. Immediate implementation of this decision was prevented by the First World War. But in 1923, Dr Johann Schober, head of the Austrian national police force, revived Prince Albert's initiative by inviting more than three hundred lawyers and police officers to participate in the second international conference on crime and police. This Vienna conference became the occasion at which the forerunner of Interpol, the *Commission Internationale de Police Criminelle* (CIPC) was inaugurated (Anderson 1989: 39–41).

The issue of international crime did not have high political priority in the turbulent period leading up to the Second World War and the Cold War which followed it. International crime was brought back to the political agenda when various locations in Europe, the Middle East and America were targeted by terrorist attacks in the seventies and eighties. Alleged cross-border links between groups such as *Action Directe* and the Red Army Faction[1]

---

[1] *Le Monde*, 19 Nov. 1986.

encouraged law enforcement and intelligence agencies to widen their operational horizon and to share intelligence with foreign counterparts. During the same period, law enforcement agencies throughout Europe began to appreciate that drug trafficking and money laundering were not isolated problems, but phenomena which could be tackled only at an international or global level. The demand for a globalization of law enforcement efforts was met by the United Nations, which provided a framework in which a number of international conventions against drugs and drug-trafficking were negotiated,[2] and by Interpol, which provided a practical global framework for the international exchange of information (Anderson 1989).

With greater political stability in Europe, it became possible to envisage a supra-regional approach to law enforcement linked to the EC or some wider grouping of countries. Problems with crime were broadly similar in EC countries, especially the North European members. Interpol responded to the need for growing regional co-operation and to dissatisfaction with the service it was providing by creating a European Regional Assembly, a Technical Committee for Co-operation in Europe and, in 1986, a European Secretariat within its General Secretariat. But its lack of operational powers and its alleged lack of efficiency created pressures in some European countries for developing other initiatives. The proposed abolition of border controls within the EC, an outcome of the 1986 Single European Act, became a further important reason for intensified cross-border policing (see chapters 1 and 4).

National perspectives on the desirability of new and more effective forms of police co-operation differed. German official and police circles have been the strongest supporters of these new forms. Fijnaut claims German politicians have been consistent in promoting European bilateral and multilateral European police co-operation. This strategy is related to Germany's central position in Europe's internal security matrix. It also flows from the general rejection within German police culture of amateurism and *ad hoc* arrangements for fighting crime (Fairchild 1988). The German government, and Chancellor Kohl in particular, was the source of the

[2] The United Nations *Single Convention on Narcotic Drugs* (1961), the *Single Convention on Psychotropic Drugs* (1971), and the more comprehensive United Nations *Convention Against Illicit Traffic in Narcotic Drugs and Psychotropic Substances* (1988).

last-minute proposal, to the surprise of the other delegations, to include in the conclusions of the 1991 Luxembourg Summit a commitment to establish a Central European Investigation Office, leaving open the option of conferring executive powers (Fijnaut 1993b: 53). Furthermore, Germany has used the negotiations of the Schengen Conventions to achieve what it could not obtain by means of bilateral negotiations with France, namely a formal structure of cross-border police co-operation (Fijnaut 1993b: 40f).

This was the broad context in which systems of European police co-operation evolved, although many more arguments and events took place which cannot be discussed here. In the next part of this chapter, 'old' systems are contrasted with 'new' systems of co-operation, with a view to identifying more general trends in police co-operation.

Old Systems I: Interpol

The first years of the International Criminal Police Commission (the forerunner of Interpol) were dominated by the Vienna police department. When Schober was elected Chancellor of the Austrian Republic, his assistant, Dr Oskar Dressler, became Secretary-General. The organization was initially a loose association of individuals and national delegations. In terms of infrastructure, the organization relied heavily on the well-developed files of the Viennese police (Bresler 1992: 24). But it was inefficient to have one independent central bureau, and in 1925 Belgium was the first member to create its own National Central Bureau (NCB). This example was soon followed in countries like Germany, the Netherlands, Spain, Romania and Bulgaria. In 1956, having an NCB became a precondition for membership of the reformed organization, the International Criminal Police Organization—Interpol.

After the Nazi takeover of Austria in 1938 the organization was chaired by the head of the German *Reichs Sicherheits Haupt Amt,* Heydrich, and the head of the Vienna police and president of Interpol, Dr Michael Skubl was kept in political detention until 1945. Interpol's headquarters were moved to Berlin and data may have been used in the Nazi campaign against Jews, gypsies, communists and homosexuals (Bresler 1992: 56f; Van der Wel and Bruggeman 1993: 20). Following a Belgian initiative, the ICPC was revived, changing its name to International Criminal Police Organization (ICPO) and moving its headquarters to Paris. The organization had to be rebuilt completely on the basis of a drastically reduced number of criminal records, a lack of financial resources, and a poor infrastructure. But in 1949, there were already 35,000 new records and a significant number of specialist crime dossiers (Bresler 1992: 113). Interpol's administration was dominated by the French until the 1980s: although a senior Belgian police officer, Florent Louwage, was elected President at the General Assembly in 1951, the first four Secretary-Generals of the organization were, as the statutes required, French police officers (Anderson 1989: 42).[3]

France made the largest contribution to the organization because it provided the headquarters and paid some of its staff. The legal status of the organization was vague. The first Headquarters Agreement between Interpol and the French government was signed in 1972, endowing the organization with an independent legal status which was enhanced by the second Headquarters Agreement of 1982 (Anderson 1989: 57-73). The United Nations and the Council of Europe had already implicitly granted Interpol the status of a public international organization through admitting its formal participation in UN business. Although problems related to Interpol's independence remained unresolved, the organization developed into a global service. Bresler (1992: 125) notes that by 1972, the NCB in Wiesbaden reported co-operation with 98 countries, the NCB in Tokyo with 55 and the NCB in New Delhi with 37. Almost 1,000 arrests were made in 19 countries (mostly West European) at the request of NCBs and information was sent to other NCBs 87,981 times and received 66,608 times. Even now, around 80 per cent of Interpol's message-traffic concerns information-exchange between European countries (Benyon et al. 1993: 126). Message traffic through Interpol increased sharply in the 1980s, when the United States started to use Interpol to a much greater extent, and again in the 1990s, when new communications technology made a dramatic impact.

Like other international organizations, Interpol has its own internal rules (the statutes approved in 1956 and supplemented by the various resolutions of the annual General Assembly). The General Assembly is Interpol's controlling body: if a Member State fails to

---

[3] The General Assembly in Vienna in 1956 adopted a new statute which ruled that the Secretary-General should preferably be a person from the country where Interpol's headquarters are seated (Bresler 1992: 117).

comply with the rules set out in the statutes promulgated by the General Assembly, other States have the right to protest but sanctions against States are extremely rare. The General Assembly also admits new membership and elects an Executive Committee (consisting of thirteen members: a president, three vice-presidents and nine delegates). The Executive Committee prepares the agenda for the General Assembly, plans Interpol's activities and controls the work of the Secretariat-General. Mr Raymond Kendall, who is an ex-United Kingdom Special Branch officer, former Head of the Drugs Sub-Division and Head of the Police Division of Interpol has been head of Interpol since 1985 (Anderson 1989: 79; Van der Wel and Bruggeman 1993: 22–3). The Secretariat-General is responsible for daily management of Interpol and is not accountable to the governments of member states: this implies that the Secretary-General of Interpol operates independently, rather like the UN Secretary-General, and the conduct of the organization is regulated in international law only by the Universal Declaration of Human Rights (Article 2 of Interpol statutes).

Although Interpol's major advantage is its global reach and membership—it currently has 176 members world-wide—there have been complaints from European Members about the service it provides and they have expressed doubts, which Interpol strongly contests, about the security of message traffic through the Interpol communications system (Home Affairs Committee 1990: xxv–xxvii). Much time is lost by the poor quality of service provided by some countries, which reflects inefficiencies in national law enforcement agencies rather than in Interpol's own procedures and practices. A considerable effort has been made to improve the effectiveness of Interpol headquarters. At the Nice General Assembly in 1987, a budget of ten million Swiss francs was approved for a five-year modernization plan that included the computerization of the archives and the links between Interpol headquarters and the NCBs (Bresler 1992: 188). Since the introduction of the Automated Message Switch System (AMSS)[4] in 1987, and the Automated Search Facility (ASF)[5] in 1992, complaints about

[4] The AMSS processes about one million messages a year, among which 350,000 messages are received and 650,000 transmitted (Benyon *et al.* 1993: 225).

[5] The ASF—to which about 25 countries now have access—enables National Central Bureaus to control information which is entered into the computerized database and to control who has access to it, granting or denying access to any other Member State (Benyon *et al.* 1993: 225f).

delays have declined. However, doubts, justified or not, about the reliability of Interpol's communication network—especially in relation to information about terrorism—have remained.

A major peculiarity of Interpol is the lack of a treaty basis for the organization, a matter which is now being seriously considered. A treaty might help to dispel popular myths (often encouraged by the mass media) about Interpol, such as the belief that it can send out agents to conduct investigations. More seriously, without a statute there are no rules binding on Member States about the communication of information through the Interpol communications system. A form of data protection, through a supervisory board, was included in the 1982 Headquarters Agreement (Anderson 1989: 65-6), but this has not offered a sufficient protection for some European States, particularly Germany. The issue of data protection is likely to be a continuing problem which can only be definitively settled by formal treaty provisions. Interpol's Executive Committee recently rejected two recommendations formulated by its internally convened European Working Party on data protection. These recommendations included the establishment of criteria according to which data can be exchanged (in compliance with national data protection legislation) and definitions of key terms to be included in the Rules on International Police Co-operation (Grange 1994).

As noted in chapter one, neutrality in political, racial or religious cases used to be an obstacle in the international co-operation against terrorism. Since this was overcome at the 1984 Luxembourg General Assembly (Bresler 1992: 170), Interpol's services have also been used for terrorist-related crimes. The Washington General Assembly in 1985 approved of a special anti-terrorist group, which was finally created in January 1987 under the name 'TE' group and initially led by FBI agent Don Lavey. Two months later, the General Assembly circulated an anti-terrorist 'manual' (*Guide for Combating International Terrorism*) among the NCBs. The TE group has since specialized in a form of proactive investigation, resulting in a series of warnings about possible terrorist actions (Bresler 1992: 241).

Faced by the challenge of new initiatives in the field of European policing—such as Schengen and Europol—Interpol is contemplating its future and trying to determine its position *vis-à-vis* new structures and organizations (see below). The traditional strength of the organization is apparently that it kept the 'informal old boy network' intact: it was an organization created by police officers and run by police officers (Bresler 1992: 30–1). This is probably eroding because of Interpol's almost universal membership and because European police officers now have many more opportunities for meetings and contacts. Although, in the early to mid-1980s, there was apprehension in the General Secretariat of Interpol that it would be marginalized by new forms of European co-operation, a new confidence is now apparent. This is based on the technical improvements in Interpol's services, a world-wide membership and the perception that professional police opinion is becoming less enthusiastic about Schengen and Europol. The delays, declining political interest in Europol, and the realization that a genuinely operational facility needs a clear legal basis (which will be achieved only with great difficulty), have resulted in a change of mood among the senior police officers in contact with Interpol headquarters. 'Professional opinion has swung in favour of Interpol', according to Raymond Kendall, because it is seen 'as the most useful instrument to hand'.

Old Systems II: Trevi

In the wake of continued indigenous and Middle Eastern terrorism, and disappointed by the refusal by Interpol's Secretary-General, Nepote, to have terrorism put on the agenda of the General Assembly, EC ministers of justice and home affairs came together in Rome in 1975 and created 'Trevi' (named after the famous fountain in Rome and after its first (Dutch) chairman, Mr Fonteijn). Trevi, under the auspices of European Political Co-operation, was an intergovernmental committee outside the EC framework, intended as a forum to coordinate an effective response to international terrorism. A declaration after a Trevi ministerial meeting on 2 June 1976 set out, among others, the following objectives: co-operation in the fight against terrorism and exchange of information about the organization, equipment and training of police organizations, especially tactics employed against terrorism. The group met biannually at ministerial level with more frequent meetings of officials and law enforcement professionals.[6]

---

[6] The organizational structure of Trevi was tripartite. The first level was the ministerial level, the second level that of senior officials and the third level that of the

Trevi soon established a number of working groups. Working Group I was created in 1977 with a membership of senior civil servants and representatives of police and security services. Its most important task was to exchange information about terrorist strategies, activities and persons, and about dangers to airline security. Security issues in relation to nuclear plants were also part of the brief of this group (*e.g.* nuclear transports and protective measures to be taken by police in the event of a nuclear fire). Other issues covered concerned the role of the media in the response to violent terrorist incidents, and the protection of VIPs. The exchange of information was facilitated by liaison offices[7] in each country and by the setting up of a secure communications network. Liaison offices exchanged both administrative and sensitive information by telephone, facsimile or telex: information about terrorist groups could be made available immediately (Van der Wel and Bruggeman 1993: 46). The link between political co-operation and foreign and security operation was made explicit in 1986 by the direct communication of Working Group I threat analyses to Ministers of Foreign Affairs. While anti-terrorist activities within Trevi I had a considerable political element, the Police Working Group on Terrorism (PWGOT), with a membership wider than the EC Member States, concentrated on practical and operational affairs. Both indicated a growing acknowledgement that internal security was no longer a purely national affair (Van der Wel and Bruggeman 1993: 47).

The remit of Trevi's Working Group II, established simultaneously with Working Group I, was co-ordination in matters of police equipment (*e.g.* police weaponry, radio equipment, forensic science), and police techniques, tactics and training. The Working

working groups. Senior officials prepared the groundwork for the Ministerial Conference. From 1986, the activities of the Trevi working groups and the senior officials were co-ordinated by the *Troika,* consisting of the current, previous and future Presidency. The Troika was extended in 1989, when it became a *Piatnika* (five chairs in chronological order). External contacts with the so-called 'friends of Trevi' were also part of the Troika's remit (Van der Wel and Bruggeman 1993: 44).

[7] These liaison offices were facilities for the exchange of information about terrorist incidents and for mutual support in anti-terrorist action more generally. In Belgium, the relevant facility was the *Veiligheid van de Staat* at the Ministry of Justice, in Germany the *Bundesamt für Verfassungsschutz,* in France, the *Unité de Coordination de la Lutte Anti-Terroriste* (UCLT), in the UK, the European Liaison Section of the London Metropolitan Police Special Branch and, in the Netherlands, the *Binnenlandse Veiligheidsdienst.* In the event of terrorist crimes, Member States were required to inform the other Member States within 24 hours.

Group organized numerous seminars about these matters (Benyon et al. 1993: 155). In the same year, the mandate of Working Group II was extended to cover information exchange in relation to public order, for example football hooliganism and demonstrations. In 1985, a new Working Group III was created to enhance co-operation in the area of serious crime other than terrorism, such as drug-trafficking, bank robberies and arms-trafficking. Among the issues discussed in Working Group III have been strategies to combat drug-trafficking, stationing of drug liaison officers, confiscation of the proceeds of crime, combating of vehicle theft, witness protection programmes, money laundering and environmental crime (Van der Wel and Bruggeman 1993: 50).

Finally, Trevi '1992' was created in 1988 to examine the consequences of the abolition of internal border controls in the European Community (Benyon et al. 1993: 152–64). This group reported to the Co-ordinator's Group, instituted at the European Council summit at Rhodes in 1988, and which drafted the Palma document containing a list of preparatory measures for the abolition of border controls (see chapter 4). Trevi '1992' also had close working relationships with the Mutual Assistance Group '92 (Customs) and the *Ad Hoc* Group on Immigration, which drafted the Dublin Asylum Convention[8] and the External Frontiers Convention.[9] It was also responsible for overseeing activities in the *Ad Hoc* Group on Europol, which reported directly back to the senior officials. An *Ad Hoc* Group on International Organized Crime[10] was added in September 1992 to propose measures to counter both the increasing influence of the Mafia across the territory of the EU and the threat of East European organized crime (Van der Wel and Bruggeman 1993: 44). Although the latter group was not established as a Trevi Working Group, it followed the Trevi cycle for practical and financial reasons. The first report of the group appeared at a meeting of the Trevi ministers on 6 and 7 May 1993 in Denmark. It contained an analysis of the structure and nature of the Mafia and other organized criminal groups, and also offered a threat assessment of organized crime (Benyon et al.

---

[8] Convention Determining the State Responsible for Examining Applications for Asylum Lodged in one of the Member States of the European Communities, Dublin, 15 June 1990.

[9] Draft Convention of the Member States of the European Communities on the crossing of their external borders (SN 2528/91 WGI 82).

[10] Also called the Anti-mafia Group; see ch. 1.

1993: 44). Trevi '1992' was disbanded in 1992 during the United Kingdom Presidency upon the completion of its main tasks, its remaining responsibilities being re-allocated to Working Group III.

Trevi did not publish many documents, an exception being the important *Programme of Action* in June 1990.[11] It envisaged the creation of the European Drugs Intelligence Unit (EDIU). The EDIU was to be supported by national drugs intelligence offices in each EC Member State. In time, the EDIU proposal was to become enmeshed with the proposal to create Europol (see below).

Because of Trevi's intergovernmental status, democratic control of its activities had a *post hoc* character. It has been criticized by the European Parliament and by civil rights groups for its lack of transparency and of external democratic control (Benyon *et al.* 1993: 168; Van Outrive 1992b; Spencer 1990; and see chapter 8). The United Kingdom Home Affairs Committee of the House of Commons was concerned that the normal consultative and democratic procedures of the EC were not applicable to Trevi, although it considered this to be compensated by accountability of national ministers to their national parliaments (Van der Wel and Bruggeman 1993: 54; Home Affairs Committee 1990: xx-xxiv). Police officers have criticized Trevi for its remoteness from the practice of policing (Van der Wel and Bruggeman 1993: 55–6). Many also considered the work of Trevi to overlap with that of other bodies, in particular Schengen, the CoE, and various more or less institiutionalized bodies involving some or all of the EC Member States (Benyon *et al.* 1993: chs. 4 and 5). The force of these criticisms has been somewhat reduced by the introduction of a new Co-ordinating Committee under the aegis of the third pillar of the TEU. Trevi has thus been 'absorbed' by the Pillar on Justice and Home Affairs, and its former tasks have been integrated in the work of newly established steering groups (see below).

New Systems I: Schengen

The most elaborate proposal yet for internal security co-operation between a majority of EU Member States is the Schengen Conventions,[12] named after the village on the Mosel where the

---

[11] Trevi Programme of Action relating to the Reinforcement of Police Co-operation and the Endeavours to Combat Terrorism or Other Forms of Organized Crime (Dublin, June 1990).

[12] Convention on the gradual abolition of checks at the common borders of

agreements were signed. Schengen is symbolically located at the intersection of the three frontiers of Luxembourg, France and Germany. The Schengen Implementing Convention of 1990[13] is a comprehensive framework to balance free movement of goods, persons and services with intensified cross-border police co-operation. The main philosophy underlying the Schengen Conventions is that when borders are opened and free traffic of persons and goods is allowed, internal security can only be guaranteed by compensatory measures.

After a series of secret negotiations, the Schengen Convention was signed in 1985 by Germany, France, Belgium, Luxembourg and the Netherlands. The European Commission had observer status in the negotiations, and encouraged the Schengen countries to have all checks on persons crossing their common land frontiers abolished by 1 January 1990. The European Commission monitored the arrangements under the Agreement to ensure they were consistent with EC rules. The 1985 Convention laid the foundation for an implementation agreement. The first part concerns short-term measures which entered into force as of January 1, 1986, dealing particularly with the free movement of goods and services (Cruz 1990: 3). The second part concerns long-term measures dealing with the free movement of persons. Short-term measures for the relaxation of border controls included the introduction of visual checks on EU citizens, the green sticker at the front window of small motorized vehicles, and joint checks at the borders (Peek 1990: 112). The Schengen partners intended to improve co-operation between customs and police authorities and to co-ordinate the fight against the illegal trade in drugs, serious international crime and illegal immigration. In the longer term, the parties undertook to harmonize their visa policies, firearms and ammunition laws, and rules on the registration of travellers in hotels (Taschner 1990: 113).

France, the Federal Republic, Belgium, the Netherlands and Luxembourg of 14 June 1985, and the Schengen Implementing Convention of 19 June 1990 (for an English translation, see *Commercial Laws of Europe*, vol. 14, Feb. 1991, Part 2).

[13] Both Conventions are now signed by all EU Member States except Denmark, the UK and Ireland. Denmark stated its interest in becoming a member of Schengen in June 1994 in view of the likely accession to the EU of three other Nordic states with which it shares a passport-free zone (Nordic Union). In the event, Finland and Sweden joined at the end of 1994, but Norway voted against accession. Denmark enjoys observer status within Schengen, and Austria became a full member on 6 March 1995 (*NRC Handelsblad*, 22 Feb. 1995). For an account about the reasons for non-accession by the UK and Ireland, see O'Keeffe (1994).

The preparation of the Schengen Implementing Convention was undertaken by four working parties; police and security; movement of people; transport; and movement of goods. The negotiations were protracted, especially with regard to police activities in foreign territory, extradition, drug policies and asylum policy (Den Boer 1991b: 4). Developments in Eastern Europe delayed the signing of the Implementing Convention, as the Federal Republic of Germany was concerned about controlling the movement of East Europeans other than East Germans across its border with East Germany (Den Boer 1991b: 6). This pause provided parliamentarians, lawyers and academics with an extended opportunity to criticize the 'democratic deficit' of the Schengen negotiations. A Resolution adopted by the European Parliament on 23 November 1989 contained a request to the national parliaments to withold approval of the Implementing Convention, until further information was given to national parliaments and the European Parliament. The Resolution suggested that a large number of issues had not been properly worked out, such as border controls between East and West Germany, refugee policy, asylum policy, data protection, hot pursuit, drugs policies, and banking secrecy. For some commentators, this merely exposed the underlying problem of the continuing absence of a common European understanding of the role of policing and judicial co-operation.[14]

Negotiations resumed in March 1990 and the Convention was signed on 19 June 1990. It contains arrangements for the pursuit of criminals across national borders, a common asylum policy, illegal immigration, resolution of the status of refugees, joint action against drug-trafficking and terrorism, and a common computerized information system (Schengen Information System or SIS) for the exchange of personal data. Some of the criticisms levelled against Schengen had been met. Before the introduction of SIS, the partners agreed to ratify the 1981 Convention of the Council of Europe for the Protection of Individuals with Regard to the Automatic Processing of Personal Data, to introduce national data-protection laws (Belgium had none), and to introduce complaint procedures if individuals considered their rights had been infringed (Baldwin Edwards and Hebenton 1994; Den

---

[14] E.g. NRC Handelsblad, 13 Dec. 1989.

Boer 1991b: 19-23; Dumortier 1992; Raab 1994). The agreements would refer more explicitly to the 1951 Geneva Convention of the United Nations on the Status of Refugees as amended by the New York protocol of 31 January 1967. Bank secrecy, an issue of particular significance for Luxembourg, would not be abolished but would be subject to important exceptions by the EC Directive on Money Laundering (Den Boer 1991b: 7). The Implementing Convention was signed in the expectation that West and East Germany would be unified, and that the external border would be relocated to the east, between Germany and Poland and Czechoslovakia.

The justification of the Schengen Conventions was twofold. On the one hand, they sought to prefigure the arrangements for a wider border-free Europe under the '1992' programme; that is to say, they provided a prototype which could be refined for use in an EU-wide context. On the other hand, the Conventions anticipated delays and difficulties in the wider EU-programme and offered a more modest interim solution. The first justification can be traced to the political declaration made by the Member States when the SEA was adopted: the introduction of the free movement of persons should be accompanied by co-operation between the Member States with regard to the entry, movement and residence of nationals of third countries, and with measures to combat terrorism, crime, the traffic in drugs and illicit trading in works of art and antiques. Another, complementary, general declaration was made with regard to Articles 9 and 13 of the SEA, reserving the right of Member States to adopt measures for the improvement of its internal security, as long as these were compatible with EC law. The second justification behind the Schengen Conventions gained prominence as the slowness of progress towards the opening of intra-EC borders became evident, making the target of 31 December 1992 look increasingly unrealistic. Some EC Member States felt it would be too difficult to reach an agreement with all twelve.[15]

The forerunners of this twin-track evolution were the 1958

---

[15] Doubts about a core group of states proceeding more quickly were sometimes expressed. In their advice on the Schengen Conventions, the Dutch Council of State (*Raad van State*) asked whether or not the other EC Member States wanted to become signatories to the Agreement, and if not, why not (*Tweede Kamer der Staten-Generaal*, Vergaderjaar 1985–86, 19 326, 29 Oct. 1985).

Benelux Treaty,[16] the 1977 Convention of Paris,[17] the 1984 Saarbrücken Agreement,[18] and, to a certain extent, the 1949 Police
Border Agreement between the Netherlands and Belgium. The
Benelux Treaty was an important precursor of the abolition of
frontier controls envisaged by the Schengen Conventions. Belgium,
the Netherlands and Luxembourg agreed on the free movement of
persons, goods, services and capital, the co-ordination of national
economic policies, and the pursuance of a common trade policy
towards other countries. Six months before the treaty came into
force, passport controls between the three countries were abolished
for Benelux nationals travelling from one Benelux country to
another. As the Saarbrücken Agreement sought a similar relaxation
between France and Germany, the Schengen Conventions can be
viewed in a clear progression from these two earlier agreements,
bringing together the various signatory states in a wider border-
free zone (Peek 1990: 112).

Schengen is, however, far more ambitious and wide-ranging than
its smaller-scale predecessors. The Police Border Agreement
between the Netherlands and Belgium of 1949, for instance, only
addressed police co-operation in the common border area. The
Benelux Treaty mainly concerns the cross-border 'hot' pursuit of
persons suspected of extraditable offences, but does not include
other forms of operational co-operation, exchange of information
or technical collaboration. The Saarbrücken Agreement concentrates on a modest level of cross-border information exchange. The
Paris Convention between France and Germany was intended to

---

[16] The Benelux Economic Union was created on 3 Feb. 1958 (in force July 1960),
the year after the implementation of the Treaty of Rome. The Treaty was extended
by the Convention on the Transfer of Control of Persons to the External Frontiers
of the Benelux Territory of 11 April 1960 and the Benelux Treaty on Extradition
and Mutual Assistance in Criminal Matters of 27 June 1962. The Schengen
Implementing Convention has been strongly influenced by the latter.

[17] Convention between the Government of the Federal Republic of Germany and
the Government of the French Republic on the Co-operation between Police
Authorities in the German–French Border Area (1977).

[18] *Abkommen zwischen der Regierung der Bundesrepublik Deutschland und der
Regierung der Französischen Republik über den schrittweisen Abbau der Kontrollen
an der deutsch-französischen Grenze, Bundesgesetzblatt,* Nr. 27, Jahrgang 1984, Teil
II, Bonn, 767–71. The Saarbrücken Agreement was concluded on 30 July 1984
between France and West Germany to relax border controls on individuals at the
Franco–German internal border. Hence, it was a bilateral realization of the statement of the Fontainebleau European Council made on 25 and 26 June 1984 (Fijnaut
1993b: 42).

develop the organizational, tactical and technical conditions necessary for effective policing on both sides of the border; the main instrument was the organization of regular meetings to discuss common police measures (Fijnaut 1993b).

Despite ratification of the Convention by all signatory states, it had still not been implemented by the end of 1994. Indeed, when the signatories could not meet the October 1994 deadline for the implementation of the Convention, it was the fifth such failure. One explanation at the time for SIS not yet being fully operational was the existence of technical problems. This may have been an excuse however, masking political disagreement about national drug policies and the effectiveness of border controls in checking illegal immigrants. Tension over these matters has been particularly marked between France and the Netherlands. However, the Netherlands introduced mobile border patrols against 'bogus' asylum-seekers and illegal immigrants, and has attempted to achieve tighter control over drugs sales to foreigners in Dutch border towns.[19] Despite delays in implementing Schengen, there has been a gradual movement to bring national internal security policies into line.

The costs and benefits of the Schengen Conventions for law enforcement agencies are difficult to assess. Opening the internal borders has certainly been exploited by police and security services in order to gain a broader mandate, more resources and better equipment (see Articles 39-47 of the Schengen Implementing Convention) (Fijnaut 1993b: 50). Whether a real increase in international crime can be established (see chapter 1), and whether a hypothesis about future crime trends can be used to justify the extension of police activities must remain open questions. Apart from gaining an important facility in the computerized SIS, law enforcement agencies will be able to exchange information much more easily through telephone, radio and telex links, to mount pro-active criminal investigation activities by means of covert cross-border surveillance[20] and the technique of controlled delivery of drugs (Busch and Funk 1995), to engage in a hot pursuit of

[19] See *De Volkskrant*, 3 and 7 May 1994 .

[20] Only applicable to extraditable crimes: murder, manslaughter, rape, arson, counterfeit, aggravated theft and fencing, extortion, abduction and hostage-taking, trading in human beings, illegal drug-trafficking, arms and explosives offences, destruction by means of explosives, and illegal transport of toxic and harmful waste.

suspects across the internal border, and to station liaison officers in the other Schengen Member States.

The operational core of Schengen is a national SIRENE office in each Member State. The principal task of SIRENE is to control the validity of 'tagged information' exchanged through the SIS. SIRENE officials may refuse to circulate a request for information if such a request is contrary to national laws. Every SIRENE office will have direct access to other SIRENE offices. This requires a secondary electronic information system which chiefly transfers supplementary information.[21] SIRENE offices may co-operate with the Interpol National Central Bureaus to avoid a duplication of information requests within the Schengen territory,[22] but requests through the SIS have priority over those made through the Interpol network. One of our informants, an executive at the Schengen Secretariat, describes SIRENE as follows:

SIRENE is the core of European police co-operation, and is a framework within which action is undertaken on the basis of information. It depends on the political will whether or not [Europol] should grow out into something more executive. But SIRENE and Europol Phase II will at some point run parallel, as they are both operational. The only difference is that Europol is primarily concerned with intelligence, and SIRENE with information . . . The problem with SIRENE is that nobody has yet discussed the education and training of the people who will work in the national SIRENE offices. Nobody knows what the requirements should be. The recruitment of SIRENE personnel will be difficult—the people will have to speak foreign languages and have technical, legal knowledge. During the Schengen negotiations, the problem of machines has been addressed, but people are also important.

The implementation of the Schengen Convention is a task of the Executive Committee, in which each signatory has a seat (usually a minister, assisted by experts). Significantly, the Schengen Implementing Convention makes an unambiguous link with the European Community. Article 134 states that the Schengen Convention only applies to the extent that it is compatible with EC law, Article 140 stipulates that all EC Member States may become

---

[21] Discussion paper of the Interlabo GERN, Louvain, 18 March 1994, unpub. paper; *Circulaire* No. SAEI 93-1-L2/27-09-93, *Ministère de la Justice*, Paris.

[22] Until SIS is fully operational, information requests under the auspices of Article 95 of the Schengen Implementing Convention may also be circulated through the Interpol channels.

parties to the Agreement, and Article 142 provides that if a European-wide Convention for the creation of an area without internal frontiers is concluded (such as the External Frontiers Convention, see chapter 4), Schengen will be subject of incorporation, replacement or alteration.[23]

Despite these points of connection, Schengen will, if fully implemented, remain an intergovernmental framework, with limited involvement of EU institutions. Whether Schengen will be absorbed by Title VI of the TEU will depend on the scope of the External Frontiers Convention and the outcome of the 1996 Intergovernmental Conferences. If it is absorbed, more democratic and judicial controls by EU institutions become possible, and the SIS will merge into the European Information System. The Schengen Conventions may, however, also be used as facilitators of bilateral agreements between the signatories. Read alongside the equivalent provision in Article K.7 of the TEU, which states that Title VI shall not prevent the establishment or development of closer co-operation between two or more Member States in so far as such co-operation does not conflict with, or impede, that provided for in this Title, this may leave room for developing aspects of Schengen, or forms of co-operation exclusive to some or all Schengen countries, alongside the Europol system.

New Systems II: Europol and the TEU

At the Luxembourg European Council Meeting in June 1991, Germany proposed the creation of a new European Criminal Investigation Office. At the Maastricht Summit in December 1991, a modified proposal was formally adopted that Europol should be recognized under the new Justice and Home Affairs Title of the TEU. Article K.1(9) of this Title refers to Europol as a system of information exchange for the purposes of preventing and combating terrorism, drug-trafficking and other serious forms of international crime. In the associated Political Declaration of the Member States, the signatories are committed to explore ways to co-ordinate national investigation and search operations, to create new data bases, and to provide a central analytical facility for the planning of criminal investigations. Further, the Declaration states

[23] According to Lensing (1993: 226), the Netherlands is lobbying to make the ECJ competent to interpret the Schengen Conventions; if successful, this would forge an even closer link with EC law.

an intention to explore Europe-wide initiatives in respect of crime prevention, and to make progress in collaborating on training, research, forensic science and criminal records.

The contents of both Article K.1(9) and the Declaration are different in the terms used and less ambitious than the annex to the conclusions of the June 1991 European Council Summit in Luxembourg. Considerable resistance was expressed against the German idea of assigning operational powers to the 'European Criminal Investigation Office', making it analogous to the American FBI (Fijnaut 1993b: 55). The name 'European Police Office', subsequently used in the TEU, is more neutral but flexible enough to allow room for a possible extension of Europol's remit in the future (Den Boer 1994b: 175). The first phase of the Europol organization, namely the Europol Drugs Unit (see below), was opened in the old CRI buildings in The Hague on 1st January 1994, with Jürgen Storbeck as its Director, and commenced operations in October 1994.[24]

According to the draft Europol Convention prepared by the German Presidency of the EU in October 1994, Europol's main objective is to improve the effectiveness of law enforcement agencies in combating terrorism and preventing and combating unlawful drug-trafficking and other serious forms of international crime. These crimes must satisfy a number of criteria—their prevention or investigation requires the involvement of two or more Member States, the criminal offences are committed within an organized criminal structure, and they are sufficiently serious to justify action at the European level (Article 2). Under the Europol Convention, the organization's initial remit will include unlawful drug-trafficking, crime connected with nuclear and radioactive substances, illegal immigrant smuggling, international motor vehicle theft, and illegal money-laundering activities in connection with these forms of crime. On the unanimous proposal of the Council, the Europol Management Board may add any of the following crimes to the list of those Europol is competent to address: terrorism; homicide; grievous bodily injury; kidnapping and hostage-taking; unlawful trade in human organs; exploitation of prostitution; illegal trafficking in arms, ammunition and explosives; illegal transfer of technology; traffic in human beings; unlawful

[24] As of Oct. 1994, it had recruited seventy personnel and had processed the first 200 requests for information.

supply of labour; forgery of official documents; environmental crime; illegal trafficking in works of art and antiquities; robbery and blackmail; forgery of money, cheques and securities, and passing off such forgeries; credit card crime; product piracy; investment fraud; other international fraud; and computer crime. Money laundering and membership of illegal organizations associated with the above mentioned activities may also be added to the list.[25]

Terrorism, despite being mentioned in Article K.1(9) in relation to Europol, was not included in the list in the original draft Convention of November 1993. The Justice and Home Affairs Council had, in principle, already agreed the eventual inclusion of terrorism at its November 1993 meeting, but the conditions of its inclusion were still the subject of intense negotiation. Indeed, at that stage, a senior German police officer predicted that terrorism was so sensitive that its inclusion in the final list of crimes was 'unlikely'. According to a senior Dutch police officer, one of the problems is the inevitable involvement of intelligence services, which would lead to the creation of two networks, one between police, the other between intelligence services; this, for a senior Belgian police officer, would involve 'stepping into a grey area'. Despite this difficulty, at the May 1994 meeting on the draft Europol Convention, the Spanish delegation proposed the inclusion of terrorism, and this was provisionally inserted in the June 1994 draft. Subsequently, the German draft proposed a gradualist approach, with nuclear crime included in the initial brief and other dimensions of terrorism to be added later.[26]

In the November 1993 draft of the Europol Convention, the vexed question of operational powers was bypassed by an evasive formula: '. . . the High Contracting Parties . . . may . . . entrust Europol with any other task not provided for' in the Europol Convention (Article 3.2). This clause was not included in the later drafts of June 1994 or October 1994. Under these drafts, endowing

[25] The list of activities capable of being brought within Europol's competence expanded greatly between the initial draft of Nov. 1993 and the German draft of Oct. 1994.

[26] In the face of continuing Spanish pressure for a clearer commitment to anti-terrorist co-operation, an early proposal was made by the subsequent French Presidency for Europol's brief to be extended to general anti-terrorist matters two years after the signing of the Europol Convention. This new proposal also addressed the relationship between policing and security service networks, suggesting that Europol should have access to counter-terrorism intelligence held by police forces, but not by security services (*Guardian*, 27 Jan. 1995).

Europol with operational powers could only be done by making use of Article 40 (Amendment of the Convention), which states that the Council, on the advice of the Management Board, can unanimously adopt modifications to the Convention accordance with Article K.1 (9) of the TEU.[27]

According to the German draft Convention, Europol's remit nevertheless includes the following wide range of tasks: collecting, collating, analysing, and disseminating criminal information and intelligence, and maintaining a central data base for these purposes: developing expertise in the investigative procedures of law enforcement agencies of the Member States and offering advice and support in investigations; facilitating national investigations by providing the national units with all relevant information; providing strategic intelligence to assist and promote efficient and effective use of national operational resources; and preparing general situation reports (Article 3). The November 1993 draft Convention expressly forbade the connection of the central data base with other international automated processing systems (Article 10). Thus there could be no computerized link with SIS or the future EIS, the CIS, or Interpol's ASF and ASS facilities. However, in the June 1994 and October 1994 drafts, this broad restriction was omitted. In more general terms, Europol should maintain relations necessary for information exchange and the pursuit of its functions more broadly with organizations such as Interpol, the UN and other public agencies within and beyond the framework of the EU (Articles 10 and 39).

It is apparent, therefore, that Europol is intended as a complex multi-functional organization, with its governing Convention required to provide a sophisticated regulatory framework. The Member States were aware that such an ambitious initiative would involve protracted negotiation and elaborate preparation. They decided, therefore, to develop a more modest and less controversial structure pending final agreement on the full Europol organization. This interim measure took the form of the Europol Drugs Unit, set up by Ministerial Agreement at Copenhagen in June 1993. Its ini-

---

[27] It is noteworthy that such a cautious position was maintained during the German presidency in the second half of 1994, despite Germany's longstanding support for operational powers. Indeed, this preference was reiterated by the Germans at the meeting of the Council of Justice and Interior Ministers in Berlin on 7 Sept. 1994, but was received with little enthusiasm by other Member States.

tial remit covered illegal drug-trafficking, the criminal organizations involved, and associated money-laundering activities. However, when it became apparent that the Europol Convention would not be concluded by the end of 1994, as promised by the German presidency, the jurisdiction of the Europol Drugs Unit was extended to cover nuclear crime, illegal immigration networks, vehicle crime, and associated money-laundering activities.[28]

Europol is not only internally complex, but also embedded within the wider mosaic of the TEU pillar on Justice and Home Affairs. This covers areas of common interest, including policies on immigration, asylum, and external borders and strategies to combat international fraud and drug addiction, as well as matters falling under the rubric of judicial co-operation in civil and criminal law, and customs co-operation (Article K.1 (1-8)). International conventions relating to any of these themes may be drawn up within the framework of the Third pillar, and these conventions 'may stipulate that the Court of Justice shall have jurisdiction to interpret their provisions and to rule on any disputes regarding their application' (Article K.3 (2) (c)).[29] There is also a more direct *passerelle,* enabling justice and home affairs co-operation in some areas, but not judicial co-operation in criminal matters, customs co-operation and police co-operation, to be brought within EU institutions generally, provided all Member States agree (Art. K.9). Title VI also contains provisions with regard to the role of other European institutions, including the European Commission, a permanent Coordinating Committee of senior officials[30] and the European Parliament[31] (Fernhout 1993; Schutte 1991: 83).

Despite its apparent heterogeneity, Title VI ties various issues together and is, at the same time, a catalyst for the transition of old systems into new systems of European police co-operation. Inter-institutional relations between the new Co-ordinating Committee (K4 Committee), the Council, the Commission and the Parliament are set down in authoritative, if general, terms. Furthermore, law enforcement efforts are linked and coordinated across a wide range of areas, including drugs, fraud and money laundering, immigration, asylum and extradition. By defining and demarcating matters of common interest, Title VI of the TEU

---

[28] *Statewatch,* Vol. 4, No. 6, Nov–Dec. 1994: 1.
[29] The role of the European Court of Justice is considered in ch. 6.
[30] See ch. 6.   [31] See ch. 8.

facilitates a more coherent formulation of policy-objectives and strategies.

The fact that categories of crime are more explicitly connected with one another indicates a strategic shift: whereas under the old systems crimes tended to be classified and dealt with by distinct bodies, under the new regime a more generalist approach to fields of crime prevails. This trend incorporates an organizational shift from 'particularist' to 'generalist', and from 'local' to 'centralist'. This tendency has emerged both at national level (through the creation of national intelligence services and national intelligence teams) and at international level (improved co-ordination leading to and reinforced by the creation of Europol and related Title VI bodies).

Each component of the old Trevi system has been replaced within the more cohesively integrated structure of Title VI. The Trevi ministers have been replaced by the EU Council of Interior and Justice ministers.[32] The Trevi *Troika* is now represented by the *COREPER* (Committee of Permanent Representatives from each EU State) which is directly accountable to the Council of Interior and Justice ministers. Senior officials are now represented in the K4 Committee, which consists of one full member from each Member State and one from the European Commission (Article K.4). The former Trevi Working Groups, the *Ad Hoc* Group on Immigration and the Rhodes Co-ordinator's Group are now replaced by three steering groups. These are respectively Immigration and Asylum; Security, Police and Customs Cooperation; and Judicial Co-operation (including criminal and civil justice co-operation). In turn, these are divided into a broad range of specialist working parties (see Table 2.1 below).

Old versus New Systems of European Police Co-operation

One of the difficulties of European police co-operation has been to co-ordinate efforts across national, organizational, jurisdictional and linguistic barriers. Law enforcement agencies have been dissatisfied with the increasing bureaucratization of cross-border policing: for them, all the conferences, meetings, courses and reports could never have the same utility as a European-wide anti-drugs team with common facilities and an operational support capacity (Van der Wel and Bruggeman 1993: 26). From the point of view of

---

[32] Sometimes called 'JHA Council' (Justice and Home Affairs Council).

TABLE 2.1.* *The Structure of Justice and Home Affairs Co-operation (Title VI, Article K.4)*

Council of EU Justice and Interior Ministers
Committee of Permanent Representatives (COREPER)
Coordinating Committee (K4 Committee)
Steering Groups

I. *Immigration & Asylum*	II. *Security, Police and Customs Co-operation*	III. *Judicial Cooperation*
Migration		Extradition
Asylum		International Organized
	Terrorism	Crime
		Penal Law/Communitarian
Visas	Police co-operation	Law
External Frontiers	(operational and	Withdrawal Driving Licence
Forged Documents and	technical)	Trial Documents
	Drugs and Serious	
Clearing Houses on		Application Brussels
Immigration	Organized Crime	Convention
and Asylum (CIREA		
and CIREFI)**	Customs	
	Ad Hoc Group Europol	

Horizontal Information Group (*inter alia* European Information System)

──

* Compiled from King 1994: 2; Peek 1994; and Drüke 1994.
** Centre for Information, Discussion and Exchange on Asylum and the Centre for Information, Discussion and Exchange on the Crossing of Borders and Immigration.

the police, the size and seriousness of the drug-trafficking problem required a co-ordinated strategy. Interpol in the first instance reacted to the growing demand for co-operation close to practical policing by instituting regional bureaus and liaison officers. But this did not satisfy the need for strategic analysis of and a concerted response to the drug trade. In Interpol's case, the lack of advanced means of communication in the non-European National Central Bureaus was an additional obstacle to practical co-operation (Van der Wel and Bruggeman 1993: 27).

Although Interpol's role and that of the now defunct Trevi were always clearly distinct, with Interpol focused on providing a service for practical policing and Trevi on policy issues, some members of the Interpol General Secretariat, as mentioned above, were apprehensive about Trevi's role. Some EC Member States found that Trevi's information exchange in the field of anti-terrorism was much more effective than that of Interpol, although not everyone shared this view (Van der Wel and Bruggeman 1993: 55). Trevi II was host to an automated system of information exchange about objects (cars, weapons, identity papers, etc.) and Trevi III's system allowed for communication between twelve liaison bureaus. Furthermore, under the auspices of Trevi I an Aeroflex network and a permanent computer-telex link enabled immediate access to information about terrorists and analyses of criminal groups (Van der Wel and Bruggeman 1993: 46). The speed with which the information was made available and the sensitivity of the information made Trevi a formidable competitor with Interpol's services in certain restricted areas.

One of the advantages of Interpol is that it can be used to combat pan-European crime. Several of our informants regarded Trevi and Europol as initiatives which do not cover the optimal geographical area. A senior British police officer observed: 'If you look at the major problems such as drugs, it makes absolutely no sense to talk about the Community. Especially now, the major routes into Europe are through the back door, the old Eastern block. It is just as important to have proper liaison with them as it is with our fellow Community members.'

The relationship between Interpol and Europol has been the subject of considerable speculation. Some of our informants deplored that Interpol headquarters in Lyons was never seriously considered as a location for Europol. A senior British police officer recounted some of the reasons:

Political jealousy was important. There was a strong feeling within the twelve that the new policing initiative had to come from the twelve and had to be divorced from previous initiatives. There was also some worry about the lack of accountability of Interpol. That was a bit of a joke, considering that the accountability of Europol had not really been considered seriously at all. Raymond Kendall was not invited into the special Trevi Sub-Committee on Europol to discuss its future. He and his organization were effectively frozen out.

It is clear that this informant, and also many others we interviewed, characterizes the relationship between Interpol and Europol as competitive (Johnston 1992; Van Reenen 1989). A British police officer responsible for the investigation of organized crime notes that 'Europol has been a culture-shock to Interpol'.

Europol may be preferred, in future, for communications because it has a stronger regional base (Benyon *et al*. 1993: 130). It may also be able to provide specialist understanding about how European police forces work, and could, therefore, as one of our informants argued, be less rule-bound and more pro-active in its relations with domestic police forces than Interpol. A senior Italian official responsible for national and international drug investigations said that: 'The added value of Europol is that it will assist us in situations where agreement could not otherwise be reached about the exchange of intelligence.' A senior British police officer was more sceptical: 'The difference between Interpol and Europol is radical: Interpol is a post-box, Europol stands for criminal investigation powers. Indeed, Europol results in problems on a large scale; investigation powers, arrest, and the interception of drugs are not possible in the actual framework.' Raymond Kendall, Interpol's Secretary-General, was also reported to have said that Europol would have difficulty getting off the ground, due to cultural and linguistic differences and the absence of an appropriate legal infrastructure.[33] On this view, Europol may be criticized as too ambitious. However, putting its long-term development to one side, in the short and medium term Europol arguably compares favourably with Interpol in terms or its capacity to develop co-operative initiatives.

Europol's advantage is that it has a smaller number of countries to mobilize than Interpol. The difficulty of achieving consensus about a data protection regime is illustrative: the Interpol Executive Committee recently rejected two recommendations formulated by its European Working Party on data protection; these suggested criteria under which data can be exchanged (in compliance with national data protection legislation and eventually resulting in a global data protection Convention), and definitions of terminology to be included in the Rules on International Police Cooperation (Grange 1994: 15). The pro-Europol campaign refers to this and other examples in criticizing Interpol's deficient personnel and material support and organizational cohesiveness for international criminal investigation, and in emphasizing Interpol's flaws with regard to accountability and data protection (Benyon *et al*.

---

[33] *Agence Europe*, 'Citizen's Europe: The Secretary-General of Interpol does not think a European Police Corps can be created at present.' London, 22 Jan. 1992. For other opinions of Raymond Kendall about Europol, see Bresler (1993: 371–3).

1993: 129; Storbeck 1994a: 81). Informants who characterized the service of Interpol as 'excellent' or 'very good' belonged to a minority.

The developing relationship between Interpol and Europol need not be viewed exclusively in competitive terms. It may also be viewed in co-operative terms. Interpol has recently been engaged in an intensive reappraisal of its role, contemplating its future and trying to determine its niche (Cameron-Waller 1994).[34] In its business plan '1992–1996', Interpol aims at forging formal relationships and at encouraging daily informal co-operation with Europol in the short term, eventually leading to a fully fledged, institutionalized working relationship with Europol and observer status in its meetings.[35] Senior informants active within one of the European NCBs wondered why Interpol could not have a general intelligence role at the European level, as it had already assumed this task in the drug field.

From an organizational point of view, it is broadly recognized as desirable that Interpol and Europol should work together: 'within the framework of a Convention of Europol maximum efforts will be made to contribute to mutually fruitful co-operation with other international police bodies, including, in particular, Interpol' (Fode 1993b: 11). A first step might be the secondment of an Interpol liaison officer at Europol's headquarters in The Hague, which could mean that officers would have direct access to Interpol's criminal records (Project Team Europol 1993: 12). However, there is an influential body of opinion which is less enthusiastic about inter-organizational co-operation. For instance, a Belgian police officer with a senior post within Europol thinks that Europol and Interpol should remain 'absolutely separate', because Interpol is not treaty-based and because it is not sufficiently regionalized.

Trends in European Police Co-operation

A number of trends in the evolution of cross-border policing in Europe can be identified. The first is that personal initiatives are less central than they were. International police co-operation used to be a cause promoted by enthusiastic individuals who created

---

[34] See Interpol/ICP, *Interpol 2000—Organizational Renewal,* General Assembly Session, Aruba, 29 Sept.-5 Oct. 1993, at 2ff, wherein in particularly the improvement of the quality of service is considered.

[35] SO12(ICS), 17 Feb. 1993.

networks and infused life into Interpol. Gradually, the institutional-ized forms of co-operation have become dominant. This *systemati-zation* runs parallel with another trend, namely, *bureaucratization* (Van der Wel and Bruggeman 1993: 55–6), which is caused by the declining impact of practitioners in policy-making. Practical police input has been overtaken by bureaucratic input from senior civil servants—a development deplored by many police officers.

Secondly, the loose structure of European police co-operation is gradually being replaced by a more institutionalized structure, which is supported by a process of *co-ordination* and *centraliza-tion*. The desire for more efficiency, cohesion and central control have been driving forces behind the third pillar of the TEU and Europol.

Thirdly, the *range* of cross-border policing activities has been *extended both qualitatively and quantitatively*. Until the late eight-ies, police co-operation was focused on the exchange of informa-tion. This is, and will remain a core activity of cross-border policing, but there is now more emphasis on more active forms of mutual co-operation, such as the joint analysis of information and intelligence, and upon the exploitation of modern technology, such as DNA profiling, smart cards, telecommunications, electronic sur-veillance and computerized data banks.

Fourthly, there tends to be more emphasis on *accountability*. 'Accountability' does not merely refer to data protection, but also transparency of activities, parliamentary control and the social legitimacy of policing (see chapter 8). Although accountability pro-cedures are frequently regarded as inadequate, the political salience of this subject has moved from total neglect to a certain promi-nence. The efforts of the Committee on Civil Liberties and Internal Affairs in the European Parliament have been particularly signifi-cant (Van Outrive 1992a; 1992b; 1992c; Walker 1993a). Fifthly, *state sovereignty* in policing matters is gradually eroding (see chap-ter 3). Politicians who are least likely to admit this development have themselves encouraged it by emphasizing the growing impact of transfrontier crime. By admitting that transnational crime is a genuine threat to the internal security of the EU Member States, politicians are forced to concede that it must be combated at the international level. The significance of this concession is underlined by the fact that the areas in which the demand for collaboration is greatest are intimately bound up with the sovereignty of the state, in particular terrorism (Den Boer and Walker 1993: 14). A further symptom of the decline of state sovereignty at the symbolic level is that border controls are gradually being replaced by controls exercised in the interior of the national territory. Further, with the Schengen Conventions, the TEU, the External Frontiers Convention and the Dublin Asylum Convention, more emphasis is laid on joint responsibility for those border and immigration controls which remain. One could argue that the defining features of the European State are being subjected to profound change.

Micro-Political Dynamics in European Policing

The form and extent of European police co-operation will, to a large extent, be determined by the outcome of negotiations involving different parties, such as politicians and the senior officials, and, to a lesser extent, police officers. From the interviews we conducted with the representatives of these parties, several opposing positions and tensions regularly emerged. These reflected and reinforced strategic stances in the negotiation process. In other words, they have become significant points of reference for the participants in the policy-making debate, helping them to define their own positions and also influencing their identification of opposing groups and what they stand for. As one informant observed, polarization along these lines became more acute during the negotiations on the Europol Convention. In the following sections, some of the stereotypes and dichotomies employed in the discourse of senior officials and police officers are analysed.

Dichotomy I: Old Boy Network versus Formalization

According to a number of our informants—especially those in the United Kingdom—the 'old boy network' still prevails in international policing, although largely outwith the official negotiations concerning Schengen and Europol. Current developments are seen by some as an enhancement or facilitation of this network rather than the birth of a genuine European police service. In interviews, the question sometimes arose whether there is a need for formalization. A senior British police officer told us that 'All police co-operation on a practical basis happens without a formal umbrella: goodwill on an operational basis is present almost everywhere; during the last ten years, the co-operation concerning drugs and terrorism at informal level has been easy.' Senior officials in Germany expressed concern that the formalization of arrangements for police co-operation in the Schengen Conventions might endanger the working of informal arrangements, which are an essential element of co-operation in the border regions; this so-called *kleiner Grenzverkehr* has operated to some extent beyond or independently of formal legal provisions, for example, in relation to information exchange. Indeed, senior German police officers with considerable experience in international criminal investigations told us that informal—sometimes even extra-legal—co-operation would continue notwithstanding the formalization of contacts represented by the Schengen Conventions.

Middle-ranking police officers with experience in the context of the Channel Tunnel project also tended to contrast informal co-operation with formal arrangements. Although the informal network is believed to work better, an Exchange of Letters[36] was seen as providing a kind of safety net for the maintenance of informal contacts between British and French police officers. In a similar vein, informants in Scotland said that 'the best thing would be to have a combined system of formal *commissions rogatoires* and informal contacts.' In Portugal, police officers in frontier regions have 'good social relations' with their Spanish counterparts, although, in principle, direct contact must always be reported to the Director-General of the Ministry of Justice and cross-border surveillance operations should never take place without prior authorization of a public prosecutor. A Dutch police officer with experience in regional co-operation with the German and Belgian police regards the balance between official agreements and informal co-operation as 'difficult to strike, but absolutely necessary: formal agreements avoid chaos, they give cross-border police activities a legitimate character.'

A senior British police officer active in the field of financial intelligence described the relationship between informal and formal co-operation as 'complementary', and conceded that informal relations are often associated with the pre-investigation stage.

Informal contacts are also seen as crucial because they bring the 'guys on the shop-floor' closer to one another; as a British Detective Chief Inspector remarked:

[36] An exchange of letters, although less formal than a treaty or convention, is capable of creating obligations in international law between the consenting parties.

It does not matter that you get a good lunch out of the *commissaire*, . . . at the end of the day it is important that the guys on the ground can talk to each other, and can accept each other. Although there are some tight controls on people [i.e. police officers] travelling—(jokingly) because on some occasions we have more people in France than in Kent—we have actually maintained the possibility for guys on the shop-floor to still meet one another.

An example of these visits, quoted favourably by another respondent, is a one-week exchange between British police officers and officers of the French *Police de l'Air et des Frontières* in order to develop language skills, to extend their knowledge about each other's judicial system, and to return with fewer prejudices about each other.

Informal networking is seen by many police officers as a key to the success of international policing activities. With regard to football intelligence, it was noted by an informant that 'It is crucial to build up trust: this is necessary for the exchange of intelligence. To this end a series of meetings has to be organized in advance . . . For example, at the time of the World Cup in Italy, 50 ground level *carabinieri* were sent to the UK and this was found to be very helpful.' Informal networking also has disadvantages. A senior British police officer active within the International Association of Police Officers (IAPC) says that 'If I'd drop dead now, the chain would break.'[37] The same point was made by informants from the Kent County Constabulary in relation to the maintenance of a European liaison unit, where all contacts have been secured by a single person. According to our informants, other disadvantages of informal networking included '*ad hocery*', a lack of proper co-ordination, lack of a legal basis and of accountability and transparency.

In conclusion, although in the 1990s there is a trend led by politicians and senior civil servants in national, European and international organizations towards formalization and centralization of systems of European police co-operation, from the police officers' perspective this will not make informal co-operation redundant. The two forms are complementary, and are both required to achieve success.

---

[37] From the European point of view, the IACP works as an umbrella for regional strategic meetings.

Dichotomy II: Practical Policing versus Politics

Police officers often deplore the fact that there seems to be a gap between 'high' politics and 'practical' policing. A Portuguese informant put it concisely: 'The decision to establish Europol and to make its first responsibilities in the drugs field were politically driven, not police-driven decisions.' Police officers accuse politicians of conducting a cosmetic exercise, and of pushing the scope of European police co-operation beyond practical limits and operational needs. 'When the politicians exercise enough pressure, it just happens: the police do not have any control', a senior Scottish police officer told us. Another senior Scottish police officer compared the most ambitious political projections of a European police organization with 'intergalactic space travel'. Another informant conceded that although 'the politicians want it to happen, it should be allowed to develop naturally'.

Police officers are also generally negative about the increasing bureaucratization of the policy-making process on cross-border police co-operation, in the sense that they are no longer consulted with sufficient frequency. Trevi was regarded by police officers as very much a 'civil servant's job'. Sir Roger Birch noted, in arguing in favour of a European Police Council, that the Trevi *Troika*, which set the agenda for the Trevi ministerial meetings, did not consult the practitioners, resulting in a 'yawning gap'. Although the police were represented in the working groups, they were left out at senior official level. Some informants considered that 'Europol was not looked at from a professional point of view, but was played as a political card' as 'added value' enhancing the 'law and order' credentials of its champions in national and international political debate. A senior Belgian police officer related the bureaucratization of the negotiation process to problems of scale and explained why this wider bureaucracy can be insensitive to specific practical policing problems: 'The idea of small-scale approaches stands diagonally opposed to international co-ordination. The larger the scale, the more bureaucratic negotiations become. At a high level, what the priorities should be can be more or less agreed, but there is less clarity about the priorities at a lower level.' In other words, broad agreements of principle in the more exalted corridors of international power can simply obscure the absence of consensus over particular operational problems.

Finally, police officers frequently blame 'politics' for creating obstacles in practical police co-operation. Governments, it was argued by some respondents, find it difficult to trust police with international relations. Conversely, the police are 'obsessed with standing back from political development'. As far as extradition procedures are concerned, the view was expressed that 'the minute you get the government involved you get problems'.

The tension between the higher echelons of the police and politics seems related to the degree of autonomy police organizations have in relation to the Interior Ministry or Home Office. In countries with a centralized system of policing (*e.g.* Portugal, Italy, France and Spain) police officers do not tend to dissociate themselves as much from ministerial and senior official levels; a senior Spanish police officer said that the participation of the most senior officials in international meetings is the 'only way of getting business done because you must have the authority to negotiate and you must have the knowledge and expertise.' In the United Kingdom, on the other hand, a decentralized service has traditionally been excluded from key national and international policy-making fora, and its representatives remain less convinced of the willingness or ability of senior officials to pursue professional police interests effectively (Walker 1992).

Dichotomy III: 'Our' Systems versus 'Their' Systems

The pessimism expressed by many police officers about international police co-operation and harmonization of criminal justice procedures is often illustrated by pointing out that there are numerous differences between 'us' and 'them'—between the familiar and the foreign. A frequently cited example is that policies on drugs and pornography are significantly different between the EU Member States. A senior Dutch police officer told us: 'We are always seen as slightly deviant abroad . . . I really think that we have a damned good system, and we also have a noticeably smaller number of heroin fatalities, and the problem does not get worse either.' By contrast, a German academic observed there was 'no likelihood of Germany adopting a more liberal policy' on drugs as the Dutch approach was now discredited.[38] Also similar laws are

---

[38] Interestingly, a senior Dutch official drew the opposite conclusion, namely that the German drugs policy was approaching the Dutch policy, in particular in

applied differently by EU Member States and investigative policies, such as whether or not to pay ransoms to kidnappers, are different. Some of our informants regarded policy differences as a serious obstacle to effective co-operation within the Schengen framework. A senior Italian official noted that 'In some European countries, for instance, all criminals have to be prosecuted, and in other countries prosecution can be waived. In Italy, if a person is found with ten grammes of drugs on him for personal use, there will be no prosecution.' Furthermore, differences between police organizations (especially centralized versus decentralized) and police cultures are seen as a fertile source of difficulty. Yet, some positive views were expressed. Some spoke of a shared 'cop culture' in Europe. As one of our informants said: 'Despite the national cultural differences, there is a shared police identity generated by practicalities.' A Scottish officer who was involved in a criminal investigation in another EU Member State observed that 'there was a tremendous sense of camaraderie among the detectives'. He was surprised to find a common culture, the briefing each morning, the drink after work and the low status of uniform officers relative to plain-clothes detectives.

Data protection rules in some of the EU Member States sometimes make co-operation difficult, and strict rules are criticized by police officers. According to a senior police officer active in the football intelligence sphere, Germany could not provide Swedish law enforcement authorities with data about football hooligans and travelling criminals (who use football matches as a front to commit crimes such as money laundering) at the time of the 1992 European Championship. Similarly, in the Netherlands, photographs of hooligans and football criminals can only be kept for the duration of the operation, so reducing the scope for effective international co-operation. One senior Dutch police officer regarded data protection in the Netherlands as 'ridiculously inflexible' and 'too strict'.

Another difficulty is that the *modus operandi* and priorities of police organizations in other countries are often perceived to be different. These perceptions are usually associated with cultural stereotyping. One of our informants observed that North European countries have a similar outlook and, for example, plan football

Hamburg, Düsseldorf and Frankfurt, where more emphasis is placed on the public health aspect, and where the soft drugs addict is seen in a different light than the hard drugs supplier.

intelligence operations and emergency responses to bomb threats long in advance. 'Functional bottlenecks' (a euphemism for excessive delays) were observed by senior officials working for the Dutch customs investigation service when cooperating with countries like Spain, Portugal and Greece. A senior German police officer said (jokingly) that the only cultural problem with the French was that they could not be reached at meal times! A senior Dutch police officer stated that the priorities of the Belgian police were occasionally different from those of the Dutch CRI: 'The Belgian police still frequently send us a police report because someone has refuelled without paying. Well, for goodness sake, we really don't have time for that kind of thing anymore.' Organizational divergences—in this case between the decentralized British policing system and the centralized French policing system—became an issue in the Channel Tunnel policing initiative:

There is one very simple difference between ourselves and the French police. We represent all national interests from a county perspective, and for the first three years, we never got to meet the right people from the French side. Because of the centralized system, everything was emanating from Paris. Some sort of power for the decisions has now been devolved down to the Pas de Calais.

The Chief Superintendent who participated in this interview added:

A prime example being that I can make decisions on behalf of the Kent County Constabulary. I have the authority from the Chief Constable to make fairly important decisions . . . If I am going to a meeting with the French, and the *Commissaire Principal* is there, he cannot do that, unless he speaks to the *préfet* of the Pas the Calais who now has more power than any other *préfet* in France, because authority has been pushed down to him from the centre.

Both the territorial and the functional division of police activities in one Member State can draw criticism from officers in other Member States. For example, senior police officers in Luxembourg said that the internal decision-making process in Germany, including that on police operational matters, had a tendency 'to be cumbersome at times, as a result of her federal system', and the co-operation with the French 'could be difficult because of the *gendarmerie*/police divide'.

Dichotomy IV: Intergovernmentalism versus Federalism

Opposed views about the place of European police co-operation within framework of the EU exist between police officers and policy makers in the different EU Member States. German and Dutch informants were the strongest advocates of federalist tendencies in European policing, while the British have been most opposed to it, and remain committed to the intergovernmentalist position. The French, too, have increasingly distanced themselves from the comprehensively federal model. But even within Member States, there may be significant differences in outlook. A senior Dutch official said that 'not many countries are prepared to make concessions about their national criminal laws and criminal justice systems'. Yet, a Dutch police officer said that 'Europol would have more chance in the context of a federal model: the current intergovernmental model is inadequate. I fear that Europol will become a bureaucratic, slow process.' A senior police officer in Luxembourg, on the other hand, did not see Europol leading to a uniform system of criminal law, which was 'light years away' and perhaps not even desirable.

The federalist position was given a new impetus by Chancellor Kohl, who at the outset of the German presidency of the EU in the Summer of 1994 relaunched his idea of a European FBI. Again, however, there is no consensus within the national policy-making community, still less at the European level, over the appropriateness of this model. In particular, there is continuing disagreement over the relevance of any domestic federal model, whether imported or indigenous, to international policing arrangements. For example, one German commentator said that, although the Germans would seek to have their federal model of policing adopted within the European framework, it was unlikely 'that an FBI model would be adopted despite the prevalence in Europe of American ideas on the combating of organized crime.' Another German informant was less sure about the application of German internal security conceptions and structures at the European level, even at the level of broad principle. In the German model, it is possible to second police officers from one of the *Länder* to the *Bundeskriminalamt* for the duration of joint enquiries and in particular criminal cases. But these commissions are much rarer than their American counterparts because of the comparatively narrower jurisdiction of German federal police authorities. More generally, the *Länder* have not refrained from passing laws on policing which in some instances threatened to overlap with federal legislation on criminal procedure, particularly when laws sought to specify police powers at the investigatory stage of the criminal process. In sum, the central police authority within German federalism may be insufficiently strong to provide an attractive level for European police co-operation.

Dichotomy V: Exchange of Information versus Operational Powers

Debate on the future of Europol has focused on this dichotomy. As suggested, only the German government is at the moment in favour of a European FBI. In most other countries opposition to operational powers prevails, varying from mild opposition (operational powers under certain conditions) to outright rejection. For some, these differences of opinion as to the optimal level of co-operation represent a key impediment to progress, while for others they are of less significance. A senior Italian official became almost poetic about the difficult negotiations over Europol and the squabbling which was caused by French criticism about drugs and immigration policies in other EU Member States, when he said: 'Love is beautiful when it is quarrelsome. Within Europol we quarrel all the time, but we don't quarrel about the general framework. In the past, integration was produced by war, now by friendship . . . We are getting to know each other very well.' There is much discussion about whether cross-border operational powers are necessary or useful. A senior British police officer confided to us that 'criminals don't give a damn about cross-border powers'. An operational European police service, he added, 'is not going to happen in a million years'. Problems of organizational difference, accountability and sensibility lie behind this position. Cross-border arrests are agreed to be a very difficult area. A senior British civil servant mentioned the problem of different national laws and judicial systems: 'How could you possibly have a common operational unit without common legal powers?' Another problem, which he pointed out, concerned conjoint jurisdiction; this caused friction in legal systems where it was already in place, such as the United States. A range of other objections was articulated by a senior British police officer:

There are those who would like to see Europol with executive powers. That seems so utopian, that it is hardly worth thinking about at the moment. Where would you get the police officers from, what would their status be? Would they have to be multi-lingual? Would they be accountable? Would their status change when they moved to a different country? I can't see the police of one country relinquishing their authority to a multinational agency within their own borders. It would cause terrible resentment. You would have to have a situation where the domestic police actually made the arrests.

Numerous informants mention the difference between judicial systems as the greatest obstacle to an FBI-style European Police Office. A very senior British police officer conceived of an operational Europol as, at best, a very limited conception: 'The legal-political framework may be a problem. But politics won't keep up with international executive investigations. The political framework may be difficult for Europol. It is only feasible if all other aspects of Europe mirror it.' In Germany, likewise, a senior police officer said that 'operational powers were not on the cards, at least not in the short or medium term' and even that it was *Zukunftsmusik* ('pie in the sky'). As suggested earlier, the drive for Europol with operational powers seems to originate from the German government rather than professionals involved in or associated with law enforcement.

On the other hand, a minority of our informants said that Europol may be redundant if its intelligence arm is not flanked by an operational unit. An informant working in the private security industry told us that a Europol without operational powers would be of no use to the banks. Although the Dutch are firmly against operational powers, a senior Dutch police officer suggested that multinational Special Task Forces could be set up for special investigations.

The June 1994 and October 1994 drafts of the Europol Convention suggest that operational powers are not on the immediate political agenda. The Schengen system will provide law enforcement authorities with certain cross-border policing powers. If, in the future, Europol is furnished with operational powers, this would be a fundamental change in three distinct ways: 1. operational powers would, for the first time, be assigned to an international police office rather than to a national law enforcement authority; 2. the powers would be used in the investigation of a category of crime which will have to be defined as 'international organized crime'; 3. the powers would have to be of a pro-active nature, particularly in the area of the law of search, given Europol's focus on generating intelligence, in the form of new data and analysis, rather than simply receiving historical data of national origin. Merely stating these requirements makes clear how much resistance might be expected to the conception of an operational Europol once it descends from the symbolic heights of European summitry.

Conclusion

Systems of European police co-operation have been established mainly on the basis of pragmatic needs. In operational circles, in the lead up to 1992, there was impatience with the slow process of criminal justice harmonization between Western states. 'Old' systems of European police co-operation—such as Interpol and Trevi—evolved from specific political initiatives and were dependant on informal networks. In the old systems, public, political and legal accountability was viewed by participants as less important than getting the job done. The co-ordination they provided was not placed on a formal footing. As a consequence of the development of the European Community and political co-operation associated with the Community the establishment of more mature systems of European police co-operation has become possible. The TEU is an important catalyst in moving towards systems of accountability and parliamentary control of European police co-operation, particularly as it leaves the door ajar for possible assimilation of criminal justice initiatives within the First Pillar of the TEU, whether through Conventions under Article K.3, the *passerelle* under Article K.9, or subsequent amendment to the Treaty.

Although the formalization of European police co-operation is sometimes regarded suspiciously by police officers, most, even in Britain, acknowledge that it is necessary because of disadvantages attached to informal co-operation. But what they most want is not coordination or the institutionalization of cross-border policing, but criminal justice harmonization and improvement of mutual judicial assistance. Police officers are sceptical about politicians, despite their acceptance that political initiative has been crucial in securing progress in European police co-operation, because they fear that the negotiations about cross-border policing will be increasingly removed from practical and operational needs. When police officers need assistance, they prefer to make direct contact with colleagues abroad, although it is not always easy to locate the right person in a foreign policing system. Furthermore cultural, linguistic or legislative obstacles to co-operation have to be overcome. Practical necessity promotes contacts between police, although there is a danger, because of previous bad experiences and negative stereotyping, that partners in foreign police organizations are chosen from a narrow selection of possibilities.

The majority of our informants regarded a Europol with operational powers as either unrealistic or undesirable. But the crucial discussion, that is, the discussion about whether or not European police co-operation should remain intergovernmental, takes place at the highest political level. These questions will be central to the Intergovernmental Conferences of 1996, when the transfer of parts of Title VI to the first pillar of the TEU will be considered. This is also a further indication that systems of European police co-operation are dynamic entities, and that they are continuously influenced by changing attitudes to co-operation and integration in domestic policy-making circles (see chapter 3) and changes in the physical and political environment of cross-border policing initiatives (see chapter 4).

3
The Political Theory of European Police Co-operation

Introduction

In the present chapter, we broaden our perspective in order to address the macro-political context of European police co-operation. Our aim is to examine the nature of the relationship between, on the one hand, new transnational and supranational initiatives in the police sector, and on the other, macro-political trends towards integration within the EU and the more general reconfiguration of international relations.

The analysis of the relationship between political integration and law enforcement co-operation within the EU contributes to a wider theoretical debate. It raises the general question of the relationship between the forms of policing and the forms of political life. To what extent, and in what manner, are policing arrangements within any society informed by, and informative of the broader institutions, practices and ideas in terms of which that society constitutes itself as a political entity? When social scientists and social theorists conduct this inquiry, they usually do so in either historical or counter-factual terms. They may engage in retrospective analysis of the manner in which the unfolding forms of political life within different societies have become interwoven with the development of a policing function (Robinson and Skaglion 1987). Alternatively, they may proceed by means of hypothetical discussion, attempting to gain insight into the broader significance of policing institutions by asking what difference it would make to the wider polity if such institutions had not evolved in their present form (Bittner 1971; Cohen 1985; Klockars 1985). Both methods have their shortcomings. The historical method risks confusing consequences with causes (Brogden 1990); just because police institutions develop in response to a particular configuration of social and political pressures, does not mean that the contemporary relationship of these institutions to the wider political domain remains explicable in terms of their origin. By contrast, the counter-factual approach focuses more closely on the contemporary relevance of policing institutions. However, the attempt to offer explanations by reference to other possible worlds is inherently speculative; the answers to the 'what if' questions—the causal models in terms of which alternative scenarios are constructed—are not susceptible to empirical refutation.[1]

If, instead, the inquiry concerned actual current developments in policing institutions against a backdrop of structural change in the wider political sphere, the limitations of historical and counter-factual approaches alike could be overcome. The underlying institutional and conceptual grid which shapes policing remains deeply embedded in the traditional structures and ideologies of the state. But the developing mosaic of the EU provides an outstanding exception. As a novel form of political order, the EU has begun to challenge the hegemony of the state and has arguably come to rank alongside the latter as a key unit of political organization. The shifting patterns of mutual influences, of legal and political competences, and of competing claims to legitimacy which characterizes the relationship between the new political order and its more traditional rival, provide a testing ground for refining our broader understanding of the relationship between policing and the political realm.

Policing, Political Theory and Political Practice

Inquiry into the relationship between police and political development in contemporary Europe also has a pressing practical significance. The piecemeal, incremental quality of police institutional development in the new Europe has been criticised (Van

---

[1] The difficulty in specifying truth-conditions for claims concerning the nature of the police function and its relationship to the wider political order helps to explain the durability of debates between those who favour public-order and crime-fighting conceptions of the police role respectively; see the review symposium on Reiner (1985) in *British Journal of Criminology* (1986), 26, 94-105; see also the defence of a theory of 'minimal policing', concerned mainly with crime-fighting, against wider public order models, in particular that of the American criminologists Wilson and Keeling (1982), in Kinsey *et al.* (1986), esp. chs. 4 and 9. The controversy caused by the UK Home Office review of core and ancillary police tasks in 1994-5 highlights the same point; see Newburn and Morgan (1994), Reiner (1994b).

Reenen 1989; Benyon *et al.* 1990; 1993). The Internal Market programme, triggered by the 1985 SEA, intimated a more coherent approach to EC internal and external economic relations, but produced a 'spillover' (Lindberg 1963: 280) of patternless institutional development in areas such as social policy, and police and criminal justice co-operation. The explanation for this state of affairs and its implications for future development are complex and controversial (Streeck and Schmitter 1991); but in the professional and policy-making community of the police and criminal justice sector structural fatalism is subscribed to widely, if often tacitly (Van Reenen 1989; Bentham 1992). This fatalism rests on an inference that the shape of policing in the Community inevitably depends on the shape of the Community itself as a political entity; since this wider vision remains hazy and contested, it is a pointless exercise to advocate and institute new policing practices and mechanisms on anything other than a provisional, flexible and modest basis.

An alternative way of thinking about police co-operation prevalent within the professional and policy-making community could be termed naïve separatism. Models of police co-operation are assessed and evaluated independently of wider political forces. The requirements of international law enforcement are seen as paramount; little attention is given to the *Realpolitik* of international relations and how this might impede the development of optimal systems of co-operation. The result, as Fijnaut has noted, is a tendency for various blueprints for European police co-operation to set unrealistic timetables and to adopt overly-ambitious standards (Fijnaut 1991). The Benelux Agreement, the Schengen Conventions, the security aspects of the 1992 Programme, and, most recently, the Europol initiative, each disappointed the policy-making élites who believed that matters intrinsic to law enforcement could be pursued in splendid isolation from wider political concerns.

These two forms of conventional wisdom within professional and policy-making communities about the relationship of policing to developments beyond the nation state have resulted in opposite errors. Structural fatalism relegates policing to the status of the dependent variable: naïve separatism fails to acknowledge the inevitable interpenetration of policing and wider political matters. Although diametrically opposed in theory, these two positions may be closely related in practice. Naïve separatism tends to beget politically marginalized policies, so encouraging structural fatalism.

However, the circumstances of contemporary Europe should provide an opportunity to challenge such attitudes. The embryonic development of new forms of policing and politics in the EC should be seen, not as an occasion to apply old orthodoxies in unreflective fashion, but rather as an opportunity to gain fresh insights and to place the debate on the future of policing in Europe on a more informed footing.

Policing and the State: Parallel Theoretical Traditions

Having re-entered the mainstream of Anglo-American social science and social theory some twenty years ago, the state remains an 'essentially contested concept' (Gallie 1956) for two main reasons. First, in empirical theory, the modern state is represented as a network of, apparently heterogeneous, institutions and capacities; this allows much scope for divergent conclusions in attempts to identify an underlying operational unity. Secondly, in normative political theory, conceptions of the state are bound up with rival notions of the good life; this provides a battleground for opposing political ideologies (Jessop 1990: 339–40).

Yet there remains an 'overlapping consensus' (Rawls 1987) about some of the characteristics of the state. This consensus has philosophical roots in Jean Bodin and Thomas Hobbes' realist account of the absolutist state of the seventeenth century, and later sociological origins in Max Weber's interpretation of the nature of the nation state of the early twentieth century. Weber's characterization of the modern state as a human community which (successfully) claims the 'monopoly of the legitimate use of force within a given territory' (Weber 1948: 78) is still a widely endorsed point of departure (Jessop 1990: 343; Giddens 1987b; Hall and Ikenberry 1989; Held 1989a; Poggi 1990). For Weber and others who subscribe to the theory of the *Machtstaat*, the direct control of the means of internal and external violence is *the* distinguishing feature of state power.

A Hobbesian teleological conception of the state has also survived because the 'finalities' (Poggi 1990: 15) of the state are often conceived as resulting from its monopoly coercive power. For Giddens, the state's coercive power provides for an 'administrative monopoly over a territory with demarcated boundaries' (Giddens 1987a: 171). For another writer, this power enables the state 'to define and enforce collectively binding decisions on the members of a society in the name of the common interest or general will' (Jessop 1990: 341). From this perspective, the state, through its dominant political élite, strives to consolidate its own power base and maintain its own integrity *qua* state.

There are parallels between theories of police and state theory. Policing theory, like state theory, typically embraces both means-centred and teleological analysis—the latter emphasizing the connection between the ends of police work and the distinctive means available to police agencies. Also, features of both the means and ends of the state conventionally conceived within state theory are claimed, in policing theory, as specific attributes of the police function. Thus, means-based analysis of policing has stressed the position of the police as 'a mechanism for the distribution of non-negotiably coercive force' (Bittner 1971: 46), and as 'the specialist repository domestically of the state's monopoly of legitimate force' (Reiner 1992a: 49); police is the label and policing the means used when asserting the state's exclusive authority to the use or threat of the use of force within its territory. Echoing the teleological approach of general state theory, Marenin has claimed that the role of the police is to protect both 'general and specific order', the former being public tranquillity and the latter the interests of dominant political and social élites. Whatever the balance struck between general and specific order, both have a conservative orientation consistent with the propensity of the state to self-preservation (Marenin 1982: 258).

Detailed examination of the key themes of police theory reveals an even closer connection between the police function and the broader function of the state. The police function of preserving specific order is directly linked to the interests of the state. Thus Brodeur talks of the tradition of 'high policing', characterized by its propensity to 'reach . . . out for potential threats in a systematic attempt to preserve the distribution of power in a given society' (Brodeur 1983: 513). High policing is about the preservation of the specific forms of order upon which the security of the state most immediately rests—combating terrorist organizations and activities or gathering comprehensive information on political dissidence, or laying contingency plans in the event of the widespread breakdown of public order (see chapter 5). Since the protection of general order involves the preservation of minimum standards of private security and public peace which are necessary for the working of *all* societies and from which all social actors benefit, it is difficult to see any more precise connection between this police task and the interests of the state. But this superficial conclusion is misleading.

First, although specific order and general order are analytically distinct, in practice, particular police activities help to achieve both. Activities which pose a direct challenge to the state, such as urban disorder or terrorist attacks on civilians, also threaten the general order and safety of the wider population. Conversely, activities concerned with the maintenance of general public security, such as preventive patrolling or the detection of ordinary criminal offences, are indispensable to specific forms of order. In addition, general policing tends to benefit disproportionately those who have the largest stake in the *status quo*, in terms of property ownership, social status, commercial security, neighbourhood amenity and so on. They have, on balance, most to gain from general policing activities and most to lose from their absence. By contrast, there is a section of society whom the police tend to do things *to*, rather than *for* (Shearing 1981: 285). As Reiner points out, 'studies of routine policing in all industrial societies and throughout modern police history show that the main grist to the mill of routine policing is the social residuum at the base of the social hierarchy' (Reiner 1994a: 728).

Secondly, apart from this conceptual common ground, the boundaries in practice between specific order and general order may be blurred in certain places. Particular crimes such as drug-trafficking may straddle the border between specific and general order, while criminal networks may embrace a range of practices located at either side of the analytical division.

Thirdly, since the maintenance of order is an extraordinarily diffuse notion, it can involve police officers in an unpredictable range of situations whose only common feature is the need for authoritative resolution, if necessary by force. The monopoly of legitimate force also indicates the key role of the police as the residual, or 'stand-in' authority in the state (Cohen 1985: 37). This role has to be understood in the context of the broader claim of the state to 'administrative monopoly' within a territory. State activity comprises a series of policy sectors—education, social welfare, industry, transport and so on—each subject to decision-making at the macro-political level with reference to matters of broad ideology

and public expenditure constraints, but each having some autonomy in terms of social function and policy choices and implementation (Dunleavy 1989). Policing stands out as an exception to this
vertical division of labour between policy-sectors and has relevance
across all of them. Police intervention may be required to deal with
threats to, or breaches of, general order across a wide range of
activities, many normally governed by a separate framework of
social control but which from time to time experience an 'authority
vacuum' (Cohen 1985: 38). As Cohen argues: 'Social workers, med-
ical personnel, teachers, probation officers, judges, parents and others in identifiable social roles have a wide range of authority they
may fail to exercise for one reason or another'; on such occasions,
it typically falls to the 24-hour versatile service, the police, to provide an authoritative, if only provisional, solution.

This connects police work with the wider interests and authority
of the state. Public policies and practices of the state in other sectors shape the circumstances in which the police may be asked to
exercise a substitute authority. The coherence and legitimacy of
police actions may depend on a degree of compatibility with the
working methods and orientations of the agencies in the policy
area in question. To take an example relevant to international
policing, the effectiveness of policing initiatives against drug-
trafficking depends on how they fit into social and public health
policies pursued by the numerous agencies concerned with the
problem of drug abuse. The police role has to be co-ordinated with
other public services, whether through a multi-agency decision-
making framework (Kinsey et al. 1986), or through a series of more
informal understandings and practices (Punch 1979).[2]

Can we conclude that policing function and state interests are in
fact inextricably intertwined? In the context of European integration, this question can be refined in two ways. First, if, in the short
and medium term, we assume a level of political and institutional
integration falling short of the emergence of a European state, can
we nevertheless conceive of the development of substantial EU-
police institutions? Secondly, if we turn the question on its head, is

---

[2] Of course, the fact that police are situated within the state provides no guarantee that they will perform their role as residual authority in a manner which meets
with the agreement of other social agencies or their clients (Kinsey et al. 1986).
However, all else being equal, the dangers of usurpation of the authority of other
state agencies by the police would seem to be greater where a police organization
does not owe exclusive loyalty to a particular state.

it possible to conceive of the emergence, in the long term, of a European 'superstate' possessing many of the attributes of a state, but without its own police force? Can we have either a police force without a state or a state without a police force?[3]

General Theories of European Integration

We have already indicated the importance for our purposes of the theoretical traditions associated with policing and with the state. But policing theory and state theory refer to old institutions and an old relationship. What of the new political order, the European Union?

A variety of different theoretical approaches to European integration, from realist to functionalist, has something to contribute to our understanding of developments in police co-operation (Anderson 1994a). One basic difficulty with integration theory, however, has been the tendency for a dichotomy to develop between agency-based approaches and structure-based approaches (Hix 1994: 3). Theoretical positions tend towards one of two diametrically-opposed ontological assumptions: first, that patterns of behaviour are basically reducible to the autonomous actions of individuals or other internally coherent agencies—a position which is variously associated with realism, pluralism and rational choice theory; or that they are determined by 'external' mechanisms of a social, cultural or institutional nature—a position exemplified by various forms of structuralism or institutionalism. Insights offered by such perspectives into dimensions of integration such as policing and criminal justice are bound to be partial. An agency-based approach over-emphasizes the influence exerted by key political and professional élites, or, in the realist view of international relations, would treat each state as an individual 'actor' with its own interests, competing with other national interests. Structural approaches pay less attention to individual actors and emphasize factors neglected in the agency-based approach, such as the role of European law and institutions, or cultural developments, political ideologies or economic trends across Europe. An acknowledgement of the significance of both agency and structure within a unified theoretical framework seems necessary in order to understand the development of European policing institutions.

[3] For earlier, and briefer attempts to address these two questions, see den Boer and Walker (1993), Walker (1994a).

One example of such an approach, neo-functionalism, has enjoyed a renewed wave of popularity in recent years. Two types of 'spillover' are identified by neo-functionalists, each of which helps to explain the expansion of the EU's activities into new domains (Moravcsik 1993: 474–8). Firstly, from a predominantly structuralist perspective, *functional spillover* occurs when the limited scope of integration undermines the effectiveness of existing policy. Functional spillover occurs because government intervention in one sector may require consequential adjustments in various other sectors if policy is to have its intended effect. Secondly, from a predominantly agency-based perspective, *political spillover* occurs when the existence of supranational organizations triggers a self-perpetuating process of institutional development. New political and administrative entities gain a stake in the system and develop a measure of policy-making autonomy, distinct from the concerns of state and sub-state organizations.

The recent renaissance of neo-functionalist theory reflected a quickening tempo in the process of European integration. Neo-functionalism struggled to account for the period of stagnation from the late 1960's to the passage of the SEA, but offered a much more convincing explanation for the new dynamism of the pre-Maastricht period when the Community developed a broader range of economic and social objectives. The growth in police co-operation is plausibly explained within this framework. As we have seen (see chapter 1), with the initiation of the '1992' programme and the planned abolition of frontier controls, many governments and police authorities viewed close police co-operation as a functional requirement, as a way of countering new opportunities for criminal profits. But so many agencies are already part of the international co-operative network; political spillover has been an untidy and uneven process. The involvement of key players in protracted negotiation and competition over the form and substance of new initiatives has disturbed, although not confounded, the incrementalist logic of economic spillover (Anderson 1994a: 6).

However, neo-functionalism does not satisfactorily explain developments in an area such as policing (Hix 1994: 4–6; Moravcsik 1993: 474–80). In the first place, the attempt to overcome the opposition between structuralism and voluntarism may amount to little more than a restatement of the problem. Functional spillover and political spillover may be twin motors of change, but in the absence of an account of their interaction, it is unclear how the determinist assumptions associated with the former can be reconciled with the voluntarist assumptions underpinning the latter (Hix 1994: 5). This leads to a more general criticism of neo-functionalism—it cannot generate an enduring research agenda and a cumulative set of findings. Such a failing may be attributable to a more general absence of theoretical clarity (Moravcsik 1993: 476).

Two other manifestations of this shortcoming are relevant to police co-operation. The first concerns the emphasis of neo-functionalism on issues of technical co-ordination rather than the broader symbolic dimension of politics, leading to an insufficient differentiation between, on the one hand, 'high politics', which embody the traditional areas of national sovereignty and are not easily merged, and, on the other hand, 'low politics', where obstacles are less prominent (Hoffman 1966). Secondly, neo-functionalists have difficulty in taking proper account of external change. Neo-functionalism tends to operate as a closed explanatory system, concerned only with variables at the European level. It pays little attention to political and socio-economic factors operating at a wider level, such as the global, even though these may feed back into the development of the EU (Hix 1994: 5).

On the positive side, the main value of neo-functionalism lies in revealing the powerful technocratic imperatives in the integration process. Unlike in classical functionalism, however, these technocratic imperatives do not have direct causal significance; rather, they are represented in the political process as the basis of a persuasive set of arguments in those public and bureaucratic fora where the issues in integration are negotiated. The tension between the determinist leanings of economic functionalist analysis and an analysis based upon the actions of strategic political agents, therefore, may begin to be resolved by identifying the importance of *functionalist discourse* in the area of police co-operation, and this is reflected in the approach adopted later in the chapter.

On the negative side, neo-functionalism can be criticized both as couched in unduly general terms and as too narrowly conceived. It is too general in that it neglects salient differences between policy domains. The notion of state sovereignty inevitably makes a difference in policy-making in areas such as criminal justice and policing policy. Therefore, sectoral analysis, which avoids the simplifications of general explanations across all policy areas, is necessary. But, neo-functionalism is narrowly conceived in the sense that it treats European integration as the beginning and end of inquiry. Paradoxically, although sensitive to the limitations of the state as the object of inquiry, neo-functionalists fail to appreciate that a concentration on European integration can induce a similar form of myopia.

A final criticism of neo-functionalism, and, indeed, of European integration theory generally, is linked to the previous argument. Analyses of developments at the European level tend to draw sparingly upon theoretical understandings of socio-political units at other levels, instead emphasizing the uniqueness of the European experience and the need to develop a distinctive explanatory framework. This is particularly evident as regards the idea of the state. It is understandable that those attempting to understand the EU as a new type of political animal would wish to eschew explanatory categories associated with the conventional type of state. But there is a danger of missing the point. The search for theoretical innovation can, paradoxically, encourage a negative form of analysis, an emphasis upon what the Union is *not,* rather than an explanation of its uniqueness.[4] A rigid dichotomy between the state and the European Union risks failing to do justice to the uniqueness of the new Europe in blending some of the qualities of the conventional state into a supranational organization with a novel structure and a distinctive dynamic. Our second question, which some may find provocative, conceives of a mature European Union as a state-like entity. The analogy between the EU and a state can be taken too far, but it nevertheless remains a useful starting-point in thinking about the various dimensions of the new Europe.

A Police Force Beyond the State?

A chorus of academic and political voices has stressed the significance of the single market programme and the broader enterprise of European integration in creating the need for some form of Union-wide policing facility (see chapter 1 and Birch 1989; Van

---

[4] This tendency to be trapped in a conventional discourse, even when attempting to transcend it, restricts the otherwise highly illuminating perspective offered in two other prominent recent studies. See MacCormick's critique of the notion of sovereignty within the new Community legal order (1993), and Weiler's critique of the idea of 'Europe as Unity' (1991: 2478–81).

Reenen 1989; Benyon *et al.* 1990, 1993; Walker 1991, 1992, 1993b; Den Boer and Walker 1993). The increasing propensity of criminals to disregard national boundaries will, it is argued, receive stimulus from a free market in goods, people, capital and services, and from the deeper process of social integration which the move towards a common European citizenship will bring (see chapter 1). This argument has been inadequately scrutinized and the rhetorical justifications for increased co-operation have received insufficient critical attention (McLaughlin 1992; Den Boer 1992, 1994*a*; Bigo 1994*b*; see chapter 5). Nevertheless, the incorporation of an embryonic Europol within the new Justice and Home Affairs (JHA) pillar established by the TEU represents a significant transformation in the political recognition of police co-operation.

The precise meaning and import of this change remains ambiguous (Müller–Graff 1994). On the one hand (see chapter 2), decision-making in police co-operation, in particular, and criminal justice policy, in general, has shifted from an intergovernmental model to one which has supranational characteristics, with the introduction of new institutions which are to some extent autonomous from the Member States in their composition and functioning (Dehousse and Weiler 1990: 250). This step towards a 'vertical integration' (Van Reenen 1989: 48–9) of policing capacities has been in conjunction with an increase in the scope of co-operation. The measures to which the Member States have committed themselves in Europol and in the arena of police co-operation more generally, involve significant initiatives in terms of mutual operational support and general policing strategy (Walker 1991: 28). In addition, the broader regulatory context is also favourable to the Europol initiative and police co-operation. The wider framework of JHA co-operation allows an integrated policy approach over a range of security issues within the Union; moreover, non-Union initiatives, such as the SIS and the criminal justice co-operation treaties promulgated under the auspices of the Council of Europe, and, to a lesser extent the UN, complement and deepen co-operation among the Member States (see chapter 7).

In each of these dimensions of police co-operation, there are other, less positive indicators. Although Europol and policing more generally are recognized in the TEU, they are not yet fully integrated in the constitutional structure of the Union. Some executive authority is conferred upon Community institutions, but they continue to lack both legislative and judicial competence in this area. The areas of operational support, strategic policy and other forms of common action made possible by the TEU, although path breaking, are limited. The black letter of the text is both laconic and vague, and does not commit Member States to a detailed plan for co-operation. Beyond a bland commitment to consider the scope for future development by 1994, there is no hint (despite the raising of the issue at the 1991 Luxemboug Council) in the Declaration on Police Co-operation that the 'second phase' of Europol would include operational capacity (see chapter 2). The cautious tone of the Maastricht Treaty is conveyed by a saving provision which acknowledges the retention by Member States of their responsibilities for law and order and internal security (Article K.2.2).

The lack of precise commitments in the Treaty is reflected in the uneven pace of post Maastricht progress. The Ministerial Agreement on the EDU was delayed beyond the due date of December 1992 because of the lack of agreement on the site of the new organization. When the agreement was finally signed in June 1993 the basic question of location remained unresolved for a further five months. The decision to draft the Convention to provide the legal basis for a fully developed Europol was delayed until after the 1992 Lisbon Council. In November 1993 the JHA ministers, in planning their first agenda under the newly implemented TEU, agreed October 1994 as the completion date for the new convention. Even this extended timetable continued to be treated with some scepticism and proved to be unrealistic, in particular because of continuing disagreement over the scope of the new agency's activities and its relationship to the main institutions of the EC (Fode 1993b; see chapters 2, 6 and 8).

In the wider context of European internal security policy, the continuing absence of direct Community legislative competence is particularly significant. Because policing and the maintenance of internal security, unlike the second pillar of the new EU, foreign affairs, are associated with the idea of general order achieved through uniform standards, they require underpinning by the general, authoritative precepts associated with law; this is a partial explanation for the crowded agenda of European law-making initiatives in areas such as asylum, external border controls and information exchange systems. Many of our police respondents have articulated the widespread belief that it is difficult to envisage any significant police *operational* role for Europol in the absence of a legal framework at the EC level dealing with police powers and procedures, and perhaps also with matters of substantive criminal law. These two areas have so far remained entirely outside the competence of the EC (Schutte 1991; Sevenster 1992; chapter 6).[5] Even in those areas where agreement has been reached by the twelve, reliance upon international law conventions which require unanimity of signatories before they are brought into force, has been featured in both pre-Maastricht and post-Maastricht periods. For example, by the end of 1994, the Dublin Convention on asylum seekers agreed by the EC immigration ministers in 1990, had still not been ratified by all twelve domestic parliaments. Delays have also troubled the ratification of a Convention on controls on persons crossing external frontiers of the Member States (see chapter 4).[6] Similarly, the slow and uneven progress which has marked the EIS and the emergence of a data protection framework for the new systems of police co-operation is yet further evidence of the limitations of existing legislative procedures (see chapter 8).

The broader framework of criminal justice co-operation has not yet made progress towards integration. The Schengen system was repeatedly delayed beyond the original implementation deadline of January 1993 for the abolition of border controls (see chapter 2). Even where the broader institutional framework is strengthened, this does not necessarily favour the harmonization of policing at the EC level. There is a tendency for the various emergent international policing and criminal justice arrangements to compete with one another (Van Reenen 1989: 49-50; Johnston 1992: 202; chapters 2 and 8). Interpol, Schengen and the Council of Europe may harbour bureaucratic interests and embody conceptions of international policing and criminal justice which are not necessarily compatible with those associated with Europol (Den Boer and Walker 1993; Walker 1993b).[7] It cannot be assumed, therefore, that

---

[5] Bilateral and multilateral agreements in international law may make progress towards criminal law harmonization. However, despite modest advances (Gilmore 1992a; Hondius 1993), which may be accelerated by the negotiation of new Conventions under the Title VI of the TEU, international law has not yet provided the means of advancing the cause of harmonization. See further, ch. 7.

[6] OJC 11, 15.1.94; COM (93) 545; Bull. EC 11-1993, 1.5.4; Bull. EC 12-1993.

[7] The public criticism of the Europol idea as premature by Raymond Kendall, the Secretary-General of Interpol, immediately after the conclusion of the draft

the relationship between the variety of international policing developments in the modern Europe is always mutually beneficial. Different institutions may pursue programmes which, at best, are imperfectly co-ordinated, and at worst, hinder the realization of each other's full potential.

We are faced, therefore, with a complex, shifting, non-linear development which yields no clear indication of the overall trend in police co-operation. It is premature to draw firm conclusions about the level of common police organization which can be sustained by a political entity falling short of a state. However, if we examine the evidence in terms of the theories presented earlier in this chapter, a clearer picture of the limits to growth emerges.

To begin with, there is the question of police protection of the 'specific order' through which dominant interests within the state are sustained. It is a central paradox of police co-operation that many areas in which demand for collaboration on functional grounds is most persuasive are also those which bear most intimately upon state-specific interests. Terrorism is the most obvious example. The organizational sophistication, contact network and scope of activities of many terrorist organizations, whether 'international' or 'transnational' (Riley 1991: 12; chapter 2) is such that international co-operation is required if they are to be effectively combated. However, these organizations offer such direct and profound threats to state interests that targeted states will jealously guard the right to control the purpose and scope of such operations (Riley 1991: 9). Although the need for co-operation in terrorist matters supplied the initial impetus for the development of Trevi and remained a priority in the Maastricht Treaty, it did not figure in early plans to develop Europol. As discussed in chapter 2, opposing perspectives on anti-terrorism continue to be evident in the debate over the final text of the Europol Convention.

agreement on the Maastricht Treaty, is an example (*Agence Europe*, 22 Jan. 1992). Another is provided by developments within Schengen. Delays in the dismantling of internal borders post-1992 mean that assumptions that Schengen would quickly be superseded by the wider security arrangements involving Europol and the other Article K institutions have been premature. The resilience of Schengen is shown by the negotiations of the Schengen Secretariat over future arrangements with various candidate states who were not scheduled to join the Community until 1995 at the earliest (interview with Jan Öhlander, Ministry of Foreign Affairs, Stockholm, 18 May 1993). Also, at the meeting of the Executive Committee of the Schengen Agreement, Bonn, 27 June 1994, Austria was granted observer status and co-operation with Switzerland was intensified; *Agence Europe*, No. 6261, 27/28 June 1994.

Public order problems may raise a similar, if less acute, dilemma. In 1991, the Trevi ministers agreed to establish national contact points for public order matters.[8] Their initiative was stimulated by football hooliganism (Home Affairs Committee 1990), although other public order problems exist. Holiday hooliganism and cross-border 'spillover' disorder may be joined by a more calculating strand of international disorder, such as fascist fringe groups seeking to stem the flow of immigration from the south and east into the territories of the Community. After a spate of attacks on Turkish communities in Germany and France in May 1993, the Trevi ministerial meeting at Copenhagen in June decided to initiate an investigation into the possibility of transnational orchestration of racist violence.[9] However it manifests itself, public disorder poses an threat to the security of the state, perceived to be all the more acute when disorder is politically motivated. Despite a functional requirement for closer collaboration in public order policing, it is difficult to envisage a state ceding authority on its own territory to an external police agency.

Are there similar obstacles to the development of operational competence for Europol in the wider sphere of police activity concerned with general order? It might seem not, since the demand for public tranquillity and the prevention and detection of certain common categories of crime transcends boundaries. There may be no immediate prospects of criminal law harmonization in the EC, but there are similarities between European states concerning what constitute the main categories of crime.[10] However, three problems associated with supranational competence in the domain of general order remain, corresponding to the general qualifications voiced earlier in discussion of general order as a neutral standard across states.

There is, first, the impossibility of isolating questions of general order from those of specific order. Even when crimes have a clear international dimension, but no direct bearing upon the specific order of a particular state, as is the case with road traffic offences

---

[8] HC Debates, 20 Dec. 1991, col 352 (WA).   [9] *Guardian*, 2 June 1993.

[10] Without these similarities, the Council of Europe Convention on Extradition, which requires broad agreement between requesting and requested state as to the definition of criminal conduct, could not operate (see chap. 7); equally, an operational role for Europol prior to criminal law harmonization would be impossible to imagine, yet this role has attracted some support in Trevi and elsewhere (Van Outrive 1992a; *The Independent*, 20 April 1992).

(Home Affairs Committee 1990: x), computer crime, or automobile and art thefts (Gregory and Collier 1992), their suppression nevertheless contributes to securing specific order. Although there may be no direct conflict of interests between states, the pooling of policing capacities is unlikely to proceed in a particular area unless and until national authorities are persuaded that operational supranational policing is more effective than national policing.[11]

Secondly, there are more specific connections between general and specific order. As a crime of considerable common concern to Member States, drug-trafficking is an obvious choice as the initial priority for Europol (Trevi 1991). However, beneath a broad consensus there exists disagreement over the scope and seriousness of the trafficking problem and the best methods of containing it. This reflects differing national attitudes to the appropriate balance between individual choice and public regulation. Indeed, because anti-drugs policy strays into the domain of specific order, this has contributed to the uncertain progress of the EDU. The protracted disagreement over its site prior to the general agreement on the location of new EU institutions by the European Council in October 1993 was in part due to the opposition to the Hague candidacy by the French government, marking its disapproval of the Dutch authorities' persistence with a policy of licensed sale of soft drugs.[12]

The networks and syndicates involved in drug-trafficking tend not to respect nice jurisprudential distinctions, as their tentacles reach across the general order/specific order divide. To maximize effectiveness, police strategies in this area concentrate on criminals rather than categories of crime (Dorn *et al.* 1992), but this may lead criminal inquiries into sensitive territory for specific order. One example is the close relationship between drug-trafficking and money laundering, recognized in various international law agreements (Gilmore 1991; 1992a), and included in the Ministerial Agreement on the establishment of the EDU.[13] But as Levi argues, there is too much potential conflict between national economic interests for the idea of an 'international Police State' (Levi 1991:

---

[11] On the difficulties of generating trust and confidence between national police forces, see Walker (1992; 1993b); Robertson (1994).

[12] *Financial Times*, 9 Dec. 1992.

[13] Indeed, acknowledgement of this nexus had prompted the Trevi ministers in their earliest discussions of the new entity to make the provisional decision to expand the remit of Europol into the sphere of money laundering (Trevi 1991).

299) to take root easily in the money-laundering field. Money laundering is one of the 'crimes of the powerful' (Pearce 1976). In a market economy, its regulation demands difficult choices between, on the one hand, the circulation of capital, and, on the other hand, the intrusion of monitoring devices to trace illicit sources and destinations. Ultimately, these choices involve questions of specific order.

Recent initiatives of Trevi and of the JHA Ministers in the area of organized crime more generally (see chapter 1) indicate that, as the level of international coordination of criminal activity intensifies, the more varied such activity becomes and the more likely it is to challenge both specific and general order. The idea of 'narco-terrorism' denotes one such bridging activity, although this remains a poorly documented subject (Anderson 1989: 28). Various other links between terrorism and other criminal activities and organizations within the EU have been noted. Examples include the link between attacks on foreigners and terrorist movements in Germany;[14] increasing concern with the illegal traffic in nuclear materials (see chapter 5); the alleged relationship between Mafia groupings and terrorist movements in Italy; and the extensive involvement of the IRA in smuggling, extortion, armed robbery and a wide range of commercial and construction industry frauds (Fijnaut 1991: 109-10; Northern Ireland Office 1993). In so far as such activities assume international dimensions, difficult questions arise as to how supranational policing can be effective without encroaching on states' conceptions of their own particular security interests.

The final obstacle to the conferring of authority on a supranational police agency within the domain of general order has to do with the capacity of the police to exercise residual authority across a broad range of policy sectors. If, as argued, there are good reasons why such authority should be exercised at the same level as the political entity which has primary responsibility across the broad range of policy sectors, the continuing pre-eminence of the state as the source of public policy militates against the assumption

---

[14] See Opinion of the Committee on Civil Liberties and Internal Affairs for the Committee on Foreign Affairs and Security, *para.* 6, appended to the Report of the Committee on Foreign Affairs and Security on terrorism and its effect on security in Europe, 2 Feb. 1994, Doc EN/RR/245/245119.

by a supranational body of the policing capacity to perform this residual role.

This point is illustrated by the example of drug abuse. Of all the areas in which a supranational law enforcement entity may play a role, this stands out as one which the EU is treating in a multi-dimensional manner. Title VI of the TEU authorizes the Commission and Member States to initiate policy to combat drug addiction by means other than through police, judicial and customs co-operation (Art. K.1 (4)). Title X, which deals with public health, envisages the pursuit of joint research into the causes of drug-related diseases and the provision of health information and education. Common foreign and security policy arrangements permit the provision of financial support to producer countries to assist crop substitution. The European Drugs Monitoring Centre, established by the Commission in 1993, could provide a vital resource in collating information and providing analysis in each of these dimensions of drugs policy (Dorn 1993: 40-2).[15]

European drugs policy nonetheless remains less than the sum of its superficially impressive parts. It may combine police, judicial, public health, educational, and economic strands. But these are more prominently present in the national and sub-national policy arena, and domestic policy instruments are even more predominant in various other spheres bearing upon the social environment of drug abuse, such as housing, environmental planning, social security, personal social services and industrial development. Even excluding the more obvious ways in which anti-drugs policy is linked to the specific order of the state, the breadth and depth of the instruments of domestic public policy with relevance to drug abuse are such that they eclipse policy-making at the European level. The domestic level, therefore, remains appropriate for the major law enforcement effort if law enforcement is to be in tune with the general orientation of public policy.

The feasibility and legitimacy of some form of supranational police capacity within the EU as presently constituted should not be dismissed, but they are limited. In the domain of general order,

---

[15] Further evidence of a generalist approach can be seen in the priority action plan drawn up by the JHA Ministers in Brussels in Dec. 1993, which included the development of a global strategy on combating drugs. The strategy on drugs was subsequently submitted to the JHA Ministers at their meeting in Luxembourg on 21 June 1994, where it was welcomed (*Agence Europe*, No. 6256, 22 June 1994).

the jurisdiction of a supranational body may be circumscribed by a number of factors. Because general order always has some bearing upon the specific order of constituent states, participants in any supranational venture are likely to insist upon very high general standards of efficiency and security. Where issues of general order shade into matters of specific order, the competence of a supranational agency may be narrowly defined and national responsibilities jealously guarded. Finally, because all policing policy and practice tends to be so interwoven with other areas of domestic public policy, any new international police organization may be subjected to monitoring at the national level to ensure that it does not develop beyond a limited specialist remit to assume the generic policing role traditionally reserved to the domestic level. As the brief history of Europol indicates, the appropriate model is one of incremental rather than exponential expansion, providing an umbrella for particular functions rather than a basis of general policing capacity.

A State Beyond Policing?

While there may be limits to the development of the policing remit of the EU in its present form, the picture may alter considerably in the future. Following the period of stagnation in the 1970s, from the mid-1980s onwards the Community developed renewed institutional momentum through initiatives such as the 1992 programme, the SEA and the Intergovernmental Conferences which preceded the TEU (Keohane and Hoffman 1991b; Weiler 1991; Nugent 1992). If this 'logic of deepening' (Nugent 1992: 313) is sustained to the beginning of the new millennium, the Union may evolve into an entity with many state-like characteristics. On the other hand, there are contrary trends in recent developments.[16] The ambivalent public reception given to the TEU, particularly in Denmark, the United Kingdom and France, gave impetus to anti-federalist political forces. The intensification of the debate between, on the one

---

[16] The case for the Union having reached the limits of its integrationist potential does not rest only upon empirical evidence of increasing resistance to integration. There are a number of more or less sophisticated theoretical positions which attribute a deeper significance to this evidence. Essentially, they argue that the development of the Union is explicable in terms of the advancement of national interests, but if the point is reached when the national and Union interests no longer coincide, national interests will prevail over Union interests (see e.g. Moravcsik 1993; Milward 1992).

hand, proponents of a 'two speed' Europe—led by an inner core of the more solidly committed—and, on the other, advocates of a Europe of variable geometry, where each state satisfies its particular taste for co-operation from an *à la carte* menu of competences, is further evidence of growing disagreement on Europe's future, particularly as *both* options concede the implausibility of a single pattern of integration for all Member States (Harmsen 1994). Also, the debate surrounding the accession of Austria and the Nordic states and the agenda of the 1996 Intergovernmental Conferences has provided, and will continue to provide, a prominent new arena for Eurosceptics. One writer has remarked that evidence of contrasting trends is only to be expected:

. . . for now we are confronted with a dialectic of integration and fragmentation, where each drives the other. Since each becomes a motive for the other, we get more of both, and it is impossible to determine any firm direction. Integration and fragmentation logic have entered a kind of loop where each swing to one side generates its opposite (Buzan 1993: 7).

Buzan also argues that given the unstable and fragile nature of the present balance of power, in the longer term, '. . . the generative . . . *logic*' is likely to flow in either one direction or the other, however obscured by the continuous cycle of action and reaction. Too much should not be inferred, therefore, from short-term trends, whether in the policing sector or within the European polity more generally. Rather, these trends should be placed within a deeper theoretical understanding and a longer historical pattern.

A Post-Hobbesian State?

In the most strongly integrationist scenario for long term change, the EU, as 'a novel form of political domination' (Bryant 1991: 204), will have a rather different profile from that of the traditional state. Monopoly control over internal security is particularly vulnerable to exclusion from this new EU.

Schmitter has recently depicted the developing Union structure as a prototype 'post-Hobbesian state', or 'European supranational non-state' (Schmitter 1990 [discussed in Bryant, 1991]; Streeck and Schmitter 1991: 152). For him, the distinctive characteristic of such an entity is 'the absence of military insecurity as the overriding motive/excuse for the exercise of political authority'. In the Hobbesian world order, although not necessarily born of military struggle, the state typically emerges 'when the accumulation and concentration of coercive means grow together' (Tilly 1990: 19), and when those who control such means assert their capacity to maintain the integrity of the new entity in the international balance of power. This implies security against threats and disruptions from both within and outside the new entity. The post-Hobbesian state, by contrast, possesses no such defining role. It emerges in a context of incremental political development where loyalty to the nation state as the ultimate source of political authority remains, and where, in the absence of the geo-political conditions which formed the Hobbesian order of states, the 'authority-legitimacy transfer' (Haas 1971; Anderson 1994a) necessary for a strong supranational policing capacity is difficult to envisage. Schmitter himself forecasts that the 'form of the post-integration Europe will lie somewhere between sovereign units each with an unambiguous monopoly on violence . . . and diffuse networks based upon multiple voluntary exchanges' (quoted in Bryant 1991: 204).

As the neologism 'supranational non-state' indicates, Schmitter's approach, while highly suggestive, shares with other variants of integration theory, a tendency to become trapped by the very terms of the statist discourse it seeks to reject. As suggested in our discussion of neo-functionalism, this can produce a falsely dichotomous style of argument, leading to a restricted appreciation of the possible development of both the EU and the Member States. In stressing the differences between the emerging form of the European entity and traditional views of the state, it risks neglecting developments on either side of the divide; both the increasingly state-like characteristics of the European Union and the evolution of the traditional state into a less cohesive political entity.

Uneven Development

If a more open theoretical orientation is adopted, the EU defies easy classification in terms of old oppositions such as federation/confederation and state/non-state. There is a major imbalance between, on the one hand, its limited 'political supranationalism', and, on the other hand, its mature 'juridical supranationalism' (Hartley 1989: 47) and sophistication as an international economic organization. In the political sphere, even after the ratification of the TEU, the two major supranational organs, the Commission and European Parliament, lack the institutional powers of the central tier of a traditional federal state, still less of a unitary state, while there also remain a strong intergovernmental flavour to arrangements within the Council of Ministers and the European Council. In the juridical sphere, however, the doctrine of direct effect of Community legislation in Member States, the principle of the supremacy of Community law over national law, and the ever-widening jurisdiction and increasingly intensive activity of the Community in legislative matters, provide a significant counterweight.

Given the context within which the new Europe has emerged, this is perhaps not a surprising trend. Compared to the older Western federations and quasi-federations of Australia, Canada, the United States and, to a lesser extent, Germany, the EU has developed in a welfarist and corporatist age where the legitimate role of government greatly expanded. Post-Maastricht Europe has either concurrent or exclusive legislative powers with states in matters as disparate as agriculture, industrial development, technological research and development, transport, education, consumer protection, environmental protection, and, more tentatively, in political and citizenship rights, and employee and social welfare rights. In economic terms, too, the EU is an expanding and more cohesive power. Although controversy over eventual monetary union remains, the achievement in 1993 of a substantially complete internal market in the EU heightened the contrast in affluence and influence with the disorganized economies of post-Communist Central and Eastern Europe.

The implications for police institution-building of this diverse and inconsistent set of trends are complex. Many of the emerging areas of regulation will require their own system of sanctions in order to enforce Union-wide norms. There have been signs of a European capacity in the domain of 'administrative policing' (Van Reenen 1989: 47; Johnston 1992: 202) in the enforcement of competition law (Lavoie 1992) and in the work of UCLAF since 1989 in co-ordinating efforts to combat fraud against the Community budget (Reinke 1991; Clarke 1993). In time, this 'administrative policing' might extend to cover matters such as environmental protection, health and safety at work, and nuclear safety. The development of an administrative policing capacity may, of course, be hampered by the absence of a general criminal law jurisdiction, but, as explained at length in chapter 6, the Commission can impose administrative fines and other civil sanctions in certain areas, and European law authorities can oblige national authorities to impose suitable penalties for infringements of European law. Also, the absence of broad jurisdiction in criminal justice matters means that the Commission has no general investigative competence, but exceptions in areas such as competition law and VAT fraud indicate a scope for future development (Sevenster 1992: 32–5).

Some of these diverse strands are being pulled together. On 15 June 1994 the Commission adopted proposals for a new general regulation on administrative sanctions at Union level, and for the preparation of a Convention under Title VI which would ensure that fraud against the financial interests of the Union is treated as a criminal offence in each Member State. These proposals, which were endorsed by the JHA Ministers meeting in Luxembourg,[17] are part of the Commission's broader anti-fraud work programme which seeks to strengthen the initiating and co-ordinating role of the Union in operations and intelligence-gathering as well as in the development of a regulatory framework (Commission 1994d).[18]

Equally important is the growing perception of a 'security deficit' within the Union (Bigo 1994b; chapter 5). The immediate catalyst was the 1992 programme which has encouraged the view that vigilance at external border controls must be extended to compensate for the loss of internal border controls (Den Boer and Walker 1993; Den Boer 1994b; chapter 4). As Bigo argues, this line of thought has stimulated the creation of an 'internal security field', a domain of practices and ideas which presupposes a single 'security continuum' along which the issues of immigration and asylum are closely linked to concerns with organized crime, terrorism and anti-drugs policy. As well as encouraging Schengen and Europol and the development of co-ordinated immigration policy, the new internal security ideology has also sustained proposals for

---

[17] *Agence Europe*, no. 6256, 22 June 1994.

[18] In the new Commission appointed in 1995, one Commissioner, Anita Gradin from Sweden, was given special responsibility for tackling the problem of fraud against the EU. In an important integrative move, she announced that all the anti-fraud units of individual Brussels directorates were being incorporated into the Commission's central fraud squad, UCLAF. This would have the effect of increasing the staff of UCLAF from 30 at the beginning of 1994 to 130, about 1% of the total administrative staff of the Commission (*Guardian*, 1 Feb. 1995).

the creation of a unit dedicated to the policing of external borders against illegal immigrants (Van Reenen 1989: 48) and has encouraged particular emphasis on the threat posed by crime syndicates from eastern Europe.[19]

The ideology of internal security, focusing on the specific order of the Union and establishing a frontier between this order and the interests of other territorial regions, may also have direct institutional implications. It could encourage the formation of an administrative élite with a strict duty of allegiance to the Union rather than to the states. Such a development is encouraged by recent Commission proposals for a new official secrecy law—subsequently reformulated as a Code of Practice—which applies to Community information and to public servants handling such information,[20] and in the insistence of the Council of Ministers that the new European Ombudsman established under the TEU should be denied access to categories of classified information.[21] If this trend towards the creation of a new ethos of secrecy, confidentiality and exclusive loyalty within the administrative apparatus of the Union continues, this may in turn encourage the institution of a security agency to police the enforcement of the new security regime.

Two other trends associated with the emergence of the internal security field may enhance the law enforcement capacity of the Union in the long term. The increased legislative and social policy profile of the EU encourages public order protests with a 'real European character' (Van Reenen 1989: 46)—directed against European institutions and policies. Potential flashpoints include co-ordinated protest against CAP, and, in the context of emergent common energy and employment policies, anti-nuclear protests and strategies of industrial action.

---

[19] The significance of this new perspective is exemplified by the Berlin Declaration on Increased Co-operation in Combating Drug Crime and Organized Crime in Europe, agreed on 8 Sept. 1994. The Declaration was endorsed by six East and Central European states alongside the twelve EU Member States.

[20] For the original legislative proposal, see *Statewatch*, vol. 2, No. 3, May–June 1992: 1; see also 'Official Secrecy Law in the European Community?', *Statewatch briefing paper*, May 1992. This proposal was dropped in the wake of the commitment of the Edinburgh European Council towards subsidiarity in Dec. 1992 (*Statewatch*, vol. 3, No. 1, Jan.–Feb. 1993: 1), to be replaced by a proposal of the Council of Ministers meeting on 6 Dec. 1993 for a Code of Practice (*Statewatch*, vol. 3, No. 6, Nov.–Dec. 1993: 1; vol. 4, No.1, Jan.–Feb. 1994: 15).

[21] *Guardian*, 11 June 1993.

Another possibility associated with the specific order of the Union concerns threats by terrorist organizations made directly against European institutions and interests. The Revolutionary November 17 Group, based in Greece, attacked the local EC offices in December 1990 in protest against austerity measures which, it claimed, sullied Greek sovereignty (Riley 1991: 23–4). The French group, *Action Directe*, or a successor, could re-emerge in conjunction with a variety of other indigenous European groups to challenge the implementation of the Single European Market (O'Ballance 1989: 120). Ideologically motivated threats to the Union may also emanate from beyond its frontiers. Notwithstanding Schmitter's prognostication, the new CFSP Chapter in the TEU indicates a significant shift toward Union competence in foreign affairs, and so towards incorporation of the second pillar of the Hobbesian state, namely external coercive potential. This may involve the Community in challenges to internal security, through both espionage and terrorism, by external hostile powers. For the first time, terrorism and strategic intelligence associated with 'state security' may become bound up with the specific order of the EU rather than its Member States.

Finally, the cumulative effect of the integration process at the institutional level is bound to produce ever greater social and cultural integration such as the spread of language skills, the growth of intra-Union travel, friendship and commercial ties between individuals and corporate bodies across state boundaries, and the development of common commodity preferences. In turn, the encouragement of a 'European civil society' may accelerate a process of internationalization of the traditional forms of national crime.

However, none of these trends makes inevitable a strong central policing capacity in the longer term. The matters involved are diverse and specialized; notwithstanding the Commission's integrative efforts, the growing demand for administrative policing may be met through a series of specialized agencies rather than through a unified police agency capable of developing generic police functions. In the high-profile area of fraud against the Community, the inability of UCLAF to develop an effective strategy has attracted mounting criticism from the European Parliament and elsewhere; the tendency of Member States to treat fraud against the Community as less serious than defrauding the state is a clear case of the specific order of the state retaining priority (Clarke 1993).[22]

In the new internal security field, the existence of a common threat at and beyond the external borders may encourage, but does not guarantee, a common solution. Indeed, as the failure to complete the dismantling of internal border controls within the '1992' deadline indicates, there is a continuing reluctance to rest the defence of internal security primarily upon the maintenance of a common external frontier for which there is shared responsibility.[23] As for the development of a new security framework for European institutions, vigorous legal and political opposition has been voiced.[24] As long as European law and policy against public order and terrorist threats are seen as mere legislative rules without a complementary central political authority, each Member State may persist in defining the Union's security profile in terms of their own specific orders and continue to treat any common problems by intergovernmental means. A common anti-terrorist capacity directed against external threats depends upon the development of a strong Union identity in international security and military matters, which, as the failure to develop a robust co-ordinated response to war in the Balkans indicates (Hoffman 1993), is as uncertain in the 'post-Hobbesian' world as the central policing

[22] See, for example, the criticisms made by the Court of Auditors of the European Community in their Annual Report to the European Parliament for the year 1993–4; the Court complained that insufficient measures had been taken to remedy deficiencies it had identified in the last ten years, including deficiencies in the system of preventing and detecting fraud against the Community. In its response, the Commission announced that as part of its new anti-fraud strategy (Commission 1994d), it was about to open a new free telephone 'hotline' which would allow citizens to report information on suspected fraud 24 hours per day (The Week in Europe, 12 Nov. 1994). For subsequent developments, see note 17 as above.

[23] On the Schengen delays, see ch. 2 and 4 and n. 8 above and associated text. Repeated delays in the abolition of border controls under the Single Market programme of the Community as a whole have prompted the European Parliament to take legal action against the Commission under Art. 175 of the EC Treaty over its failure to act (OJC, No. C1/12, 4.1.94 (Case C-445/93); see also Statewatch, vol. 3, no. 4, July–Aug. 1993: 7).

[24] Political misgivings over the Code's non-legal status have been expressed through COREPER by German, French and Italian representatives (Statewatch, vol.4, No. 2, March-April 1994: 10). The Danish and Dutch Governments have also voiced strong objections; indeed, the decision is under legal challenge from the Dutch Government, while the Guardian is also challenging a refusal to disclose background documents for a meeting of the JHA Ministers (Statewatch, vol.4, No. 3, May–June 1994: 10–11; vol. 4, No. 5, Sept–Oct. 1994: 10).

capacity itself. Finally, the growth of social and cultural ties within the Community may be reflected in gradual development of the predominantly intergovernmental structures of police co-operation and not generate a demand for a new European operational police force.

But the whole picture may prove greater than its parts, and the cumulative effect of various factors may provide the conditions for a gradual transformation of the basis for European policing. Echoing the conclusions of the neo-functionalists, some have argued that the propensity of the EU's governing institutions to develop into new areas despite the absence of strong popular or political initiatives from constituent states should not be dismissed (Bulmer 1993). However, in each of the areas discussed, precisely the same impediment arises, namely the absence of the preconditions of the 'authority-legitimacy' transfer which would allow 'Brussels' to claim the right to defend its own conception of specific order. This is the all-pervasive problem and, unless and until it is overcome, there seems little prospect of the Union developing an autonomous policing capacity, whether by incremental development or radical innovation.

Bridging the Legitimacy Gap

What are the preconditions of the requisite authority-legitimacy transfer, and what are the prospects of these being met? Are there any social and political developments which make the state a less authoritative site for policing institutions than before, and are there are any developments which make the EU an increasingly attractive site? In addressing these questions, we may distinguish 'push' factors from 'pull' factors.

On the one hand, there are the 'push' factors. By depicting the conventional Hobbesian state as an entity which emerged in the context of a general struggle over security, writers such as Schmitter and Tilly assume that the legitimacy of policing within such a state has tended to be closely linked with its basic *raison d'être*. However, As Waever *et al.* (1993) have argued in an analysis of the origins of the modern state system, the Hobbesian state has undergone important internal transformations with implications for its continuing capacity and legitimacy to perform certain functions, including the policing function.

The territorial state—the original Hobbesian state—is a creature of the 16th century, predating the 'nation state' by two centuries. The development of the idea of the nation state, influenced by the enlightenment search for a non-religious cosmology (Waever 1993: 28-30), brought together political identity with cultural identity; the nation state provided not only the institutions and coercive support of political authority, as with the original territorial state, but also a sense of 'imagined community' (Anderson 1991)—a common heritage and a mass culture associated with a myth of nationhood. Waever *et al.* contend that we are now entering a third phase in the development of the state, when 'the coupling state-nation is weakened without a new synthesis being achieved at the European level' (Waever and Kelstrup 1993: 69). The potency of tradition in the construction of identity myths means that in this third phase cultural identity remains predominantly at the national level (with a tendency to move down towards 'micro-national "regional" identity' (Waever and Kelstrup 1993: 69)); but political identity is dispersed across a number of levels—national, subnational and supranational. In other words, the nation state is gradually becoming more 'nation' and less 'state'.

In demonstrating the separability of cultural identity from political identity, this analysis allows the relationship between the state and policing to be viewed more contingently than if the two forms of identity are treated as inexorably linked. The policing function may be intrinsic to the political authority of the state, but it is not essential to the cultural package of the nation. But there may remain a powerful symbolic link between policing and the modern Western European nation state, even if its political authority is in secular decline. Although state sovereignty is no longer exclusive, the nation state still retains a significant political authority, and therefore remains a legitimate locus for a strong policing capacity. Also, although analytically separate, cultural identity and political identity have become interwoven in the historical context of the nation state. The idea of nation, although separate from that of the state, flourished in the political environment of the sovereign state. Some of the practical attributes of statehood, including the military function and the policing function, were used in the symbolic development of national identity. Indeed, the development of the nation state in many cases coincided with the development of specialized police institutions and thus has helped to create a legacy linking police institutions with national unity (Emsley 1993; Reiner

1994a: 755-6). But his link, however strong, is severable. It will tend to weaken as political authority shifts, and as the evidence accumulates that the location of policing functions at national level is not an inevitable part of a social order but merely a product of particular historical circumstances.[25]

There is, therefore, no insurmountable obstacle to the disassociation of the policing function from the nation state, but current trends suggest only the mildest 'push' away from the state level. Much, then, depends upon the strength of the 'pull' factors attracting policing functions toward the higher level. To understand how the post-Hobbesian state might acquire the authority to police its territory, the conditions under which the Union emerged and is sustained must be appreciated. The defining context for the EU has been the history of post-war Western European democracy. Originally charged to pursue the economic benefits of free competition in a common market, the Union has gradually assumed a wider range of social and welfare objectives. Further, it has pursued these objectives against a background of widespread expectations that important decisions which distribute key resources and influence life-chances must be controlled by representative and participatory democratic institutions.

Unlike the Hobbesian state, therefore, the link between the integrity of the political entity and the policing function is not a direct one. Can sufficient indirect links be forged to legitimate the policing function? One possibility concerns the functional link between policing and economic prosperity. The Union's modest advances in the field of administrative policing result from its contribution to a system of fiscal regulation through which the Union's economic objectives are advanced. Similarly, the threat from immigrants as a justification for an increased policing capacity, is based on the perception that the material welfare of EU citizens might be undermined by mass immigration. However, a rationale which is purely economic, and which is seen as an objective imposed from above, is insufficient to support supranational policing.

Meehan has argued, in her discussion of citizenship in the

---

[25] The symbolic link between policing and nation is undermined by objective developments in international policing, and also, as Reiner argues, by the fragmented and pluralist cultural conditions of 'postmodernity', which militate against the more homogeneous conception of national identity with which the imagery of the police has tended to be associated; see Reiner (1992a; 1994a: 756).

European Union, that the legitimacy of the European order rests upon an indivisible 'cluster of meanings' (Meehan 1993: 177). The Union originated as a series of voluntary agreements between states which shared a common recognition of individual rights and obligations; the legitimacy of the Union depends upon its regulation of the economic, social and political domains being couched in terms of individual rights and obligations.[26] As Meehan puts it, an updating of Marshall's analysis of citizenship (Marshall 1950), there was in the EC from the beginning a strong connection between civil rights (and associated economic freedoms), political rights and, to a more limited extent, social rights of the citizen, and an expectation that such rights should be granted conjointly. Arguably, such a holistic treatment of citizenship rights may in time persuade EU citizens of the legitimacy of EU political authority, and to accept that EU institutions, *including policing institutions,* are required to enforce such rights and obligations.

This line of argument does not support the complacent conclusion that the population of Europe will only legitimate the transfer of policing authority to the EC in return for a full set of citizenship rights. But it supports the contention that, without some expansion of citizenship rights to supplement the functional economic arguments, such a shift will not be accepted easily. Some expansion of citizenship rights is taking place. Civil and economic rights have always been linked to the purposes of the EU: both the completion of the 1992 programme, and the general reception of fundamental rights and freedoms into Community jurisprudence culminating in formal recognition of the ECHR in the TEU (Art. F.2), have consolidated this. In the social field, the TEU has embraced a broad vision of entitlements in employment and social security through the 1989 Social Charter. In the area of political rights, the Treaty establishes the new status of citizenship of the Union; the right to vote and stand for election in local and European Parliament elections anywhere in the Community, to receive diplomatic protection from other Member States' representatives in third countries, to petition the European Parliament, and to apply to a new ombuds-

---

[26] Thus, although not set out explicitly in the original Treaty framework, the doctrine of the direct effect of Community law, which allows individuals to enforce Community rights against Member States, was confirmed by the European Court of Justice in an early case. See *Van Gend en Loos*, Case 26/62 (1963) ECR 1. See also Meehan (1993: 178).

man of the Community (Title 11, Art.8), build upon the modest foundations of the earlier Citizen's Europe programme (Closa 1992).

European citizenship, however, remains incomplete. The recognition of fundamental rights by the European Court of Justice remains uneven (Coppel and O'Neill 1992). The United Kingdom has refused to accept the Social Charter, which, in any case, is concerned more with Community powers rather than individual entitlements to welfare provision. The unevenness of economic development across the Community militates against the provision of uniform welfare standards (Majone 1993: 167–8). The new political rights, too, are not comprehensive. They contain no entitlement to participate in national general elections. They do not address the democratic deficit of the Community, namely the denial of an effective legislative role for the only directly elected European institution, the European Parliament (see chapter 8).

Whether or not the sorts of development outlined above will lead to a strong EU policing capacity in the longer term remains a matter of speculation. We can, however, contemplate alternative scenarios to identify possible developments which will make supranational institutions either more or less likely, and also identify some wider social and political implications of different outcomes.

If a strong police capacity fails to emerge, this may be because EU citizenship is destined to be insufficiently robust to legitimate the development of European policing institutions. Even if a rounded conception of citizenship is developed which endows the EU with legitimate authority, however, this does not mean that all important rights and duties need be articulated at the European level. Meehan argues that in Western Europe there is developing 'a kind of three-dimensional framework for the exercise of the rights, loyalties and duties of citizenship' (Meehan 1993:173), with the regional, national and supranational levels each legitimate within its own sphere. In such a scenario, there is no compelling reason why powerful policing institutions should be appropriate and acceptable at the supranational level. That police institutions have been traditionally located at the other two levels may argue against such a shift. Equally, however, as the link to the national and subnational levels is contingent rather than necessary, there is no compelling reason why powerful policing institutions should *not* be appropriate and acceptable at the supranational level. The absence of any sacred tie between nation and policing means that more profane arguments, in particular those of a neo-functional variety, will determine which, if any, policing functions will be raised above the nation state.

However, even when functional arguments favour elevation, we should not assume that the institutions of the EU as presently conceived will be seen as the appropriate level at which a new policing capacity should be organized. The limitations already noted of European integration theory in general, and of neo-functionalism in particular, are a tendency to assume that the EU marks the boundary of feasible development of international political organization and that its development is explicable exclusively by reference to endogenous factors. But 'pull' factors might cause policing and other policy functions to gravitate to an even higher (global) level. Although there are many variants (Giddens 1990; Robertson 1992), a common thread runs through the 'globalization' approach—namely, that a number of geo-political shifts, such as the development of a world capitalist economy, a greater international division—and interdependence—of labour, and the evolution of a world military order, have produced an ever more closely interwoven and centralized world political order. Globalization progresses in a dialectical manner (Giddens 1990: 73), and, as the 'deepening *versus* widening' debate in the EU indicates, an intermediate entity such as the EU is both a product and a potential casualty of the globalizing trend.

A similar tension is revealed when policing is viewed as a discrete policy sector. The same pressures which encourage EU initiatives also cast doubt on whether a narrow regional solution is sufficiently flexible and effective. The competition between the EU level and agencies with wider scope, such as the Council of Europe and Interpol (chapter 2), has already been mentioned.[27] Within the EU itself, relations of individual Member States and the EU collectively with third countries in the area of JHA are a matter of acute political concern. The collapse of the Warsaw Pact created oppor-

---

[27] Raymond Kendall, Secretary General of Europol, has sought to develop the themes of wasteful inter-agency rivalry and the limitations imposed by the narrow territorial boundaries of Europol (Interview with Raymond Kendall; see also, *Agence Europe*, 22 Jan. 1992). The fact that later drafts of the Europol Convention have recognized the need for closer links with Interpol suggests a growing awareness of the need for a regional police organization to develop a global network of allegiances and communications (see ch. 2).

tunities both for international criminals wishing to take advantage of deregulated economies and minimally controlled borders, and for political interests keen to set the ideological tone of reconstruction in the area of security policy. There was extensive involvement by Member States in law enforcement co-operation initiatives in Eastern Europe prior to Maastricht (Gregory 1994). More recently, the JHA ministers have placed the question of external relations at the top of their agenda, with particular reference to the position within the new structure of the longstanding 'friends of Trevi', including Canada, United States, Morocco and Switzerland, and to the most appropriate co-operative arrangements with the numerous central and eastern European States with whom the EU already has association agreements, and who are emerging as candidates for full membership (see chapter 4). However this debate is resolved, the fact that it is taking place so soon after the development of the third pillar suggests the provisionality and fragility of the current settlement.

The dynamic of globalization may pose an even more direct challenge to the prospects of police co-operation in Europe. In a corrective to the Euro-centric approach which has dominated in much discussion of European police co-operation, Nadelmann has argued that the post-Second World War era has been marked by the 'Americanization of foreign criminal justice systems' (Nadelmann 1993: 11, 136). Prompted by political concerns over the domestic implications of the development of transnational drug-trafficking and money laundering, the United States has taken a leading role in promoting international agreements, locating agents and agencies abroad, and influencing the contents of the criminal law and the methods of law enforcement in foreign legal systems. Whether the United States' interests have been as predominant as Nadelmann suggests is controversial, although his account is persuasive. His approach suggests that, if policing requires an exclusive or predominant jurisdiction in Europe (however broadly defined), this will be resisted by a powerful international actor which retains an interest in international crime control in both Western and Eastern Europe (Nadelmann 1993: 153).

This scenario suggests an image of European policing dominated by global forces, but there is an alternative scenario which assumes a more self-assertive EU, but which has different and equally alarming implications. This scenario marginalizes questions of the broad EU legitimacy gained from developing citizenship rights, and envisages a narrow and direct appeal to material interests. The economic functionalist rationale for institutional growth in 'the internal security field' may achieve wide acceptance and this may diminish acceptance of wider citizenship rights and of giving rights to immigrants. The new status of European citizenship may remain narrowly state-derivative; in a context where the theme of security threats—fiscal and otherwise—is the only basis on which the argument is made for new European police institutions, the 'denizens' and 'margizens' of Europe (Martiniello 1995), whose interests are directly threatened by an exclusionary security policy, will be deprived of the framework of rights upon which the broader legitimacy of European policing institutions rests.

Conclusion

The experience of the EU reveals a complex relationship between police institutions and the socio-political environment in which they are located. Police institutions are not simply epiphenomena, to be 'read off' from the broader social and political framework, whether this takes the form of a state or some novel political arrangement. Indeed, as Europe progresses from the sovereign state, to the nation state, to the post-Hobbesian political order, the relationship between policing and forms of polity becomes looser and more influenced by other considerations. Policing institutions nonetheless remain linked to wider political forms, which promote and set limits to developments in the policing domain. Policing is aptly described as a 'semi-autonomous social field' (Falk Moore 1978: 720; Goldsmith 1990: 93) to which the contrasting orientations of structural fatalism and naïve separatism are equally inappropriate. Instead, the main requirement to build effective and legitimate police institutions in the new Europe is a framework of analysis which remains sensitive to the influence exerted and restrictions imposed by the political context and also includes consideration of matters intrinsic to the policing sector.

4
Frontiers and Policing

Introduction

Effective and harmonized administration of controls at the external frontier and the abolition of internal frontier controls are essential requirements for the completion of the Single European Market (SEM). The SEM required the full implementation of the four freedoms agreed in principle by the Member States by the signing of the Treaty of Rome and re-confirmed by the 1985 Single European Act—freedom of movement of persons, goods, services and capital. *Inter alia* this required the dismantling of customs checks on goods and police controls on persons at the internal frontiers as well as the abolition of the non-tariff barriers to trade within the EU, embedded in different health and industrial standards, professional and trades qualifications, specifications of goods and administrative procedures. Sharp differences of opinion were expressed by Member States, interest groups and individual members of the public about how much harmonization was necessary, particularly over rates of indirect taxation and Community-wide definitions of goods such as beer and ice-cream. Freedom of movement of goods within the SEM, which is less politically sensitive than freedom of movement of persons except where unfair competition or traffic in illegal goods are suspected, also depended on making the external frontier the customs collection point for all Member States, and an effective barrier to smuggling of goods. Controls at all crossing points of the external frontier should be equally effective in preventing the entry of illegal immigrants so that, within the external frontier, there could be free movement of persons. Differences of view have already emerged about the amount of common or joint police co-operation necessitated by the new freedoms and new systems of regulation.

The Single European Market and the 1992 programme (the detailed measures to implement the SEM) were intended to result in the abolition of all internal frontier controls by 1 January 1993. Because of delays in implementing the Schengen agreements and in ratifying the External Frontiers Convention, those controls on persons have remained in place. Despite pressure from the European Parliament,[1] the abolition of checks at all internal frontiers remains a matter of legal and political controversy.[2] Controls are exercised systematically at certain internal frontiers, such as those of the United Kingdom and Brussels airport, and intermittently at others; where there is a limited amount of traffic, they have disappeared.[3] Those on goods have been abolished, although random police[4] and customs checks for illegal goods are more frequent in the frontier

[1] The European Parliament adopted a strongly worded resolution in 1991 (Official Journal No. C 267, 14 Sept. 1991: 197) criticizing the Commission and requiring it to submit proposals for the implementation of free movement of persons before the end of the year. In 1993, it initiated an action against the Commission under article 175 of the EC Treaty citing the Commission's failure to comply with Article 7A at the EU Treaty. O.J.E.C. No. C1/12, 4-1-94 (Case C.445/93). See also n. 2 below.

[2] The controversy between the UK and other Member States and European institutions reached new heights in February 1995. A British Home Office Minister, Charles Wardle, resigned in anticipation of Britain's inability to maintain border controls in the light of its legal obligations under Article 7A. Thereafter, the British Government claimed that the General Declaration attached to the SEA which allowed Member States to maintain control of immigration from outside the EC was sufficient to justify the retention of internal border controls. This claim was disputed by the Commission, and in a speech to the European Parliament on 15 February 1995, the new Commission president, Jacques Santer, promised that the Commission would use its legal powers to achieve a border-free Europe in the near future (*Guardian*, 16 Feb. 1995).

[3] The interpretation of Art. 8A (now 7A) of the EC Treaty is a matter of dispute. Different views are taken on whether it commits Member States to remove all controls at the frontier. The European Commission's position is that it does and that it allows no discretion. The Commission declared that it would use all available legal means to do away with all checks and verifications at internal frontiers (*Abolition of Frontier Controls*, Commission Communication to the Council and Parliament, 8 May 1992 SEC (92) 8777 Final; *Europe* (5726 new series), 9 May 1992). The Select Committee Report on European Legislation of the House of Commons (14th Report, 4 March 1992: viii) carried a clear statement that the Department of Trade and Industry did not agree with the Commission's view and British ministers have made repeated statements to the effect that they will never end controls on persons at the internal frontiers.

[4] For example, on the frontier between France and Spain, there was in 1994 a permanent police presence at the heavily used frontier posts of Hendaye-Irun and Perthus, intermittent police presence at others such as the Col de Somport and the Col de Puymorens, and none at all on little frequented crossing points such as Pierre Saint Martin and the Col d'Orrhy. Also some forms of transport, such as first-class only Trans Europe Express trains are virtually exempt in most places from frontier checks.

zone than in the interior of countries. It has also proven impossible to date, to abolish the notion of export and import of goods in the Single Market, because of difficulties in enforcement of the collection of indirect tax; the administration of value added tax still requires certification of origin in a Member State, because VAT fraud is otherwise too easy if points of manufacture, wholesale and retail sale are located in different countries.

In order to assess the implications of the changing regime of police controls at EU frontiers, this chapter explores a number of themes. These are first, certain general characteristics of the international frontier; secondly, the few (and very distant) analogies with the EU frontiers in the contemporary world, such as the frontiers of the United States; thirdly, the doctrine of compensatory measures; fourthly, the proposed External Frontiers Convention, which, with related agreements, will influence the ground-rules and the spirit of police co-operation; fifthly, the practical implications of the symbolic role of frontier controls; sixthly, criminal threats coming from across the external frontier of the EU; and lastly, myths of frontier control.

The General Problem of Frontiers

Frontier policy, because of the nature of the contemporary international frontier, is one of the important indicators of the political cohesion of the European Union. Frontiers mark the geographical limits of states but they are not unproblematic demarcation lines where one political authority runs out and another begins; they are important political institutions, and complex processes take place on, and across, frontiers. As institutions they are established by customary international law and legal texts—treaties, conventions, agreements, arbitrations, judgments, letters of understanding—and by political decisions to reach and enforce these agreements. The text of agreements is subject to changing interpretations according to political circumstances. But where a treaty has been concluded which establishes a boundary, that boundary is subject to special protection.[5] Territory is central in international law and it is, for example, a basic criterion of the legal definition of statehood. Numerous legal rules exist to protect the inviolability of territory,

---

[5] For example, a fundamental change of circumstances may not be regarded as a ground for terminating or withdrawing from a treaty establishing a boundary. See Vienna Convention on the Law of Treaties, Art. 62(2)(a).

including the exclusive territorial nature of law enforcement jurisdiction.

Executive action is commonly taken by governments to police or to protect frontiers and, according to customary international law, international agreements may be suspended if national security is at risk. Frontiers are used in various practical and symbolic ways as instruments of government to gain advantages and defend interests. They are also a constraint on the liberty of action of states; their location cannot be changed at will when they become inconvenient or obsolescent, and many aspects of the management of frontiers are regulated by formal agreements which are costly to ignore. In the contemporary world, frontiers are also markers of nationality and citizenship; on one side of a frontier citizens or nationals enjoy certain rights and privileges which they do not have on the other. Rules of citizenship and nationality include some human groups and exclude others.

Frontiers have an important psychological and symbolic dimension because they are the boundaries of political identities. Living in a specific territory with well-established frontiers is part of what it is to be British or French or Italian. Frontiers are part of political beliefs and myths about the unity of the people (and sometimes myths about the 'natural' unity of a territory) which the frontiers enclose. These 'imagined communities', to use Benedict Anderson's phrase concerning nations, are a world-wide phenomenon and often have deep historical roots (B. Anderson 1991; see also Gellner 1983; Hobsbawm 1991; Smith 1986; Smith 1991 and the discussion in chapter 3). Myths of unity are linked to the most powerful form of ideological bonding in the modern world: nationalism. But myths of unity can be created or transformed with remarkable rapidity after war, revolution and political upheaval. Although imagined communities are usually associated with nations, they may escape the confines of the nation state. Myths of regional, continental and hemispheric unity have also marked boundaries between friend and foe (Connor 1969). These myths and symbols are linked to, and often serve, material ends: the maintenance of inequalities of wealth and power between states or groups of states.

Meanings are attributed to frontiers, and these meanings change over time. The term 'frontier' is part of the language of law, diplomacy and political debate, and used differently in different contexts. In European political debate, 'frontier' has many rhetorical contexts, ranging, at one end of the spectrum, from statements about the 'opening' or abolition of frontiers, implying some kind of liberation, to, at the other end of the spectrum, frontiers being essential protection for identities or interests, preventing the destruction of cherished ways of life or economic activities on which particular types of community or social categories depend. People who live in frontier regions, or whose daily life is directly affected by frontiers as obstacles, have a more specific image of them, informed by the (sometimes irksome) rules imposed at the frontiers, mixed with popular symbolism based on how the frontier is perceived, as barrier or junction between peoples, or as a protection from external dangers. Within law enforcement milieus, frontiers are associated with controls; loss of these controls mean that the frontier as an instrument of law enforcement vanishes.

The frontier has throughout modern European history been part of the discourse of military or external security. It is now very much part of the discourse of internal security. A senior police officer expressed a view widely endorsed within the élite law enforcement community, when he said to us:

For those who are bound by convention, by political influence, by national borders and by laws and procedures, the future changes daily. But what of the future for the thoughtful criminal? He has never had regard for borders, he is not bound by laws. He has regard only for his criminal enterprise. In this respect, he always has the advantage and our criminals are already looking for the opportunities presented by the changing face of Europe. If we are wise, we need to do the same and with some urgency. [It is my belief], shared by many European colleagues, that there are many good class criminals who will be encouraged to expand their activities across internal boundaries in the belief that January 1993 will produce a sudden relaxation in police and customs activity. I accept that the perception may be more significant than the reality, but nevertheless, there is a danger that the criminal will feel less restricted and act accordingly.[6]

Frontiers in general, as well as particular internal and external frontiers of the EU, have, therefore, different meanings and significance for different categories of people. Attitudes towards frontiers, their relationship with the identities which they help to frame, and the institutional development of frontiers form a complex environment within which the policing of Europe's border

[6] Interview with Sir Roger Birch in 1992. Similar statements were made to us many times.

areas takes place. Dismantling frontier controls has been made possible by more relaxed attitudes, especially among élite groups, towards territory, and the weakening of protectionist attitudes; absolute control of territory is less frequently seen as essential to physical security and international trade is no longer regarded as a zero sum game in which one country's gain is another's loss. Frontiers remain nonetheless symbols of state sovereignty and, in practice, are the limits of executive police powers. In contemporary Europe, the symbolism of frontiers and the practical effects of frontiers affect all aspects of policing of frontiers and transfrontier co-operation between police forces. Also, policing of frontiers cannot be treated in isolation from other policies regarding frontiers. These policies concern immigration and asylum, prohibited goods, illegal movement of goods (to evade taxation), trade policy, and security and foreign policy (especially with regard to immediate neighbours). In principle, according to the Treaties of Rome and Maastricht, policies on all these subjects should be either common or harmonized EU measures.

The interpretation of the changing nature of the frontiers of the EU must be related to general perspectives on European integration (discussed in chapter 3). But whatever theoretical perspective on integration is adopted, one general proposition remains valid—the core institutions and practices of a state, or a union of states, are always influenced by the degree of control which governments exercise over their frontiers. The claim (never fully realized) of the modern sovereign state to be 'the sole, exclusive fount of all powers and prerogatives of rule' (Poggi 1978: 92) could only be put into practice if its frontiers were made impermeable to unwanted external influences. The inability of states in the recent history of Europe to police much of the traffic of persons, goods and information across their frontiers has changed the nature of both states and frontiers. The threat which this poses to the interests of the state is a double-barrelled one. Governments have become, through force of circumstances, less able either to rely upon the security traditionally afforded by borders or to make independent use of the classical instruments of absolute territorial sovereignty in order to redress the security deficit. All governments of EU Member States are exposed to an external environment which limits, sometimes severely, their options in frontier control and many other aspects of government policy linked with the frontier. The Member

States, in principle, retain territorial sovereignty in police and criminal matters and all the instruments of state sovereignty are at their disposal. They are reluctant to loosen their grip on these powers, without gaining important benefits, because of implied loss of autonomous control of activities within their territory; and relinquishing territorial sovereignty represents an important political and psychological threshold. Governments have even been slow to agree a general harmonized EU frontier regime, although elements are already in place such as a common external tariff and customs procedures, and other policies are edging closer to agreement, such as admission of third country nationals.

Comparison with the United States

A difficulty in analysing the policing of frontiers in the EU is the absence of comparable situations elsewhere in the world. The closest international comparison is with the United States. The internal frontiers of the United States Federation create difficulties for law enforcement and the external frontier does not mark the limits of the criminal activities which United States law enforcement agencies face.[7] Internal frontiers within the United States are important in law enforcement because most criminal laws are state and not federal laws, and most police forces, too, are not federal but state and local. Like the EU, the United States acts as a magnet for criminal activities because of the large illegal profits to be made. Repression of international 'organized crime' has been a priority of United States' law enforcement and this has influenced European thinking. The United States is adjacent to countries to the South with very different standards of living and social patterns. The problems of illegal immigration into the United States, despite the mechanisms put in place by the 1986 Immigration and Refugee

---

[7] A parallel with the CIS could emerge where the Russian Federation has attempted to take the lead in establishing close police co-operation and proposals have been made for an economic community along the lines of the EU. Germany also provides an analogy because competence in criminal justice policy rests mainly with the Länder, and because of the volatile nature of Germany's frontiers; there are attempts, particularly by Germans, to draw on the German experience in the development of EU internal security policy. The Hong Kong-China border provides a more distant analogy. The vast difference between the economic and social situations of the two countries has encouraged an extensive trade in smuggling and illegal immigration, and has led to significant cross-border involvement in armed robbery (Vagg 1992). The advent of 1997 will pose complex regulatory problems if the political border disappears but the social and economic disparities remain.

Control Act (IRCA), and the 1993 strengthening of the Border Patrol, are in some respects similar to the issues facing the European Union. Furthermore, the general debate above the security implications of the liberalization of border controls between the United States, Canada and (more recently) Mexico, in the North American Free Trade Area established under the Free Trade Agreement of 1988, echoes many of the concerns expressed in the 1992 debate in Europe (Taylor 1992).

The unresolved problems of law enforcement across internal boundaries and the external frontier of the United States are not an encouraging precedent for the EU. The United States is a mature federal system and, over two centuries, much serious thought has been given to state/federal relations; many constitutional developments have taken place concerning these relations. But difficulties remain concerning the responsibilities of law enforcement agencies and the overlapping jurisdictions of state and Federal courts. There are federalizing elements in Europe,[8] but the EU has a long way to travel before it could be considered a mature federal system. There are 'two Europes' relevant to law enforcement. First, the European Convention of Human Rights with the European Court of Human Rights are increasingly influential over criminal law procedure and penal policy in the signatory states (Gearty 1993). Secondly, there are the legislation of the EU and the jurisprudence of the European Court of Justice (which overlaps with the first because the EU has recognized the European Convention on Human Rights as a source of law).[9] In principle, the EU does not have criminal law jurisdiction but nonetheless imposes sanctions and increasingly is prepared to deal with cases with criminal law implications in the Member States (see chapter 6).

The basis of the development of the criminal law competence of the United States' Federation rested on two foundations—the first ten amendments to the Constitution, collectively known as the Bill of Rights, together with the Fourteenth Amendment, which applies the Bill of Rights to the states; and the Federation's exclusive constitutional authority to regulate inter-state commerce (Art 1, Section 8). While these two precedents seem to be relevant to Europe there are many important differences. For example, the

---

[8] For an extended discussion, see Lensing 1993. See also ch. 3.

[9] TEU; Title 1 (Common Provisions), Art. F(2).

federal monopoly over mail in the United States, derived from the inter-state commerce clause of the United States' Constitution, was the key to the expansion of federal criminal law competence because most offences can be linked to the mail; there is no analogy for this in the Treaties of Rome and Maastricht, although the protection of the financial interests of the European proto-federation may be the foundation on which an EU system of criminal law will be built. Although there is clearly an overlap between both the ECHR and the ECJ and national jurisdictions in Europe, this overlap is likely to develop differently from the one between Federal and state jurisdictions in the United States. In the more specific field of law enforcement agencies, the history of the United States may indicate some difficulties to be avoided.

In very different economic and social circumstances the United States did not (apart from United States' Customs, established by the second Act of Congress) establish a significant law enforcement capacity until the twentieth century. When it did so, specialized law enforcement authorities were set up to enforce specific areas of Federal law (Federal Bureau of Investigation (FBI), Drug Enforcement Administration (DEA), United States' Marshals Services, Internal Revenue Service (IRS), Immigration and Naturalization Service (INS), Secret Service and the special investigators attached to Federal regulatory agencies such as the Securities and Exchange Commission, the United States' Postal Service and the Inter-state Commerce Commission).[10] The result was overlapping responsibilities between Federal law enforcement agencies as well as between them and over 1,500 state and local police forces (S. Walker 1992: 35), resulting in rivalries (the celebrated 'turf battles') and thorny problems of co-ordination. In 1967, the President's Crime Commission concluded that a 'fundamental problem confronting law enforcement today is that of fragmented crime repression efforts resulting from the large number of unco-ordinated local governments and law enforcement agencies (President's Commission on Law Enforcement and Administration of Justice, 1967). Although more recent research suggests that the traditional position was overstated (Ostrom *et al.* 1978), there is no doubt that

---

[10] In 1988, there were an estimated 65,297 full-time federal law enforcement employees, at the annual cost of $3.5 billion. This figure represented about 12.5% of all expenditure for police protection in the US (S. Walker 1992: 481).

fragmentation has contributed to lack of co-ordination, duplication and inconsistent standards (S. Walker 1992: 52–7). If, in future, specialized law enforcement agencies are established in the EU, experience in the United States suggests that these internal difficulties should be considered before, and not after, their establishment (see discussion in chapter 8).

Because of the size and wealth of the United States and the nature of its legislation, federal law enforcement agencies have also taken a great deal of interest in activities across the external frontier of the Federation. Under the 1984 Crime Control Act, the United States claims extraterritorial criminal jurisdiction for certain categories of crime—assassination of diplomats, air piracy, piracy, kidnapping and hostage taking (of United States' citizens). The size and wealth of the country make it vulnerable to international criminal enterprises and illegal immigration. Its prohibitionist drugs laws have created the largest illegal market in history. The international ramifications of criminal enterprises in the United States has made federal law enforcement agencies aware of the global environment. The international activities of these agencies reflect the domestic organization of United States' law enforcement. Each agency has developed an international presence—agents of the FBI, DEA, United States' Customs, INS, IRS, United States' Marshals (because of their responsibility for the fugitive criminal) and Secret Service, are to be found as liaison officers in United States' embassies. The FBI was the first in the field immediately after the Second World War, followed by the Secret Service but the DEA with, by the late 1980s, over sixty permanent offices in 43 countries (and a presence in up to 70 countries) is by far the largest overseas presence. DEA agents have conducted investigations, sometimes with the co-operation of foreign jurisdictions, sometimes with their tacit consent, sometimes without their knowledge. Problems of sovereignty and legality are posed by these operations (Anderson 1989: 160–5; Nadelmann 1993). Sometimes the fight against drugs, it has been argued, serves as a pretext for establishing an American presence in politically fragile regions of the world and for justifying intrusive policies in Latin America.

Is the EU likely to follow the example of the United States in any of these respects? It has already done so in that Member States have posted police liaison officers abroad, more often to each other, but also in the United States, South America, Africa and

Asia, with some co-ordination between them.[11] For legal, technical and political reasons the extra-territorial jurisdiction and law enforcement presence of the EU and its Member States are likely to be much more limited. But just as the EU is developing a buffer zone for confronting the problem of immigration (see below), and close co-operation with Hungary and other East-Central European countries for combating the 'Balkan route' for drug-trafficking, instruments of European police co-operation (particularly Europol)[12] will almost certainly develop a close interest in states immediately bordering the EU, and more distant states, when they seem to be at the origin of criminal traffics. The development of federal operational powers of law enforcement, with consequent overlap of competences, is a probable long-term development (see discussion in chapter 6).

Compensatory Measures

Two themes are at the core of the debate on removing systematic checks[13] on persons and goods at the internal frontiers. The first concerns the doctrine of compensatory measures, while the second concerns frontiers as the limits of criminal justice and police systems. The first theme marks a particular stage in the integration process, although the compensatory measures can have long-term consequences. The doctrine of compensatory measures was a temporary political necessity to gain political acceptance for the Single European Market. No one knew, and there were no means of forecasting, the internal security consequences of the freedom of movement of goods and persons. But pressures from within law

[11] For example, in the UK, the overseas drug liaison officer network is spread over both EU and non-EU States. The non-EU officers report to HM Customs and Excise whilst the EU-based officers are located in NCIS International Liaison Unit. Intelligence from all overseas liaison officers is also channelled through the NCIS International Liaison Unit (National Criminal Intelligence Service 1993: 17).

[12] The list of forms of serious crime contained in the annex to the draft Europol Convention (see ch. 2) makes this virtually inevitable.

[13] The ECJ (27 April 1989, Case 321/87, *Commission* v. *Belgium* [1989] ECR 997) considered a Belgian law which required Community immigrants and other foreigners to have their residents' permits on their persons at all times and to produce them on demand to the relevant authorities, on pain of a fine. The Court held this not to be incompatible with EC law, despite the fact that checks were sometimes carried out at frontiers. The Court added, however, that frontier checks of this kind could constitute a violation of EC law if carried out systematically, arbitrarily or to no useful purpose. See also Weatherill and Beaumont (1993) ch. 18; Green, Hartley and Usher (1991: 131–4).

enforcement establishments, and the anticipated political reactions if problems arose after '1992', required that precautions be taken. Two contingent factors encouraged the adoption of the doctrine. These were increasing hostility towards immigration in some countries and alarm at deteriorating reported crime rates throughout the EU which in some countries gave rise to demands for more effective 'law and order' policies.

The second theme will last into any future that can be foreseen; frontiers are 'hedges' between criminal justice systems which create problems relating to arresting persons, transferring evidence from one jurisdiction to another, subpoenaing witnesses, adapting to differences in criminal law procedures and varying law enforcement policies; these difficulties, while not insuperable, are bound to cause expense, delay, misunderstanding and friction (see chapters 2, 6, and 7).

The spectre of loss of control over terrorists, drug-traffickers, money launderers, fraudsters and illegal immigrants is directly linked with the policing of frontiers in the debate on policing and internal security (see chapter 5). Prime Minister Margaret Thatcher, in her noted Bruges speech, referred to the maintaining of frontier controls as 'plain common sense'.[14] This 'common sense' has often been supported by superficially convincing statistics about drug seizures at frontiers and the apprehending of illegal immigrants by authorities (Butt Philip 1991; Latter 1991).[15] The *Police de l'Air et des Frontières* (PAF) in France claimed that the majority—64 per cent in 1992—of illegal immigrants were stopped at the internal frontiers of the EC. A scenario of increased danger from external criminal dangers was assumed if the internal frontier controls were completely dismantled.[16] The consequence was that

[14] The UK has consistently resisted abolition of systematic frontier controls at its own borders (see n. 2 above) and, therefore, never seriously considered joining Schengen. It was joined in this attitude by Denmark (for a time) and the Republic of Ireland. These three countries have, however, no objections in principle to the adoption of standard border control regimes for the external frontier.

[15] Customs services published impressive figures of drug seizures without indicating how many were the result of tip-offs, intelligence and undercover operations rather than routine border checks (for a discussion about statistics on European crime, see ch. 1).

[16] As argued in ch. 5, the major external threat is widely assumed in political and law enforcement circles to emanate from East Europe. However, this is by no means perceived to be the only source, even within Europe, For example, a significant criminal threat is also believed to come from Austria, whose candidature for the membership was successful in 1994, because of a reputation for laundering

the doctrine of compensatory measures underpinned the Palma Document, the Schengen Agreements and, to a lesser extent, the draft External Frontier Convention.

Some harmonization of policing practices and a high degree of mutual trust in authorities of all twelve Member States is necessary to manage effectively the evolving system of frontier controls. In December 1988 the EU Member States made the first collective move towards a harmonized frontier control policy at the Rhodes summit. National co-ordinators were appointed to oversee the measures necessary to implement the 1992 programme. These measures were set out in the Palma document, originally intended as a confidential working paper of the European Commission. The document was published first by a United Kingdom's House of Lords Committee (House of Lords 1989), during a period of tension between Prime Minister Thatcher and the Irish and Belgian governments over the extradition of an Irish priest, Father Ryan, wanted by the British authorities on arms-trafficking charges. However, lack of confidence in the treatment of Irish nationalist suspects by British police and courts, and the poor reputation earned over the years by the United Kingdom in the field of extradition, manifested both by the legal difficulties faced by European countries in securing the return of fugitives and by the failure of the United Kingdom over many years to ratify the 1957 CoE Convention on Extradition, reduced international support for the position adopted by the Thatcher government.

Despite this *contretemps,* work proceeded on the Palma document. The document stated, in general terms, that there should be an approximation of national laws in certain fields, collaboration between national administrations, and a prior strengthening of controls at external frontiers.[17] The areas covered, in response to the envisaged abolition of internal frontier controls, were stated to be the combating of terrorism, drug-trafficking and other illicit trafficking, improved co-operation in law enforcement, development of judicial co-operation, standard rules covering articles (*e.g.* firearms) accompanying travellers, and matters deriving from family problems (*e.g.* abduction of children and trafficking in minors).

money, with 7 million inhabitants and 49 million bank accounts, 90% of which were secret numbered accounts (République Française—Sénat 1994: 23).

[17] The Commission agreed (7 Dec. 1988 COM (88 final)) that Member States should proceed by way of intergovernmental agreements (Timmermans 1993: 363).

For the external frontier, a set of legal, administrative and technical instruments would be established. *Inter alia,* these include a European visa, with the establishment of a common list of countries whose nationals require visas, harmonization of criteria for the granting of visas, a common list of persons to be refused entry, acceptance of identical international commitments with regard to asylum, a simplified or priority procedure for the examination of clearly unfounded requests, conditions for governing the movement of an applicant between Member States, and study of the need for financing the consequences of implementing a common policy in these fields.

The document defined measures which were essential and those which were merely desirable for both the external and the internal frontiers. Most of these were either straightforward to agree in principle, such as the definition of common measures in respect of checks to be carried out at the external frontier, or expressed in vague and relatively uncontentious terms, such as the commitment towards co-operation between law enforcement agencies, and between law enforcement agencies and customs authorities, in border regions at the internal frontiers. Others, for example the commitment of Member States to ratify the European Convention on Extradition, were explicit enough but, as shown in chapter 7, the impact of ratification could be very uneven owing to the reservations entered by the ratifying state and owing to the various procedures for integrating treaties into domestic law. In the more detailed recommendations concerning matters such as co-operation in the field of drug-trafficking, terrorism, visa policy, asylum and refugee status, judicial co-operation in civil and criminal matters, and common rules on articles carried by travellers, some recommendations were so general that it would be difficult to establish with any precision when and if they had been put into effect; examples are the study of the desirability of harmonizing laws and their implementing procedures on narcotic and psychotropic substances and a commitment to expedite ratification of the agreements concluded between the Member States to improve judicial assistance in criminal matters.

The Palma Document pointed out the diversity of forms and fields of co-operation which the new frontiers made necessary, and progress was made on key areas for police co-operation such as the EIS on wanted persons and illegal immigrants (see chapter 8).

Although a timetable, subsequently updated during the 1992 United Kingdom's presidency, was included in the document for the implementation of the measures, the way in which the text was drafted makes it difficult to measure how successfully this schedule has been adhered to.[18] The contents of the document indicates that the notion of compensatory measures will, in due course, be dissolved into a number of specific areas in which, in the light of experience, co-operation needs improvement.

The clearest expression of the doctrine of compensatory measures is found in the Schengen Conventions. The explicit purpose of these agreements was to compensate for the 'security deficit' created by the abolition of internal frontier controls by enhancing the quality of police co-operation among the signatory states, *inter alia* to ensure effective control of their common external frontier (see chapter 2). The long-term future of these agreements is uncertain but their repeated postponement[19] highlighted the problems of abolishing police controls at the frontiers. Part of the reason that the agreements encountered difficulty lay in the increase in the number of participants from the original five to nine. Establishing a common frontier could have been regarded mainly as a technical-administrative matter by a small group of like-minded states but expanding the group so considerably, in radically altered political circumstances, changed the implications of the agreements. Among other matters, issues were raised about the competence and integrity of the southern European frontier police, about the possibility of the spread of Mafia-type organizations into northern Europe, about relations between members and non-members of Schengen, about the new issues of frontier control with the ending of the Cold War division of Europe, and about the accountability and supervision of the Schengen system (Den Boer 1991a; 1993a).[20]

Both the Palma Document and the Schengen Agreements possess

[18] It was claimed by MAG 92 (Mutual Assistance Group for Customs Cooperation) that it had completed all the measures for abolition of customs controls by the due date and customs controls at the internal frontiers were discontinued on 1 Jan. 1993.

[19] The start date was postponed on five occasions before the agreement by the Schengen Executive Committee meeting at Bonn on 22 Dec. 1994 to implement the Conventions between seven of the nine signatory states as of March 1995 was finally honoured.

[20] Among the many reservations expressed about Schengen, the French Parliament, at end of the ratification debate in Dec. 1991, set 30 preconditions for implementing the Conventions.

the virtue of emphasizing the linkage between policy for the internal and the external frontiers. Development of secure and uniform external frontier controls strongly influences practical measures concerning the internal frontiers and, consequently, the nature of police co-operation. To the extent that the external frontier can be policed efficiently according to uniform rules, controls can be removed at the internal frontiers. The abolition of internal frontier controls and the 'hardening' of external frontier controls require a more flexible and efficient police response to transfrontier criminal activities. Three major sets of issues for police co-operation are posed by the external frontier: its location, the relationship of the EU (and its Member States) with neighbouring states across the frontier, and the development of new controls on persons to prevent the movement of illegal immigrants or criminals across the external frontier.

If frontiers are changed and the political map is redrawn, how does this affect co-operation between criminal justice systems and police co-operation? Does it result in transitional difficulties or longer term structural problems? Answers to these questions are highly speculative. But where the external frontier is,[21] and where it may be located in the foreseeable future, has profound implications both for the general internal development and for the external relations of the EU; both directly affect police co-operation. In the immediate future the bringing into force of the EEA on 1 January 1994, extending many elements of the SEM to the members of the EEA, including free movement of persons, complicates the external borders compensatory measures strategy. If these states form part of an area in which systematic frontier controls are abolished—and the legal argument for this conclusion is just as strong as the parallel argument that the post-1992 EU should comprise a border-free zone—various initiatives such as the Dublin

[21] Considerable territorial complexity on the fringes of the EU raises problems of administration and control of frontiers, which have not yet been resolved. This complexity is composed of several components—sovereign micro-states which are enclaves in EU territory (Andorra, Monaco, San Marino, the Vatican); enclaves of Germany in Switzerland and in Italy; 'free zones' which are not considered part of national territory for customs purposes (Gex, Haute-Savoie in France, Gorizia and Livigno in Italy); territories which, though linked to Member States, are not considered part of the EU (Channel Islands, Faroe Islands, Greenland); dependencies and overseas territories which may or may not be part of the EU or its customs territory. No one individual case is important but collectively they pose considerable difficulties.

Agreement on Asylum, the External Frontiers Convention and the common visa provisions will have to be extended to them.

There was some anticipation that the 1995 extension of the EU would lead to a realignment of frontiers. However, the new EEA external boundary does not coincide with the 1995 EU external boundary, nor even the external boundary of the European Free Trade Association (EFTA). Iceland and Liechtenstein are EEA states, but were not candidates to join the EU during its most recent cycle of enlargement. Norway, too, remains an EEA state, although it was a candidate member of the EU but chose not to join after a referendum in November 1994. For the most part, the EEA is made up of Member States of the EU together with members of EFTA, set up in 1960 by those European states who wished to benefit from a free trade area but did not favour the Community method of economic integration. Switzerland, however, although a member of EFTA, decided in a referendum in December 1992 not to join the new EEA. As its continuing membership of EFTA gives rise to certain rights and obligations in respect of free movement with other EU and EEA states, this further complicates the development associated with the EU external frontier. The problem of the relations between the legal regimes of the EU and associated free trade associations has not, therefore, been resolved by the widening of the EU in 1995.

In more general terms, the location of the EU frontier influences the degree of political integration possible, the 'constitution' of the EU, the workings of EU institutions, the extent of policy co-ordination and harmonization, the nature of political alignments and the balance of economic interests. These effects are the basic themes in the so-called 'widening or deepening' debate about the future of the Union (Harmsen 1994; McMahon 1994; Nugent 1992; Duff et al. 1994). They all affect, in a general way, the nature of police co-operation, the system of accountability and supervision of Europol and related institutions, the operation of common or harmonized practices in policing external frontiers, and many other matters. Enlargement will complicate the operation of EU institutions of police co-operation. The same difficulties faced by other European institutions will be encountered—even more official languages, more participants in the consultative and decision making processes, more divergent interests. In addition, within the police field, the more cumbersome and ineffective European institutions of police co-operation become, the more informal systems of co-operation or bilateral arrangements will be encouraged (Anderson 1993b). Bilateral co-operation dominates relations between EU Member States and former communist bloc countries, with Germany having the most case-related co-operation.[22] The provision by Germany of specifically targeted material and technical assistance (often initiated by informal bargains) facilitates practical co-operation in investigating specific criminal networks (Gregory 1994). Other countries such as Britain, France and the Netherlands have separate programmes of training and technical assistance. Complaints have been made by France and by the United Kingdom[23] about the lack of coordination, even lack of knowledge about each other's efforts, and suggestions made about co-ordination.[24] Former communist countries, however, find advantages in being able to select from different donor countries for different types of aid and, for political reasons, in not being reliant on one source of assistance.[25]

Systematic and efficient criminal law enforcement co-operation depends on stable and friendly relations between states. The absence of these relations means, at best, grudging and intermittent co-operation, at worst, the active encouragement of activities which the neighbouring state regards as criminal. Inclusion of East-Central European countries within a larger EU will result in its proximity to politically unstable countries, and will place a premium on the formulation of an agreed European political strategy for each sensitive frontier. The absence of such a strategy will compromise law enforcement co-operation to the extent that the state on the other side of the external frontier could be transformed into 'bandit country' where criminals operate with

---

[22] There have been some indications that multilateral systems of co-operation may counter the predominance of bilateralism. The systematic consultation of East and Central European countries on justice at home affairs within the framework of the third pillar of the TEU was called for by the 'Hurd-Andreotta' initiative of Dec. 1993 and ministers from these countries were invited to the Conference on Drugs and Organized Crime held in Berlin in Sept. 1994.

[23] Interview with Mr Trefor Morris, Her Majesty's Chief Inspector of Constabulary for England and Wales, Oct. 1993.

[24] Requests for assistance have frequently been made to Interpol and have been passed on by the organization to the appropriate national authorities. The Secretary General of Interpol, Raymond Kendall, considers that there is a coordinating role for Interpol in this field and has suggested this to Member States (interview).

[25] Head of the Judicial Police of Hungary, Police Major General Dr Antal Kacziba, interview 23 Aug. 1993.

impunity. The problems are already clearly apparent over the Greek frontiers—in Epiros with Albania, in Macedonia, and in Thrace and in the Ægean with Turkey. The result is that some minimal law enforcement co-operation takes place with Turkey but virtually none with Macedonia and Albania, apart from the expulsion of undesirables.

Immigration control is a crucial dimension of policing the external frontier and will cause intractable problems if more members are accepted in the EU. Strategies for controlling immigration are deeply enmeshed in relations with immediate neighbours. Even when illegal immigrants come from distant origins they frequently attempt to gain access to the EU via immediate neighbouring countries: for example, arrivals in Germany from Asia, the Middle East and Africa have used Polish and Czech Republic territory as staging posts before claiming political asylum in the Federal Republic. The German government has reached two types of agreement to counter this. The first is bilateral treaties with Hungary and the USSR in 1991, followed by similar treaties with Bulgaria, the Czech Republic, Poland and Slovakia to fight organized crime and drug-related crime; this also facilitated co-operation with these countries for the repression of organized groups which smuggled immigrants into Germany. The second type was a series of readmission agreements[26] in which neighbouring countries agreed to take back illegal immigrants and deport them to the countries whence they came. Poland and the Czech Republic were naturally reluctant to do this without financial compensation but eventually agreements came into force in 1993 and 1994 respectively. The prospects of joining the EU and of German financial aid were factors in reaching these agreements.

These agreements also implied a tightening of Czech and Polish admissions policies; for this reason, Poland put a limit of 10,000 individuals in the first year (unlimited numbers thereafter) so that it could put more stringent frontier controls in place. Readmission agreements effectively turn immediate neighbouring states into buffer zones. This has been emphasized by the so-called cascade readmission agreements, exemplified by the Poland-Bulgaria agreement of August 1994 in which Bulgaria agreed to accept all individuals of Bulgarian nationality who had been returned to Poland

---

[26] The Palma document envisages mutual readmission agreements between all Member States of the EU.

under the German–Polish readmission agreement of 1993. The generalization of this kind of agreement results in a domino effect of individuals returned through two or more countries and the shift of problems eastwards (King 1994). Unless these agreements can be turned into multilateral treaties, they do not help the EU to come to a general agreement on immigration, refugees and asylum because they put in place a series of bilateral understandings based on mutual adjustment of national interests, rather than a settled collective regional interest between EU Member States and their eastern neighbours. If the frontier of the EU is moved further to the east it is unlikely that the buffer state strategy could be reproduced in the same form because the neighbouring states are likely to be less stable and less amenable to EU pressure. The responsibility of policing the eastern frontier of the EU will be placed on some of its most fragile Member States.

The External Frontiers Convention

Many Palma document measures concerned police and administrative matters which lay within the scope of executive action or were already agreed in international treaties and conventions. But to support the document, a general legal framework for frontier control was a basic requirement, although this was not mentioned in the Palma document itself. Harmonized police controls of the external frontier would be difficult to sustain in the medium term without a treaty basis because Member States would inevitably react to short-term pressures and difficulties by taking unilateral measures. In addition, a general framework would affect the spirit in which the external frontier was policed, because of the symbolism of a common legal document.

A legal vacuum for the nine signatory states was created by the postponement of the Schengen Conventions and, for the whole Union, by non-ratification of the External Frontiers Convention. In June 1991, agreement had been reached by the European Council on a draft External Frontiers Convention. In the final stages of the negotiation a difference arose between Britain and Spain over the territorial extent of the EC with regard to Gibraltar which, despite two years of attempts to reach a compromise, prevented the Convention being signed. After the ratification of the TEU, speedy acceptance of an External Frontiers Convention became a priority for the Member States. The governments agreed to deem the

Convention accepted *de facto* and undertook to abide by its conditions. After Maastricht, the Copenhagen summit in June 1993 decided that the draft Convention should be modified to bring it into line with the Treaty. It could then be introduced as a legal instrument under title VI of the TEU (Art. K.1(2)), in which rules governing the crossing of external frontiers were stated to be 'matters of common interest'. In late 1993, it was the Commission, given a broader right of initiative by the Treaty, that submitted to the European Parliament and to the European Council a revised version of the Convention, intended to preserve the political consensus between the Member States reached during the previous negotiation on the Convention. The closely related matter of issuing visas to third country nationals was placed on an even more substantial legal foundation by the TEU. It was henceforth to be treated as a matter of EC competence according to the new Article 100c of the EC Treaty, to be dealt with through decisions taken under the procedures of the Treaty of Rome. The Commission has since issued a proposal for a resolution on this matter.[27]

The amendments to the text of the draft Convention were both formal and substantive to take account of developments since the Convention had been drafted, such as the EEA Agreement already referred to. To bring the draft Convention into line with the rest of the EU decision making procedures, a qualified majority rule for decision making in the Council concerning the external frontier was introduced, the requirement of unanimity being retained only for exceptional circumstances. On the controversial matter of the territorial extent of the Union, the relevant article remains blank until bilateral discussions between Britain and Spain resolved the issue of Gibraltar. The original draft Convention included articles concerning the passage of goods at the external frontier; since all outstanding issues on goods had already been agreed, the new instrument referred only to persons. In an important amendment, making possible a genuine Europeanization of the frontier regime, the new draft allowed for recourse to the European Court of Justice to ensure uniformity of interpretation. [28]

The text of the proposed External Frontiers Convention begins with a series of definitions on such matters as residence permits,

[27] COM 94 287 final, 13 July 1994.
[28] This amendment takes advantage of a facility made available in Article K.3(2) (c) of the TEU.

different types of visa, and local frontier traffic. The basic definition was that of the external frontier itself, which was stated to be:

– a Member State's land frontier which is not contiguous with a frontier of another Member State, and maritime frontiers;
– airports and seaports, except where they are considered to be internal frontiers for the purposes of instruments enacted under the Treaty establishing the European Community.

According to the Convention, the crossing of external frontiers is to remain controlled by national authorities and carried out in accordance with national law, but with due regard to the provisions of the Convention. The draft lays down general principles concerning the nature of the controls at external frontiers, such as that all persons crossing the external frontier shall be systematically subject to visual controls to establish their identity. Special arrangements for airports are envisaged to ensure that flights internal to the EU are kept rigorously separate from flights connecting with third states. The criteria for refusing entry are specified as the lack of the necessary documents, or a threat to the public policy or to the national security of Member States. In addition, a list of persons to whom entry is to be refused will be constantly updated by the Member States. Rules are laid down for resident non-citizens crossing internal border, stays of non-citizens other than for a short time, and the issue of residence permits.

The Convention states in its preamble that Member States are to conduct controls in compliance with the 1951 Geneva Convention as amended by the 1967 New York protocol on refugees. Whether some states' legislation is in conformity with the letter, let alone the spirit, of these international undertakings is doubtful (d'Oliveira 1993). These include: Britain with its discretionary procedures for dealing with applications for asylum and limited rights of appeal against refusal;[29] Germany, with the removal by the 1993 Asylum Law of the possibility of applying for asylum at the frontier and the introduction of an extensive list of countries whose nationals are not considered for asylum; and France where summary expulsion of

---

[29] Reinforced by the Asylum and Immigration Appeals Act 1993. Section 8 read together with Sch. 2, para. 5, allows the Secretary of State to designate certain applications as without foundation, or as 'frivolous or vexatious', in which case the applicant may be denied a right of appeal against refusal of entry to a special adjudicator.

undocumented aliens is permitted by the 1993 Pasqua Law and arbitrary deportation is used under the procedure of 'extreme urgency'. Carrier liability imposing sanctions on companies, already effected at the national level, was included in the draft Convention, requiring airlines and shipping companies to refuse undocumented refugees. A systematic exchange of information is envisaged, in particular by Article 13.2, which states that 'the creation, organization and operation of a computerized system will be the subject of the Convention on the European Information System'.

Despite the new enabling legal framework of Title VI of the TEU, the proposed External Frontiers Convention remains politically controversial and has not yet been agreed by the Member States.[30] Enhanced legal competence has proved to be similarly ineffective in the face of political opposition in related areas. The Commission appended to the amended Convention an explanatory memorandum and a draft Regulation drawn up in accordance with the new Article 100c of the Treaty of Rome concerning the issuing of visas valid in all Member States.[31] This provided for a uniform visa, the conditions under which it would be issued, and a provisional list of countries (based on the list previously drawn up by the Schengen countries) whose nationals would be required to have visas. The suggested list contained 129 countries, including virtually all Third World and Eastern Europe (but excluding the Visegrád and the Baltic States) as well as, to the irritation of the United Kingdom, South Africa and the majority of Commonwealth countries. Spanish and Portuguese-speaking South American countries and the whole of the highly industrialized world were excluded from the list. The experience of the Schengen group of countries shows that administrative inertia on this matter flowing from a reluctance to relinquish national control over policy can be a serious cause of delay.[32]

---

[30] Indeed, at the Essen meeting of the JHA Ministers in Dec. 1994, Padraig Flynn, the outgoing commissioner for JHA matters, claimed that the Member States were further from agreement on an External Frontiers Convention than before Maastricht. The Gibraltar problem remained, but additional obstacles, such as the role of the European Court of Justice, had arisen (*Agence Europe*, No. 6369, 2 Dec. 1994).

[31] After 1 Jan. 1996 the common visa could be adopted by a majority vote (*European Report*, (1967) 16 July 1994).

[32] At the time of writing, there is pessimism about the outcome of the negotiations for a common visa because states wish to retain the right to withdraw unilaterally from the arrangements.

The successful resolution and implementation of the draft
External Frontiers Convention may also be obstructed by the failure to overcome political disagreement over linked conventions.
For example, the draft Convention leaves virtually all police,
administrative and legal control in the hands of the Member States,
but the Member States agree to certain common principles in order
to harmonize their practices. Although less ambitious in this
respect than the 1985 and 1990 Schengen Conventions, the effective
implementation of the Convention depends on preparation of an
acceptable legal instrument for the EIS, and police co-operation
through Europol, after a Convention for Europol has been prepared. Much work has been done on an agreed document for the
EIS. Early in 1994, the EIS draft Convention was under negotiation
in an intergovernmental working group, reporting to the K4
Committee. The draft is modelled on the SIS and its data protection provisions, in effect extending them to all EU Member States.
However, the final stages of negotiation were plagued by delay. In
particular, the United Kingdom's Home Secretary took the view
that any EIS agreement should be ratified according to the normal
procedures of international treaties and not as an EU Council decision under Title VI of the TEU which would be directly applicable
in the Member States.[33] As discussed elsewhere, the Europol
Convention has also been the subject of extensive delays.[34]

A more general uncertainty characterizes the current situation.
The TEU contains all the areas of co-operation envisaged in the
Schengen Agreements except operational cross-border policing
activities such as hot pursuit. If both were implemented at the
same time, problems of consistency and coherence between them
could arise. The counter-argument is that two out of the three
Member States which remained outside Schengen, Britain and
Ireland,[35] are intent on maintaining systematic controls at the
internal frontiers and would hinder attempts at establishing a genuine control-free area for EU citizens. Influential opinion in some
of the other Member States is reticent about dismantling internal
frontier controls; the idea of having the Union as an area of free

---

[33] UK legislation will also be required in order to give the police powers to detain
for 24 hours persons for whom there is an EIS entry requesting provisional arrest
for the purpose of extradition.
[34] See in particular chs. 2 and 6.
[35] Denmark signalled accession to Schengen in June 1994.

movement of people could fade unless a group of states takes the initiative.[36] If the initiative is taken then the two systems of Schengen and the EIS/External Frontiers Convention, in time, may merge although this would require amendment of the Schengen agreements to remove the exclusive character of certain provisions (for example in data control). An alternative, more pessimistic but more probable, scenario is that both the EIS and SIS come into existence and remain parallel but compatible systems. A genuine two-speed Europe would be a reality with frontier controls maintained by a small minority of Member States.

Administration Implications of Frontiers as Symbols

The practical questions of how to administer frontier controls are invested with symbolic meaning. How and by whom[37] individuals are checked, and even the procedures used in handling goods, involve a symbolic demonstration of state authority as well as serving specific policing objectives. Frontier controls symbolize the belief that institutions and arrangements within the confines of a state have a higher degree of legitimacy and attract more trust than those on the other side of an international frontier. Cherished practices within European states are regarded as hallmarks of identity and cultural difference. The unanswered questions, which we sought to address in chapter 3, are when and how a European political identity will command similar loyalties.

Sensitivity about the way in which goods are handled is generally much less acute than about the way people are policed. The introduction of EUROSCAN for checking containerized goods was not controversial and passed virtually unnoticed. The use of technology to check baggage such as X-rays and magnetometers, the computerized organic tracer (COT), the hydrogenous explosive detector (HED) and the development of new technologies such as thermal neutron activation (TNA) are accepted as an inevitable

---

[36] Renewed controversy over the abolition of internal controls in the early months of 1995 testifies to this. See n. 2 above.

[37] Different kinds of law enforcement agencies have been responsible for policing ports of entry into the territory of European states. Sometimes these are specialized police forces such as the *Police de l'Air et des Frontières* in France. For historical reasons, militarized police forces such as the *Bundesgrenzschutz* in Germany and the *Guardia Civil* have had a central role in securing the frontier. In some northern European countries, particularly Britain, this would be politically unacceptable because deep-rooted suspicions of paramilitary police forces exist.

consequence of the activities of terrorists (Clutterbuck 1990).
Control on goods, except where it impinges on certain aspects of
criminal law enforcement in the fields of drugs, pornography and
arms smuggling, has a much lower political profile than immigration control. European customs co-operation has been much less
controversial between and within states than co-operation over
immigration. In addition to an on-line customs intelligence system,
exchanges of customs officers were put into effect with a pilot
scheme in 1990 and a much more ambitious three year programme
in 1991 (Vergnolle 1992).[38] The establishment of a single administrative document for all goods originating in a Member State
required time and patience because of the complexity of administrative practices which had grown up in the Member States.
Residual distrust remained about whether goods were produced in
all countries according to the agreed health and safety standards,
and whether some countries were more open to fraudulent descrip-
tions of goods. Questions are regularly raised in national parliaments about safety and public health checks on goods, and on
control of smuggling of illegal goods and substances.
Counterfeiting high value products is a continuing problem and is
a *sotte voce* argument against extending EU membership to Turkey.

The control of citizens by foreign jurisdictions, and domestic
police forces, is a highly sensitive area. Apparently innocuous
administrative matters such as documents which allow the checking of a person's identity at frontiers and inside states can arouse
strong feelings. The long and difficult negotiation over the common format of passport for EU citizens showed how even the
appearance of these documents can be controversial. Most
European countries, including the overwhelming majority of the
EU Member States, have national identity cards. But there has been
public opposition to proposals for schemes in countries, notably
Britain and Ireland, which have not yet adopted them, as there was
in Germany when they were introduced in 1987 and in the
Netherlands where, in 1994, compulsory identification was introduced for certain purposes. This apparently minor issue of personal identity cards can assume major symbolic importance.

The technological possibilities of 'smart cards' increase the likeli-

---

[38] British customs officers were the most enthusiastic about gaining experience in
another European country before the exclusively European customs regime came
into effect (*Independent*, 28 March 1991).

hood of a common personal identification for all EU citizens; such cards could initially be available to business travellers, which would give an élitist dimension to free movement.[39] 'Smart cards' would be useful for European police co-operation, particularly for EIS and SIS, because, with a 30 Kilobyte memory, they can hold a person's health, social security, and tax record as well as confirmation of personal identity.[40] Arguably, this could help to combat fraud[41], tax evasion, illegal immigration and criminal activity in general but it would undermine, and probably destroy any claim to confidentiality and privacy of personal information. The risk, which already exists,[42] of people being arrested through erroneous or out-of-date information on a data base would be increased exponentially unless new systems for checking the validity of information were put in place.

The United Kingdom will, almost certainly, be the last Member State to introduce national identity cards. The British debate, often couched in parochial terms, is important because its resolution could open the way for a common pattern of European cards and could influence the form these take. British and (formerly) Dutch reticence about these cards is based in part upon fading memories

[39] In conjunction with John F. Kennedy airport, Schiphol airport issued volunteers with smartcards which, together with a digitized reading of an individual's 'hand-geometry', allows immediate passage through immigration control.

[40] France announced early in 1994 that it would replace all paper identity cards by smart cards, with this potential, by the end of 1995.

[41] One pressure for identity cards is fraudulent social security benefit claims (which, given free movement of persons, is a potentially European problem). A solution proposed is unique personal identifiers encoded in electronic 'smart cards', perhaps with accompanying photographs (C. Brown, 'ID Cards will be issued for job-seekers' benefit', *Independent*, 24 Dec. 1993). The increasing computerization of state administration strengthens the argument that convenience as well as fraud control may be served by an unique personal identification number which can be used for a variety of purposes. The UK Data Protection Registrar expressed authoritative misgivings about piecemeal drift into national identification schemes in which National Insurance and National Health numbers may increasingly be used for general identification purposes. This could happen with government decision and parliamentary debate, and with inadequate privacy safeguards (Data Protection Registrar 1989, 1991, 1994).

[42] For example, the Italian writer and journalist, Pino Cacucci, was held for four hours while in transit at Roissy-Charles de Gaulle on 29 July 1994. As a result he missed his connection to Mexico and had to return to Bologna. No explanation by the French authorities was given, although his name was on their computer records, even though he had never been subject of a criminal prosecution or investigation (*Le Monde*, 5 August 1994; for a discussion of data protection see ch. 8; see also J. Jenkins, 'Jeux sans frontières', *New Statesman and Society*, vol. 5, No. 226, 30 Oct. 1992, pp. 22 and 23).

of wartime experiences, in part upon civil libertarian grounds, and in part upon cost. Ethnic and political minority groups, including immigrant populations, feel particularly vulnerable to identity checks. There are reports of police harassment in countries where identity cards are in use, and civil libertarians as well as the groups themselves fear that these minorities will face further intimidation if they are introduced in Britain (Spencer 1990).[43] Scepticism about the efficacy of identification schemes is sometimes linked with apprehensions in police circles about the adverse effects which identification schemes may have on the relationship of the police to groups in the community. For example, the Association of Chief Police Officers (ACPO), although it subsequently (1992) has become united in support, was divided in 1988 when the idea of identity cards was floated (Lyon 1991). Influential Conservative Members of Parliament often press for identity cards and they have been under consideration by the Home Office for many years. Voluntary identity card schemes have been suggested but such schemes are inherently unstable and, to all intents and purposes, are likely to become compulsory within a relatively short time. Civil libertarians have found it difficult to convince a wide public of the dangers of surveillance systems which increase the ability of the police and other agencies to identify individuals. They are often made to seem 'friends of the criminal'.

British parliamentary and governmental opinion shifted in the 1990s in favour of identity cards. The House of Commons Home Affairs Committee supported machine readable identity cards and a central register of DNA profiles for the British male population. Critical evidence from the Data Protection Registrar (Home Affairs Committee 1991) that the Data Protection Act would be unable to guard against matching and disclosure of data was not considered sufficient to outweigh the advantages for crime control. The cost (the recent Home Office estimate being £475 million to introduce the cards and £50-100 million annual running costs) and the inevitable controversy the introduction of identity cards would cause, stayed the hand of successive Home Secretaries. But Prime Minister Major, in June 1994, came out strongly in favour of personal identifiers saying that they had the potential for countering

---

[43] A. Dummett, letter to the *Independent*, 15 Aug. 1992; C. Moraes, (Director, Joint Council for the Welfare of Immigrants), letter to the *Independent*, 18 Aug. 1992.

crime and would have popular support.[44] No mention was made by Prime Minister Major of the European implications of a national identity card because, while the right of the Conservative Party may be in favour of identity cards, it would become hostile if a suggestion was made that these were introduced as a result of membership of the EU.[45]

The moves towards introducing identity cards in Britain is part of a general tendency towards reinforcing controls within countries, of moving controls formerly exercised at the frontier away from the physical frontier.[46] Increased police surveillance in frontier regions has been noted in several countries. Mobile patrols operating in frontier zones in France (the first country to adopt this procedure)[47] and Germany regularly apprehend illegal immigrants; regular vehicle checks for offence such as overloading, which used to be conducted at the frontier posts are now done on motorways leading to the frontier. The Dutch ministries of Justice and Home Affairs have instituted new immigration patrols, called flying brigades, a few kilometres from the Belgian and German borders to intercept illegal immigrants entering the Netherlands by car. Drug law enforcement has been intensified in Dutch border towns in discos, bars and cafes. Customs in the United Kingdom have moved a substantial number of staff to inland locations.

The most powerful instrument of control is, however, large computerized data bases of the kind represented by the police data bases operated by the German INPOL and the United Kingdom's National Criminal Intelligence Service. The fear of civil liberties groups is that procedures for accountability and privacy protection are likely to lag behind the development of such databases. Civil libertarians are also concerned that the various data bases available

[44] *Daily Telegraph*, 8 June 1994. This view was reiterated at the Conservative Party Annual Conference in Oct. 1994.

[45] There had been hints of possible EC pressure. EC Commissioner Martin Bangemann said that Britain might have to introduce identity cards if it lost its attempt to retain border controls (*The Times*, 26 February 1992).

[46] In certain countries, such as Belgium, tight legal controls of immigrants inside the border, going as far as limiting their rights of movement were already in place (Nayer 1994).

[47] In particular, one of the missions of the *Direction Centrale de la Lutte contre l'Immigration et le Travail Clandestin* established in 1993 is to control a 20 kilometre wide zone adjacent to the frontiers. Similarly the PAF is empowered by articles 78–2 and 79–2 of the *Code de Procédure Pénal* to control personal identities within 20 kilometres of the frontier and up to 60 kilometres if an offence is suspected.

to the public authorities, including those in the private sector, could be accessed by law enforcement officials to establish a general profile of individuals through 'data-matching', thus throwing a dragnet over large categories of the population without cause or suspicion (Lyon 1994). Preventive policing, especially in the field of so-called organized crime, where reactive policing is thought to be ineffective, and criminal 'threat analysis' is an increasingly popular approach, can lead to serious misuse of data bases in which innocent individuals are subjected to intensive investigation and surveillance. Together with other intelligence-gathering through undercover policing (Fijnaut and Marx 1995), electronic eavesdropping (including telephone tapping)[48] and video cameras, the new widely networked data bases have the potential to create a much more controlled society than has existed in post-1945 western Europe.

Frontiers and the Threat of Crime from outside the EU

Difficulties over the draft External Frontiers Convention and Schengen are, in part, the result of the great changes wrought by the collapse of communist systems in Eastern Europe, and other geo-political developments in Asia and Africa which destabilized various existing regimes. These changes created great uncertainties about the security needs of the EU Member States. Two themes in the debate related directly to frontiers. First, new connections were seen between internal and external security (discussed in chapter 5); new threats from the outside were identified in the form of the spread of 'disorder' from regions adjacent to the territory of the EU (Eastern Europe, North Africa and the Middle East), through the violent activities of political groups. The second theme which was amplified by changes in the wider international order was that of 'organized crime';[49] the main focus was on the enhanced threat of drugs-trafficking, but the heightened sense of apprehension encompassed other criminal traffic from which profits could be derived—stolen works of art, export of stolen cars, traffic in

---

[48] The Justice and Home Affairs Ministers' Meeting at Essen on 30 Nov. and 1 Dec. 1994 discussed the introduction of a scheme whereby telephone-tapping could be authorized on a transnational basis, allowing a tap to be placed on a telephone in one Member State in order to assist investigation of a crime in another Member State (*Guardian*, 2 Dec. 1994).

[49] For the extent to which organized crime is seen as an external threat, see Anderson (1993a).

women, illicit trade in radioactive and nuclear materials, fraud and extortion[50]

Once discussion of external criminal threats from outside the EU became a part of political debate, additional attention was drawn to the weaknesses of policing arrangements for the external frontier. The French Senate committee of enquiry into the application of the Schengen Conventions sharply criticized them. Germany's land frontiers were seen as highly permeable.[51] The 450 kilometres of border territory with the Czech Republic are probably relatively secure[52] because of good bilateral co-operation, but the 420 kilometres with Switzerland are lightly policed, the 800 kilometres with Austria are subject to a free circulation agreement of August 1984 (and virtually unpoliced), and the 430 kilometres shared with Poland (the old Oder-Neisse line) are very difficult to control: 80 per cent of the asylum seekers arrived across the latter border in 1992. More than one million people entered Germany in 1992 across all its frontiers with the intention of staying permanently; some of them, the French *Police de l'Air et des Frontières* (PAF) feared, might reach other countries in the EU. Spain had in 1992 significant clandestine immigration from North Africa and these immigrants frequently reached France before they were apprehended. Italy has a very difficult coastline to police and was administering strict immigration legislation for the first time in the early 1990s (Den Boer 1993a). After the arrival of increasing numbers of people from the former communist states, Greece, with

[50] At a meeting in Berlin on 8 Sept. 1994 of EU ministers of Justice and Home Affairs, ministers from the four candidate members of the EU and the six Central and Eastern European countries with Association Agreements issued a declaration of intent 'to enlarge and reinforce co-operation to strenuously fight against drugs and organized crime in Europe' and which included all these other criminal activities (*Agence Europe*, 9 Sept. 1994).

[51] For a detailed study of the German frontier controls until 1990, see Kühne (1991). Since then Germany has made considerable efforts to improve the quality of its policing of frontiers. It has increased the establishment of the *Bundesgrenzschutz* by the integration of 7,000 members of the former GDR Border Police, and stationed more of the BGS on the frontiers, purchased new surveillance equipment (thermal, radar and infra-red), initiated mobile patrols, and entered into cooperative agreements with Poland and the Czech Republic (including exchange of officers, technical assistance and co-ordinated patrols). Anything which could reasonably be done without being seen to copy the lethal practices of the old GDR has been done.

[52] Although one estimate gave a figure of 200,000 illegal entrants across this border (*International Law Enforcement Reporter*, 5, 1992, pp. 195–7) and some reports suggested that Prague was becoming an important centre of organized crime (*Tijdschrift voor de Politie*, 54, 9, 1992, p. 384).

1,180 kilometres of land frontiers in difficult terrain, 15,021 kilometres of coastline and more than 2,000 islands, could be represented as a threat for the whole EU (République Française—Sénat 1993).[53]

One reason for the United Kingdom's desire to maintain frontier controls is the belief that they are more efficient than in the rest of the EU. Historically, there may have been substance in this belief, partly because Britain's island location made control of ports of entry easier. Confronted by mass movements of population and containerized goods transport, it is harder to sustain. Heathrow airport faces the same problem as other major European airports, as it can only provide very cursory inspection of individuals and goods originating in the EU (as well as the rest of the highly industrialized world). This inspection is of dubious value in crime control and it is likely to become an increasing source of irritation for the travelling public.

The idea of an hermetically sealed frontier which would prevent undesirable foreigners from intruding into the territory of the EU Member States cannot bear serious scrutiny. There have been many cases of 'closed' frontiers which have failed to prevent large-scale movement of refugees.[54] Doubtless, seas, barbed wire, guard dogs, electronic and visual surveillance, frontier guards with orders to shoot to kill, and even automatic killing machines restrict the numbers of unofficial border crossings. The western frontiers of the German Democratic Republic had these features, between the building of the Berlin Wall in 1961 and the collapse of the regime in 1989, but remarkably, the flow of emigrants did not cease—it was reduced but it continued (Funk 1994). The frontier was surprisingly permeable in both directions and in several ways. The western frontier of the GDR was so open to the trade in goods that the GDR was, in effect, a shadow thirteenth member of the European Economic Community. Many other examples illustrate the same point: in contemporary circumstances, the potential of frontiers for strict control of persons and goods is severely limited.

Conclusion

A myth of control of frontiers is essential to the maintenance of state authority and the credibility of state sovereignty. State

[53] République Française, *Op. cit.*, 23 June 1993, No. 384 53.
[54] One case in 20th century Europe was the Franco-Spanish frontier on the Pyrenees which was closed during and after the Spanish Civil War (1936–9).

authority would not be undermined if there were a widespread confidence that controls at the external frontier of the EU were as effective as those of the most efficient Member State. The policing of frontiers would then be a reciprocal service states provided for one another (precisely the principle on which the draft External Frontiers Convention is based). This is a principle, and a practice, which the United Kingdom government openly espouses[55] and to which other governments of Member States give more muted support. Some, particularly Germany with its vulnerable eastern frontier, would prefer to spread the burden and seek the protection of a genuine European regime for the external frontier and for internal security. Of course, as the United Kingdom example demonstrates, support for an intensive system of policing the external frontier does not necessarily imply acceptance of a generally more integrated framework of legal and police co-operation. Transforming the intergovernmental regime envisaged by the draft External Frontiers Convention into a genuine European regime in which policing of persons would become subject to European law (in the same manner as clearing goods through customs) adjudicated by the European Court of Justice would be a psychological, political and legal breakthrough, marking the arrival of a predominantly federal element in the constitution of the EU, and perhaps providing a sounder practical basis for the maintenance of an effective 'outer shell' for the EU.

Until this happens, the international frontier between European states remains a crucially important legal and political institution. Despite the development of European law and the vast tranfrontier flow of persons and goods, the territorial principle associated with state sovereignty remains intact in a crucial respect—the exclusivity of law enforcement jurisdiction of the state. In addition to this basic legal principle, entrenched political identities remain associated with the territorial state and are not yet counter-balanced by a European identity strong enough to permit the transfer of important policing authority from the states to the EU (see chapter 3). The experience of the only, and distant, analogy with the United

---

[55] Although, as we have seen, the UK Government is not convinced the control of external frontiers is capable of reaching the level of efficiency required to abolish all internal frontier controls. Paradoxically, therefore, the state which is possibly more favourably disposed to the development of a secure external frontier, is also most committed to the maintenance of secure internal frontiers. See n. 2 above.

States gives little guidance as to how and when this might happen. The characteristics and historical experience of the United States federation and the proto-federation of the EU are too divergent for the analyst and European policy-maker to draw any direct lessons from the United States.

The core of the debate on the abolition of frontier controls within the EU has centred on the doctrine of compensatory measures. This doctrine was an essential political complement to the completion of the internal market and was intended to counter the concerns in law enforcement and political circles, as well as wider public opinion, about the loss of control over serious crime and criminals as a result of easing or abolition of checks at frontiers. Certain agreements such as the Schengen Conventions, the Palma Document and the draft External Frontiers Convention are practical expressions of the doctrine. An aspect of the doctrine was the linkage between policy on the internal and external frontiers— controls could be removed at the internal frontiers to the extent that the external frontier could be policed according to uniform rules and common standards. The lack of progress on the External Frontiers Convention, the frequently stated British opposition to removing internal controls and the complications resulting from enlargement of the EU, indicate that a strong political resolve is necessary to achieve the aims of the SEA and the TEU.

The most sensitive questions raised in the debate on abolishing frontier controls is the manner and the location of checks on individuals. A consensus is emerging that some kind of personal identifier is essential for policing illegal immigrants and persons suspected of criminal offences. Identity cards were controversial when introduced in Germany, and they still have not been introduced in the United Kingdom. Civil libertarian arguments against personal identifiers are losing ground but the cost and form of personal identifiers are still contentious in the United Kingdom. Their necessity has been buttressed by claims, common to arguments supporting proposals for other kinds of improved police co-operation, of threats coming from non-EU nationals in the form of illegal immigrants and organized crime. In turn, this has focused attention on the effectiveness of checks on individuals at the external frontiers. Hermetically sealed frontiers, which prevent crossing by any suspect individuals, are impossible in contemporary circumstances. But for political, resourcing and geographical reasons, not all external frontiers can be policed with the same degree of rigour. This is likely to provoke suspicions and tensions between Member States.

Arguments about control of frontiers relate to so many dimensions of European security that they are unlikely to be resolved unless there is some form of federalizing of EU territory in which a high level of legal and political integration is achieved. This federalizing would involve the establishment of a European police authority to control the external frontier, perhaps with operational police powers in all Member States. A European frontier and immigration administration would have to be introduced. Governments and public opinion are not yet ready for these innovations. In the nationalist atmosphere which characterized the anti-European campaign during the ratification debates of the TEU, and in light of the apathy, compounded by outright hostility to European integration on the part of a strong minority of the electorates of virtually all Member States shown in the June 1994 European elections, further Europeanization of frontier policing in the near future is improbable.

5

The Merging of Internal and External Security

Introduction

The legal and organizational lines between internal and external security, between security of the individual within the state and security of the state itself, and between the police and the military have historically been drawn differently in the European countries. Under the pressure of events since 1989 radical changes have taken place and the relationship between internal and external security is being redefined. The changes since 1989 have been the subject of optimistic and pessimistic interpretations, some believing that they represent the triumph of western values and western liberal democracy, others regretting the loss of a bi-polar world in which the distribution of international power and influence between the two super-powers was more or less stable and predictable. Commentators and politicians agree, however, that the post-1989 situation has suggested new scenarios and posed new challenges: there is now a more dynamic situation with unpredictable security threats, which requires the planning of flexible responses to a variety of dangers (Van Ham 1993).

The rethinking of European security has had a number of repercussions on European police co-operation. Broadly speaking, these repercussions can be classified in four groups. The first is that the pattern of criminality may change as a consequence of changing macro-politics and macro-economics in areas neighbouring the European Union. The transfrontier aspect of criminality may expand because of developments in East Europe (see chapter 1). Secondly, the disappearance of the 'iron curtain' has opened up new possibilities for interaction between law enforcement agencies in East and West. With the prospect of enlargement of the EU with membership of the EEA states and eventually Central and East

European states, European police co-operation will have to be superimposed on a greater variety of policing traditions and systems (Anderson 1991). Thirdly, as a consequence of a waning state-controlled security and the redundancy of some state security agencies, security will become a concern of more organizations and agencies, including those in the private sector. Fourthly, increased anxiety about the socially destabilizing potential of international organized crime and the employment of pro-active policing techniques have produced a situation in which internal security is no longer a matter which can be separated from issues of external security, and policing will become an increasingly diffuse and open-ended concept. At the centre of EU politics, then, lies a crucial question: to what extent will EU Member States be prepared to institutionalize and regulate collectively home affairs and foreign policy? In this chapter, we further assess the repercussions of the events of the late 1980s in the light of distinctions habitually made between internal and external security, and between police and military functions.

In analysing developments in European policing in the light of the changing security agenda, it would, however, be a mistake to assume that the channels of influence flow in only one direction. The policing agenda is not merely 'acted upon' by outside forces: European police co-operation has in recent years developed into a semi-autonomous social field (Goldsmith 1990; Walker 1994a), with its own policy network and discourse (Den Boer 1994b: 174; Den Boer and Walker 1993: 20). Certain fora, such as Trevi, have been influential in 'pushing' the agenda beyond traditional policing concepts, for example by taking on board 'high policing' (Brodeur 1983) issues such as terrorism and new 'security threats' such as immigration. As a consequence, the definitions of policing and security have therefore become closely linked and mutually influential.

Changing Definitions of Security

The notion of security is constituted by a number of different elements, and can be looked at from a variety of points of view. From a realist starting point, Buzan (1991) has characterized the security threats in the post-Cold War situation as being of five broad types. The first is military threat, which relates exclusively to the level of external security; the second is political threat, which is associated with both external and internal security and which includes subversive or anti-democratic activities against the institutions, symbols and ideology of the state; the third is societal threat, such as a threat to the cultural integrity of ethnic or other socially-cohesive groups; the fourth is economic threat, including the security risks arising from competition and unemployment; and the fifth is ecological threat, which again combines elements of internal and external security, as for example transfrontier pollution. This redefinition of security threats illustrates a partial merger between the domains of internal and external security. The implications of this conceptual merger for police organization and practice may be profound. The wider definition of security and the broader range of threat analyses which this produces is likely to encourage pro-active policing, undercover policing and the more systematic targeting of social categories—a shift in emphasis from modes of policing which may pose new problems of abuse of legal powers and avoidance of accountability (see chapter 8).

A number of further observations about Buzan's classification may be made. In his terms, 'security' seems to coincide with 'threat' or 'insecurity', rather than with 'control', 'law enforcement' or 'public policy'. In our view, security should include the level and form of military control or policing, as well as the *raison d'être* of control. This should constitute a two-dimensional view of security, in which subject and object-related aspects of security are highlighted. Next, Buzan makes use of a clear distinction between internal and external security, but they should not be viewed dichotomously. In the real world, security concerns are diffuse and cannot be precisely categorized (Berki 1986). The distinction between internal and external security, which is usually parallel with the distinction between home affairs and foreign policy domains of politics, is one which is commonly employed rhetorically, but which, if treated with caution, may also be of heuristic value. Indeed, we maintain the distinction between external and internal security throughout this chapter for heuristic reasons. A third and final observation, which underlines the permeability of the distinction between internal and external security, is that the threat of crime touches and even pervades all five domains defined by Buzan.

Organized crime, in particular drugs and arms-trafficking, have been defined as external security threats, *inter alia* because they are associated with guerilla warfare, terrorism and aggressive forms of international economic competition and imperialism. These particular crimes may be subjected to semi-military types of control; examples are the United States' military operations in drug-producing Latin American countries (Bullington 1993). Large-scale and professional crime have the potential to corrupt governments and public administration, particularly in politically fragile states, and thus constitute a political threat. The link between societal threat and crime is more apparent, both in terms of cause and effect; for example, the evidence is abundant and compelling that drug addiction has had devastating effects on individual lives and local communities, and also that it is fostered by other conditions of social deprivation (South 1994). Economically, crime is parasitic upon the legitimate activities of manufacture, trade and banking. Organized crime and the turnover of the black economy are sizeable components of national economies in many parts of the world (Hobbs 1994; Taylor 1994). It has even been suggested that the legalization of drugs and other commodities might endanger the stability of the world's major stock exchanges and trading centres. Ecologically, organized crime is now a major threat because it exploits the loopholes in environmental legislation and because it seeks to corrupt officials in public administration (Van Duyne 1993); the dumping of chemical and nuclear waste has already become a thriving business in transfrontier organized crime (Pearce and Tombs 1993), while the sale of plutonium and uranium on the black market has recently emerged as a threat of even greater dimensions.[1] Furthermore, immigration and asylum, which, like crime, are increasingly defined as a threat to the internal and external security of western states, are phenomena related to each of Buzan's five dimensions of security.

Cumulatively, these developments imply that the notion of security is shifting in three important and related ways: internationalization, de-territorialization and internalization. The collapse of the

---

[1] 'The European Union and a number of Central and East European states recently decided to co-operate against the smuggling of nuclear substances ('European Ministers probe nuclear crime issue'; informal Council meeting on 7–8 September 1994 in Berlin, *European Report*, No. 1973, 6 Sept. 1994, at 2; German Police Criminal Statistics 1993, *Bulletin*, 30 May 1994, at 464; *NRC Handelsblad* 8 and 15 Sept. 1994). At the subsequent European Council in Essen on 9-10 Dec. 1994, the trade in radioactive and nuclear substances was one of the areas of crime to which the mandate of the Europol Drugs Unit was extended (*Guardian*, 12 Dec. 1994; see also n. 4 below).

bi-polar system is only one undercurrent to these changes. The emergence of new security communities, the erosion of the significance of national borders, and the gradual displacement of responsibilities for security from the state to the private sector and the individual citizen, have also been important influences. The emergence of new security communities is partly a side-effect of the bi-polar collapse (Buzan 1991: 208) as external security strategy which was previously dominated by the Cold War super-powers has either been delegated to other structures or, as the Balkan crisis has graphically demonstrated, has been left to develop in an *ad hoc* manner without clear lines of responsibility or points of initiative. The EU, which has just started to assume intergovernmental responsibility for home affairs, foreign policy and security, is a candidate to become a security community (see below). The emergence of new security communities and new security partnerships to deal with external security threats, such as the association of East European states with NATO, is paralleled by the increasing internationalization of previously domestic forms of security control. The latter is based on a growing awareness that the control of multinational systemic crime (see chapters 1 and 4), and international migration, solely at the level of the nation state is insufficient. In regions with a long history of political co-operation between states, such as between the Member States of the European Union, the state of international anarchy (Bull 1977) and divergent national interests may be replaced by institutionalized security partnerships.

The decreasing significance of the monopoly of military force—the supreme symbol of national sovereignty—and the associated idea of national borders, adds an additional argument to the pressure for internationalization. Indeed, we may observe a general de-territorialization of security controls, with physical controls at national borders and other controls premised upon exclusive jurisdiction within national territory giving way to a more diffuse set of arrangements as the nature of political authority changes. The potential transfer of national border control responsibility to a regional security community increases both the significance of the 'external' borders of the EU and of police controls within states (see chapter 4).

Internalization is the final factor underpinning the shifting notion of security, in the sense that security is becoming more and more foregrounded as a responsibility of the individual citizen. Many West European states admit an inability to control crime by conventional policing. This has led to numerous crime-prevention programmes and information campaigns. Citizens are expected to lock everything behind them, to carry their handbags diagonally around their shoulder, to fit alarm systems, to leave the curtains open and to leave a light on when they go on holiday, to remove their radios from their cars, to use inside pockets in their jackets and to keep their cheques separate from their bank cards; they are also, in some cases, encouraged to participate in or finance neighbourhood-watch schemes. This new focus is closely associated with the development of late modern society as a 'risk society' (Beck 1992). Community is no longer characterized by exchanges that include quality face-to-face relationships and local organization tied to direct results. Instead, in an era of impersonal communication and electronically-mediated transactions, risk assessment and the maintenance of security is less a matter of personal trust relations and more a matter of resort to impersonal techniques, expert systems and institutions which specialize in risk management. The insurance industry and the manufacturers of security devices thrive on the need to find reliable and systematic means to prevent crime. The recognition that the police cannot provide a comprehensive service has resulted in a burgeoning demand for services provided by private security firms by banks, financial institutions, commercial and industrial firms, as well as institutions in the public sector. As crime prevention and security maintenance techniques no longer flow naturally from the pattern of routine activity of individuals in their communities, with the state police as a sufficient back-up, security control has become a more apparent and pervasive problem, and, as such, has become the subject of internalization (Ericson 1994; Giddens 1991; Gyomarch 1991; Hoogenboom 1991; Johnston 1992; Reiner 1991; 1994a).[2]

The Changing Nature of External Threats

External security threats are no longer, for the moment, primarily military, but lie in mass migration, drugs and arms-trafficking, and criminal networks expanding across frontiers. One dramatic example of the way in which the collapse of the communist regimes of

---

[2] See ch. 8 for a discussion of the declining status of public policing.

Eastern Europe has resulted in the merging of internal and external security is in the menace of trade in nuclear materials. Prior to 1989, the major concern of the NATO powers was that the massive nuclear arsenal of the USSR would be unleashed against the West. Arms limitation agreements were designed to reduce the possibility of this happening, and a nuclear non-proliferation agreement was intended to ensure that nuclear weapons would not fall into the hands of 'rogue' powers. As the bipolar system began to fragment, the clandestine trade in nuclear materials by individuals for private profit became a serious possibility, and thus nuclear weaponry entered the domain of ordinary criminality. There are suggestions that Russian criminals have made pacts with Italian Mafia groups to share trade in drugs and nuclear material.[3] Although the number of discoveries of nuclear material registered by the *Bundeskriminalamt* has been relatively small, there has been an increase: seven cases were reported in 1990, twelve in 1991 and seventeen in 1992, until in 1994 a number of more serious incidents increased the public profile of this type of criminal activity. For the first time, in August 1994, three people of various nationalities were arrested in Germany in the possession of 350 grammes of pure plutonium 239, a material used directly in nuclear weapons.[4]

The converse is also the case: activities previously considered within the domain of ordinary criminality are now sometimes regarded as matters of state security. The most obvious example is organized crime, above all 'international organized crime' (see chapter 1 for a discussion of this concept). The United States' government promoted this redefinition with President Nixon's slogan of the War Against Drugs as a national priority; President Reagan mobilized the navy, airforce as well as the security service to interdict the import of drugs (McGaw 1991; Nadelmann 1993). Organized crime is regarded as a specific category of crime[5], sub-

---

[3] *Independent*, 11 Oct. 1993.

[4] It was claimed this seizure would have been impossible if German criminal investigators had not used infiltration methods. *Le Monde*, 17 and 25 Sept. 1994; *Independent* 18 Sept. 1994. See also n. 1 *above*.

[5] Federal criminal enterprise statutes target criminal behaviour conducted like a legitimate business. The Racketeer Influenced and Corrupt Organizations Act (RICO), since 1970 incorporated in the Organized Crime Control Act, is the most prominent of these statutes, as it targets offenders working at the top of various kinds of criminal organizations. The Continuing Criminal Enterprise Act (CCE) 1984 targets drug-traffickers who are responsible for long-term and elaborate conspiracies. The criminal enterprise statute has the potential to break up associations

ject to special legislation and specialized investigative teams or task forces. These are justified by the argument that organized crime penetrates public institutions and private corporations very much in the manner of organizations which seek to subvert the authority of the state. A pro-active law enforcement strategy, in which intelligence-gathering and undercover operations play key roles, is considered necessary; organized crime could flourish without the nature of the criminal conspiracy being uncovered if policing was confined to purely responsive investigations of individual criminal acts. Against a background of similar arguments, in which the experience in the United States is frequently invoked, European policing has been moving in the same direction (Busch and Funk 1995; Cooney 1992: 66).

The difficulty with this approach is that it requires the targeting of criminal 'threats' on an *a priori* basis. The definition of targets by law enforcement agencies is influenced by public policy objectives, and they take into account influential or allegedly representative views or forcibly expressed opinion. The views of the public are to some extent constituted by and inferred from the preoccupations of the mass media, which in turn both influence and are influenced by the immediate concerns of populist politicians (Herman and Chomsky 1988; Schlesinger and Tumber 1994; Sparks 1992). In the same way, the manufacturing of consensus about the 'new threat' of criminal enterprises from the East has been a discursive process encouraged by the military planners and intelligence services. The difference in emphasis that could previously have been observed—at least in the British model of policing—between the way in which military planners establish 'threats' and the way in which police respond to crime and disorder, is no longer so apparent.[6] This blurring is even more evident at the level of European police co-operation which is more obviously concerned with grand strategies of 'fighting' crime and with targeting certain activities for intelligence-gathering, rather than reacting to an agenda largely controlled by others.

The battle for control over aspects related to external security

of highly placed drug-traffickers or to neutralize criminals who direct complex illegal activities. From Bureau of Justice Statistics Clearing House, Nov. 1993.

[6] Although the capacity even of a non-military, decentralized police service such as the British to influence the public agenda and define its own priorities should not be underestimated. See Reiner (1992b: chs. 2 and 5).

also encourages overlap and rivalry between police services, as their efforts are increasingly directed towards the range of threats offered by terrorism, organized crime (Bögl 1994: 30)[7] and extreme right-wing movements (Gill 1994: 72). In France, for example, the question about who takes control over high policing causes considerable rivalry between two or three directorates general of the National Police and the *Gendarmerie* as well as some sectors of the National Police which stand to gain more than others from closer European and international law enforcement co-operation. Likewise, in the United Kingdom, the replacement in May 1992 of the Metropolitan Police Special Branch by the Security Service, MI5, as the lead agency in gathering intelligence on PIRA in mainland Britain, and the subsequent suggestion that MI5 was seeking to expand its activities yet further into the areas of drugs and major fraud, illustrates a new competitiveness within the United Kingdom's law enforcement circles (Walker 1993b; 1994b; see below).

The Security Continuum

The linkage between security fields lies at the core of the redefinition of the West European security situation. Integration of the tasks and functions of police services, immigration services, customs and intelligence services (Den Boer 1994c: 7; Walker 1995), is supported within high policing discourse by the gradual shaping of an 'internal security continuum' (Bigo and Leveau 1992), connecting terrorism, crime, immigration and asylum-seeking. Indeed, a crucial factor behind the merging of internal and external security has been the definition of immigration and asylum-seeking as problems for the internal security of West European states. This linking process operates at the level of cultural meaning and is associated with a variety of discursive techniques (Bigo 1994c; Den Boer 1994c; Brion *et al.* 1994: 38; Solomos 1993). The image of migratory flows jeopardizing internal security is often integrated into the vocabulary of law and order (Bigo and Leveau 1992: 9, 29). There is an increasing tendency to view immigrants as pre-

---

[7] Bögl asserts that organized crime groups increasingly try to corrupt political and economic élites; he argues that the objective of organized crime groups to infiltrate national financial institutions must be regarded as a *political danger* (our emphasis), which can be regarded as a sufficient justification for action by the intelligence services.

sumptively deviant (Goldstock 1991; Zachert 1992a): this builds on an existing tendency to link indigenous coloured minorities with crime (Bunyan 1991: 19-27; Keith 1993; Werdmölder and Meel 1993). Other discursive features are the association between immigration and unlawful social benefit claims, the fear, nurtured by xenophobes, of a connection between mass immigration and social instability (Castles and Miller 1993: 13; Heisler and Layton-Henry 1993: 162), the blurring of the distinction between refugees and immigrants, and the insertion of provocative terms like 'manifestly unfounded' into official discourse on asylum (Den Boer 1995).

There are three modes in which internal security concerns have become amalgamated with immigration and asylum. The first of these is ideological merging: law enforcement agencies in Europe started to redefine internal security threats. The old external threat of communism was replaced by an external threat established by mass immigration, organized crime, and imported terrorism, the penetration of which would, like the old threat, lead to the destabilization of 'well-balanced' western societies. The second component—instrumental merging—is to be found in the range of instruments which are employed against illegal immigration. There is an increase in the use of intelligence (House of Commons 1992: 10, 11), of 'high-tec' detection equipment, and of concerted proactive investigation generally by all agencies involved in immigration control.[8] The EU Ministers of Justice and Interior have negotiated the introduction of joint compensatory measures and instruments of control. Striking examples are international information systems (such as the SIS, and in the future, the EIS), fingerprint systems, carrier sanctions and visa requirements (Ogata 1993: 10-11). Law enforcement officials will have on-line access to these international information systems. These instruments used for migration and asylum controls will simultaneously be used for crime control. The third component is institutional merging: institutions engaged in international police co-operation and immigration, such as Trevi and the *Ad Hoc Group* on Immigration are—as a consequence of the Treaty on European Union—reconstituted and merged into the K4 Co-ordinating Committee (see chapter 2).

[8] According to the *Guardian* of 24 March 1992, the Home Office in Great Britain was considering the use of heat detectors to prevent illegal immigration from the Continent in trucks and vans; a week's trial of detectors at Dover in 1991 apparently led to ten arrests.

Indeed, the third pillar of TEU may be seen as the culmination of the integration between international law enforcement concerns and concerns about migratory movements and asylum seekers (Ford 1991: 128).

The creation of the security continuum is also apparent in a narrower organizational sense. The association between organized crime and ethnic groups (Cooney 1992: 28-37) encourages a linking of law enforcement agencies: co-operation between ordinary police forces, immigration services, customs and intelligence agencies, therefore, is based on and reinforces the continuum which runs from terrorism to immigration, and from ordinary crime to political and subversive crime. In most European countries, immigration control is a shared responsibility of a variety of law enforcement agencies. Although this does not result in a merging of institutions, close relationships must be maintained on a daily basis. Immigration services, customs services and border control agencies, and regular police forces are all involved in certain stages of immigration control. Police services have assumed an expanding role in this field. In addition to enforcing the criminal law against illegal and clandestine immigrants, police officers also tend to perform the administrative function of registration, and to play a co-operative role alongside the immigration service in the enforcement of immigration law in areas such as housing and employment. But even where the police are entrusted with administrative functions, they often retain a level of discretion normally associated with the policing function.

International co-operation may be facilitated by the creation of domestic police special units and surveillance forces to combat immigration fraud (Den Boer 1993a) and human smuggling.[9] Following the American practice, internal controls may be stepped up in restaurants, hotels, bars and horticultural industries, as these are thought to be the typical workplaces or residences of illegal aliens.[10] The introduction of wider and tougher statutory powers for the police has already occurred in some EU Member States. For

[9] *Financial Times*, 17 Feb. 1993.

[10] *Ad Hoc* Group Immigration (1993: 12). Research in the Netherlands has demonstrated that police officers are most likely to ask for identity documents when they suspect an alien of infringement of the penal code or of illegal residence; internal immigration control performed by police officers is thus regarded as an extension of primary law enforcement tasks (Aalberts 1989: 2). See ch. 4 for a discussion of ID cards.

example, in the UK the 1984 Police and Criminal Evidence Act gave the police new powers of detention, questioning and search, which may be used to investigate immigration offences more intensively and to gather information more systematically (Gordon 1985: 98). Police powers in respect of asylum-seekers are further increased under the 1993 Asylum and Immigration Appeals Act, which allows the fingerprints of all applicants to be taken.

The ideological implications of attempts to identify and group security risks are inevitably of significance, especially when the 'external threat' of immigration is amalgamated with the 'internal threat' to the stability of West European economies and societies. The political repercussions may be wider than intended by mainstream political forces who have developed the new security agenda. The increased intake of immigrants and asylum-seekers and their presence in EU Member States has been exploited by right-wing extremists who advocate overtly racist policies and attempt to steer European law enforcement more strongly in the direction of zero immigration and draconian controls of non-EU nationals within 'Fortress Europe' (Harris 1994: ch. 2).

The Fading Distinction between 'High' and 'Low' Policing

In all police institutions in western Europe there is a strong pull of tradition in the form of laws and practices, norms and values, disciplines and expectations. Some of the most influential of these concern the relations of the police to government and the state. Brodeur's conceptual scheme (1983: 514-15) has provided an analytical framework for the relationship between state and police with a distinction between 'low' and 'high' policing, to which Marenin has added policing of the 'general' and the 'specific' order of the state. The essence of the distinction drawn by these two authors is between policing which is concerned with the protection of the state, and of dominant political actors, and policing which is concerned with the maintenance of order and suppression of crime more generally (see chapter 3; Marenin 1982). This classification can be applied to any policing system, but it is less suited to countries with 'Napoleonic' and 'gendarmerie' traditions. This is because Gendarmeries have always provided, without making any distinction between them, high and low policing functions. A gendarmerie tradition is one in which a corps of armed police—organized along military lines and under the hierarchical control of the

Ministry of Defence—is responsible for the general policing of parts of the national territory. In all their activities, including the investigation of ordinary crime, police in the *gendarmerie* tradition regard themselves as serving the state. France, Italy, Spain, Portugal, Greece, Luxembourg, Belgium, and to a certain extent the Netherlands have been marked by the *gendarmerie* tradition. Germany, with a federal constitution, Britain, with a decentralized police system, but also Denmark and Ireland with national police forces, have civilian policing traditions. In this tradition, the distinction between high policing and low policing is readily understood in the police and security communities (Benyon *et al.* 1993: ch. 3). Indeed, one of the few generalizations that can be made about the legacy of the past in policing systems within the European Union, is the existence of a marked institutional and organizational difference between the *gendarmerie* and civilian police traditions. This distinction is, however, becoming increasingly blurred as law enforcement agencies in both traditions gradually embrace the same wide range of functions, from the 'highest' form of state security to enforcing the 'lowest' form of road traffic regulation.

A related institutional trend apparent right across Western Europe, is the tendency towards centralization of previously decentralized policing systems, particularly exemplified by the establishment of national intelligence services.[11] Increasingly, specialist policing capacities are concentrated in central agencies. In France, Belgium, Spain and, even more in Italy, this has always been the case by virtue of the strong hierarchical structure of their policing systems. The creation of the anti-Mafia directorate (DIA) in Italy, a National Criminal Intelligence Service (NCIS) in the United Kingdom, a national police unit (KLPD) with its own crime investigation team in the Netherlands, and the possible setting up of an anti-Mafia unit in France are among current high-profile examples of new or reinforced centralization (Rosenthal and Cachet 1992: 141). European integration and anticipation of the creation of EDU/Europol has encouraged some centralization in the form of

[11] There are also decentralization tendencies. In France, there is a greater devolution to the *départements* and the municipal police is growing (Anderson 1991; Journès 1993). In the UK, Basic Command Units have been created beneath the traditional unit of the Division and there is more financial decentralization (McLaughlin 1992; Walker 1991).

national drug (intelligence) units, and more recently, national criminal intelligence units (Den Boer 1991a; Walker 1994b). The EU also exercises a more general centralizing pressure on national criminal investigation apparatuses in Member States by encouraging the co-ordination of national effort and the representation of coherent national positions in the various structures established and initiatives made under Title VI of the TEU (Hoogenboom 1994: 331; Walker 1994b: 27-30). The influence of the Schengen Conventions, the TEU, and European discussions of crime control is shown in domestic political debates by the frequent explicit references to the internationalization of crime and policing. Of course, there are noticeable differences in levels of knowledge and of enthusiasm for police co-operation between the various national policy communities.[12] However, this is not to deny that the centralizing tendency has had the general effect of encouraging a more holistic conception of policing in which the distinction between high and low policing becomes less relevant.

The lines between low and high policing, and between internal and external security provide only very general guidance for the understanding of policing issues thrown up by the very complex array of policing organizations and policing cultures. In everyday operational terms, the significance of the distinction is often remote, but they still function as useful markers between the different competences of police, military and security services. But, quite apart from the general influence of centralization, there are indications that the practical importance of the distinction is fading. Faced by particular actions involving foreign nationals, intelligence services, 'political police' and ordinary police often have to co-operate: the interpenetration of internal and external security is an everyday phenomenon. The conceptual distinction between 'high' and 'low' policing, therefore, has a limited and declining effect on police organizations. Vested interests of police and security agencies (see chapter 2) and the fluctuations of the macro-political agenda for the process of European integration may, on the other

[12] Our interviews suggest that developments in European police co-operation have been primarily driven by a north European coalition for three main reasons: fear of increase in crime as a consequence of European integration, lack of faith in the competence of southern allies on the part of the UK, France, Germany, Belgium, the Netherlands, and greater, albeit uneven enthusiasm for the idea of European union in Germany, France, Belgium, the Netherlands, and Luxembourg.

hand, be of considerable significance for the evolving division of competences between the different agencies.

The Changing Horizon of Low Policing

Indicative of the narrowing conceptual and practical distance between 'low' and 'high' policing within the national law enforcement bodies throughout Western Europe is that the ordinary police services have begun to shift their focus from local crime to regional, national and transnational crime.[13] Crime with more than local ramifications includes serious crimes of dishonesty and violence, such as bank robbery and kidnapping, the various activities of organized crime, including illegal trading enterprises, environmental crime, organized prostitution, human smuggling, counterfeiting of currency and identity documents, and political crime, such as subversion and terrorism. The shift of emphasis from local crime runs parallel with the creation of specialized central police units and with the increased employment of controversial pro-active policing techniques and instruments, such as wire-tapping, covert surveillance, entrapment and the use of paid informants. 'High' policing, together with the techniques traditionally associated with its practice, is therefore increasingly entering the realm of 'ordinary' policing. This is especially the case since organized crime has begun to be targeted by police organizations throughout Europe.

There is currently a second wave of legislation in various EU Member States aimed at enlarging police powers in the sphere of pro-active criminal investigation. During the late seventies, there was a spate of anti-terrorist laws in several European countries: in the nineties, the fight against organized crime has provided political support for the introduction of new legislation. The first wave in the seventies was marked by the introduction of legislation in Italy, Germany, the United Kingdom, and to a lesser extent France, aimed at both domestic and 'imported' terrorism. Italy provides an extreme example. The Italian *Reale* Laws of 1975 (extended in 1977) increased police powers of search, arrest, detention on suspicion, and the tapping of telephones, which required the written consent of a magistrate. Law 191 of 18 May 1978 went further and

---

[13] For a discussion of this development in the Netherlands, see the Report of the *Bijzondere Onderzoekscommissie IRT* (1994).

permitted magistrates to approve telephone taps verbally, so that police could act immediately. The notorious *Cossiga* Law (Law 15 of 6 February 1980) authorized police to search houses or apartment blocks without prior authorization of a magistrate, if there were reasonable grounds for believing they harboured someone wanted for a terrorist crime. Other legislation facilitated intelligence gathering by approving the establishment of a computerized data base within the Ministry of Interior (Clutterbuck 1990: 37–9; 154; 186).

After the kidnap and murder of Dr Schleyer in 1976, German laws enhanced police powers in dealing with terrorist suspects. Police were permitted to search all apartments in a block if they suspected that terrorists and hostages were there, and they were empowered to set up road-blocks to establish the identity of people passing through neighbourhoods in the vicinity of terrorist incidents. In addition, a powerful computerized data bank was set up within the BKA (Clutterbuck 1990: 58). The 1974 Prevention of Terrorism Act in the United Kingdom authorized police to demand evidence of identity and arrest people without warrant if suspected of any of the offences covered by the Act, such as membership of the PIRA or involvement in the commission, preparation or instigation of acts of terrorism. When the Act was reviewed in 1989, police were given extended access to bank accounts and business records anywhere in the United Kingdom: they were empowered to share information with each other and with the social security authorities; and the onus was placed on suspected racketeers 'to prove that there was a legitimate source for their funds'. (Clutterbuck 1990: 93). The 1989 Act also differs from its predecessors in that it does not automatically expire after five years, so conveying the sombre message that the problem of terrorism is no longer considered a temporary one.[14] In France, police powers were increased in 1986 to permit police officers to prevent people from leaving the scene of the crime if they required information (Clutterbuck 1990: 78).

The campaign against multinational systemic crime is gradually beginning to take shape with an enlargement of police powers in

---

[14] Whether the 'peace dividend' resulting from the PIRA ceasefire in Aug. 1994 and the commencement of political talks with the British Government in Dec. 1994 will include the review and repeal or reduction of anti-terrorist legislation remains to be seen.

pro-active policing. In Germany, customs investigators are now empowered to tap telephones and intercept mail of firms suspected of illegally exporting components and software to countries like Libya and Iraq for use in their nuclear and chemical weapons programmes.[15] The German 1992 organized crime statute authorized the use of undercover agents, video techniques, and electronic surveillance (Kaiser 1990; Lüderssen 1985).[16] In Britain, the majority of interception warrants issued under the 1985 Interception of Communications Act are now used to combat drug-trafficking, rather than counter-terrorism and subversion.[17] In the Netherlands, parliamentary interest has been aroused by police searches of private property and other pro-active investigation methods; there is a growing consensus to create a new legislative framework to control the use of pro-active investigation methods (Corstens 1994; Hoogenboom 1994: 32 and 304; Werkgroep Vooronderzoek Opsporingsmethoden 1994). In Belgium, proposals have been made to establish a new legislative framework for police powers in general, which also includes methods such as infiltration of criminal organizations (Fijnaut et al. 1990: 78). One feature common to Italy, Germany and the Netherlands is the criminalization of 'acts of preparation of and participation in a crime' in much broader terms than has hitherto been the case.

The Moving Target of Intelligence Services

Just as the sites of agencies traditionally engaged in 'low' policing have been raised, those of agencies traditionally engaged in 'high' policing are gradually being lowered. Intelligence services have begun to redefine their targets in a way which overlaps with traditional policing functions. The 1989 destruction of the Berlin Wall removed traditional targets and activities of the national security and intelligence services, such as espionage and counter-espionage directed at the USSR and Soviet dominated countries, and of domestic left-wing subversives. The end of the external and internal communist 'threat' has precipitated 'a sometimes frantic search for a new *raison d'être* for these agencies' (Klerks 1993b: 66). In

---

[15] *Guardian*, 24 Jan. 1992.
[16] *Gesetz zur Bekämpfung des illegalen Rauschgifthandelns und anderer Erscheinungsformen der organisierten Kriminalität* (OrgKG 15 July 1992; NJW 1993, Heft 4, 237).
[17] *Independent*, 20 April 1991.

order to legitimize their activities and to ensure greater public acceptability, security services in Europe started to enter domains which previously belonged to the higher echelons of ordinary policing, such as organized crime[18] and right-wing extremism (Gill 1994: 72; Klerks 1993b). For example, since the ending of the Cold War, the British Intelligence Service (MI6) changed its role to concentrate more on countering the threat from terrorism and the proliferation of nuclear and chemical weapons.[19] Members of the Dutch security service, the *Binnenlandse Veiligheidsdienst* (BVD), have infiltrated extreme right-wing parties to find out whether there were links with neo-nazi groups outside the country.[20] The German Intelligence Service, the *Bundesnachrichtendienst* (BND), was slimmed down in 1992 and changed its priorities to international drug-trafficking, trade in nuclear weapons, terrorism and illegal technology transfers.[21] Changes in French intelligence have also highlighted the importance of the suppression of domestic crime in the pursuit of the national interest. The political intelligence police, the *Renseignements Généraux* (RG), has increasingly concentrated in recent years on the surveillance of gambling rackets alongside its anti-terrorist and anti-subversion roles (Klerks 1993b: 70).

The increasing involvement of security and intelligence services in ordinary policing sharpens inter-agency friction and competition. The London Metropolitan police, for instance, have criticized the security service (MI5) for 'hijacking' control of terrorist-related intelligence: the semi-public contest between MI5 and the Special Branch of the London Metropolitan Police for Irish terrorism-related intelligence has been one of the indicators of the changing responsibilities of intelligence services (see above; Gill 1994: 125).[22]

---

[18] *Financial Times*, 22 Nov. 1993.   [19] *The Independent*, 25 Nov. 1993.

[20] See *Staatscourant*, 20 Sept. 1994 for the focus on activities of the extreme right.

[21] *Guardian*, 25 April 1992.

[22] *Central Intelligence Machinery* (1993) (London); *The Security Service* (1993) (London). Since gaining control of terrorism-related intelligence on the British mainland in 1992, MI5 has sought to extend its remit into areas such as drugs, organized crime and money laundering. This was the barely hidden agenda of its Director, Stella Rimington, in the annual James Smart lecture delivered in November 1994. Relatedly, MI5 is attempting to take over from the Metropolitan Police Special Branch's European Liaison Unit the right to nominate one of the British representatives on the Europol Drugs Unit (*Guardian*, 23 Nov. 1994). A similar problem exists in relation to MI6 and the Government Communications Headquarters (GCHQ). Sections 1 and 3 of the Intelligence Services Act 1994 (c.13), which places the intelligence services on a statutory footing for the first time, state that the functions of the

The redefinition of the role of European secret services from being important actors in a bipolar security competition to the more modest one of attending to the consequences of the disappearance of this competition (such as the problems of a possible black market in nuclear and chemical weapons) will have consequences for the evolution of cross-border policing in Europe.

The relationship between the security services and arrangements for European police co-operation, particularly Europol, is bound to be uncertain and untidy, and, at least in the early years, is likely to be punctuated by a series of 'turf battles'. Given its primary orientation towards the collection and analysis of intelligence on drug-trafficking and related forms of criminality, Europol is set to occupy a position at the intersection between low and high policing. But evolution towards other domains of criminality, such as terrorism and right-wing extremism, the acquisition of operational powers and involvement in the deployment of sensitive policing techniques, is undecided (see chapter 2). Europol's policing tasks and powers at the end of this century depend on where EU Member States decide to locate it on the continuum between high and low policing. If high policing dominates, it may result in a highly secretive organization resembling the model of an intelligence service; an intermediate possibility is the development of a European Criminal Intelligence Service along the lines of the United Kingdom's National Criminal Intelligence Service; if the low policing theme dominates, we are more likely to witness both transparency and the development of operational powers.

Under the traditional policing philosophies of Western Europe, public consent is the single most important source of legitimacy for the police, and effective accountability mechanisms help to secure this. Under a system dominated by high policing concerns, an informed and consenting public would be less crucial. Protecting the constitutional public authorities, rather than bringing criminals to court, would have priority. The more secretive and élitist ethos of the security services would gain ground, and the ideal of a transparent, rule-governed and politically neutral system would

Intelligence Services (MI6 and GCHQ) shall be exercisable 'in support of the prevention or detection of serious crime'. Furthermore, Section 2 allows the heads of MI6 and GCHQ to provide information 'for the purposes of any criminal proceedings', a power which is extended under sched. 4 of the 1994 Act to the head of MI5. This will permit encroachment on the traditional police preserve of collecting evidence for the purpose of prosecution (Wadham 1994).

become no more than a remote possibility (see chapter 8; Gill 1994: 62; 121).

The European Union as a Security Community

Title VI of the EU represents a key convergence of ideological, instrumental and institutional dynamics. In addition to the superficial imposition of more coherence on cross-border law enforcement co-operation, Title VI creates a link between various security issues. As we have seen in chapter 2, these include asylum policy, external border controls, immigration policy, drug addiction, fraud, judicial co-operation in criminal and civil matters and customs co-operation. Last but not least, it includes police co-operation.[23]

On closer examination, however, the TEU presents a confused picture. On the one hand there is convergence, but, on the other, divergence of the security issues. The overlap between JHA and Common Foreign and Security Policy (CFSP) concerns internal security issues with a potentially international dimension, such as immigration (Cremona 1994: 253; Lacaze 1994) and asylum, external border controls, drug-trafficking, terrorism, and forms of organized crime which are characterized as politically or economically harmful to the Union as a whole (Bögl 1994: 47). Although Title VI may be represented as a seamless range of internal and external security matters, it is still formally restricted to JHA, and there is no bridge between it and Title V (the 'second pillar'), which is the formal agreement for external security matters under the TEU.

From an integrationist perspective, this may be viewed as a retrograde step, since between 1976 and 1993, there was such a bridge built onto the framework of European Political Cooperation (EEC). There is now a possibility of a new breakthrough, as the European Commission and the European Parliament are exerting increased influence over both immigration and foreign policy. A key issue is whether, during the 1996 intergovernmental conferences, there will be a proposal for formal links between the second and third pillar, given that current issues such as terrorism, immigration, extreme right-wing groups, former Yugoslavia, and organised crime throw up obvious links in practice. In criticizing the obvious overlaps and potential conflicts between second and third pillar activities, it has

---

[23] Art. K.1(9), Title VI, TEU.

been suggested that Article J.4 (1) of the second pillar, which includes the 'security of the Union', may overcome the 'artificial and unworkable distinction hitherto made between political and economic aspects of security on the one hand and military aspects of security on the other' (Neuwahl 1994: 232). Although formally, drug law enforcement, asylum policy and anti-terrorism are integral parts of the third pillar, they may also be covered by the second pillar 'whenever policies of third countries are involved'. Similarly, foreign policy aspects of terrorist threats could be dealt with under Title V, but not when it concerns internal mechanisms to combat them (Neuwahl 1994: 234). From the point of view of institutional co-ordination of European internal and external security issues, however, the EU is just one part of a larger jigsaw. Just as the internal structure of the EU is crucial for the development of an integrated approach to security, so too is the extent of co-ordination between the EU and agencies such as NATO and WEU.

These important structural transformations and possibilities lend new urgency to the question marked at the beginning of this chapter: whether and to what extent the EU can become a security community? This question recalls the fundamental debate over whether the notion of the European nation state is losing ground (chapter 3; Buzan 1991: 158). Buzan notes that although West European states admit their inability to fulfil independently many economic and defence functions, they are reluctant to break away from the familiar forms of the state-action. But he predicts that, if the EU states continue to integrate politically, the Union can pass 'beyond the structure of an anarchic sub-system into the grey zone of semi-statehood' (Buzan 1991: 194) where the pressure from outside the Union to treat it as a single actor will begin to outweigh the pressures towards internal divergence. Although the EU has failed to define a coherent and decisive policy vis-à-vis former Yugoslavia (Keohane 1993), this does not mean that security threats outside the EU cannot be responded to collectively.

If the EU is gradually identified by élites and governments as a security community, it will confront directly certain key questions of internal security in the light of this very broad understanding of its jurisdiction. Three issues stand out. The first, very much in line with national law enforcement strategies, is the political question whether the EU should adopt a coherent criminal justice strategy with a predominantly preventive or repressive orientation (Walker

1993b: 113-17). To the extent that a preventive policy is chosen, the links between crime and insecurity, and the wider socioeconomic environment would have to be analysed, after which a comprehensive 'European Crime Prevention Programme' could be drawn up by combining and integrating European amelioration policies and crime control policies. To the extent that a repressive approach is adopted, the methods and techniques of crime-fighting would be the major focus rather than the deeper causes and motivations behind crime and deviancy. Organized crime, fraud, terrorism, drug-trafficking and other multinational crimes would in that case be seen as phenomena to be suppressed with an increased and intensified use of intelligence, internal controls and operational powers (Den Boer 1994a: 283–4; 1994c).

The second issue is the current interpretation of the existing legal and political framework of internal security by the EU Member States. With the failure to meet the 1992 deadline on the abolition of internal border controls, there has already been much disagreement about the interpretation of Article 7A of the TEU[24] and about what, if anything, constitutes a sufficient danger to public security to justify the retention of controls; in the future more controversy may be expected about the detailed enforcement of internal controls and intra-European checks on EC citizens. In the context of the Schengen Conventions, there have already been political disagreements about the level and quality of immigration and drug enforcement controls, resulting in modification of border control policies and drug control policies in certain countries.[25] The Committee on Civil Liberties and Internal Affairs of the European Parliament has pointed out that the Schengen countries have not yet even tackled the interpretation of the terminology in Articles 95-100 of the Convention Implementing the Schengen Agreement, including open-textured terms such as 'danger to internal security', 'public policy' and 'serious criminal offence' (Van Outrive 1992c). Such terminology and the issues underpinning its use are a source of great controversy in domestic immigration debates. When a number of countries attempt a common definition of the difficult themes associated with the concept of internal security, the scope for disagreement is even wider.

The third issue concerns the consequences of the current and

---

[24] Formerly Art. 8A of the Single European Act (see also ch. 3 and 4).
[25] See ch. 2.

future enlargement for the cohesiveness of the EU as a security community. The 1995 enlargement of the EU from twelve to fifteen members may change external security threats and make policing within the Union more heterogeneous (see chapter 4). We have already alluded to some current and future repercussions of the opening up of the EU beyond the Fifteen to incorporate many Central and Eastern European states. If and when these states accede to the European Union, the territory of the Union will expand considerably. It will have new external borders and will face new threats from regions adjacent to the territory of the EU (see chapter 4); and it will inherit security concerns already present in these regions, such as control over the strategically important area between the North Atlantic Ocean and north-western Russia. Tensions between EU Member States because of different national interests could become so serious that the idea of the EU as a security community could be undermined.

A second significant consequence of enlargement of the EU is the growing cleavage between policing systems in Europe. With the accession of three of the EEA states to the EU, the balance has been tipped marginally in favour of countries with a civilian policing culture as opposed to the *gendarmerie* traditions which dominate the south of Europe.[26] Even prior to the incorporation of the EEA states there was already a perception of a 'North-South divide': in southern Europe, a predominantly repressive approach prevails and there is a high level of tolerance with regard to information exchange unregulated by data protection legislation (even though such legislation exists). In northern Europe there is a more professionally detached and institutionally autonomous approach (Zanders 1994: 14). Other differences which cut across the North/South axis to a greater or lesser extent concern the nature of institutional links between prosecution and police (a crucial matter for the improvement of judicial co-operation), the relationship between police and public, and the emphasis on generalism versus specialism.[27] These differences are reinforced by divergent

[26] Two of the new Member States, Finland and Sweden, have a strong civilian tradition, while the third, Austria, has both a civilian national police force (*Bundespolizei*) and a paramilitary national police force (*Bundesgendarmerie*).

[27] There has been a tendency in most EU countries, encouraged by EU policy on police co-operation, to create specialized police units against organized crime, terrorism and drug-trafficking, while in the EEA states this has been somewhat delayed.

public and political attitudes to organized crime and immigration, resulting from different geographical locations and socio-economic interests.[28]

Conclusion

Internal and external security in Europe are in the process of redefinition. The collapse of the bi-polar system has played an important role in this. Military threats have been replaced by lower intensity and more nebulous security threats from international organized crime and illegal immigration. This does not imply that security matters occupy a less prominent position in national and international political agendas. If anything, the merging of security issues and the internalization of security anxieties in the 'risk societies' of late modernity have lent a new urgency to the whole question. Responses to the new security threats have become increasingly interconnected; common institutions, instruments and ideologies have been developed to combat them. As the European Union is tending to develop into a common security area and security community, this has also encouraged a redefinition of security. A gradual transfer of internal and external security control is taking place from the nation state to international institutions, and the embryonic institutions of the EU may be undermined by 'globalization' as much as by residual loyalty to the nation state.

The changing perception of security threats has considerable repercussions on the definition of tasks and responsibilities of police and intelligence services. Intelligence services are increasingly penetrating fields which used to belong to the realm of 'ordinary' policing, such as organized crime and right-wing extremism, while the police services are also beginning to shift their priorities away from local crime and to the use of pro-active policing methods. Political decisions will determine whether these national policing developments will be reflected in European police co-operation.

The events in 1989 and after demonstrated the contingency of security arrangements and concepts: the balance of global power can change suddenly and unexpectedly, but not necessarily with apocalyptic consequences. Changing global balances inevitably influence internal security arrangements and political calculations

---

[28] Two useful recent reviews of national policy systems within the EU are Benyon *et al.* (1993) and Klerks (1993a).

about international police co-operation. Politically motivated abuse of European policing arrangements is possible and the current demand for improved accountability shows awareness of this. The tension between the political and practical pressures exercised on law enforcement organizations and the need for a regulatory framework which facilitates and monitors police co-operation is evident. The next three chapters are concerned with the legal and political arrangements which both reflect and seek to resolve this tension.

6

The European Union and Criminal Law

Introduction

This chapter examines the jurisdiction of the European Union in criminal justice matters. Cross-border police co-operation in the EU is hampered by the diversity of national rules concerning police powers, substantive criminal offences and criminal procedures (Zachert 1992: 32–33). Some physical barriers at the frontiers between EU Member States may have been abolished but national borders continue to mark important dividing lines between them from a legal point of view. In principle, the jurisdiction of the police and criminal authorities of each Member State begins and ends at the frontier. The reluctance to depart from this expression of state sovereignty was very well illustrated by the tortuous negotiations surrounding the regulation of the right of hot pursuit in the Schengen Convention.[1] The basic agreement to allow hot pursuit has been made subject to a large number of national reservations (Kühne 1991: 155-8) and, according to Article 41(5) of the Convention, 'pursuing officers must comply with the provisions of . . . the law of the Contracting Party in whose territory they are operating'. In other words, Schengen does not allow police powers to be 'transported' from one Contracting State to another.

European Community law has, to date, shown little interest in police powers, except in the context of legal proceedings before the ECJ concerning the legitimacy of controls on personal identity carried out at the border.[2] But the same does not apply to criminal law as such. The first part of this chapter will show that Community law was already having an impact upon the

---

[1] Interview, BKA, 30 Sept. 1992.
[2] Case 321/87 *Commission* v. *Belgium* [1989] European Court Reports (ECR) 997.

application of national criminal laws some time before the entry into force of the TEU in November 1993, and that it has developed its own form of quasi-criminal sanctions, albeit in limited fields, in order to combat certain breaches of Community law. The introduction of legal provisions on co-operation in the field of JHA and the establishment of common European policing institutions such as Europol further challenge the widely-held assumption that the criminal law remains the exclusive province of the Member States.

All EU members recognize that the rule of law in democratic societies demands that police forces must be subject to effective legal controls sufficient to prevent abuse of powers. Although the balance between the state's interest in the prosecution and detection of crime, on the one hand, and the protection of civil liberties, on the other hand, is not struck in identical ways throughout the EU, each Member State has undertaken to comply with the essential substantive and due process guarantees set out in the European Convention on Human Rights. In order to conform to the constitutional traditions common to the Member States, Europol would, therefore, have to satisfy a number of minimum requirements concerning the protection of human rights and the legal control of police action. The role of the courts, especially at European level, is of special significance in this regard and judicial control will, therefore, be an important theme of this chapter.

Community Competences and Criminal Law

Most legal opinion takes the view that the European Community lacks the competence to prescribe criminal offences or sanctions or to impose or enforce such criminal sanctions (Sevenster 1992; Tiedemann 1993). The 'legal opinion' referred to includes Advocates-General of the ECJ,[3] although it is unclear whether it includes the Court of Justice itself. That institution, while to date declining to support any argument pled to the effect that a Community institution was seeking, in the case before it, to prescribe or impose a criminal penalty, has expressly reserved its view on the question of a Community competence in the criminal or penal domain.[4] In a number of cases brought before it, the Court has, however, confirmed that national criminal law cannot be

---

[3] *Cf.* Advocate-General Verloren van Themaat in Case 117/83 *Karl Könecke GmbH* v. *BALM* [1984] ECR 3291: 3315.

[4] Case C-240/90 *Germany* v. *Commission* [1992] ECR I-5383: 5431.

applied in isolation from its possible effects upon Community law. It has held, by implication, that Member States may be required to enforce the performance of Community obligations by use of their own systems of criminal law, because of the so-called 'assimilation principle'. That principle, developed by the Court, has now received a blessing in Article 209a of the EC Treaty,[5] in relation to countering fraud against the Community's financial interests. The principle requires Member States to punish breaches of Community law as strictly as they would penalize breaches of equivalent national law. This, if not an EC criminal competence, certainly amounts to Community 'interference' in the criminal sphere. Community law may also affect national criminal laws by placing limits on the extent to which, and the manner in which, Member States may apply their national criminal provisions in contexts where Community law applies. It is more uncertain whether it may also require harmonization of national criminal laws of the Member States in order to further the objectives of the European Community.

We begin our examination of these issues with an analysis of Community 'penal sanctions' in the fields of the Common Agricultural Policy (CAP) and competition policy. Developments in these areas raise the question whether there is any general legal basis upon which Community sanctions may be introduced more widely. Thereafter, the effect of Community law upon the application of national criminal laws will be considered, with reference to the jurisprudence of the European Court and recent legislative developments at Community level. There are indications that, with the completion of the Internal Market, Community law is becoming more bold in its efforts to put national criminal laws to use in the protection of Community interests.

Community Penal Sanctions

It is important to distinguish between the prescription, imposition and enforcement of sanctions. There are very few examples in Community law of sanctions which may be imposed directly by the Community itself. There are rather more instances of sanctions being prescribed by Community law for imposition by the Member States. In the vast majority of cases, however, both the prescription

---

[5] Inserted by Title II of the TEU.

and imposition of sanctions to secure the effective application of Community law is left to the Member States. This is in keeping with the general practice in the Community whereby the administration of Community law is a matter for the Member States and direct Community administration remains exceptional (Louis 1990: 157–61). The notion of 'administration' of Community law includes the enforcement of Community obligations which is, therefore, also, in general, a matter for the Member States (Vervaele 1992: 14). Enforcement in the narrow sense of securing the application of pecuniary sanctions imposed by 'decisions of the Council or of the Commission' is expressly assigned to the authorities of the Member States under Article 192 of the EC Treaty, at least in so far as sanctions imposed on persons other than States are concerned.

Although the general practice in the Community is national enforcement of Community norms, this does not necessarily mean that the Community lacks a general legal competence to prescribe sanctions for the breach of Community norms. Advocate-General Jacobs asserted in a recent case concerning a challenge by Germany to the legal validity of certain punitive sanctions prescribed by Community law under the CAP that 'it would be natural to suppose that the Community is competent to specify, in any legislation it adopts, those sanctions for its infringement or abuse which are to be regarded as sufficiently effective, proportionate and dissuasive'.[6] This is a rather brave assertion, to say the least. As Mr Jacobs himself notes in his opinion, there is no clear legal underpinning in the EC Treaty for a power on the part of the Community institutions either to prescribe or impose sanctions. The Court has stressed the need for penalties for the infringement of Community law to be founded on 'a clear and unambiguous legal basis'.[7]

The penalties in question in the *Germany* v. *Commission* case had been prescribed under secondary Community legislation. They were of two types: first, penalties of one year's exclusion from the receipt of transitional aids to agricultural income or of premiums paid to offset income loss by sheepmeat producers, in the event of a farmer providing the Commission with inaccurate data; and, sec-

---

[6] Case C-240/90, *Germany* v. *Commission* [1992] ECR I-5383: 5410–11.
[7] Case 117/83 *Karl Könecke* v. *BALM* [1984] ECR 3291: 3302. In this case such a basis was found to be lacking.

ondly, a penalty of repayment of such premiums plus a surcharge, in the event of their having been improperly paid. Germany accepted that the surcharge penalty was legitimate but challenged the competence of the Community (and, secondly, the Commission) to prescribe the penalty of exclusion. The Court of Justice held that Articles 40(3) and 43(2) of the EC Treaty were appropriate and sufficient legal bases for the sanctions. But these provisions merely refer to the adoption of measures by the Community—and, in the case of the latter provision, specifically by the Commission— in order to 'attain the objectives' or secure the 'implementing' of the CAP. They make no express reference to sanctions and it is difficult to follow how the Court could see in them the 'clear and unambiguous' legal basis for the prescription of Community penalties which it had called for in the *Könecke* case.[8] Articles 40(3) and 43(2) of the (then) EEC Treaty had, however, already been relied upon by the Court of Justice to justify the system of mandatory deposits set up under various common market organizations of Community agricultural markets (Barents 1985: 239f). The Court upheld the legality of the system in the famous *Internationale Handelsgesellschaft* case, stating that the forfeiture of deposits 'cannot be equated with a penal sanction, since it is merely the guarantee that an undertaking voluntarily assumed will be carried out'.[9] Litigants have frequently sought to invoke principles of criminal law such as *nulla poena sine lege* or *in dubio pro reo* and other principles deriving from their national criminal jurisprudence before the Court, in order to attack the type of sanctions imposed under the CAP rules.[10] These arguments have been conspicuously unsuccessful. As the Court has always held that the sanctions are not penal in character, it refuses to apply these principles. The only grounds of challenge to the legality of such Community sanctions readily accepted by the Court are the lack of legal basis and the principle of proportionality.[11]

---

[8] *Ibid.*

[9] Case 11/70 *Internationale Handelsgesellschaft mbH* v. *Einfuhr-und Vorratsstelle für Getreide und Futtermittel* [1970] ECR 1125: 1136.

[10] Case 137/85 *Maizena Gmbh* v. *BALM* [1987] ECR 4587 provides an example of this. The principle *nullum crimen, nulla poena sine lege* is the principle according to which no punishment may be laid down or applied other than by law (also known as the principle of legality). The *in dubio pro reo* principle is an evidential principle which entails that the burden of proof should be on the prosecution and that the defence should be given the benefit of any doubt.

[11] The latter principle has been interpreted widely by one of the Court's

It is clear, then, that in the context of the CAP, the Community has claimed and exercised the authority to prescribe sanctions for the breach of Community rules which the Member States are required to impose. The Court of Justice has defended this power of sanction by reference to the terms of the EC Treaty which call for the effective implementation of the CAP. In the *Germany* v. *Commission* case the Court confirmed that the sanctions may be of a punitive character, going further than the forfeiture of a deposit or security. It expressly recognized the advantages of a system of Community-prescribed sanctions over penalties laid down by the laws of the Member States, stating that 'the application of national sanctions would not guarantee the same uniform application of measures against persons seeking to commit fraud'.[12]

In its development of new forms of financial sanction in respect of CAP obligations in recent years, the European Commission has always been careful not to assert a criminal competence. In rejecting the penal character of sanctions imposed in the agricultural sector both it and the Court of Justice have sometimes stressed the administrative context within which the sanctions are imposed rather than the character of the sanctions themselves. In the *Germany* v. *Commission* case, for example, the Court held that the sanction of exclusion 'must be seen as an administrative instrument forming an integral part of the aid regime and one which is designed to assure the good financial management of Community public funds'.[13] In the *Maizena* case on the other hand, the Commission sought to designate the sanctions concerned as clearly different in character from penal sanctions, pointing out that the imposition of a sanction of forfeiture of a deposit as a result of failure by a party to comply with an undertaking to the Commission did not attract any 'unfavourable moral judgment', or imply that serious 'opprobrium' attached to that party's action.[14]

A recent study sponsored by the European Commission has shown how systems of 'administrative penalties', subject to their own substantive and procedural rules, have emerged as alternatives

---

Advocates-General to include protection against double jeopardy (Verloren van Themaat, in Case 117/83 *Karl Könecke* v. *BALM* [1984] ECR 3291: 3317).

[12] Case C-240/90 [1992] ECR I-5383: 5430. Similar reasoning can be found in another recent case (Case C-326/88 *Anklagemyndighede* v. *Hansen & Son I/S* [1990] ECR I-2911: 2934–35).

[13] Case C-240/90 [1992] ECR I-5383: 5431.

[14] *Maizena* (n. 10 above), p. 4592.

to the ordinary criminal law in the laws of the Federal Republic of Germany, Italy and Portugal. Such rules apply in a number of economic sectors, e.g. the competition field (Commission 1993: 34). In Member States which have not seen the emergence of such clear distinctions, the criminal law nevertheless reflects the more lenient public attitude towards certain types of criminal conduct. The modern notion of a 'regulatory offence'[15] or a 'public welfare offence', which is often a creation of statute, e.g. breach of health and safety at work regulations or breach of traffic regulations, may be seen as a product of the older distinction between *mala in se* and *mala prohibita*[16] (Gordon 1978: 17f). The crucial issue seems to be how to distinguish 'public welfare' or 'administrative' sanctions from 'criminal' or 'penal' sanctions. The factors which may be pointed to from the European case law and Commission statements include: the administrative character of proceedings under which such sanctions are imposed, the nature of the bodies (such as the Commission) imposing the sanctions, the relative or complete lack of moral culpability associated with the transgression in question, the absence of any official recording of the transgression as criminal, and the absence of any custodial penalty as an alternative to a pecuniary sanction.

The last point focuses on the severity of the sanction. In general, the sanctions prescribed by the Community in relation to the CAP are not severe when one compares them to the criminal sanctions known to national laws. This is less true, however, of the penalties at the Commission's disposal in anti-trust proceedings under Regulation 17/62,[17] which vests in the Commission its most draconian powers of sanction. The Regulation, which is based on Article 87 of the EC Treaty, provides that the Commission may

[15] There is a burgeoning socio-legal and criminological literature on the special characteristics of so-called 'regulatory offences'. In particular, these offences tend to be distinguished from other crimes in terms of the nature of the criminal class, the difficulties associated with detection, and the accent on compliance rather than deterrence within enforcement philosophy and practice. See *e.g.* Miers and Page (1990); Hawkins (1984); Hopkins (1994). 'Public welfare offence' is the equivalent term used by Gordon, writing from the perspective of a substantive criminal lawyer (1978: 17).

[16] *Mala in se* refers to actions which are wrong in themselves; *mala prohibita* refers to matters which are merely prescribed as illegal under the positive law of the state.

[17] Council Regulation No. 17, First Regulation implementing Arts. 85 and 86 of the EEC Treaty, OJ Special Edition 1962, No. 204/62, p. 87.

impose fines of up to one tenth of the previous year's turnover on undertakings which are found to have contravened Article 85(1) or 86 (the Treaty's anti-trust rules) intentionally or negligently. But such fines are expressly held by Article 15(4) of the Regulation not to be of 'a criminal law nature'. This form of words indicates that the drafters of the Regulation were, at best, uncertain whether Article 87 of the EC Treaty, which refers only in general terms to 'provision for fines and periodic payments', is sufficiently broad to encompass 'criminal fines'.

The Court of Justice has consistently held that the Commission is an executive body and not an impartial tribunal within the meaning of Article 6 of the European Convention on Human Rights.[18] In *Germany* v. *Commission*, Advocate-General Jacobs similarly argues that "Community law . . . does not confer on the Commission (or on the Court of First Instance or the Court of Justice) the function of a criminal tribunal.'[19] The decisions in these and other cases indicate that the Court views Commission proceedings as administrative rather than penal in character. This approach, and the similar statement in Regulation 17, may be justified if one's attention is focused on the nature of the investigating body and the investigative procedures. It is less convincing if one concentrates on the quality of the sanction itself.

Under Regulation 17/62 daily penalty payments may be imposed alongside or as an alternative to fines. The European Court has drawn a distinction between the two, pointing out that the fine has a repressive character,[20] fulfilling a deterrent function. Recent fining policy of the Commission has emphasized this function of the fine. Fines of several million ECU are no longer a rare occurrence and in its Report on Competition Policy for 1991 the Commission declared its intention to make fuller use of its power under Article 15 to fine up to ten per cent of annual turnover (Commission 1992b: point 139). It seems clear that the Commission, by imposing high fines, wishes to publicize and stigmatize particularly serious breaches of its competition rules and highlight the illegal conduct of specific undertakings.[21] In practical

---

[18] E.g. Cases 209-15, 218/78 *Van Landewyck* v. *Commission* [1980] ECR 3125: 3248.

[19] Case C-240/90 [1992] ECR I-5383:5408.

[20] Case 41/69 *ACF Chemiefarma et al.* v. *Commission* [1970] ECR 661: 701.

[21] A fine of approximately £25 million was imposed recently on British Steel (*Independent*, 17 Feb. 1994), and at the end of Nov. 1994 the Commission imposed

terms the Regulation 17 fine can be as harmful to an undertaking's financial position as a criminal fine (Kerse 1994: 246). Neither fine nor penalty payment are comparable with compensation for private law wrong, as the sum concerned is not paid over to the damaged competitor of the offending undertaking. Such an analysis of Regulation 17 fines, which takes account of recent Commission practice, results in the conclusion that it is very difficult to distinguish these sanctions from sanctions of a penal or criminal character.[22]

There is now some authority from the European Commission of Human Rights in Strasbourg to support this conclusion. In the case of *Société Stenuit* v. *France*, the European Commission on Human Rights found that the fine imposed on an undertaking in a decision by the French Minister of Economic and Financial Affairs under the French laws governing anti-competitive behaviour amounted to the disposal of a criminal charge.[23] The fines were of a similar character to Regulation 17 fines, but with a somewhat lower maximum fine of five per cent of annual turnover. If we take seriously the reasoning of the European Commission of Human Rights, this highlights the uncertainty surrounding the adequacy of Article 87 of the EC Treaty as a legal basis for fines such as those provided for under Regulation 17. Unlike Regulation 17 itself, Article 87 does not say that fines imposed under the competition procedures may not be criminal in nature. But there would certainly be a case for revising the treaty article to make it more explicit on this question. Such a revision would also offer the opportunity to spell out in the treaty the rights of the defence which should be complied with when such fines are available.[24]

In discussing the penal sanctioning powers of the Community, the new version of Article 171 of the EC Treaty should be mentioned. It remains to be seen how the Luxembourg Court will deal

its highest ever fine of 248 million ECU on an alleged cartel of cement producers and associations in the EU (see European Commission (London Office), *Week in Europe*, 41/94, 1 Dec. 1994).

[22] This now seems to be accepted by some members of the Court: see Advocate-General Vesterdorf in Case T-1/89 *Rhône-Poulenc* v. *Commission* [1991] ECR II-867:885 and Advocate-General Darmon in Case C-89 etc./85 *Ahlström* v. *Commission* [1993] 4 CMLR 407: 539.

[23] *Société Stenuit* v. *France* (1992) 14 EHRR 509.

[24] It is not obvious why the EC Treaty should continue expressly to protect professional secrets against disclosure by the Community institutions and their staff (Art. 214) but not equally important rights of the defence.

with penalty cases brought under this provision. In its revised form, it enables the Commission to recommend to the Court that a 'lump sum or penalty payment' be imposed on a Member State which has failed to respect a judgment of the European Court that it was in breach of its obligations under Community law, following an enforcement action under Article 169 or 170 of the EC Treaty. Any fine recommended by the Commission would have to be a very substantial one in order to have the required deterrent effect. The amended Article raises a number of questions similar to those posed by the Regulation 17 fine. Member States at the wrong end of the new article might be inclined to argue that the Commission is assuming quasi-criminal powers, not authorized by the Treaty, if an unduly heavy-handed approach is taken.

If, as argued here, Regulation 17 fines, if not the sanctions imposed under the CAP, should be classified as of a criminal nature, one must then ask whether the legal guarantees available to persons exposed to criminal sanctions are being respected by Community law. Article 6 of the European Convention on Human Rights sets out certain requirements regarding a right to a fair trial or hearing.[25] The Community's procedural rules, including the system of judicial protection, seem in general to satisfy the requirements of Article 6. The establishment of the Court of First Instance in 1989 has greatly enhanced the scope of judicial protection of the rights of parties and the substance of these rights has been elaborated in a rather generous fashion by the Court of Justice.[26] The Court of First Instance and Court of Justice's thorough exercise of their powers of review and scrutiny over Commission decisions (including decisions to impose sanctions under Article 15 of Regulation 17) mean that a hearing by 'an independent and impartial tribunal established by law' in terms of Article 6(1) of the European Convention on Human Rights is guaranteed.

[25] Art. 6(1) of the Convention may in fact apply to Community competition procedures by virtue of their involving a 'determination of . . . civil rights and obligations', even if suspected infringements of Articles 85 or 86 are not classified as equivalent to criminal charges: see Case 374/87 ORKEM v. Commission [1989] ECR 3283: 3350.

[26] See Kerse 1994: 298 (and preceding discussion at 295–8). These points were recognized by the competition law practitioners who gave evidence to the House of Lords Select Committee which reported on Community enforcement of competition policy at the end of 1993 (House of Lords 1993a: 37–38). For a more detailed analysis of the jurisprudence of the European Court of Justice concerning the protection of fundamental human rights, see Weatherill and Beaumont 1993: 220–3.

Recently, however, some new concerns have been raised about the level of protection of certain fundamental rights, in particular due process rights in Regulation 17 proceedings. These have focused on the jurisprudence of the European Court of Justice concerning the privilege against self-incrimination in Regulation 17 proceedings and access to business premises by Commission investigators. Some observers have detected discrepancies between the Luxembourg court's case law on these matters and the demands of the European Convention on Human Rights, as applied in the Funke[27] and Chappell[28] cases (Van Overbeeck 1994; Schermers 1992: 54). As the Community seeks to extend its powers of sanction and as they become ever more difficult to distinguish from penal or criminal sanctions, it also becomes more important that the guarantees insisted upon by the European Convention on Human Rights, as interpreted by the European Court of Human Rights, are fully protected by Community institutions. This task would be facilitated by the formal accession of the Community to the Convention, which would mean that decisions of the Community's institutions could be directly reviewed by the European Court of Human Rights for their compatibility with the European Convention on Human Rights (Schermers 1992: 54–7; Twomey 1994: 126). In relation to Regulation 17 matters, we have seen that there is a need for the European Court to pay closer attention to the development of Strasbourg's jurisprudence. The extent of the 'problem' should not, however, be exaggerated. The ECJ accepts the European Convention as 'a direct source of Community law' (Edward 1990: 391) to be applied in its own review of Community action, and this development also now finds direct expression in the TEU (Article F(2)).[29]

Even if the procedural context in which they are applied is clearly regulated by the European Convention on Human Rights, arguably it remains anomalous that new forms of sanction in relation to the CAP have been developed by the Commission in the absence of a strong mandate in the treaties. Here, one may question whether the Court of Justice has applied its own test of 'clear

[27] *Funke* v. *France* (1993) 16 EHRR 297.
[28] *Chappell* v. *United Kingdom* (1990) 12 EHRR 1.
[29] For a recent discussion of the Convention by the Court of Justice see Case C-159/90 *Society for the Protection of the Unborn Child* v. *Grogan* [1991] ECR I-4685; [1991] 3 CMLR 849.

and unambiguous legal basis' rigorously enough. As we have observed, unlike the Advocate-General, the Court in *Germany* v. *Commission* did not address the question of the Community's general sanctioning power and it refused to be drawn into debate about the Community's competence in the criminal sphere. The Commission Legal Service is said to be of the view that Article 172 gives it the authority to impose punitive sanctions (Vervaele 1992: 24–5). This Article states that: 'Regulations adopted jointly by the European Parliament and the Council, and by the Council, pursuant to the provisions of this Treaty, may give the Court of Justice unlimited jurisdiction with regard to the penalties provided for in such regulations.' However, to take Article 172 as general authority for the prescription or imposition of Community sanctions would be to put the cart before the horse. It is extremely doubtful whether the Article purports to confer general Community jurisdiction in criminal matters. Literally interpreted, it merely means that, should such jurisdiction otherwise be found to exist under the EC Treaty, the Court of Justice would enjoy full jurisdiction to review, and if necessary alter, any penalties.[30]

The Commission has now taken the debate on the sanctioning powers of the Community a very significant step further by proposing a Regulation on protection of the Community's financial interests, in which it intends to establish a general system of 'Community administrative penalties' (Commission 1994c). These may be imposed, by the Commission or the Member States, in order to deter and punish conduct by natural or legal persons amounting to fraud against the Community's financial interests, abuse of Community law or 'any other failure to discharge an obligation provided for in rules governing Community revenue or the grant of aid, a subsidy or any other benefit'. The scope of the proposed legislation is, therefore, broad. The Commission states in its accompanying Explanatory Memorandum that: 'The objective is

---

[30] It should be noted that the Treaty establishing the European Court and Steel Community (ECSC Treaty) contains a similar provision, Art. 36, which was discussed by the Court of Justice in an early case, Case 8/56 *Acciaierie Laminatoi Magliano Alpi (ALMA)* v. *High Authority of the ECSC* [1957 and 1958] ECR 95. The ECSC Treaty is more precise in its attempts to regulate the behaviour of Member States and undertakings than the EC Treaty and contains several references to sanctions of a 'pecuniary' character. But neither Art. 36 nor any other provisions of the ECSC Treaty (*e.g.* Arts. 64, 66, or 82) define the nature of such penalties; *cf.* Advocate-General Roemer in Case 1/63 *Macchiorlati Dalmas & Figli* v. *High Authority of the ECSC* [1963] ECR 303: 319–20.

to establish horizontal Community rules that . . . would apply across the board to the general management of the Community's finances.' (Commission 1994c: 2) Examples of such penalties are given in the draft and include 'administrative financial penalties', which may take the form of fines, or temporary or permanent exclusion from eligibility for Community aid (Article 7(1)). The draft contains a number of important restrictions on the sanctioning power, including the limits on penalty proceedings. It also enshrines the principle of non-retroactivity in Article 10. Where no fault is shown, liability to serious penalty sanctions such as the 'administrative financial penalties' will, in general, be excluded (see Articles 4 and 7).[31]

The suggested legal basis for the proposed measures is Article 235 of the EC Treaty (and its equivalent in the Euratom Treaty), *i.e.* the 'default' legal basis of the EC Treaty which may be used, in the absence of an express power in the treaty, to allow the Council of Ministers to act in order 'to attain, in the course of the operation of the common market, one of the objectives of the Community . . .' Article 235 has attracted criticism for being used rather indiscriminately to found new Community competences (Weatherill 1994: 15). The TEU left the wording of this provision of the Treaty of Rome untouched but the Member States have sought to narrow its potential field of application in some areas by introducing new fields of activity in the revised EC Treaty (Lane 1993: 979). In fact, however, the introduction of new activities may have the opposite effect, by providing a wider base line of Community objectives to which Article 235 may be linked. The 'Community objective' whose attainment would arguably be furthered by the draft Regulation on fraud is the protection of the Community financial interests. When discussing the legal basis for its proposal in its Explanatory Memorandum, the Commission points to Article 209a of the EC Treaty, which was introduced by the TEU; as we have seen, it obliges Member States to protect the Community's financial interests in the same way as their own financial interests. On the face of it, Article 209a offers a rather flimsy basis to support an Article 235 measure of this importance. The use of Article 235 requires unanimity in the Council. If it can be obtained in this instance, the Member States will have signalled

---

[31] The origin of some of these proposals can be traced to the recommendations of the Delmas–Marty report (Commission 1994c: 2).

a willingness to extend Community sanctioning powers to a significant extent.[32]

National Criminal Laws and the Protection of the Market

Following the completion of the Internal Market at the beginning of 1993, the attention of the regulators is now focused on ensuring that this market functions as intended. The enforcement of internal market rules poses a particularly important challenge for national and Community authorities alike (Commission 1994b: D). As we have seen, the enforcement of Community rules is, in general, a matter for the Member States. Given the limited powers of sanction which the Community enjoys, it falls to domestic law, in the main, to secure compliance with Community law through the application of effective remedies and sanctions. Under Article 5 of the EC Treaty the Member States are bound to 'take all appropriate measures . . . to ensure fulfilment of the obligations arising out of [the EC Treaty] or resulting from action taken by the institutions of the Community'. This provision has a specific bearing on remedies and sanctions for the breach of Community law. The Court of Justice set out the position forcefully in Case 68/88 *Commission v. Greece*:[33]

It should be observed that where Community legislation does not specifically provide any penalty for an infringement [of Community law] or refers for that purpose to national laws, regulations and administrative provisions, Article 5 of the Treaty requires the Member States to take all measures necessary to guarantee the application and effectiveness of Community law . . . whilst the choice of penalties remains within their discretion, they must ensure in particular that infringements of Community law are penalized under conditions, both procedural and substantive, which are analogous to those applicable to infringements of national law of a similar nature and importance and which, in any event, make the penalty effective, proportionate and dissuasive.

This is the authoritative statement of the 'assimilation principle', which seeks to ensure that the Member States penalize similar infringements of national and Community law equally severely. The Court's language in fact suggests the need to go beyond assim-

---

[32] At its meeting in Essen, Germany, in Dec. 1994, the European Council called upon the Council of Ministers to adopt the draft Regulations on the protection of the Community's financial interests as soon as possible.

[33] [1989] ECR I-2965: 2984–85.

ilation (Lensing 1993: 223). It implies that a national court may be required to disapply a national sanction if it fails 'effectively' and/or 'proportionately' to 'dissuade' an accused from breaching Community law. This, of course, begs the question how one judges whether a particular sanction meets these criteria. It will be interesting to see if the Court offers further criminological advice to national courts. It is unlikely to want a 'free for all', with national judges across the EU applying their own tests of 'effectiveness' according to lessons learned from their own systems. Indeed, Court of Justice case law since the *Commission* v. *Greece* case suggests that Luxembourg is becoming much more inclined to intervene in the prescription of remedies and sanctions at national level. The European Court of Justice has always been concerned to secure the effectiveness of Community law. Indeed some of its most famous jurisprudence relates to the achievement of the *effet utile* or 'useful effects' principle (Weatherill and Beaumont 1993: 289–314). But in a string of recent cases the Court has become very specific in stressing the obligations of national courts to give full effect to Community law by the imposition of appropriate remedies.[34]

Such cases show that the 'assimilation principle' enunciated in the *Commission* v. *Greece* case is part of a trend whereby national procedural laws affecting the forms of redress for the breach of Community obligations are coming under the increased influence of European Community law. This development is obviously of significance for the application of national criminal laws, which are the most forceful expression of national sanctioning authority. As has been noted elsewhere, such intervention highlights a tension between 'uniformity of protection and diversity of national remedies' (Sharpston 1993: 200). The European Court's increased

---

[34] Most notably in Case C-6/90 and 9/90 *Andrea Francovich et al* v. *Italy* [1991] ECR I-5357] the Court held that Community law may require national courts to grant the remedy of damages in favour of an individual who has suffered loss as a result of the failure of a Member State properly to implement a Community Directive. In a 1993 decision it empowered an English court to override a compensation limit in a UK statute in order adequately to compensate an individual who had been discriminated against on the ground of her sex in contravention of Community law (Case C-271/91 *Marshall* v. *Southampton and South West Hampshire Area Health Authority* [1993] 3 CMLR 293). In R. v. *Secretary of State for Transport, ex parte Factortame Ltd.* (Case C-213/89 [1990] ECR I-2433) the House of Lords was told by the European Court that, in order to give effect to Community law, it could overturn an ancient common law rule that an injunction could not be granted against the Crown. The British courts gave precedence to Community law over English or UK law in each case.

'interference' in the domain of national procedural laws appears to be partly motivated by the concern that the implementation of internal market measures should not be distorted by the application of significantly divergent national remedies.[35] The diversity of criminal laws and systems of criminal justice across the Member States of the Community represents a particular threat to the treaty goal of undistorted competition (Sevenster 1992: 56, 58f). Although their range may be growing, Community penal sanctions are limited in scope (see above). As a result, the Community still has to rely on national enforcement. It is arguably not enough for it simply to have 'access' to national criminal laws for enforcement purposes. In order to give effect to the unity of the market and the principle of non-discrimination on grounds of nationality, some degree of equivalence, if not harmonization of national criminal rules may be desirable. To date, Community legislative measures which aim at such harmonization have been few and far between.[36] One of the reasons is uncertainty about the correct legal basis, or whether any such basis exists.[37]

The extent of fraud against the Community budget has grown to such proportions in recent years that it has become an issue of major political concern in the Community (Prieß and Spitzer 1994: 297). The Commission has come under increasing pressure to take or encourage the Member States to take effective legal steps to combat such fraud. The United Kingdom government has been one of the strongest supporters of tougher action. The adoption of the new Article 209a of the EC Treaty, incorporating the assimilation

[35] See Case C-326/88 *Anklagemyndighede* v. *Hansen & Son I/S* [1990] ECR I-2911: 2934-35.

[36] Apart from the money laundering and insider dealing Directives (referred to below), one may also cite the directive concerning firearms (Council Directive 91/477/EEC of 18 June 1991 on control of the acquisition and possession of weapons, OJ L 256, 13.9.1991, p. 51), the precursor chemicals Regulation (Council Regulation (EEC) 3677/90 of 13 Dec. 1990 laying down measures to be taken to discourage the diversion of certain substances to the illicit manufacture of narcotic drugs and psychotropic substances, OJ L 357, 20.12.90, p. 1) and the Directive concerning items of cultural heritage (Council Directive 93/7/EEC of 15 March 1993 on the return of cultural objects unlawfully removed from the territory of a Member State, OJ L 74, 27.3.93, p. 74). While having implications for national criminal laws, these measures do not seek harmonization but attempt to co-ordinate the application of such laws. The precursor chemicals Regulation (Article 8) uses the neutral term 'penalties' when referring to the sanctions to be applied in the implementation of the Regulation.

[37] See below concerning the scope of Art. 100a, EC Treaty.

principle in primary Community law, with regard to fraud against the Community budget, may help to ensure that the principle is respected in every Member State. Concern that this is not happening was expressed in the Delmas-Marty report, in relation to measures taken to protect Community contributions and grants (Commission 1993: 30–1). This report also demonstrates the great diversity of national legal approaches to the combating of fraud against the Community budget. National criminal laws are employed in order to protect that budget in a variety of contexts. In the VAT field, the eleven Member States having criminal offences of domestic VAT fraud have applied them to the Community dimension. This is in conformity with the assimilation principle, but the penalties applied to such offences vary considerably. Moreover, Luxembourg has no criminal law provisions at all in this area (Commission 1993: 9–10). Significant differences among national laws are noted by the report in relation to the definition of offences related to Community grants and subsidies: here, the view is taken that 'there are valid grounds for proposing measures to harmonize national legislation to narrow the differences between definitions of offences aiming to secure the Community's financial interests'. (Commission 1993: 39). No empirical evidence was available to Professor Delmas-Marty on the actual application by national authorities of (criminal) penalties sanctioning breach of the rules against Community fraud. But her theoretical discussion of the systems of such penalties in the different Community countries refers to a number of important discrepancies regarding the availability and severity of custodial sentences as alternatives to pecuniary penalties for evasion of payment of customs duties. Large discrepancies such as these can 'create incompatibilities such as to impede mutual assistance and [may] allow offences to go unpunished . . .' (Commission 1993: 48).

The latest proposals to introduce 'Community administrative penalties' to combat fraud against the Community budget, which have already been discussed,[38] may be seen as an attempt by the Commission to iron out some of these discrepancies. Neither these measures, nor the steps proposed under Title VI (see below), would, if they came into effect, bring about anything approaching a complete harmonization of national penal laws in this field. They

[38] See the draft Regulation on protection of the community's financial interests, referred to in the previous section.

aim rather at achieving a greater convergence of national approaches. Harmonization of criminal laws or procedures at European level requires, as a first step, a willingness on the part of the Member States to accept that Community law may compel national criminal laws to be employed in the interest of the Community. The case of the money laundering directive revealed a reluctance on the part of some of the Member States, notably the United Kingdom, even to accept this much.

The Commission's original proposal for a directive on the prevention of the use of the financial system for the purpose of money laundering contained a clause (Article 2) which would have required the Member States to 'ensure that money laundering of proceeds from any serious crime is treated as a criminal offence according to their national legislation.' British objections were entered to this on the basis that it amounted to an assertion of Community legislative competence in the criminal sphere (Cullen 1993: 37). But these objections seemed to ignore the implications of the Court's judgment in the *Commission* v. *Greece* case (see above). The Court stated explicitly in *Cowan* v. *Trésor Public*[39] that Member States' criminal laws could not, in principle, remain unaffected by Community law (House of Lords 1990: 15). It had already noted on a number of occasions that the application of national criminal laws must take account of Community principles or rights acquired under Community law.[40] The money laundering proposal was, thus, arguably only placing the Court's case law in legislative form. It did not seek to prescribe the nature of the criminal offence to be created or the level of the penalty which should be attached to it. In the event, in the face of the opposition, the Commission withdrew the draft article and followed the line it had taken in the earlier insider dealing directive[41] by merely requiring the Member States to prohibit the offensive conduct.[42]

---

[39] Case 186/87; [1989] ECR 195.

[40] Case C-265/88 *Criminal Proceedings against Lothar Messner* [1989] ECR 4209.

[41] See Art. 13 of Directive 89/592/EEC of 13 Nov. 1989 co-ordinating regulations on insider dealing, OJ L 334, 18.11.1989, p. 30; Hopt (1990), comments on this directive.

[42] A statement by the Representatives of the Government of the Member States meeting within the Council (*i.e.* acting outside the EC framework) was, however, agreed which indicated that the Member States would 'take all necessary steps by 31 Dec. 1992 to enact criminal legislation to comply with their obligations' under the directive (see OJ L 166, 28.6.91, p. 83).

The money laundering and insider dealing directives share Article 100a of the EC Treaty as a legal basis. This indicates that they are designed to facilitate the establishment and functioning of the Internal Market by 'approximating' national laws. Article 100a makes no distinction between the types of laws which may be 'approximated' in furtherance of Internal Market objectives. So, at first sight, it may be argued that there is no logical reason to exclude criminal laws from this category. The Court of Justice's reasoning in *Cowan*[43] might be cited in support of this. But as the article's concern is with national laws which 'have as their object the establishment and functioning of the internal market', its *principal* application would seem to be to substantive laws of the Member States concerning the 'four freedoms'.[44] The question of the extent of 'approximation' is not discussed in Article 100a. It is, therefore, doubtful that the Article can be regarded as offering a clear legal basis for harmonization of criminal laws.

Like the anti-fraud measures, the money laundering rules do not purport to harmonize national penal laws. As argued above, it would be stretching Article 100a to the limit to assert such a competence. In fact, Article 14 of the directive states that the Member States are free to 'determine the penalties to be applied for infringement of the measures adopted pursuant to this Directive', and the next article allows them to 'adopt or retain in force stricter provisions in the field covered by this Directive to prevent money laundering'. It is clear, therefore, that Member States may apply different penalties to combat money laundering under their national systems of criminal law, though the criteria set out by the Court of Justice in the *Commission* v. *Greece* case would have to be respected (Cullen 1993: 37–8). Although the Contact Committee set up under Article 13 of the directive may review the operation of the directive and arrange consultations between the Commission and the Member States to 'facilitate harmonized implementation', this does not give it any authority to harmonize national penalties.

The harmonization of national criminal laws may, at first sight, offer an attractive solution to the obstacles to effective police co-operation presented by divergent national laws. Some degree of

[43] See n. 39 above.

[44] *Cf.* the very wide construction given to Art. 100a in a case concerning environmental matters: Case 300/89 *Commission* v. *Council* [1991] ECR I-2867 ('Titanium Dioxide') and comment thereon by Barents (1993).

harmonization of the categorization of particular types of conduct as criminal has already taken place in the EU. Even if the Community directive did not *de jure* require this in relation to money laundering, *de facto* it has helped, along with other international measures, to bring about such a situation (Gilmore 1993c: 9). The same applies to insider dealing (Hopt 1990: 72–3). Increasing convergence in the legislative definition of certain other categories of transnational criminal conduct has already occurred as a result of international law conventions adopted under the auspices of the CoE or the UN (see chapter 7). Further developments of this kind within the EU are more likely to come as a result of Title VI measures than from instruments of Community law, since under the latter there would be no clear legal basis for the harmonization of criminal laws regarding, for example, terrorism or organized crime (see chapter 1). Nor does Community law at present offer any obvious, or even tenuous, legal basis for the harmonization of police powers.

The Third Pillar of the TEU

As set out in chapter 2, the treaty basis for JHA in general and Europol in particular is provided by Title VI of the TEU concerning co-operation in the fields of Justice and Home Affairs (Beaumont and Moir 1994: 32–6 and 32–92; Müller–Graff 1994: 496–503). The basic obligation on the Member States imposed by Article K is contained in Article K.3(1), *i.e.* co-ordination of action in the areas of common interest set out in Article K.1. The Council of Ministers (in the guise of the Ministers of Justice and Interior of the Member States) provides the forum for the processes of mutual information and consultation which should enable this obligation to be fulfilled. Article K.3 also makes clear that, in so far as the Member States decide to go beyond co-ordination and approve 'joint positions' or 'joint actions' (the legal nature or effect of these measures is not defined) or agree conventions (instruments binding under international law by analogy with Article 220, EC Treaty), such measures shall be adopted or drawn up by the Council. It is also the Council which may decide to apply the Article K.9 procedure (so-called *passerelle*) to transfer Title VI matters into Community jurisdiction. As has been pointed out elsewhere, the Council's central institutional role in Title VI reflects the essentially intergovernmental character of the Article K provisions (Müller-

Graff 1994: 497). It is also designed to facilitate the 'consistency' of action across the range of Union activities (Neuwahl 1994: 239).

The Commission's right of initiative, the centrepiece of its legislative jurisdiction in Community matters, is shared with the Member States on most questions arising under Title VI, including asylum, immigration, external frontiers policy and anti-fraud measures, but excluded entirely in relation to judicial co-operation in criminal matters, customs co-operation and police co-operation. Otherwise it is 'fully associated' with work under Title VI. It is unclear exactly what this means; for example, will Commission officials be permitted to sit in on the meetings of the K4 Committee, which reports to the Council on *all* matters falling under the remit of Title VI? Given that the Commission was admitted (albeit grudgingly, and rather late in the day) to the intergovernmental fora, such as Trevi, which the new Title VI structures are designed to replace, it would be surprising if this were not the case, though the Commission's role would probably be confined to that of observer.[45] The Commission does not enjoy any powers as law enforcer similar to those which it exercises over Member States in the context of Articles 155 and 169 of the EC Treaty (Müller–Graff 1994: 499). Certainly in comparison to the role of the Council of Ministers, the role and jurisdiction of the Commission in JHA matters is weak.

The K.4 Committee, which co-ordinates policy initiatives and helps prepare decisions by the Council of JHA Ministers, has a role both in Title VI matters and in relation to visa policy, a matter assigned to Community competence under Article 100c of the EC Treaty. This means that distinctions between Community and intergovernmental matters within the committee are almost certain to become blurred, as jurisdictional 'hats' are swapped from one minute to the next. Such blurring will also be likely within the Council of JHA ministers to which the committee reports (House of Commons 1993: 34). Despite the crucial differences between the role and jurisdiction of Community institutions in Community and Title VI matters there is, therefore, overlap and there is no doubt that the Community institutions intend to make full use of the

---

[45] With regard to Europol, it may be noted that the German draft of Oct. 1994 envisages that the Commission would be invited to attend, but could not vote at, meetings of the Management Board, and that the latter could decide to meet without the Commission representative (see Art. 25 (4)).

powers granted to them. The Commission has already made this clear in relation to its shared right of initiative on immigration and asylum policy matters (Commission 1994a: 5–6). It sees a clear link between measures which may be adopted under Title VI, such as the adoption of an External Frontiers Convention, and Community measures such as steps towards achieving a common visa policy under Article 100c. In its 1993 report on the completion of the Internal Market, it stated that its recent proposals on these matters must be seen 'as an integral part of an overall and consistent approach to attain the abolition of identity checks at internal frontiers.' (Commission 1994b: 26).

Apart from the Court of Justice (see next section) the other main Community institution which has a role to play under Title VI is the European Parliament. The nature and extent of the Parliament's role is controversial but will not be discussed here. As the involvement of the Parliament bears directly on the question of accountability, discussion is postponed to chapter 8.

Legal Nature and Judicial Control of Third Pillar Measures

In evidence to the Home Affairs Committee of the United Kingdom's House of Commons, a senior civil servant in the Home Office indicated that 'the treaty [*i.e.* convention] would be the main form of legislative instrument under the third pillar' (Home Affairs Committee 1993: 37). This is borne out by the practice to date. Conventions on a wide range of matters including Europol, External Frontiers, the European Information System, the Customs Information System, Fraud and Extradition have either already been drafted or are being prepared under Title VI.[46]

The convention offers the clear prospect of a legally binding instrument which joint positions or joint actions may not; there is uncertainty as to the legal effects of these measures as this part of the Treaty itself is silent on the question. Measures adopted under Title VI are not equivalent to legislative acts of the European institutions as defined under Article 189 of the EC Treaty, which are capable of applying directly in the legal order(s) of the Member States, *i.e.* without legislative transformation. The latter may also give rise to individual rights which may be invoked in the national courts and, furthermore, such measures, like the provisions of the

---

[46] *Agence Europe*, 2 Dec. 1994, p. 5.

Community treaties on which they are based, take precedence over conflicting norms of national law. Community legislative measures must also be interpreted with regard to the jurisprudence of the ECJ which emphasizes the primacy of the teleological approach, that is, the need to give full effect to the purpose of Community measures.

Because Title VI falls outside the field of Community competence, the special properties of Community law are denied to Title VI measures. The Europol Convention would have the status of any other instrument of general public international law. To the extent that changes in the domestic legal orders of the United Kingdom are required to give effect to its terms, legislative incorporation will be required. For some of the EU Member States with written constitutions, the Europol Convention will rank behind national constitutional provisions in the hierarchy of legal norms.[47] As to joint positions or joint actions, these are more difficult to classify (Müller–Graff 1994: 509–10). It is unlikely that any legal effect will attach to the former, which may be regarded as analogous to the non-binding recommendations referred to in Article 189 of the EC Treaty (Müller–Graff 1994: 509). It is more likely, however, that the Council may use instruments of joint action referred to in Article K.3(2)(b) to bind the Member States (Müller–Graff 1994: 509).

Although the third pillar, unlike the CFSP pillar,[48] does not stipulate the character or legal effects of joint actions, there is already some evidence to support this view. Early in 1994, the British government proposed that joint action be adopted pursuant to this article in order to compel Member States to punish fraud against the Community budget under their criminal laws (Commission of the European Communities 1994c: 2). The Commission responded in June 1994 by incorporating the British proposal in a draft Fraud Convention.[49] This may have been mainly because it wanted to

[47] For Germany, see Hesse 1993, pp. 117–18.

[48] See Art. J 3(4) of the TEU which, in the context of the CFSP provisions of the TEU, states: 'Joint action shall commit the Member States in the positions they adopt and the conduct of their activity.'

[49] The substance of this draft will be discussed in more detail below. It is important to distinguish this proposal from the proposed Regulation concerning 'Community administrative penalties' which derives its legal basis from the EC Treaty (see above). The European Council meeting in Essen of Dec. 1994 endorsed the idea of *either* joint action or a Convention to tackle fraud against the EC budget, as well as calling for the Regulation to the adopted. It is clear then that such fraud will be tackled by both Community and intergovernmental instruments.

invoke the jurisdiction of the ECJ (see below), but it probably also reflected uncertainty about the legal nature of joint actions. At present, one may classify joint actions and the measures which the Council may adopt to implement them as manifestations of a new category of European law called 'Union law', or perhaps even 'Union quasi-legislation', whose exact relationship with both Community law and national law remains to be determined.

One of the important differences between the Convention as a legal instrument under Title VI, and the joint position or joint action, concerns the means of its coming into force. Pursuant to Article K. 3(2)(c), a convention only takes effect when approved by the Member States in accordance with their constitutional requirements, *i.e.* after national ratification procedures. Experience with the Schengen Convention and the External Frontiers Convention, in particular, has shown that this process can be a tortuous and protracted one, with no guarantee of ultimate success. Given what happened with the Schengen Convention, with whose content the Europol Convention is likely to overlap significantly, it is probable that national parliaments would subject the Europol Convention to close scrutiny. As argued below, its terms may also give rise to legal challenges on the basis of national constitutional laws. Unlike conventions, joint positions or joint action may simply be adopted at European level, albeit by unanimity in most cases (Articles K.3 and K.4).

The Court of Justice is the Community institution which is most clearly marginalized in the JHA field. It enjoys no mandatory jurisdiction in Title VI matters; only if the conventions envisaged under Article K.3 expressly stipulate that the Court should have jurisdiction does it have a role. Heated discussions have taken place over a number of draft conventions based on Article K.3, including the draft Convention on the establishment of Europol, as to whether or how the Court should be involved in their interpretation.[50] Views among the Member States differ widely on this point, with the British in the vanguard of opposition.[51] The British government would appear to be afraid that Court of Justice jurisdiction may

[50] *Agence Europe*, No. 6255, 20 June 1994.

[51] See the Explanatory Note on work carried out under Title VI (Justice and Home Affairs) of the Treaty on European Union which the Home Secretary signed and submitted to Parliament along with the German draft text of the Convention on the establishment of Europol of Oct. 1994.

lead to expansive interpretation of the powers of the Community institutions in this area, or would favour the legal rights of individuals against the interests of the Member States, though it is difficult to trace any direct or full explanation of the reasons for its view that there 'is no necessary role for the European Court of Justice' in Title VI matters.[52]

Article 11 of the draft Fraud Convention stipulates that the Court of Justice may interpret the provisions of the Convention by way of a preliminary ruling procedure in accordance with Article 177 EC Treaty, and that it may deal with disputes arising out of the Convention, on application by a Member State or the Commission. The reference to the preliminary ruling procedure indicates that the Commission foresees actions being raised in national courts concerning either the interpretation or validity of the Convention. Such actions could quite easily arise in the context of the imposition, under national criminal law, of one of the penalties stipulated in Article 4 of the draft (which may include a custodial sentence). This is important because it means that the Court could be called upon to deal with the protection of fundamental rights (see below). Given their resistance to attempts to extend the Court jurisdiction to other Title VI matters, the British government, along perhaps with a minority of other Member States, is likely to object to Article 11.

Should the European Court be given jurisdiction under the Fraud Convention, or, for that matter, the Europol Convention, two basic questions arise: first, what powers would it have to grant redress or impose sanctions and, secondly, what law would it apply?

First, according to Article L of the TEU, the whole of the powers conferred upon the Court under the Community treaties may apply in the event of its jurisdiction being invoked under Article K. 3(2)(c). This means that, when interpreting conventions adopted under Title VI, the Court could exercise the panopoly of judicial powers set out in Articles 164 to 188 of the EC Treaty, including judicial review of legislative acts at the instance of natural and individual persons, and the new power under Article 171 of the EC Treaty to fine Member States who fail to implement its judgments. But Article L must be read in conjunction with Article K.3(2)(c)

---

[52] Explanatory Note on work carried out under Title VI (Justice and Home Affairs) of the Treaty on European Union (see n. 52 above).

itself, which indicates that the extent of the Court's jurisdiction may be regulated by the individual convention, 'in accordance with such arrangements as [it] may lay down'. The idea is that the framers of such conventions should be able to choose to use the whole or such elements of the Court's treaty jurisdiction as they consider appropriate. Were a convention simply to invoke the jurisdiction of the ECJ without further specification then one could assume that the full gamut of the Court's powers would apply. Otherwise, it will require careful drafting to define the extent of the Court's jurisdiction.

The language of the Commission's draft Fraud Convention on this issue is vague, especially in relation to the second head of jurisdiction, where it is stated merely that the Court 'may hear and determine disputes arising out of the operation of this Convention, on application from a Member State or the Commission'. This makes some things clear, for example, that the European Parliament will not have legal capacity to sue, but it also leaves a number of questions unanswered. It fails to stipulate the procedural rules under which such actions may be heard, including the grounds of appeal; it also fails to specify against whom an action may be brought and the consequences of a successful action.

Article 20 of the first draft of the Europol Convention of November 1993 stipulated the European Court of Justice's jurisdiction with greater precision. Under the proposed draft, the Court would be able to determine 'disputes regarding the legality of decisions of the Europol Management Board . . . on grounds of lack of competence, infringement of an essential procedural requirement, infringement of this Convention, or misuse of powers'. It was also spelt out that one High Contracting Party, but not the Commission, may take another to the European Court if it believes that the latter has failed to fulfil an obligation arising from the Convention. A right of action was conferred on the Europol Management Board for the same purpose. In addition, the draft specified that jurisdiction should be conferred upon the ECJ to hear preliminary rulings on the interpretation of the Europol Convention and on the validity and interpretation of the Management Board's decisions. The draft failed, however, to go into specifics about the procedural rules to be applied and the extent of the Court's sanctioning powers.

The subsequent draft texts of the Convention on the establishment of Europol prepared under the German Presidency in October 1994 (English and German versions) show considerable differences from the November 1993 version. In particular, one can no longer find any reference to a general jurisdiction on the part of the European Court of Justice to review the legality of decisions of the Europol Management Board. The draft does, however, envisage that an individual may bring proceedings before his or her national court in respect of infringement of rights relating to personal data held by Europol. The draft would also allow the national court to refer a question which arose in such an action concerning the interpretation of the Europol Convention to the European Court of Justice. Unlike Article 177 of the EC Treaty, however, the draft refers only to questions of interpretation of the Treaty (Convention) itself, not measures taken to implement it. Following on from this omission, no jurisdiction is conferred on the Court to test the *validity* of implementing measures; this is probably a deliberate attempt to limit the scope of the Court's jurisdiction. The effect of a successful application by an individual will, in the absence of any jurisdiction on the part of the Court of Justice to declare void any measures adopted by the Europol Management Board, depend on national law. In other words, the national courts will be left to decide how to implement any interpretation given by the Court of Justice and any sanction or remedy given will be governed by national law. The English version of the October 1994 text makes clear that, if necessary in order to secure enforcement of rights under the Convention, all Member States must be joined in actions against Europol and each Member State must enforce the decision of any national court of another Member State concerning the infringement of the Convention. This solution is likely to prove cumbersome in practice. It is certainly less straightforward than the direct action jurisdiction conferred upon the Court under Article 173 of the EC Treaty, which the November 1993 draft text of the Europol Convention appeared to mirror.

That considerable disagreement continues among the Member States, on the matter of Court of Justice jurisdiction over the Europol Convention, is amply illustrated by the alternative versions presented by the current drafts of provisions relating to the resolution of differences of opinion on the application of the Convention between Europol and the Member States or between the Member States themselves (Article 37). The German text of the draft

Convention of October 1994 provides a fuller impression of the state of play and the extent of disagreement on this issue than the English version (of the same date). It shows that some Member States would prefer any disputes to be resolved by the Council of Ministers, if need be by two-thirds majority, *i.e.* politically, rather than judicially. But reference is also made, in one of the alternative options set out, to the possibility of the Court of Justice being called upon in the event of failure by the Council to reach agreement, and, in a further option, referral of these disputes to an arbitration tribunal (*Schiedsgericht*), consisting of the President of the Court of Justice and two other legally qualified and independent persons, is envisaged. The English version presented to Parliament refers only to 'discussion' within the Council of Ministers 'using the procedure set out in Title VI of the Treaty on European Union' of differences of opinion between Member States, or between Member States and Europol, on the application of the Convention. Title VI does not, however, provide any indication of how the Member States or Europol should resolve disputes about the Europol Convention or, for that matter, how disputes concerning any other Title VI convention may be resolved, apart from the general Article K.3(2) provisions on the Court of Justice. The English version of the draft Convention is, thus, inconclusive on this point.

Judging by the above drafts, it is quite possible that the extent of European Court of Justice jurisdiction over Title VI conventions—assuming such jurisdiction is agreed in the first place—will vary from one convention to the next. The terms of Article K.3(2)(c) clearly do not prevent this.[53] Apart from adding to the confusion likely to be caused by giving the European Parliament different rights of participation in Title VI matters, depending on the Convention concerned,[54] and thus frustrating the development of institutional transparency in this field, such a state of affairs would be a most unsatisfactory outcome from the point of view of judicial protection. It would arguably infringe constitutional princi-

---

[53] Suggestions have been made by Padraig Flynn—the Commissioner for JHA Matters during the 1994 negotiations—among others, for a separate solution for each Convention. In his case, this suggestion appears to have been motivated by a desire to avoid delay in the negotiation of particular conventions due to an inability to agree on a general formula; see *European Report*, 22 June 1994, No. 1960, p. 2.

[54] This is being resisted by the Parliament; EP Resolution on participation by Parliament in international agreements in the fields of justice and home affairs, A3-0436/93, OJ C44, 14 February 1994, pp. 180–2. See ch. 8 for details.

ples of equality of treatment and legal certainty and would certainly result in uneven application of the terms of Title VI conventions across the EU. One of the principal advantages of Court of Justice jurisdiction is the potential it offers for uniform interpretation and application of European law. The role of the European Commission as plaintiff in enforcement actions against Member States has proved crucial in this respect (Hartley 1988: 290–4). It appears, however, that the Member States are willing to forego this advantage in relation to Europol, fearing that Commission legal jurisdiction would lead to unwelcome political interference by it. But the alternative solutions being proposed do not offer any convincing prospect of effective enforcement of the Convention. The suggestion that legal disputes could be resolved by political bargaining would be unacceptable from the standpoint of the doctrine of the separation of powers, and likely to create constitutional difficulties in a number of Member States.

With regard to the law to be applied, the Court of Justice would look first at the terms of the relevant convention. However, Article K.3(2)(c) of the TEU allows the jurisdiction of the Court to be invoked not only in order to interpret Title VI conventions, but also to judge 'any disputes regarding their application'. Were it to be given jurisdiction over the Europol Convention, the Court would not be permitted to apply Community law, because that falls outside Title VI. It would be able to apply, and indeed be bound to respect, the provisions of Title VI itself. Of particular relevance in this regard would be the provisions of Article K.2(1), which requires that the matters of common interest referred to in Article K.1 (including police co-operation) be dealt with in compliance with the European Convention on Human Rights and the Geneva Convention relating to the Status of Refugees of 28 July 1951 and having regard to the protection afforded by Member States to persons persecuted on political grounds. The Court of Justice may, therefore, assess the convention concerned, and any steps taken to implement it, in the light of fundamental human rights which may not be afforded full protection under the domestic law of certain Member States. This is almost certainly one of the reasons why the United Kingdom and some other Member States are anxious to ensure that its jurisdiction is not invoked under Title VI conventions.

Before considering the implications for the protection of human rights of exclusion of the European Court of Justice from any role in Title VI matters, the possible indirect effect of the Court's interpretation of Community law on such questions must be referred to (Dehousse 1994: 10-12). There is a clear functional overlap between Community law affecting the free movement of persons and the policy issues addressed in the third pillar. There is, therefore, a possibility of conflict between action under the Community legal order and measures adopted under Title VI (Union law). Such conflicts should, in principle, be resolved in favour of the Community dimension because, as the TEU makes clear, the third pillar provisions are 'without prejudice to the powers of the European Community' (Article K.1) and nothing in the TEU should affect the Community treaties (Article M of the TEU; Müller–Graff 1994: 503-6). The ECJ has already been called upon to rule on the competence under Community law of action by the Commission in relation to immigration questions;[55] on that occasion it adopted a restrictive interpretation of Community competence. More recently, it has been asked by the European Parliament to adjudge whether the European Commission has failed to secure the implementation of Article 7A of the EC Treaty (formerly 8A of the EEC Treaty) with regard to the free movement of persons in the internal market (European Parliament 1993: 183–5). Were the court to hold that this provision of Community law requires the complete abolition of border controls in the European Union, this would have far-reaching implications for some of the policy matters addressed in Title VI; the court's judgment might prevent Member States from controlling the movement of third country nationals across internal Community borders. The conditions of entry and movement by third country nationals to the territory of Member States is one of the subjects supposedly reserved for Union action under Title VI (see chapter 2).

The absence of any mandatory Court jurisdiction in respect of Title VI measures may pose constitutional problems within some Member States. It has been observed elsewhere that the TEU does not change but only reinforces 'the current approach of incremental development of rights protection under the aegis of the Court of Justice' (Twomey 1994: 121). But in so far as Court of Justice jurisdiction over Title VI matters is made only permissive and not

---

[55] Cases 281–5 *Germany* et al. v. *Commission* [1987] ECR 3203.

mandatory, the Title VI provisions of the TEU may be regarded as a regressive step in human rights' protection. The German Federal Constitutional Court argued recently in its Maastricht judgment that the intergovernmental character of Title VI means that it only applies to rights and obligations affecting the Member States, not individuals. The implication of this is that no authority is given by Article K to the European Union to take measures which would directly affect basic rights. The German Court added, however, that, should such measures be envisaged at a later date, the Federal Republic would be bound on constitutional grounds to seek further approval for this from the German Parliament.[56] It should now be apparent that the measures being prepared for action under Title VI, in particular the draft conventions currently under consideration, do raise questions of fundamental rights, such as access to asylum, family reunion, data protection and even issues of individual liberty in the field of national criminal law. If the Court of Justice is not available to offer judicial protection in respect of these matters, then the only alternative institutional means of adequate protection for the individual lie with the national courts and/or the European Court of Human Rights in Strasbourg.[57]

National courts may become involved in Title VI matters in a variety of ways. Title VI measures may require domestic legislative incorporation. For example, national legislation may be required to regulate police powers of data-gathering, collation, exchange, *etc.*, to be exercised in relation to Europol. The draft Fraud Convention explicitly envisages the enactment of national criminal measures to combat fraud against the Community budget. Questions of fundamental rights are therefore likely to arise out of the application of national implementing provisions. A number of the Member States' courts may, for instance, be concerned about the application of the principle of proportionality to investigatory powers or the imposition of criminal sanctions (Pitschas 1993: 863-4). These questions will be answered differently depending on the balance struck by national constitutions between state and individual interests. It will be interesting to see whether national courts attach importance in this weighing up exercise to the terms of Article K.2(2) of the TEU

[56] *NJW* 1993: 3049; *CMLR* 1994, 1: 79-80.
[57] See also the limited possibilities relating to the jurisdiction of the International Court of Justice at The Hague (Schermers 1990).

which emphasizes that Title VI shall 'not affect the exercise of responsibilities incumbent on Member States with regard to the maintenance of law and order and the safeguarding of internal security'. In the light of the Federal Constitutional Court's above remarks in the Maastricht judgment, there would clearly be scope for litigants in Germany to challenge national measures implementing the Europol Convention were it demonstrated that any such measure breached the basic rights enshrined in Germany's constitution.[58]

The extent to which national (constitutional) courts would apply the European or Geneva conventions in their review of national measures implementing Title VI conventions such as the Convention on the establishment of Europol is likely to vary according to the status given to such conventions under domestic law. In the United Kingdom, in the absence of domestic legislative incorporation, the provisions of the European Convention on Human Rights may only serve as an interpretative guide for national courts.[59] In other Member States, while they may form a direct source of law, they may rank lower in the national hierarchy of norms than the state's own fundamental rights.[60] National courts may not seek guidance directly from the Strasbourg-based Court on Human Rights on the interpretation of the European Convention on Human Rights in the way that they may refer cases to the European Court of Justice concerning points of Community law under Article 177 of the EC Treaty.

The European Convention institutions may accept jurisdiction in a case only once all domestic remedies have been exhausted (Article 26 of the Convention). The European Court of Human Rights in Strasbourg is therefore unlikely, in the short term, to be an important forum for the resolution of questions of human rights protection arising under Title VI. If intergovernmentalism of the type arising under Title VI is to be confirmed at the 1996 Intergovernmental Conference as the most politically acceptable way of dealing with issues of criminal justice co-operation in the

---

[58] *NJW* 1993: 3049; *CMLR* 1994: 79–80.

[59] See *R. v. Home Secretary*, ex parte *Brind* [1991] AC 696. Article K.2(1) of the TEU, not being itself applicable in the laws of the Member States, may not serve as a 'back door' means of incorporation of the European Convention on Human Rights for the purpose of review by national courts of Title VI measures, in the way that the general principles of Community law may function in Community matters (see also Wade and Bradley 1993: 423-4).

[60] For Germany, see Hesse (1993: 117); Wade and Bradley (1993: 421-3).

EU, then one could envisage cases eventually coming before the Strasbourg Court. Questions would then arise as to the binding effect of that Court's judgments on the institutions with Title VI responsibilities. If the Court were to hold that a fundamental right had been breached as a result of the application of a Title VI measure, then Article K.2(1) of the TEU would provide a persuasive basis on which to seek compliance by the Council of Ministers, say, or by any institution such as Europol, which had been created under Title VI, with the judgment. But Article K.2(1) clearly does not by itself bring about accession by the Community or the TEU to the European Convention on Human Rights, without which the terms of the Convention are not directly binding on EC or EU institutions.

The judicial burden of dealing with any Title VI cases is therefore likely to rest with the national courts. References under Article 177 of the Treaty of Rome provide a mechanism, in the European Community context, for overcoming the often substantial procedural, evidential or linguistic difficulties which national courts may encounter when dealing with cases involving transnational elements.[61] This option will only be open to the national courts in the context of JHA matters where a Title VI convention expressly so provides. Without the assistance of the European Court of Justice, the interpretation and application of Title VI measures and their national derivatives will prove to be uneven across the Member States. This will not only be the case with regard to the importance attached to human rights when weighed against the security and other public interest considerations behind such measures. The effective enforcement of Member States' obligations under Title VI would also be endangered by the exclusion of Court of Justice jurisdiction: national courts cannot provide an adequate answer to enforcement problems beyond the territory of their own Member States.

---

[61] See Judge David Edward in Case T-24/90 *Automec Srl* v. *EC Commission* [1992] 5 Common Market Law Reports 431: 458–9. Judge Edward, acting here as Advocate-General in the Court of First Instance, was commenting on the problems national courts have to overcome before they are able to grant relief in cases involving breach of the Community's competition rules (Arts. 85 and 86 EC Treaty), but his comments can also be applied more generally to the capacity of national courts to deal effectively with cases involving transnational elements. He reminds us that part of the value of the European Court of Justice lies in the fact that it, unlike the national courts, enjoys 'supranational jurisdiction'.

Harmonization of Criminal Laws under Title VI

The matters of 'common interest' referred to in Title VI of the Maastricht Treaty show a close connection with questions of criminal law. This connection is most obvious with regard to the matters set out in Article K.1(9) as subjects for police co-operation within the framework of Europol: 'the prevention and combating of terrorism, unlawful drug-trafficking and other serious forms of international crime' are expressly mentioned in this provision. Also particularly relevant, and already the subject of proposals for action, is Article K.1(5), which refers to the combating of fraud on an international scale. The draft Fraud Convention proposed by the Commission on the basis of this clause has revealed the potential offered by Title VI for narrowing certain gaps between national criminal laws. The draft proposes that all Member States should be obliged to make fraud against the Community budget a criminal offence, punishable by penalties which to some extent are determined in the convention (Article 4). The Commission thus seeks not only to ensure the criminalization of Community fraud but also some harmonization of sanctions imposed at the national level. This goes further than the proposal under the original draft of the money laundering directive which sought only criminalization. Given the hostile reception which that proposal received, it may be that the terms of the Fraud Convention will encounter similar resistance from Member States concerned at intrusions into their national criminal laws. But the crucial difference here, which is likely to encourage the acceptability of the Commission's proposals, is that they do not come in the form of draft Community legislation based on the EC Treaty and generated through a supranational law-making machinery. The United Kingdom's concerns about the money laundering proposals do not, therefore, apply here. Indeed, the Commission's proposals build upon similar United Kingdom proposals for joint action on this question.

It is by no means a foregone conclusion that the Fraud Convention will be adopted in its draft form. It may go too far in the prescription of penalties to be completely acceptable at national level. It does, however, illustrate interesting possibilities regarding the extent to which Title VI may be used to affect national criminal laws. At present, the Commission cannot make proposals for action in relation to police co-operation matters. Member States, however, can. Assuming that the Europol Convention is agreed initially with limited jurisdiction over drug-trafficking, money laundering and certain other categories or organized crime, as the draft Convention itself anticipates, certain Member States are likely to push, in the not too distant future, for extension of the remit of responsibilities of Europol to cover a much wider range of matters, including terrorism (see chapter 2). Pressure is also likely to continue from some quarters to give Europol operational powers. But any central police agency, even if it were entrusted with operational powers which it could exercise in the investigation of serious crime across national frontiers, would, in the absence of some harmonization of substantive or procedural criminal laws in the Member States, find its investigations hampered by significant divergences in the classification and treatment of offences like terrorism (Salisch and Speroni 1994: 9, 17). Title VI provisions provide a basis for proposals to reduce, if not eliminate such differences. The intergovernmental character of Title VI currently seems better suited than Community legislation to encourage convergence of criminal laws in the EU, though any proposals would still face the difficulties which apply generally to questions of harmonization (see chapters 7 and 9).

The limitations of Title VI with regard to harmonization of criminal laws should not be overlooked. The treaty provisions are primarily aimed at improving co-operation between national systems of criminal justice, not at unifying them. The European Union remains far from the situation where it might contemplate the establishment of a 'European Criminal Court' to try common 'Community' or 'Union' crimes (Vercher 1992: 356–62). Article K could be said in a sense to assert the primacy of national institutions in the fight against transnational crime. Successive drafts of the Europol Convention show that it is rather doubtful that Europol will possess any significant autonomous powers. Its effective functioning will depend crucially on the co-operation of national police forces, thus emphasizing national institutional autonomy.

Conclusion

Any European police agency which comes into being in the near future will clearly not find itself embedded in a framework of uniform European criminal laws. The criminal law environment in the

European Union is, however, undergoing a process of limited 'Europeanization'. While the influence of the Community and the Union on national criminal laws is at present not great, developments at both levels show such influence to be increasing. On the basis of rather tenuous treaty foundations, the European Community has acquired an independent sanctioning power which is reflected in penalties which are in some respects indistinguishable from national criminal sanctions. The European Court of Justice has recently lent its support to the Commission's development of new punitive sanctions in the context of the CAP. That Court has also stressed the role of national criminal laws in the enforcement of internal market rules. It is no longer possible for national legislators, or courts, to enact or apply their criminal laws without regard to the implications of Community rules. Community competence falls short, however, of providing any general legal basis for the establishment of a code of Community criminal sanctions or substantive laws.

As in the Community field, the task of combating fraud against the Community budget has prompted developments at EU level which may encourage some limited harmonization of national criminal provisions. More generally, apart from providing a treaty basis for the establishment of Europol, Title VI of the TEU has opened up a number of possibilities for legal steps which may bring about greater convergence of the definitions, and possibly also the punishment, of transnational criminal conduct. The intergovernmental character of Title VI may make progress in these areas more politically acceptable. There are, however, considerable uncertainties and justified worries about the legal acceptability and, therefore, enforceability, of Title VI measures. Many of the concerns relate to the protection of individual rights, both with regard to the question of access to the courts and to substantive questions. Mechanisms of judicial and parliamentary control of executive action under Title VI show serious deficiencies, viewed from the perspective of accepted national constitutional standards. These problems have not been resolved in the Community context either. They may well threaten constitutional acceptability of the Europol Convention in the Member States and, if left unattended to, would deprive Europol of legitimacy.

Member States may have good reasons to leave the legal basis of their actions in JHA matters rather vague or 'fuzzy'. The lack of clear legal obligation attaching to a particular form of action may attract itself to governments. It has been noticeable that in the immigration field Member State governments have been wont to coordinate restrictive action in relation to immigrants from outside the Community by means of 'flexible agreements with political, but no legal, force' (Collinson 1993: 46). Another example of this was provided recently by the 'resolution' limiting access of third country nationals to work in the Community.[62] The objective in such cases may be to alter administrative practice (including cross-border co-operation) without going through the legislative or treaty-making process, though such measures may also pave the way for more formal legal changes. This practice clearly does nothing to enhance legal certainty and blurs lines of accountability (see chapter 8).

---

[62] *European Report*, No. 1960, V, 22 June 1994, pp. 7–8.

7

European Police Co–operation in Criminal Matters

Introduction

Although the need to act to counter transnational crime within the European Union is now acknowledged to be a matter of common concern, developments to date have not departed significantly from the fundamental international law doctrine that enforcement jurisdiction is strictly territorial. Progress has been made in areas such as the sharing of intelligence and the production of common threat assessments. Very modest advances have been made, in the contexts of the Benelux and Schengen arrangements, in facilitating operational cross border policing (Gilmore 1993d: 1962–4). But a general rule, for the members of the EU, as for the rest of the international community, it remains 'a breach of international law for a state without permission to send its agents into the territory of another state to apprehend persons accused of having committed a crime' (Jennings and Watts 1992: 387–8).

Traditional conceptions of international co-operation, such as extradition and mutual legal assistance, retain their centrality in the investigation and prosecution of those involved in criminal activities with an international dimension. Such a legal framework is, however, not a substitute for practical police co-operation. It is a supplement to it; one which is essential where powers of coercion such as search and seizure or arrest need to be exercised in the absence of any indication of a violation of national law. The present chapter examines the most important aspects of the existing framework in relation to the EU Member States and assesses the prospects for future progress.

First it is important to recall what was said in chapter 6 about the limited legislative competence of the EU in criminal matters. The unification of the law through regulations or the approximation of legislation in Member States which flows from the use of directives will only occasionally be available to facilitate law enforcement co-operation (Dine 1993; Schutte 1991). However, as the British Home Office stated in evidence to the Home Affairs Committee in 1989: 'Effective practical police co-operation does not require the laws of every member state to be identical. It is necessary, however, for there to be the maximum possible co-operation in the investigation and prosecution of offences, and that any barriers to effective law enforcement flowing from national boundaries should be identified and tackled' (Home Affairs Committee 1990: 2).

In seeking to provide an appropriate legal environment to combat cross-border crime, some progress can be made through unilateral legislative measures with an extraterritorial reach. In the United Kingdom, for example, the legislature has demonstrated increasing willingness to relax the normally strict emphasis on the principle of the territorial nature of the criminal law. Part I of the Criminal Justice Act 1993 extends the jurisdiction of the courts of England and Wales to try offences of dishonesty which involve significant international elements. A broadly similar approach was adopted in section 71 of the same Act in connection with the important issue of fraud against the Community budget (Warbrick and Sullivan 1994: 460–3).

The domestic courts can also make a contribution by adopting a creative view of the reach of existing law in appropriate cases. This is evident in the 1990 advice of the senior United Kingdom Court, the Judicial Committee of the Privy Council in *Liangsiriprasert* v. *United States Government*[1] and the judgment rendered later the same year by the English Court of Appeal in *R.* v. *Sansom*.[2] As has recently been pointed out elsewhere: 'If Britain, one of the strictest States in matters of jurisdiction, is seen to be moving in this direction, then it can only mean that there is a general acknowledgement of the need for improved systems of international law enforcement.' (Gilbert 1992: 439). Increasingly, however, it has been accepted that national measures are in and of themselves insufficient when seeking to come to terms with modern and sophisticated forms of transnational criminality. Greatly increased international co-operation to co-ordinate law enforcement

[1] [1990] 2 All ER 866.
[2] [1991] 2 All ER 145. But see *R.* v. *Atakpu* [1993] 4 All ER 215.

strategies and promote innovation are viewed as critical (Muller–Rappard 1989: 95).[3]

Finally, although our focus is on European co-operation in criminal matters, developments in other fora, such as the United Nations and the OECD, can also be of considerable relevance, in the area of drug-trafficking in particular. For example, by 31 March 1994, all twelve EU Member States had signed and ten had ratified the 1988 UN Convention Against Illicit Traffic in Narcotic Drugs and Psychotropic Substances. Belgium and Ireland expect to complete the process of bringing the Convention into force in the near future. This treaty instrument, to which over 100 states and the EU itself have become parties, has transformed the landscape of international co-operation in this central area of concern (Gilmore 1992d). Among its innovative features are the obligations imposed to criminalize drug-related money laundering and to provide assistance in the tracing, freezing, seizing and confiscation of the proceeds of such activities. In these areas, and in others, the 1988 Convention has established international minimum standards. It has therefore constituted a common base line from which both the EU and the Council of Europe (CoE) have worked in seeking to articulate more ambitious initiatives.[4]

The Role of the Council of Europe

The EU Member States have contributed to enhanced co-operation in criminal matters on an *inter se* basis since the 1970s, but the leading role in this area has thus far been played by the Strasbourg-based Council of Europe (Carlson and Zagaris 1991). This body, established in 1949, has for long given priority to activities in the legal sphere. Its efforts to promote the modernization of the law and closer co-operation between its members (which include, among others, the fifteen current members of the EU, have resulted in the conclusion of more than 145 treaties and conventions (approximately 20 relate to the penal field). The CoE has also been in the forefront of developments concerning international data protection rules and principles, including those in the police sector.

Given the overlap in membership, both the CoE and the EU have recognized the need for co-operation in areas of mutual inter-

---

[3] For the basis of Community competence see, Art. 209(a). For its relevance to Title VI, see Art. K.1.(5).

[4] See ch. 6 for a discussion of the EU directive on money laundering.

est. The current arrangements for co-operation are detailed in an exchange of letters of 16 June 1987 between the Secretary-General of the CoE and the President of the EC Commission. This, in general terms, sought to enhance existing relations between, on the one hand, the CoE Committee of Ministers and the Secretary-General, and, on the other, the EC Commission, to ensure good liaison and co-operation, and to improve the exchange of information on matters of common concern. The importance of intensifying co-operation with Brussels was emphasized on 5 May 1989 by a resolution and a declaration of the Committee of Ministers of the CoE.

The CoE has, in recent years, been concerned about how best to accommodate EU interests in both the elaboration and entry into force of its multilateral treaty instruments. The then Secretary-General of the CoE, Marcelino Oreja, undertook in the June 1987 exchange of letters to invite the EC Commission to participate in the work of the committees drafting texts on matters of common interest and to facilitate Commission participation at the meetings of ministers' deputies at which draft treaties were discussed. Finally, he undertook in new multilateral initiatives to consider 'the appropriateness of inserting a clause allowing for the EC to become a Contracting Party to the convention or agreement: it is understood that the insertion of such a clause would in no way prejudice the decision which the competent bodies of the Community might finally take with regard to the conclusion of the convention or agreement by the Community.' The EC subsequently participated in the work of the committees which drafted the 1989 Convention on Insider Trading and the 1990 Convention on Laundering, Search, Seizure and Confiscation of the Proceeds from Crime. Interestingly, Article 15(1) of the former 'is aimed at allowing, *inter alia*, the accession of intergovernmental organizations such as the European Economic Community' (Council of Europe 1989: 15).

Some CoE Conventions seek to counter specific forms of criminality of European concern, such as terrorism and money laundering, but the organization is better known for the promotion of traditional mechanisms of inter-state co-operation sometimes known as procedural regimes (Nadelmann 1990). Its initiatives in such areas as the transfer of criminal proceedings and sentenced persons have helped to ensure 'blanket cover' (Wilkitzki 1992: 276);

its instruments dealing with extradition and mutual legal assistance are, as we have seen, of particular importance in assisting law enforcement co-operation (Home Affairs Committee 1990: xxxi).

The traditional process of extradition may be increasing in importance as informal law enforcement practices come under increased judicial scrutiny. For example, in 1986 the European Court of Human Rights held that the strategy of resorting to deportation as a disguised form of extradition was incompatible with the European Convention on Human Rights.[5] Similarly, in its consideration of an application made by Walter Stocke against the Federal Republic of Germany, the European Commission of Human Rights concluded that the state-sponsored abduction of a fugitive from the territory of a third country may be incompatible with Article 5 paragraph 1 of the Convention.[6] Reflecting a changed climate, in June 1993, the House of Lords,[7] moved away from the preponderant practice of domestic courts in the United Kingdom and held that in instances involving either collusive deportation or abduction the courts possessed a discretion to stay proceedings on the ground of abuse of process (Gilbert 1991: 183–94; Gilmore 1993e; Choo 1994).

The Council of Europe and Mutual Assistance in the Administration of Justice

Extradition

Although extradition is a mechanism of co-operation of great antiquity, the underlying approach of customary international law has retained a disturbing simplicity. In particular, it is accepted that a state has no duty to extradite in the absence of a treaty. However, there is no rule of customary law which precludes extradition in the absence of a treaty and many countries within the civil law tradition provide for this in their domestic laws. By contrast, law in the United Kingdom has only allowed for such *ad hoc*

---

[5] *Bozano Case* (5/1985/91/138).

[6] Report of the Commission of 12 Oct. 1989 (Application No. 11755/85) at paras. 167–8.

[7] *Bennett* v. *Horseferry Road Magistrates* [1993] 3 All ER 138, at 155. But see, *In re Schmidt*, (*The Times*, 1 July 1994) in which the House of Lords restricted this doctrine to pending trials in England. It was thus not available in relation to extradition proceedings from the United Kingdom to third countries—in this case Germany.

procedures since the entry into force of the Extradition Act, 1989 (Gilmore 1990: 370–1).

Long before this change in British practice members of the international community, especially within Europe, had however developed an extensive network of bilateral extradition agreements. As Stein has noted, 'by the end of the 19th century a coherent body of legal rules governing extradition had developed whose major principles still apply in contemporary extradition law' (Stein 1985: 223).

No global, comprehensive extradition convention has yet evolved. Only in 1990 did the UN system produce, as part of a wider effort to promote international mutual assistance in the administration of justice, a model bilateral extradition treaty (Clark 1993: 141–6). At the global level, there have been two emphases: a range of crime-specific multilateral agreements in relation to forms of criminality have been developed; for these forms of criminality, mechanisms have been put in place to minimize the possibility of offenders escaping justice through the mere expedient of crossing an international boundary (Clark 1988). The requirement for state parties to either extradite or prosecute the alleged offender is central to both these objectives.

Crime-specific global agreements have played a positive role in international criminal law enforcement co-operation, but the need to co-ordinate and standardize extradition practices and procedures has been pursued by other means. Europe has been the site of the most developed practices and procedures. As Gilbert notes: 'Europe for these purposes should be seen as a series of concentric and overlapping circles, with various extradition arrangements in force and some states belonging to more than one grouping. The outer circle with respect to extradition would encompass the CoE's European Extradition Convention of 1957' (Gilbert 1991: 27). This regional agreement has over time become the central and single most important initiative relating to extradition within Europe. It sets out in some detail, in a manner which demonstrates the influence of the civil law tradition, provisions governing all important aspects of extradition practice. As indicated in Table 7.1, all EU Member States prior to the 1995 expansion have signed and all, except Belgium, have now ratified this pan-European instrument. All three countries involved in the latest round of expansion of EU membership (Austria, Finland and Sweden), together with Norway, which had candidate status but declined to join, are also parties.

TABLE 7.1. *Participation in European Convention on Extradition 1957** *(Status as of 7/10/94)*

Member State	Signature	Ratification or Accession	Reservations (R) and Declarations (D)
Belgium	1957	–	–
Denmark	1957	1962	R/D
France	1957	1986	R/D
Germany	1957	1976	R/D
Greece	1957	1961	R
Ireland	1966	1966	R/D
Italy	1957	1963	R
Luxembourg	1957	1976	R/D
Netherlands	1965	1969	R/D
Portugal	1977	1990	R/D
Spain	1979	1982	R/D
United Kingdom	1990	1991	R/D

* Entered into force 18/4/1960.

Two basic decisions were taken by the Committee of Experts which drafted the 1957 Convention. First, in order to ensure that the system was sufficiently flexible and sensitive to national needs, states were permitted to enter reservations to the Convention (Bartsch 1991: 500). This practice has been so extensive that it has come to form a barrier to ratification by other states. As Karle points out: 'The situation which has arisen through the use of reservations has aroused the profound concern of the Belgian authorities, who cannot help fearing that the European Convention on Extradition, instead of simplifying and improving communications with the other European countries regarding extradition, will merely render them more complex and, in certain cases, constitute a direct impediment to sound justice' (Karle 1970: 67). Secondly, while the major motivating factor behind the Convention was to promote international co-operation to counter crime, a major effort was made to ensure that this goal was balanced by provisions to protect the fundamental interests of the individual in extradition proceedings (Council of Europe 1985a: 9–10). Subsequent jurisprudence of both the European Court of Human Rights and the Strasbourg-based Commission have reinforced the importance of the protection of the individual in the extradition process (Van den Wyngaert 1990).

A central provision of the Convention is an obligation of surrender only for the specified categories of offences and, as is common, subject to the requirement of double criminality[8] (Schultz 1970: 13). It embraces the modern 'no list' or 'eliminative' method in defining extraditable offences and sets a minimum sentencing threshold for those accused of criminal offences of at least one year's deprivation of liberty in both the requesting and requested states.[9]

The requesting state need not demonstrate before the courts of the requested country that it possesses sufficient evidence of the guilt of the accused to justify the initiation of criminal proceedings (Wilkitzki 1991: 285). Under the Convention this question is, in principle, to be determined by the requesting country. This provision is fundamental to the efficiency of the extradition system. However, Denmark has reserved the right, in special circumstances, to require the production of 'evidence establishing a sufficient presumption of guilt on the part of the person concerned. Should such evidence be deemed insufficient, extradition may be refused'. Generally speaking, however, extradition requests only need to be supported by limited categories of documentary information.[10] The Convention also envisages urgent requests for the provisional arrest of the person sought pending the initiation of formal extradition procedures (Article 16). This facility has, however, been resorted to so frequently that it has given rise to official concern and calls for restraint (Bartsch 1991: 509).

The 1957 text also embraces the well-established principle that 'the requested state should exercise some control over the prosecution of the surrendered fugitive for other crimes committed before his surrender' (HM Government 1985: 13). Article 14 accordingly gives expression to the rule of speciality whereby the extradited person may not be proceeded against for offences committed prior to extradition 'other than that for which he was extradited' save with the prior consent of the party which surrendered him or 'when that person, having had an opportunity to leave the territory of the Party to which he has been surrendered, has not done so

---

[8] *i.e.* that the conduct in question is prohibited by the criminal law in both the requesting and the requested state.

[9] See also Art. 25 for the definition of a detention order. The system is, however, flexible enough to permit the use of a method of listing extraditable offences. This method is applied by Israel and was formally adopted by Switzerland.

[10] Art. 12(2)(b). See also, Art. 13.

within 45 days of his final discharge, or has returned to that territory after leaving it'.[11] This rule, designed to minimize the opportunities for abuse, is reinforced by Article 15 which provides for a similar element of control over the possibility of the individual in question being subject to re-extradition to a third state.

The Convention also contains a number of articles which provide for exceptions to the obligation to extradite and these have a major impact on the availability of this procedure in individual cases. Article 4, following the generality of the modern practice, excludes purely military offences from the scope of application of the Convention, while Articles 9 and 10 provide the individual concerned with protection against extradition in certain cases involving the principle *non bis in idem*[12] and the acquisition of immunity from prosecution by reason of lapse of time. Similarly, by virtue of Article 5 extradition is available in respect of fiscal offences 'only if the Contracting Parties have so decided in respect of any such offence or category of offences.'

Important though these restrictions are, greatest concern has been focused on the extradition of nationals and on the operation of the political offence exception. On the first, Article 6(1)(a) states simply that: 'A Contracting Party shall have the right to refuse extradition of its nationals.' This approach is buttressed, in Article 21(2), by a provision permitting a state to decline to grant a request for the transit of its nationals through its territory for extradition.[13]

Civil law jurisdictions, unlike those in the common law tradition, are normally prevented for constitutional, legal, or policy reasons from extraditing their own citizens (Duke 1970) thus expressing an historic lack of trust in foreign legal systems (Gilbert 1991: 96-7). In the case of Germany, for example, a declaration was lodged when ratifying the Convention in 1976 to the effect that the extradition of its nationals 'to a foreign country is not permitted by virtue of Article 16, paragraph 2, of the Basic Law for the Federal Republic of Germany and must, therefore, be refused in every case'. Even in cases of transit through German air space without any intention to land, 'an assurance will be required to the

---

[11] Art. 14(1)(b).

[12] *i.e.* no one should be prosecuted more than once for the same offence.

[13] In becoming a party to the Convention the UK entered a reservation to Article 21 to the effect that it is unable to accept any of its provisions.

effect that, according to the facts known to the requesting Party and the documents in its possession, the extradited person is not a German and does not claim such status'.[14] Where extradition is precluded on the basis of the nationality of the accused, the Convention, in Article 6(2), resorts to the concept of the vicarious administration of justice as expressed in the principle *aut dedere, aut judicare*[15] (Meyer 1990; Council of Europe 1985a: 17). Civil law jurisdictions make very extensive use of the nationality principle of jurisdiction in relation to criminal matters and normally have a legal basis for bringing prosecutions against their nationals charged with offences committed abroad (Gilbert 1992: 417-18). Although the possibility often exists of initiating proceedings against nationals for extraterritorial offences, a number of practical difficulties, including those relating to the location of evidence and the availability of witnesses, frequently arise and adversely affect the ability to secure convictions, however.

The other major obstacle to a comprehensive extradition framework is the contentious issue of political offences, which is dealt with in Article 3. The idea that individuals who have been accused or convicted of offences of a political character should not be subject to extradition originated in the liberal democratic political theory of the late 18th and early 19th centuries (Van den Wyngaert 1980). As Abraham Soafer, Legal Adviser to the United States Department of State, explains: 'The great 18th century revolutions were based, in part, upon the notion that individuals have the right to engage in revolutionary political activity in pursuit of liberty . . . In the wake of those revolutions the emerging democracies of Western Europe did not want to surrender to foreign sovereign's revolutionaries who had committed offences in those nations in the course of exercising their political rights' (Soafer 1985).

This position is expressed in paragraph 1 of the 1957 Convention as follows: 'Extradition shall not be granted if the

---

[14] Although such declarations are not strictly required by the terms of Art. 6 a number of countries have elected, for the avoidance of doubt, to formulate them. These include, among others, France, Greece, Luxembourg and Portugal. Denmark, in order to comply with its obligations under pre-existing Nordic arrangements has, by formal declaration, provided for a very extensive definition of nationals for this purpose. Luxembourg has reserved the right not to extradite its nationals which, by declaration, are deemed to include 'foreigners integrated into the Luxembourg community in so far as they can be prosecuted within Luxembourg for the Act is respect of which extradition is requested'.

[15] *I.e.* extradite or prosecute.

offence in respect of which it is requested is regarded by the requested party as a political offence or as an offence connected with a political offence.'[16] The term 'political offence' is not subject to definition elsewhere in the text and is left to the requested party to determine in each case; this was a reflection of the near universal practice, both internationally and domestically. Unfortunately, some of the difficulties and disputes which have arisen are attributable to the lack of an agreed international definition and the differing approaches which have evolved at the national level (Stein 1985: 226; Van den Wyngaert 1991: 295; Gilbert 1991:120–31; Gilmore 1992b; Delany and Hogan 1993).

Although the political offence exception has been widely provided for, it has always been the subject of controversy and calls have been made for its restriction or abolition. The demand for restriction can be traced back to 1854 when France failed to secure the extradition from Belgium of two individuals who had attempted to assassinate Emperor Louis Napoleon on the grounds that their offence was of a political character. Belgium amended its legislation to ensure that the same difficulty could not arise again. This particular restriction, commonly known as the 'attentat' clause,[17] is reflected in Article 3(3) of the European Convention. A number of states, including Denmark and France, were not prepared to accept this article and reserved the right to consider each case on its merits.[18]

The 1957 Convention, in one sense, has the effect of extending the scope of protection available in cases which have wider political ramifications. This flows from the decision to include a 'non discrimination' or 'asylum' clause; Article 3(2) provides that extradition shall be refused 'if the requested Party has substantial grounds for believing that a request for extradition for an ordinary criminal offence has been made for the purpose of prosecuting or punishing a person on account of his race, religion, nationality or political opinion, or that that person's position may be prejudiced for any of these reasons'. This innovation had a major influence on

---

[16] See also Art. 21(1) concerning transit for political offences.

[17] *i.e.*, a clause to the effect that assassination of a Head of State, whatever the motive of the perpetrator, is deemed never to fall within the political offence exception.

[18] The UK has reserved the right to apply this provision 'only in respect of States parties to the European Convention on the Suppression of Terrorism'. For the saving of the obligations contained in other international agreements see, Art. 3(4).

world-wide extradition practice and in the formulation of much domestic legislation. It extended the scope of protection for the individual because, while it overlaps with the traditional political exception rule, it does not fully coincide with it (Young 1984: 220; Home Office 1982: 36).

The Convention, though clearly an imperfect compromise, constituted a step forward in terms of international co-operation (Bartsch 1991: 500). Furthermore, in the years since 1957 the CoE has sought to improve upon it. This has been done in a series of recommendations by the Committee of Ministers on a variety of issues relating to its practical application. In addition, the CoE has promoted the elaboration of two additional formal agreements designed both to amend and to supplement the original. Both, though not widely ratified, are now in force (see Table 7.2).[19]

The most significant innovation in the scope of extradition is contained in chapter II of the Second Additional Protocol concluded in 1978. This brings fiscal offences (*i.e.* those relating to taxes, duties, customs and like matters) fully within the system (Council of Europe 1978a: 8).[20]

A concern with administrative efficiency is reflected in the 1978 text. Article 12(1) of the 1957 Convention established the general rule that requests for extradition should be communicated through the diplomatic channel. Experience demonstrated that reliance on diplomatic communications frequently gave rise to delays while direct contact between Ministries of Justice, utilized in the 1959 European Convention on Mutual Assistance in Criminal Matters, functioned in a more satisfactory manner (Council of Europe 1978a: 13). Chapter V of the 1978 Protocol provides for the alternative system to be used.

The Protocols contain a number of provisions which affect the level of protection afforded to the individual. Chapter I of the 1975 text restricts the level of protection provided by the political offence exception. It stipulates that crimes against humanity and war crimes 'shall not be considered' to be political. As the official Explanatory Report noted, this approach 'was in line with what

---

[19] Austria and Finland have ratified only the Second Additional Protocol. Norway and Sweden are parties to both.

[20] Ch. I of this Protocol extends the scope of the Convention to what is known as accessory extradition. The UK ratified this Protocol in 1994 but accepted its obligations in respect of fiscal offences only.

TABLE 7.2. *Participation in the 1975 Additional Protocol* and the 1978 Second Additional Protocol** to the European Convention on Extradition (Status as of 7/10/94)*

Member State	Additional Protocol			Second Additional Protocol		
	Signature	Ratification or Accession	Reservations (R) and Declarations (D)	Signature	Ratification or Accession	Reservations (R) and Declarations (D)
Belgium	–	–	–	–	–	–
Denmark	1976	1978	D	1982	1983	–
France	–	–	–	–	–	–
Germany	–	–	–	1985	1991	–
Greece	1980	–	–	1980	–	–
Ireland	–	–	–	–	–	–
Italy	–	–	–	1980	1985	–
Luxembourg	1975	–	–	–	–	–
Netherlands	1979	1982	D	1979	1982	–
Portugal	1977	1990	–	1978	1990	–
Spain	1983	1985	–	1983	1985	–
United Kingdom	–	–	–	1992	1994	R

* Entered into force 20/8/79
** Entered into force 5/6/83

was considered to be a current trend towards defining political offences and regarding certain crimes as so abominable that no immunity could be granted' (Council of Europe 1975: 7). In spite of the relatively limited amendment of the Protocol's restriction on the political offence exception, a clear majority of CoE members have yet to accept it. The record of the EU Member States is particularly poor. Table 7.2 shows that only four of the twelve Member States prior to the 1995 expansion have ratified the 1975 instrument, of which two (Denmark and the Netherlands) have declined to accept its obligations in the political offence area.[21]

Prior to the finalization of the Protocol both the Consultative Assembly and the Committee of Ministers of the CoE gave consideration to the growth of transnational terrorism and the effect of the political offence exception on efforts to ensure that those responsible for terrorist acts were brought to justice (Council of Europe 1979: 5–6). This consideration initiated a review culminating in the drafting of the 1977 European Convention on the Suppression of Terrorism (Vercher 1992: 350–2). This Convention quickly attained the necessary degree of support and entered into force in September 1978. Among others, all twelve members of the EU prior to the 1995 expansion (see Table 7.3) as well as the three new members, Austria, Finland, Norway, and Sweden have ratified it.

This instrument builds upon the 1975 precedent by defining as 'non-political a list of specified offences of the type used by violent terrorists' (Gilbert 1985: 712; Council of Europe 1979: 5–6). Article 1 enumerates serious offences, including those involving the use of bombs and automatic weapons, which shall not, for purposes of extradition between contracting parties, be regarded as political offences, or offences connected with political offences, or as having been inspired by political motives (Dowrick 1987: 640). This is supplemented by Article 2 which, framed in discretionary terms, permits each party to treat certain other offences similarly, including acts of violence 'against the life, physical integrity or liberty of a person'. The United Kingdom has exercised this option when giving domestic legal effect to the Convention.

The effect of the 1977 Convention is that the political offence exception is withdrawn in relation to Article 1 type activities but

---

[21] Art. 6 permits contracting parties to opt to accept either of the substantive Chs. or both.

TABLE 7.3. *Participation in European Convention on the Suppression of Terrorism, 1977* (Status as of 5/11/93)*

Member State	Signature	Ratification or Accession	Reservations (R) and Declarations (D)
Belgium	1977	1985	R
Denmark	1977	1978	R
France	1977	1987	R/D
Germany	1977	1978	–
Greece	1977	1988	R
Ireland	1986	1989	–
Italy	1977	1986	R
Luxembourg	1977	1981	–
Netherlands	1977	1985	R
Portugal	1977	1981	R
Spain	1978	1980	–
United Kingdom	1977	1978	–

* Entered into force 4/8/78.

the accused may be afforded another kind of protection by Article 5, in the form of an 'asylum' or 'non-discrimination' clause. Furthermore, while the Convention is designed to facilitate extradition it does not require it. However, where extradition is not possible due to the nationality of the accused or other factors, Article 7 resorts to an extradite—or prosecute—obligation. Article 6 imposes certain obligations to create extraterritorial jurisdiction over Article 1 offences in order to ensure that prosecutions can, in fact, be launched in these circumstances.

It is often claimed that the conclusion of this Convention is evidence of the closer co-operation in the fight against serious transnational criminality. This co-operation, it is asserted, is made possible by 'the special climate of mutual confidence' which exists among members of the organization 'based on their collective recognition of the rule of law and the protection of human rights . . .' (Council of Europe 1979: 10). While there may be some truth in such assertions, very real limits to mutual confidence continue to exist. Within the overall framework of the 1977 Convention, this is well demonstrated by the facility, provided in Article 13, to make extensive reservations to the central obligations contained in Article 1 (Lowe and Young 1978: 318; Van den Wyngaert 1991: 301). When extradition is refused on account of an Article 13 reservation, the obligation to submit the case to the domestic prosecutorial authorities for the purpose of instituting criminal proceedings, contained in Article 7, is triggered.

The reservations procedure has been heavily used by participating states. Of the twelve members of the EU prior to the 1995 enlargement only five (Germany, Ireland, Luxembourg, Spain and the United Kingdom) declined to take advantage of Article 13. A further five (Denmark, France, Greece, Italy and the Netherlands) reserved the right to refuse extradition in respect of all Article 1 offences. Portugal, in an action with much the same effect, made its participation in the Convention subject to its constitutional provisions relating to non-extradition on political grounds. Belgium reserved its right to decline to extradite in respect of offences which it considers political excepting those 'committed upon the taking of hostages'. Unsurprisingly, commentators have generally concluded that the 1977 Convention has not had a significant practical impact on European extradition practice (Van den Wyngaert 1991; Bartsch 1991: 504; Gilbert 1991: 142).

Mutual Legal Assistance

Mutual legal assistance means the process whereby one state provides assistance to another in the investigation and prosecution of criminal offences. This form of inter-state co-operation is of relatively recent origin, but a general consensus has developed about its scope. It includes unglamorous, but highly practical matters, such as providing written and documentary evidence for use in foreign court proceedings; the service of summonses and other judicial documents on behalf of another country; making arrangements for the personal attendance of witnesses at court hearings abroad (including that of persons in custody in the requested state); and, the search for and seizure of materials for use in evidence in overseas proceedings. More recently, a trend has developed, in response to the perceived need to target the financial base of organized criminal activity, to extend its reach to encompass the tracing, freezing, and confiscation of the proceeds of crime. Mutual assistance is the process used 'to unlock similar laws between countries on behalf of one another' (Kriz 1992: 729). It does not include arrest or detention with a view to extradition, the transfer of persons in custody to serve sentences abroad, the transfer of proceedings in criminal matters, or, outside of the area of confiscation of criminal proceeds, the enforcement of foreign criminal judgments. One leading commentator has stressed: 'Obtaining evidence from abroad . . . is as essential to the success of criminal prosecutions as collecting intelligence and obtaining the offender. It is also the most dependent upon legal formalities and affords the least latitude for the sorts of informal measures and understandings upon which police normally rely in their international dealings' (Nadelmann 1993: 313).

Although such forms of co-operation are of clear practical value, the attitude of the international community slowed its development. A number of factors, including a strong disinclination to enforce the penal laws of third countries, account for this (McClean 1992: 120-1). The orthodox international law position can be summarized as the absence of a duty to render assistance in the absence of a treaty (Geiger 1986: 249), coupled with a customary law rule that judicial and enforcement activities in a foreign state, in the absence of consent, constitutes a violation of territorial sovereignty (Dussaix 1971: 38).

The first major advance in this area at the multilateral level came with the conclusion in 1959 of the European Convention on Mutual Assistance in Criminal Matters. This Treaty, which entered into force in 1962, has been ratified by all members of the EU prior to the 1995 expansion with the exception of Ireland (see Table 7.4).[22] The three new members are among the other states which have become parties to it. Under its terms the contracting parties undertake to afford each other a broad range of measures of mutual assistance.[23] It contains detailed provision for all of the core elements of mutual assistance with the exception of the tracing, freezing, and confiscation of the proceeds of major crime. It also allows for a range of additional forms of co-operation including the periodic exchange of information concerning the conviction of nationals of other parties and the laying of information by one state with a view to the taking of proceedings in the courts of another. The latter, which reflects the influence of the civil law tradition of continental Europe in the drafting of this Convention, 'refers in particular to cases where a person, having committed an offence in the requesting country, takes refuge in the territory of the requested country and cannot be extradited' (Council of Europe 1969: 23).

---

[22] Ireland has recently enacted legislation, the Criminal Justice Act 1994, which makes extensive provision for mutual legal assistance.

[23] See Arts. 1(1), 15(4) and 24.

TABLE 7.4. *Participation in European Convention on Mutual Assistance in Criminal Matters, 1959* (Status as of 7/10/94)*

Member State	Signature	Ratification or Accession	Reservations (R) and Declarations (D)
Belgium	1959	1975	R/D
Denmark	1959	1962	R/D
France	1961	1967	R/D
Germany	1959	1976	R/D
Greece	1959	1962	R
Ireland	–	–	–
Italy	1959	1961	D
Luxembourg	1959	1976	R/D
Netherlands	1965	1969	R/D
Portugal	1979	1994	–
Spain	1979	1982	R/D
United Kingdom	1991	1991	R/D

* Entered into force 12/6/62.

The 1959 Convention has a number of characteristics which are important for law enforcement co-operation. First, the rules for mutual assistance are made less restrictive because, unlike extradition law and practice, the liberty of the individual in the requested state was not at issue. For example, assistance is granted in cases involving proceedings against nationals of the requested state. It was, however, 'still felt to be advisable to exclude military offences, and to allow discretion in relation to the more contentious areas of political and fiscal offences' (McClean 1992: 131). A second feature was to distinguish the formal provision of mutual assistance in criminal matters from operational forms of police and customs co-operation. A majority 'thought it best not to force the existing practice of the police into a rigid mould, besides which, the Statute of the International Criminal Police Organization (Interpol) already regulated mutual assistance between police authorities' (Council of Europe 1969: 8). The Convention neither regulates nor precludes operational assistance between law enforcement officials.

The CoE has kept the operation of this Convention under review. A number of recommendations have been made by the Committee of Ministers and in 1978 an Additional Protocol was concluded. The latter contains measures on the extension of the

Convention to fiscal offences, the provision of mutual assistance concerning the enforcement of sentences and similar sanctions, and the communication of information from judicial records (Council of Europe 1978b). Eight of the existing members of the EU (see Table 7.5) as well as all three states included in the 1995 expansion have ratified it.

TABLE 7.5. *Participation in the 1978 Additional Protocol to the European Convention on Mutual Assistance in Criminal Matters* (Status as of 7/10/94)*

Member State	Signature	Ratification or Accession	Reservations (R) and Declarations (D)
Belgium	1978	–	–
Denmark	1982	1983	–
France	1990	1991	–
Germany	1985	1991	R/D
Greece	1980	1981	–
Ireland	–	–	–
Italy	1980	1985	D
Luxembourg	–	–	–
Netherlands	1979	1982	–
Portugal	1980	–	–
Spain	1985	1991	R
United Kingdom	1991	1991	D

* Entered into force 12/4/82.

Other CoE instruments to support the efficient administration of justice include the 1989 Convention on Insider Trading and its Protocol. This instrument was designed to combat multi-jurisdictional insider trading and, as such, is part of a wider recent international trend to promote enhanced co-operation between business regulatory authorities confronted by the problems of global trading in securities (Gilmore 1994). A structure of administrative co-operation has been established, based on the exchange of information between designated authorities relating, in the words of Article 2, 'to matters establishing or giving rise to the belief that irregular operations of insider trading have been carried out'. Article 3 provides the option for state parties, on the basis of reciprocity, to extend the scope of these exchanges to encompass certain broader stock market regulatory matters such as price manipulation. In these specialized areas the scheme embodied in the 1959 Convention and the 1978 Protocol remains relevant. This is especially the case when the information obtained through these administrative exchanges is needed for use in criminal prosecutions. Under the terms of Article 7(4) such information may be so used only if it could also have been obtained within the framework of the 1959 and 1978 treaties or other mutual assistance in criminal matters agreed between the parties (Council of Europe 1989: 12–14).

The most recent and most important initiative taken in Strasbourg to promote co-operation in respect of crime taken is the 1990 Convention on Laundering, Search, Seizure and Confiscation of the Proceeds of Crime (Carlson and Zagaris 1991: 567–72). Adopted by the Committee of Ministers in September of 1990, it entered into force three years later. Of the six states which have ratified it thus far, four (the United Kingdom, the Netherlands, Italy and Finland) are members of the EU. This Convention is intended to undermine the financial power of those involved in highly lucrative forms of criminal activity. Its ambitious text builds upon the precedents established by the 1986 Commonwealth scheme (McClean 1992: 234–5) and the 1988 UN Convention Against Illicit Traffic in Narcotic Drugs and Psychotropic Substances (Gilmore 1992d: 13–18), but is more elaborate than the former and more ambitious than the latter. The 1990 Convention represents the current state of the art in giving formal expression to this increasingly important law enforcement strategy.

The text imposes obligations on participating states at the domestic level and in international co-operation. In the former domain, the parties are required to adopt legislative and other measures to enable them to confiscate both the proceeds and the instrumentalities of crime. Countries must, in addition, be able to identify and trace property liable to confiscation and to take other provisional measures. In an approach similar to the 1988 UN drugs Convention, Article 4(1) seeks to ensure the necessary access to banking, financial and commercial records and stipulates that: 'A Party shall not decline to act under the provisions of this article on grounds of bank secrecy.'

The intention of the drafters was to extend the requirements of confiscation, and the associated obligation to criminalize money laundering contained in Article 6 (Gilmore 1993c: 4–5), beyond drug-related offences but not to impose such duties in relation to all forms of crime. The formulation of reservations as to scope was permitted in Articles 2(2) and 6(4). The approach adopted is an invitation to make domestic legislation as wide-ranging as possible. The Committee of Experts, established by the European Committee on Crime Problems, agreed that states which took advantage of this facility 'should review their legislation periodically and expand the applicability of confiscation measures, in order to be able to restrict the reservations subsequently as much as possible. They also agreed that such measures should at least be made applicable to serious criminality and to offences which generate huge profits' (Council of Europe 1991: 17).

Chapter III of the Convention contains detailed provisions on international co-operation for the purposes of both investigations and proceedings directed towards the confiscation of proceeds and instrumentalities. Parties are obligated in Article 13, upon receipt of a request from another participating nation for confiscation of proceeds situated in its territory, either to enforce an order to that effect already made by a court of the requesting country or to 'submit the request to its competent authorities for the purpose of obtaining an order of confiscation and, if such an order is granted, enforce it'.

Article 8 of the Laundering Convention goes further in facilitating investigative assistance than the 1959 arrangements for mutual assistance. The Secretary to the Committee of Experts noted: 'The paragraph is to be interpreted broadly. It allows for police co-operation that does not involve coercive action' (Nilsson 1991: 434)—a point reinforced by the wording of Article 24(5) on direct communication between competent authorities. Parties are obliged to consider the domestic adoption of a number of special investigative techniques including 'monitoring orders, observation, interception of telecommunications, access to computer systems and orders to produce specific documents' (Article 4(2)). Any techniques adopted could also be used to advance the process of international co-operation (Council of Europe 1991: 18). A further innovation permits the spontaneous provision of information thought to be of assistance to another party in initiating or carrying out relevant investigations. Nothing prevents this permissive provision being made obligatory under domestic law (Nilsson 1991: 435).

The Inner Circles of European Cooperation

The CoE has sought to recognize the need for flexibility in promoting enhanced co-operation in the administration of justice. However, only occasionally has this taken the form of an explicit recognition of the direct interest of the EU in the subject matter of agreements. One example is the September 1989 Convention on Insider Trading, the Protocol of which was specifically designed, at the request of the EC Commission, to accommodate the special position of EU Members which become parties to it (Council of Europe 1989: 4).

It takes the form of a 'disconnection clause' and is designed to afford full protection to the *inter se* relations of EU Members which are governed by the Council Directive of 13 November 1989 on coordinating regulations on insider dealing (McClean 1992: 297). As the official CoE explanatory report makes clear, under the Protocol EU Members shall, in their mutual relations, 'apply Community rules and shall not therefore apply the rules arising from the Convention except in so far as there is no Community rule governing the particular subject concerned' (Council of Europe 1989: 16). The Convention proper, however, governs the relationship between relevant EU Members and other states which become party to it.

More commonly, however, the flexibility of Strasbourg Conventions is achieved in other ways. One such mechanism, mentioned earlier, takes the form of permitting the formulation of often extensive reservations. More constructively, it is often achieved by safeguarding certain advanced or simplified forms of co-operation contained in pre-existing arrangements, and by permitting the subsequent conclusion of supplementary strengthening agreements. For example, both the 1957 and 1959 Conventions save the system of co-operation in operation between the Nordic countries and recognize the special tradition in United Kingdom-Irish relations of reliance on relatively uniform domestic legislation (Council of Europe 1985a: 28-9; Council of Europe 1969: 36–7; Gilmore 1993b: 51–4).

The strategy of permitting supplementary agreements has proved useful both in dealing with both bilateral relationships and in allowing progress at the sub-regional level. Germany has taken advantage of the permissive wording of Article 28(2) of the 1957

Convention to conclude a number of bilateral extradition treaties (Langfeldt 1991); it has also entered into five bilateral agreements to improve the efficiency of mutual legal assistance. That there is scope for such a strategy even in the most advanced CoE texts is shown by the 15 September 1993 Agreement between the United Kingdom and the Netherlands to supplement and facilitate the operation of the 1990 Laundering Convention.

Belgium, Luxembourg and the Netherlands have taken full advantage of this dispensation in the context of the Benelux Economic Union. The preamble to their Treaty of 27 June 1962 Concerning Extradition and Mutual Assistance in Criminal Matters states, 'by reason of the close ties uniting their countries and particularly in consequence of the abolition of the examination of persons at the internal frontiers, it is necessary to extend the extradition of offenders to a larger number of offences, to simplify the formalities connected therewith and to permit mutual assistance in criminal matters to a greater extent than is provided for in the existing treaties'.[24] The 1962 Convention has, among other things,[25] increased the range of extraditable offences, provided for direct communication between Ministries of Justice, relaxed the speciality rule, and included a summary or simplified procedure to expedite extradition with the consent of the individual concerned. Both Luxembourg and the Netherlands therefore lodged reservations, on becoming parties to the 1957 Convention, to save the Benelux arrangements. Both also reserved their freedom of action in respect of their future relations with other EU Member States.

The experience of the Benelux countries under this arrangement was particularly influential in the negotiation of the Schengen Accords. The 1990 Convention contains detailed treatment of a range of key issues including the regulation of the crossing of both the internal and external frontiers, the establishment of the Schengen Information System, and, in Title III, a number of important police and security measures (Den Boer 1991b; Benyon et al. 1993: 133-51; O'Keeffe 1991). The latter 'contains provisions aimed at harmonizing domestic policies concerning narcotic drugs,

---

[24] This sub-regional agreement contains a number of innovative provisions on police co-operation including hot pursuit of fugitives across their common borders (Geysels 1990; Fijnaut 1993b: 48–9; see also ch. 2).

[25] This 1962 instrument has been supplemented and extended by the treaties concluded in 1969 and 1974.

firearms and ammunition' (Schutte 1991: 81), promoting police co-operation, regulating the operation of the principle *non bis in idem*, and facilitating mutual assistance in criminal matters and the transfer of the execution of criminal judgments.[26]

Extradition, regulated by chapter 4, provides an illustration of the progress which can be secured at the sub-regional level (Baauw 1991). In approaching this issue Article 60 of the 1990 Schengen Convention adopts a highly innovative approach to the difficulty that Belgium has not yet become a party to the CoE Agreement. It provides simply that the provisions of the 1957 Convention 'shall be applicable, taking account of the reservations and declarations made either when that Convention was ratified or, for Contracting Parties which are not parties to that Convention, on the ratification, approval or acceptance of the present Convention'.

Having ensured a degree of commonality of approach, the Schengen Convention sets out to ease the extradition process in a number of ways. The extension of extradition to offences of a fiscal character is particularly significant; *i.e.*, customs and excise duties and value added tax (Article 63), as is the agreement to extend the range of circumstances in which France is prepared to co-operate (Article 61). The decision to include a simplified system available for use when the individual concerned does not intend to contest extradition should have a positive impact on the speed and efficiency of the process (Article 66). For example, Greece has not previously made provision for such an expedited process in its law. The concern with speed and efficiency was also central to the treatment of the issue of channels of communication (Article 65) and to the decision, reflected in Articles 64 and 95, to regard a report in the Schengen Information System, relating to persons wanted for arrest for the purpose of extradition, as having the same effect as a formal request for provisional arrest (O'Keeffe 1991: 204; Benyon, *et al.* 1993: 230).

Co-operation within the EU: Developments and Prospects

A number of proposals have been made to promote closer co-operation among the EU Member States, the majority of which seek to utilize intergovernmental mechanisms and structures. Prior

---

[26] Articles 67–9 on transfer of execution of criminal judgments help to close a loophole in cases in which a convicted person escapes to his country of nationality and cannot be extradited because of his national status.

to the entry into force of the TEU on 1 November 1993, discussions took place primarily within the framework of European Political Co-operation (EPC). There has been one major effort to elaborate a EC-wide instrument in the criminal sphere which involved amendments to the treaties establishing the European Communities.[27] This was intended 'to permit the adoption of common rules to enable the financial interests of the Communities to be adequately protected under criminal law and to facilitate prosecution in cases of infringement . . .' The draft Protocol envisaged the operation of two forms of co-operation previously included in CoE instruments: mutual assistance and the transfer of proceedings in criminal matters. The latter, regulated by a 1972 Strasbourg Convention, facilitates prosecutions where extradition is not possible due to the nationality of the accused person (Council of Europe 1985a). For a variety of reasons, including differences of view over the jurisdiction of the European Court of Justice, it proved impossible to reach final agreement (Schutte 1991: 73–4).

Some limited progress was, however, secured through the EPC Judicial Co-operation Working Group (JCWG) (HM Government 1993), including the elaboration of conventions between EU Member States on the enforcement of foreign criminal sentences and on the transfer of criminal proceedings. According to Schutte: 'These treaties . . . are not considered to be replacements of the corresponding Council of Europe conventions but, rather, as instruments that should facilitate their application for states parties to the latter' (Schutte 1991: 72). Both have, however, attracted disappointing levels of support so far (Delmas-Marty 1993: 22–4).

In addition to the above, the JCWG has acted as a forum for the discussion of a range of criminal matters and co-operative strategies to combat fraud against the Community budget and to improve mutual legal assistance (Wilkitzki 1992: 281). Its unfortunate history of underachievement in the extradition sphere is due, at least in some measure, to the fact that the initial focus in the mid-1970s was on the emotive and sensitive issue of the political offence exception in terrorist cases (Nuttall 1992: 294; Vercher 1992: 352–7).

The EPC concern was contemporaneous with progress on the 1977 CoE Convention on the Suppression of Terrorism, and the

[27] 1976 O.J. (c. 222) 2.

relationship between the two soon became central to the debate. Belgium proposed that the EU members should formally agree to apply the CoE instrument *inter se* without reservations. As has been noted: 'This work was already underway when President Giscard d'Estaing took a much bolder initiative, which for a time monopolized the attention of the Nine and delayed progress on the Belgian proposal' (Nuttall 1992: 294). This was the proposal for a common European Judicial Space which envisaged a more extensive set of EC arrangements in the extradition field (see also chapters 1 and 9). The Belgian proposal was opened for signature at the Dublin European Council on 4 December 1979, while the wider French initiative was still being formulated in treaty text form for presentation to a meeting of Ministers of Justice in Rome in June 1980. But it failed to attract the support of the Netherlands and was not formally adopted. This had a negative impact on French support for the 1979 Dublin Agreement which never received sufficient ratifications to permit its entry into force.

The fiasco over the 1979 Dublin Agreement diminished enthusiasm for judicial co-operation among the Member States. The JCWG was reconstituted only in the mid-1980s with its work divided between a group dealing with criminal matters and another with civil judicial co-operation. Since that time extradition has remained at the top of the JCWG agenda. Improved extradition arrangements were given a high priority by European Interior and Justice ministers at a meeting in Athens in December 1988 following severe political strains over two highly publicized cases. One of these, which greatly soured relations between the United Kingdom, Belgium, and Ireland arose out of the Father Patrick Ryan controversy. The other related to the equally contentious Abdel Osama Al Zomar case in which a Palestinian wanted by the Italian authorities for alleged involvement in the bombing of a Rome synagogue was deported by the Greek government to Libya rather than being extradited to Italy.

After discussion of extradition was revived, a twin-track solution emerged. The first strand of activity was to seek ways to improve the efficiency of the process, and this has been moved forward in recent years in two distinct ways. First, the EC Telefax Convention was concluded, designed to speed up the procedures for transmitting extradition requests and accompanying documents, and to permit the use of facsimile transmission for extradition-purposes

(Spencer 1990: 94). Secondly, an effort has been made to improve the effectiveness of existing arrangements. For example, in the course of its Presidency in 1992 the United Kingdom hosted a seminar in London for extradition practitioners from all Member States. This resulted in agreement on a number of practical steps which could be taken 'to remove avoidable delays from the extradition process' (Gilmore 1993b: Appendix A). A number of improvements were made, including the publication by the International Criminal Policy Division of the Home Office of guidance notes, flow charts and a listing of contact points for all twelve Member States (Home Office 1993). The reaction to this practical measure was positive and in early 1994 the European Committee on Crime Problems Committee of Experts on the Operation of European Conventions in the Penal Field (PC-OC) instructed the Secretariat of the CoE to extend this text to include all parties to the 1957 Convention. The second, and more problematic, approach was to discuss again the prospects for progress on the reform and modernization of the legal aspects of the extradition question. Initial discussions, in which the United Kingdom and Spain played leading parts, resulted in a measure of consensus, prior to the entry into force of the TEU on 1 November 1993, on the future programme of work to be undertaken.

As noted in chapter 6, Title VI of the TEU makes extensive provision for intergovernmental co-operation in the fields of justice and home affairs. Among the matters of 'common interest' Article K.1(7) lists 'judicial co-operation in criminal matters'. Under the third pillar arrangements, ministerial authority is exercised by a Council of Interior and Justice Ministers which is, in turn, serviced by a committee of senior officials—the K4 Co-ordinating Committee. One of its Steering Groups (III) is devoted to judicial co-operation and replaces the JCWG (Home Affairs Committee 1993: 27). At its first meeting, on 29 and 30 November 1993, the Council of Interior and Justice Ministers stressed the importance of judicial co-operation and adopted a statement requesting that possible improvements in both extradition requirements and procedures be examined.[28] This plan, subsequently approved by the European Council of 10–11 December 1993, required senior officials to produce a final report on the subject by the end of

---

[28] 27th GEN. REP. EC, p. 344.

1994. In setting out an ambitious work programme ministers had in mind, 'the expediency of having a new convention to supplement and amend the CoE Convention of 13 December 1957'.[29]

Officials within a Working Group on Extradition reporting to Steering Group III have undertaken an examination of the grounds for denying extradition and the reservations which have been made by EU countries in this regard. Consideration has been given to relaxing and standardizing the threshold for extraditable offences, to assimilating fiscal offences to ordinary criminal offences, to lessening the severity of the lapse of time rule, to the removing of obstacles to extradition involving possible life imprisonment (a particular problem with Portugal), and to refining the scope of operation of the speciality rule. In addition, they have tackled the two most politically sensitive areas of extradition; namely, the non-extradition of nationals and the operation of the political offence exception.

Following the European Council in December 1993, Steering Group III was requested to examine the prospects for the 'extradition of nationals, possibly with conditions'. Ministers are understood to have had in mind some instances in which the traditional severity of the rule has been relaxed. Perhaps the best known, and most innovative, example is that of the Netherlands, which involved both the revision of the Dutch Constitution in 1983, and a 1988 amendment to its domestic extradition legislation. Under the latter a national may be returned to a third state if, 'in the opinion of the Dutch Minister of Justice there is sufficient guarantee that if the national should be sentenced to an unconditional custodial sentence in the requesting State for the offences for which his extradition is granted, that national would be able to serve such sentence in the Netherlands' (Paridaens 1991: 515–16). Both the concept of the transfer of sentenced nationals and the requirement of the affected individual's consent thereto are widely accepted in international practice. By 23 September 1993 all current members of the EU with the exception of Ireland, as well as the three countries which were to join in the 1995 enlargement, had become parties to the 1983 CoE Convention on this subject. Unlike the Dutch law, however, this procedural framework agreement makes compliance with a request for transfer discretionary (Council of Europe 1983:

---

[29] Bull. EC 11-1993, point 1.5.9. See also, Bull. EC 12-1993, point 1.8.

7). Consequently, further arrangements need to be in place before the Dutch requirements can be fully satisfied. This is nonetheless an illustration of how an innovative combination of differing mechanisms can help to remove traditional impediments to international co-operation. Countries such as Germany, where constitutional amendment are required, may have difficulties in giving similar proposals serious consideration (Wilkitzki 1991: 287).

The outcome of deliberations on the future of the political offence exception is very uncertain. The Working Group on Extradition was asked to examine the possible 'exclusion of the political nature of the offence as a ground for refusal of extradition in connection with requests submitted between Member States for one of the offences defined in article 1 or envisaged in article 2' of the 1977 CoE Convention. A more radical proposal calling for total abolition of the exception, supported by Germany, Italy, the Netherlands, and the United Kingdom, has also been discussed by the Group.

The thorny questions of the extradition of nationals and the operation of the political offence exception continue to represent the most significant obstacles to progress among the EU Member States and were specially selected, at the insistence of France and the Netherlands, for discussion by Ministers at the Justice and Home Affairs Council on 23 March 1994. No resolution of the difficulties involved emerged and no clear political direction seems to have emerged to guide future consideration by Steering Group III.[30]

At a less contentious level, the Working Group on Extradition is also engaged in a review of existing extradition procedures, including the prospects for 'simplification of the procedure when the person agrees to extradition'. This is, as we have seen, an area in which some progress has been made in both the Benelux and Schengen contexts. It has, in addition, received the support of the Committee of Ministers of the CoE and is in the draft comprehensive convention, currently being negotiated in Strasbourg.[31]

[30] Although a fairly optimistic progress report was tabled at the meeting of the JHA Ministers at Berlin in Sept. 1994 (*Agence Europe*, No. 6311, 9 Sept. 1994), the absence of any reference to extradition either in the reported proceedings of the JHA Ministers meeting at Brussels on 30 Nov.–1 Dec. 1994 (*Agence Europe*, No. 6368, 1 Dec. 1994, No. 6769, 2 Dec. 1994) or in the Presidency Conclusions following the European Council at Essen on 9–10 Dec. 1994, indicate failure to meet the commitment to produce a final report on extradition by the end of 1994.
[31] See, Art. II.8 of the Draft European Comprehensive Convention on International Co-operation in Criminal Matters as approved by Committee PC-OC in March 1994.

Conclusion

The treatment of issues relating to mutual assistance in the administration of justice within the EU Member States is at present both inefficient and unsatisfactory. Current arrangements, characterized by a lack of uniformity and an extreme complexity, do not make a significant contribution to efforts to combat crime in a Europe without internal borders. Indeed, the present chaotic situation in the field of extradition has been characterized by some commentators as constituting an independent incentive to cross border criminality (Butt- Philip 1989: 17). It is in this sphere that the subject of judicial co-operation has greatest public visibility and where insufficiencies in the existing arrangements have had the greatest negative political impact. Despite longstanding concerns over the erosion of national sovereignty (see chapter 3), there is an emerging consensus that '. . . the Community cannot tolerate a situation in which individuals wanted on terrorist offences in one member state may find safe haven in another member country' (Latter 1991: 11). The case for change is now widely accepted.

The perception of the need for action is supported by the common participation of all EU Members in the system of protection of human rights and fundamental freedoms reflected in the European Convention of 1950, which reflects in their shared commitment to democratic institutions and the rule of law. These circumstances make timely a move towards the reduction and removal of some of the traditional barriers to co-operation, many of which have their origins in the law and practice of the second half of the 19th Century. These barriers were created when absolutist views of state sovereignty prevailed and confidence in the standards of justice and penal administration in other countries was largely absent. Justifications for collective action are reinforced for some by the recent expansion of the CoE 'to include new members, some of which have only limited experience with pluralistic democracy, [which] makes some Community Member States query whether the Council continues to be the most appropriate forum for the development of instruments promoting international co-operation in criminal matters' (Schutte 1991: 72).

No clear consensus has yet emerged about the eventual goal for the modernization of mutual legal assistance. However, given the limited Community competence in criminal matters and the continued attachment of the TEU to intergovernmentalism, the time is not yet ripe to entertain some of the more radical proposals such as the creation of a '*Espace judiciaire européen*' (Home Affairs Committee 1990: xxxiii). A pragmatic strategy is implied by the current agenda of the judicial co-operation Steering Group III. The objective of the Group is to identify and minimize or eliminate the major obstacles to efficient operation of current pan-European schemes rather than to alter the nature of the processes in any fundamental way. Making incremental progress may well be the most realistic way forward. The agenda in areas such as extradition contains a number of difficult issues which have defied solution on many occasions in the past. The outcome of these EU discussions will have to be taken in conjunction with the modernized version of the CoE texts on extradition, mutual assistance, transfer of proceedings, and enforcement of sanctions currently under discussion by Committee PC-OC in Strasbourg. The Comprehensive Convention on these subjects was scheduled to be submitted to the CoE European Committee on Crime Problems for approval in June 1995.

The outcome of the extradition discussions, coming so shortly after the entry into force of the TEU, will provide an early indication of whether the political will exists to make a reality of the proclaimed 'common interest' in judicial co-operation in criminal matters. If a convention text emerges from the current negotiations, incorporating significant improvements in extradition arrangements, scepticism will remain until it finally enters into full force and effect. Such EU agreements normally require ratification by all members before they become operational and this process can take years to complete. Even the less demanding CoE instruments have encountered major problems in attracting prompt governmental action. Few people in European criminal justice circles will forget that it took the United Kingdom until 1991 (over 30 years after it was opened for signature) to ratify the CoE Conventions on extradition and mutual legal assistance.

Improving judicial co-operation *inter se* may secure major improvements in current levels of effectiveness but it does not eliminate the need for some harmonization of the criminal law among member countries. This is illustrated by the discussions surrounding another priority—action to combat fraud against the financial interests of the European Union (see chapter 6).[32] A common approach to the definition of relevant offences is a necessary component both to the formulation of effective counter-measures and to co-operation between Member States (Schutte 1991: 74). Harmonization of approach would remove difficulties surrounding the satisfaction of the rule of double criminality which plays an important role in all judicial co-operation and is a fundamental requirement in the field of extradition (Delmas–Marty 1993: 35). The restriction of the scope of double criminality is not a separate item on the agenda in the present discussions taking place within the K4 structure. Such a shared perception of the goal is reflected in the new Commission proposals in this area[33] which were unanimously welcomed by EU ministers of the interior and of justice at their meeting in Luxembourg in June 1994.[34] The prospects of progress are, therefore, moderately good but whether decisive steps are taken depends crucially on the political climate and whether substantial progress is made towards political union in the intergovernmental conferences of 1996.

[32] See, e.g. 'How to make money from Europe', Economist, 26 March 1994: 50; and 'EU farm fraud growing fast', Independent, 25 March 1994.

[33] See COM (94) 214 final, Brussels 15.06.1994. Despite this enthusiastic reception, little progress was made during the remainder of 1994, and at the JHA meeting in Brussels on 30 Nov.–1 Dec. 1994, it was conceded that the finalization of the new legislative programme would be delayed until 1995 (Guardian, 1 Dec. 1994). Ch. 3, n. 18, reports some early initiatives against fraud by the new Commission in 1995.

[34] It has been discussed in the Extradition Working Group under the general agenda heading of extraditable offences. Italy, the Netherlands and the UK are believed to support at least a relaxation of this rule among EU members.

8

Controlling European Police Institutions

Introduction

Police officers in police forces throughout the world are held accountable to internal supervisory officers for their conduct with respect both to the law and to organizational procedures and disciplinary standards. This internal monitoring is uncontroversial in principle. By contrast, the issue of external accountability to the courts and to other public agencies is much more complex and politically sensitive. As Reiner asserts, the question of who should guard the guardians, and how, 'is one of the thorniest conundrums of statecraft' (Reiner 1993: 1). In recent years, the external accountability of domestic policing systems has become a matter of considerable public debate in many Member States. This may be related to a more general erosion of confidence in national police institutions, for as Brogden *et al.* argue, 'police accountability becomes an issue when there is public concern that the arrangements for ensuring the police perform satisfactorily any part of their role are not working' (Brogden *et al.* 1988: 153).

The aim of the present chapter is to examine the extent to which accountability is also at issue at the European level, and to evaluate the effectiveness of the mechanisms which presently exist for holding European police institutions to account. A brief critical overview of the current position is first provided. Next, an attempt is made to explain why these co-operative arrangements have emerged and continue to develop in such a limited form, leaving great uncertainty about how, to whom, and for what these organizations are accountable. In the light of this assessment, the chapter concludes by examining how the accountability of the developing network of European policing institutions might be improved.

Present Arrangements

As previously noted, the relationship of Interpol, Trevi, Schengen and Europol to the institutions of the European Union is very different in each case (chapter two). However, they have all contributed significantly to the emerging profile of transnational policing arrangements within the Community. It is these four institutional networks which provide our main focus, with particular attention devoted to Europol as the most ambitious framework for European police co-operation.

To determine the adequacy of the arrangements for holding these four institutions to public account, the key dimensions of accountability must be identified. Drawing upon Baldwin's analysis (Baldwin 1987), there are three criteria for assessing the accountability, in its broadest sense, of an activity such as policing. The first concerns the extent to which the institution and its practices are authorized by a legislative mandate; the second concerns the arrangements made for holding the institution to regular account by a broad democratic constituency; the third concerns matters of 'due process', rules and procedures whereby individuals and groups affected by specific institutional practices may influence such practices or otherwise ensure that their interests are safeguarded in the pursuit of these practices (Den Boer and Walker 1993: 19–24).

Most domestic policing systems have statutory underpinnings—albeit often open-textured—provided under the law-making authority of national Parliaments. Similar authoritative legislative foundations have been largely absent in the European and broader international domain. Interpol is notorious for its lack of a treaty basis in international law (Anderson 1989). Although Interpol is now recognized in practice as having the status of an intergovernmental organization, an examination of the form and substance of its governing statutes suggests an entity which 'still retains important characteristics of the more or less private international association of chiefs of police that was set up in 1923' (Fijnaut 1993a: 77). The anomalous character of the present position, however, has been acknowledged by the current Secretary-General, Raymond Kendall, who has indicated support for the negotiation of a new convention.[1]

---

[1] Interview with Raymond Kendall, Secretary-General of Interpol, 25 Feb. 1994.

At no stage, after it was established between the Member States in 1975, was Trevi accommodated within the EC legal framework, or even within the secondary framework of European Political Co-operation. Over its 18 year lifespan, Trevi acquired a degree of autonomous influence on the coat-tails of a major supranational institution. It benefited from the co-operative structures, political networking and institutional status associated with the EC Treaty framework, despite the lack of formal recognition within that framework. As a relatively informal intergovernmental agency, it lacked the discipline of statutorily imposed terms of reference, and it was not even obliged to make public its own self-authorized terms of reference. The publication of its 1990 Action Programme provided a rare insight into the workings of a secretive institution.

Schengen is constituted on the more formal footing of a Convention, but the regulatory régime under which it operates is one of international law rather than directly applicable EC law. Its formal legal status rests on the somewhat fragile and uneven basis of national ratification procedures. Indeed, various measures for the implementation of Schengen, including the establishment of several working parties to prepare detailed operational plans and the construction of the SIS headquarters at Strasbourg, were undertaken prior to such ratification by the national parliaments of all Member States (Van Outrive 1992c). Responding to these developments, and to a more general concern with securing national lines of accountability, a number of domestic parliaments, notably in the Netherlands, have now demanded oversight of the workings of Schengen's Executive Committee.

As we have already discussed (chapters 2 and 6), Europol, although recognized within the EU Treaty framework under the TEU, will operate only at the margins of the main EC institutions, governed by the terms of a separate convention to be ratified by Member States. It has been said that '[w]ith a little goodwill the option chosen for the [JHA Title] could be described as a "mixed model"' (Robles Piquer 1993: 14), partly intergovernmental and partly supranational in character. In terms of its basic constitutional pedigree, Europol lies somewhere between the outsider position of Trevi and Schengen on the one hand, and full integration within the EC on the other. One major institutional actor, the Council of Ministers, is accorded executive, but not legislative authority (Art. K.3). Two others, the Commission and the

European Parliament (see below), are also accorded formal recognition, albeit in somewhat lesser roles. The precariousness of the legal mandate within Title VI is confirmed by the fact that international agreements in the form of joint positions and joint actions, which have a lesser degree of formality than conventions, are also competent (see chapter 6). These relatively informal agreements may not require ratification by national parliaments under domestic constitutional procedures, and are less likely to require alteration of domestic law; just as the role of EC institutions is restricted, the function of domestic political institutions within Europol's overall accountability framework will probably be limited (House of Lords 1993b: 5).

Popular accountability controls over the relevant institutions are equally meagre. Neither Interpol nor Trevi has been accountable to a separate agency for most of their functions. A Joint Supervisory Authority will monitor Schengen, but only in respect of activities associated with the central technical support function (which oversees and monitors input of data) of the SIS (Baldwin-Edwards and Hebenton 1994: 142). Exchanges of information outside the automated channels are not subject to any equivalent form of control. Also, since the Supervisory Authority of the Schengen system comprises representatives from the national authorities involved in implementing the agreement, it lacks supranational status and independence from the system it is required to oversee.

The main lines of accountability for Europol will follow an attenuated course through existing national practices (Trevi 1991). As suggested above, the capacity of domestic political institutions to monitor Europol and associated Title VI activities is restricted in that much of what they do may not require domestic enabling legislation, or even ratification: indeed, if the pre-Maastricht practice is a guide, many intergovernmental procedures may remain entirely confidential until final agreement is reached between the national parties (House of Lords 1993b: 6).[2] The marginalization

---

[2] In the UK, the government has agreed to the request of the House of Lords Select Committee to make available draft conventions and 'other documents of significant importance (subject to possible exceptions arising out of the need for security or operational matters)'; HM Government (1994), Cm 2471, (1993–4). During the 1994–5 session of the UK Parliament, the House of Lords European Communities Committee (Sub-Committee E (Law and Institutions)) made use of this information in conducting a systematic enquiry into the progress made on the draft Convention to establish Europol.

of domestic methods of accountability, confronted by a powerful central European executive, is underlined by the key role given to the new Co-ordinating Committee under the JHA Chapter. Staffed by senior officials from the various Member States, its role is to assist the Council of Ministers and even to take policy initiatives (Art. K.4); as discussed in chapter 2, it has already consolidated its position by developing a formidable network of committees and sub-committees to run its affairs.

Although modest compared to more central areas of Community activity, there is a marked centripetal tendency in the development of Europol, to which primarily domestically-based systems of accountability, even if more closely involved, are an inappropriate response. This has been partially acknowledged in the Ministerial Agreement establishing the Europol Drugs Unit, which supplements the supervision of national liaison officers by national Ministers by empowering the JHA Ministers as a body to oversee the Unit; this is to be achieved through periodic reports from the Co-ordinator of the Unit. Similarly, under the draft Europol Convention, a degree of central accountability is provided through the duty imposed upon the Europol Management Board, comprising one representative from each Member State, to submit reports of its activities for the approval of the Co-ordinating Committee and the Council of Ministers (Art. 16). Although these devices seek to introduce an element of collective monitoring, once again, this is internal, not external, to the system.[3]

The European Parliament could provide some control: under the TEU it has the right to be informed by the Presidency of the Council and the Commission of discussions on Title VI matters, to be consulted by the Presidency 'on the principal aspects' of activities under Title VI, to ask questions of and make recommendations to the Council, and to hold an annual debate on progress within Title VI as a whole (Art. K.6). However, the Presidency need only ensure that the Parliament's views 'are duly taken into consideration'. This compares unfavourably with the powers of co-decision and veto which the Parliament now possesses in legislative and financial matters in economic and social policy (Raworth 1994). The European Parliament may nonetheless exercise its functions with some vigour and its recent record suggests that it will. Its

[3] For analysis and evaluation of the distinction between internal and external control mechanisms, see Bayley (1985).

growing awareness of the increasing criminal justice dimension of Community activity led it, in January, 1992, to institute a Committee for Civil Liberties and Internal Affairs (renamed the Committee for Civil Liberties in 1994), which has produced a number of useful reports in this area (Van Outrive 1992a, 1992b, 1992c, 1992d; Robles Piquer 1993; Tsimas 1992), in turn stimulating lively debate and critical resolutions in the full Parliament.[4]

However, the enthusiasm of the European Parliament is in danger of outstripping its legal powers: in 1992 a Green MEP failed to obtain substantive answers to any of the 65 detailed written questions submitted to the Council of Ministers on the workings of Trevi.[5] The reason given for refusal was the absence of competence on the part of the Council in these matters. Under the post-Maastricht regime the powers of the Council and Commission remain limited, and the Parliament may be similarly obstructed in future efforts to gain enlightenment (Millar 1992). The problem has been graphically exposed in a recent series of disagreements over the interpretation of the powers of Parliament under Title VI and over its role under the Europol Convention and related agreements.

In a debate in the European Parliament on 15 December 1993, the representative of the Council Presidency, Mr Dehaene, refused to answer the direct question of an MEP whether the Council would inform and consult the Parliament before it takes decisions in the field of internal security.[6] As noted earlier, Article K.6 implies that this need only apply in the case of consultation on the 'principal aspects' of Title VI activities. In a resolution adopted on 20 January 1994, the Parliament indicated that it considers the negotiation, adoption and implementation of the conventions envisaged under Article K.3 of the TEU, and the joint positions referred to in the same article 'in so far as they concern regulatory matters', to fall among the main or principal aspects of Union activities and thus to be subject to the prior consultation requirement.[7] In fact, this resolution goes much further in its claims for parliamentary

[4] A separate Committee of Inquiry reported to Parliament, in April, 1992, on the question of the spread of drugs-related organized crime.

[5] Jenkins, J. (1992), 'Jeux sans frontieres', *New Statesman and Society*, vol. 5, No. 226, 30 Oct. 22-3.

[6] European Parliament Debates, 1993-4 Session; Report of Proceedings from 13-17 Dec. 1993, *OJC*, Annex No. 3-440, 148-50.

[7] Resolution on Participation by the European Parliament in international agreements in the fields of justice and home affairs *OJC* C44, 14 Feb. 1994, pages

involvement in international agreements in the fields of JHA than the Treaty, on the face of it, would allow. The resolution also calls for parliamentary involvement in the drawing up of conventions ('. . . full participation in deliberations between the Member States, the Council and the Commission on the contents of . . . such agreements.') and even goes so far as to demand a right of parliamentary assent before the agreements may enter into force.

The expansive attitude of the Parliament towards its role within the emerging system of accountability stands in stark contrast to that of some Member States. The British government, in particular, is not favourably disposed to giving the European Parliament these broader rights of participation in Title VI matters. It takes the line that accountability is owed to national parliaments alone, stating unambiguously in its response to a House of Lords report on scrutiny of the intergovernmental pillars of the European Union that: 'The government believe that it is an important feature of the inter-governmental process that national governments of member states should be accountable to national parliaments, not to the European Parliament, on business under these pillars.' (HM Government 1993: 1).

The extreme view that the governments of the Member States are not accountable in any shape or form to the European Parliament in respect of Title VI matters is difficult to reconcile with the express terms of Article K.6. Furthermore, it is curiously inconsistent, as well as a questionable interpretation of the principle of separation of powers, to agree, on the one hand, to the strengthening of the European Parliament's legislative powers in relation to Community matters (e.g. the co-decision procedure introduced under the TEU), and, on the other hand, to threaten to refuse to provide Strasbourg with the basic information it requires to carry out the complementary constitutional task of controlling the exercise of power by the executive branch (JHA Ministers and K.4 Committee) within the EU.[8] The executive branch seems, how-

180–2. Presumably, the European Parliament would also therefore regard joint actions, a more intensive form of co-operation than the joint position, to be caught by the prior consultation requirement which it derives from Art. K.6, although joint actions are, rather curiously, not expressly mentioned in the resolution.

[8] Even from the perspective of national parliaments, an increased supervisory role for the European Parliament is arguably advantageous, as scrutiny of EU activities might be effectively carried out in co-operation with a strong European Parliament. See also Robles Piquer (1993) and n. 25 below.

ever, already to have followed the British line by making clear that it intends to adhere to a narrow interpretation of the terms of Article K.6, thus giving the Parliament much more limited powers than it would like. At the Luxembourg European Council in June 1993, there was significant disagreement between some national representatives who insisted on the Parliament's right to receive all relevant documentation and to be formally consulted on all important developments—including the draft Conventions on Europol, the European Information System and the Customs Information System—and others who argued that the Presidency and the Commission could discharge their legal responsibility to Parliament merely by submitting a short report of their activities.[9] Despite strong support from the European Commissioner for JHA matters, Padraig Flynn, for a larger role for the Parliament, the guidelines suggested by the subsequent German Presidency for consulting the Parliament were limited in scope. Its proposals that the European Parliament should be informed only once action plans had been adopted by the Council, and that each six-monthly presidency should gather the views of the Parliament on the initiatives of that presidency, fell well short of a guarantee of prior and separate consultation on all major initiatives. Also, the German Presidency preferred the accountability question to be addressed by a code of conduct rather than a binding inter-institutional agreement[10]—an informal arrangement which would further weaken the position of the Parliament.[11]

In this climate of disagreement, it is hardly surprising that the negotiation and drafting of the Europol Convention has taken place largely without the participation of the European Parliament. The Belgian Council Presidency did, however, state in 1993 that the views on Europol expressed by the Parliament's committee on civil liberties had been considered by the Council of Ministers. Furthermore, the Parliament as a whole has debated the development of Europol, for example in the context of the regular debates on the activities of the presidency, in which questions may be

---

[9] *Statewatch*, vol. 4, No. 4, July–Aug. 1994, 10–11.

[10] The preferred option of the European Parliament itself. See note 24 below.

[11] *Statewatch*, Vol. 4, No. 5, Sept.–Oct. 1994, 10–11. A final agreement on the general role of the Parliament under Art. K.6 was still not forthcoming at the subsequent meeting of the JHA Ministers in Berlin on 7 Sept. 1994 (*Agence Europe*, No. 6311, 9 Sept. 1994, 8).

asked of the Council.[12] As to parliamentary scrutiny of the operation of Europol, this is a matter which may be regulated in the Europol Convention itself. However, mirroring the general controversy over the role of the Parliament in supervising the executive under Title VI, this has been the subject of protracted disagreement. Indeed, Article 31 of the German draft of the Europol Convention of October 1994, which envisaged rights of prior consultation for the European Parliament in respect of important decisions to implement or to amend the Convention, generated such discord that it was deleted from the version considered by the JHA Ministers in Brussels in November 1994.[13] This impasse lends credence to the view of Europol's co-ordinator, Jürgen Storbeck, that in the medium term parliamentary control of Europol will remain in the hands of national parliaments, with only long-term prospect of the European Parliament being involved more closely (Storbeck 1994b: 462).

The final method of accountability is due process protections, and here again the various safeguards are underdeveloped. International police co-operation as presently practised, already impinges on individual rights and freedoms, especially in the field of computerized information exchange (Spencer 1990; Benyon et al. 1993). Where forms of operational aid short of a supranational unit with full operational powers are in existence, information technology systems have assumed a pivotal function as methods of practical co-operation which may become embedded in mainstream operational practice across the EU (Sheptycki 1994).

There are almost as many proposed or recently established international information systems as there are international police agencies. Interpol underwent an extensive computerization programme in the 1980s, and following its 1989 move to new 'high-tech' headquarters in Lyons it has recently established an automated search facility allowing direct access by national central bureaus to a central pool of criminal intelligence, subject to restrictions imposed by the supplier country (Harrison 1992; Kendall 1992). The SIS, based at Strasbourg, will include information on wanted and convicted persons, undesirable aliens, and persons whom it is suspected may commit serious crime in the future (Den Boer 1991b). Other major

---

[12] See e.g. European Parliament, 1993–4 session. Report of Proceedings from 13-17 Dec. 1993 *OJC* Annex No. 3-440; 149.

[13] *Statewatch*, vol. 4, No. 6, Nov.–Dec. 1994, 16–17.

information technology initiatives include the proposed EIS, a possible successor to the SIS, which has been under consideration by the K.4 Co-ordinating Committee, and the Customs Information System, which, from October 1993, has provided a data base and network for the pooling and exchange of information among European Customs Officers on drugs smuggling, fraudulent export certificates, illegal trafficking in arms, endangered species, and related matters (Miles 1993). At the end of 1994, the scope, content and precise articulation of the proposed Europol central computer data base with other information systems had not yet been finally determined in the draft Convention.[14]

Before the implementation of these ambitious systems there were a growing number of cases of individuals subjected to oppressive or intrusive treatment or at risk of interference from law enforcement authorities, as a result of false information relayed about them across national borders and not subsequently corrected.[15] As denser and more systematic computer links between national forces are set up, there is a risk that such abuses will increase dramatically. Under such a regime, false information is far more easily disseminated, and the burden of apathy tends to weigh against its speedy removal. The confidentiality of these systems, as well as variations in national data protection laws and the relationships of such laws to international information systems, make it very difficult for individuals to gain access to their data in order to check their accuracy. There is also the perennial danger, amplified in an increasingly IT-friendly, 'informatized' environment, that computerized information might assume a spurious objectivity in the eyes of those to whom it is disseminated. Those who receive information relayed transnationally may act upon it, despite their

[14] Three matters in particular remained controversial in the data protection provisions (Arts. 5–23) of the German draft Convention of Oct. 1994 which was considered at the Brussels meeting of JHA Ministers on 30 Nov. 1994. First, there was disagreement over access to Europol intelligence: the French authorities wanted general access to all types of intelligence for national police agencies, whereas the other Member States wanted to restrict access where intelligence was generated by Europol's own analysts. Secondly, there was continuing disagreement over access to other computerized data systems. Thirdly, the standards of data protection remained controversial, in particular the extent to which the 1981 Council of Europe Convention on Data Protection and the 1987 Recommendation on the use of personal data in the police sector whould be taken into account, and whether these should provide minimum or optimum standards (*Statewatch*, vol. 4, No. 6, Nov.–Dec. 1994, 16–17).

[15] See n. 5 above.

ignorance of the wider operational context within which the computerized text was produced, a knowledge which is necessary for adequate interpretation.[16]

Existing safeguards may not be sufficiently robust to counter these difficulties. Interpol has a rudimentary complaints system in the form of a supervisory board to examine internal files, but substantial internal control is retained over board membership (Anderson 1989: 65-6). All EU Member States are signatories to the 1981 Council of Europe Convention on Data Protection and the 1987 Recommendation No. R (87) 15 on the use of personal data in the police sector, both of which contain provisions pertinent to the various computerized information systems mentioned above.[17] Both instruments allow wide scope for derogation in matters of state security, public safety and crime prevention, reducing their capacity to prevent abuses in individual cases (Baldwin-Edwards and Hebenton 1994; Norman 1992; Raab 1994). In addition, not all Member States have ratified the Convention, and it was not until very recently that some brought general legislation for data protection into force (*e.g.*, Ireland and the Netherlands 1989; Portugal 1991; Belgium, Greece and Spain 1993), while Italy has yet to legislate.

For the moment, a specifically EU data protection regime is lacking. A draft Directive on Data Protection was published in 1990 and revised in 1992, following widespread criticism (Commission 1992a). Protracted negotiations within the European Commission and the Council exposed national differences over crucial provisions. Its final endorsement is still awaited, and its implementation in national regulatory systems (with many allowable exceptions) and the creation of some central EC machinery, will not finally take effect until some two years thereafter (Raab and Bennett 1994). Whether and to what extent police files will fall under its rules is also uncertain (Baldwin-Edwards and Hebenton 1994; Lloyd 1994; Raab 1994). The *lacunae* which remain have prompted the Committee on Civil Liberties and Internal Affairs of the European Parliament to call for the appointment by the Commission of a Community Data Protection Officer (Van Outrive 1992c: 8).

---

[16] See note 5 above.

[17] On the treatment of these agreements, within the draft Europol Convention, see n. 14 above.

In addition, various Conventions currently being negotiated under the authority of Title VI promise more detailed regulation of EU-wide information systems accessible to police and other law enforcement agencies. In the draft Europol Convention, a Joint Supervisory Body is envisaged, comprising representatives of the relevant supervisory authority in each Member State, which will oversee the processing of personal data in the Europol central computer data base (Art.22).[18] Similar oversight is proposed for the EIS and the CIS in the draft conventions under negotiation. However, the final form of these regulatory regimes will be a compromise between law enforcement priorities and individual rights of privacy. The effectiveness of the proposed supervisory agencies will be limited by the investigative resources and the legal powers granted to them.

Issues about the protection of civil liberties are not confined to the question of protection of automatically processed data. Much police co-operation within the EU remains of the informal, 'low-tech', variety. The confidentiality of manually-held files, which are excluded from some existing data protection legislation but which were included in the draft EC directive (against the opposition of the United Kingdom government) will, therefore, remain an important concern, particularly prior to the introduction of major new automatic systems.

If, in the longer term, Europol were to acquire operational powers, in the longer term, especially those of search, questioning and arrest, the need for corresponding rights of due process would become urgent. The basic statement of principle in European jurisprudence concerning individual rights, including privacy and procedural rights, is the European Convention on Human Rights (ECHR), specifically endorsed in the JHA Title of the TEU (Art. K.2(1)). However, whether the ECJ is to have jurisdiction over JHA matters is left open, to be resolved in any particular area in the negotiation of the terms of its governing Convention (Art. K.3(2)(c)). This procedure first generated strong disagreement between the Commission and the Council over the matter of the

---

[18] The German draft Convention of Oct. 1994 states, *inter alia*, that individuals shall have the right to request the Joint Supervisory Authority to examine the permissibility of the collection, processing and utilization of her/his personal data by Europol (Art. 22(4)).

Community's external border controls,[19] and is proving controversial between the institutions and the Member States more generally.[20] From the perspective of the aggrieved individual, unless the EU becomes a party to the European Convention on Human Rights, there may be no effective judicial forum within which the rights enshrined in the ECHR can be enforced against an EU agency such as Europol (see chapter 6).

In any event, as with many domestic systems (Goldsmith 1991), it is arguable that a special complaints process and tribunal are required through which general rights can be put in context and enforced. The European Parliament has again been prominent in advocating reform in this area. In January 1993, in response to a report received from its Committee on Civil Liberties and Internal Affairs (Van Outrive 1992d), it resolved that Europol should be treated as a Community body against which individual complaints might be made to the new European Ombudsman provided for in the TEU. However, this proposal is unlikely to be implemented in the near future. In any case, doubts remain about the potential efficacy of the Ombudsman in the face of what may be regarded as matters of overriding public or intergovernmental interest.

Accounting for Limited Accountability

Why are current accountability standards deficient, and why are there only modest signs that these standards will be enhanced in the foreseeable future? To answer this question a wide range of factors must be taken into account. These may be grouped under four main headings: political marginalization, bureaucratic momentum and the development of policing markets, alternative sources of legitimacy, and occcupational culture.

Political Marginalization

The absence of a mature framework of political institutions for holding European police co-operation to account is closely linked

[19] *Independent*, 25 Nov. 1993. See now, 'Communication from the Commission to the Council and the European Parliament: proposal for a decision, based on Art. K3 of the Treaty on European Union, establishing the Convention on the crossing of the external frontiers of the Member States'.

[20] At the meeting of the JHA Ministers in Luxembourg on 20 June 1994, the Commissioner for Justice and Home Affairs, Mr Padraig Flynn, was in disagreement with certain Member States over the role of the Court of Justice. He is said to favour a selective approach, with the jurisdiction of the Court assessed on its merits for each Convention; *European Report*, June 22, 1994. See also, ch. 6, n. 54.

to the general lack of institutional development of international co-operation in policing matters. As historical treatments of both pre-Interpol (Nadelmann 1995) and post-Interpol (Anderson 1989) phases have graphically demonstrated, international police co-operation has long been characterized by light regulatory regimes at best, and by informality and '*ad hocery*' at worst. In such barren terrain, there is little opportunity for robust systems of account-ability to take root.

At the heart of this tradition of informalism lies a tension in international relations (chapter 3). On the one hand, national police forces must devise ever more extensive methods of mutual international assistance and information sharing if they are to deal effectively with deviant activity. This is expanding in line with the increased density of global economic, political and cultural transac-tions (Latter 1991). On the other hand, the modern sovereign state grew out of the absolutist state of the 16th and 17th centuries whose defining characteristic, for thinkers such as Jean Bodin and Thomas Hobbes, was its control of the means of violence against threats from both within and without the state territory (Giddens 1987b; Jessop 1990: 343). Despite some erosion, the idea of an *independent* police power as a symbol of statehood persists as a legacy of the Hobbesian world view.

This tension is exacerbated by the fact that many of the areas in which demand for international police co-operation is greatest are also those where the autonomy of the state and the protection of its 'vital' interests are most directly at stake (Walker 1994a). Terrorism, which falls squarely within the domain of 'high polic-ing' and specific order, is the best known example. The strong desire of states to control anti-terrorist operations has to be bal-anced against, and to some extent defer to, the need to co-operate internationally to resolve specific problems. The priority given to counter-terrorism led directly to several initiatives, for example: first, the reinterpretation of Interpol's constitutional restriction pro-hibiting involvement in political, religious and racial cases in a sufficiently flexible manner to allow anti-terrorist co-operation (Anderson 1989); secondly, the establishment of Trevi; and thirdly, the inclusion of terrorism in Art. K.1(9) of the TEU.

As the EDU's brief indicates, drug-trafficking, money laundering and other associated activities of 'criminal organizations' impli-cated in the drugs' trade, is currently perceived to constitute the most significant common threat to the criminal laws of the EC states. As with anti-terrorism, a broad consensus obscures important differences in national perspectives. The drugs trade has had such significant repercussions for national economies, and, in the case of the supply of hallucinogenic drugs, their regulation is so closely influenced by national attitudes about the optimal balance between license and repression, that considerations of specific order can impede the development of common institutions.[21] Further examples of how tensions and conflicts between the specific orders of different states tend to militate against formalizing co-operation in new areas of international crime may be noted in matters as diverse as public disorder (Den Boer and Walker 1993: 14-15) and EC subsidy fraud (Clarke 1993; Passas and Nelken 1993).

Recent developments under the JHA Title of the TEU might seem to break free from these constraints. However, tension between functional and ideological considerations remains, and has perhaps become more firmly entrenched due to a widespread perception of the need to compensate for the 'security deficit' flowing from the abolition of border controls in the Single Market Programme. However, the doctrine of compensatory measures (discussed in depth in chapter 4) relies on doubtful assumptions and in any case, it is a very narrow base upon which to found common security institutions.

These institutions would have greater legitimacy if they were justified by appeal to their importance as an integral component of the unique supranational EU order. However, this justification is unlikely to gain currency in present circumstances because of the continuing strong belief in the state as the proper source and repository of political authority. This traditional view is currently reinforced by general uncertainty over the pace and direction of institutional growth within the Community. A new nationalism born of economic recession has spread across Western Europe and, with it, a preoccupation with political problems within Member States, most notably in Italy, Germany and the United Kingdom (Hoffman 1993). One of the expressions of this climate is concern

---

[21] For example, an underlying factor in the prolonged negotiation to decide the location of the EDU's headquarters and the failure to meet the deadline for the dismantling of the internal borders of the Schengen states, was French unease about the comparatively liberal Dutch anti-drugs regime (*Statewatch*, 'Internal border controls', vol. 3, No. 3, May–June 1993, pp. 7–8).

over the loss of national sovereignty to European institutions. Resistance to attempts to reduce the 'democratic deficit' at the Community level—generally understood as the inability of the European Parliament to control the executive European institutions adequately—occurs because the strengthening of any European institution is perceived in narrow zero-sum terms as contributing to the erosion of the capacity for national self-determination (Weiler 1991: 2472-4). The efforts of the Dutch European Minister, Piet Dankert, during the Maastricht negotiations illustrate the effect of this attitude. He provided for the fuller 'communitization' (Fijnaut 1993a) of the JHA Chapter in a draft TEU, published six months before the final version, but it was summarily dismissed by Member States, even though this draft would have enhanced the accountability of the new institutions.

Closely related to the anxiety about erosion of national control is a concern about the appropriate political objectives of a mature EU. Schmitter proposed an interesting conceptualization of the EC as the prototype 'post-Hobbesian state', (Streeck and Schmitter 1991: 152; see also chapter 3), an entity distinguished by 'the absence of military insecurity as the overriding motive/excuse for the exercise of political authority'. Unlike the Hobbesian state, it has not emerged in circumstances where 'the accumulation and concentration of coercive means grow together' (Tilly 1990: 19). Instead, it developed as a unit of political organization primarily inspired by economic, and, increasingly, social and cultural objectives (Majone 1993; Meehan 1993). A diverse range of scenarios was rehearsed in chapter 3, but it remains likely that Member States' apprehension over the loss of sovereignty to the Community will be particularly apparent in policing which, although central to a Hobbesian conception of the state, is peripheral to the context of the new *supranational* order (Walker 1994a). If this view is correct, scepticism over the acceptance of EU jurisdiction over policing is more durable than the present general crisis of legitimacy affecting the Community and will check federalist ambitions in this domain, even in a more favourable international environment.

Bureaucratic Momentum and the Development of Policing Markets

An important consequence of the tendency to view police co-operation in functional terms has been to grant to the functionaries—the senior civil servants and professionals involved in law enforcement—a key role in developing frameworks of co-operation and in defining agendas. One commentator has developed this theme in forceful terms, talking of 'a virtual revenge against the world of politics perpetrated by a 'self-motivating bureaucracy' (Bigo 1994b). The development of a bureaucratic momentum has a number of negative implications for accountability.

The emergence and constant evolution of so many different institutions of police co-operation in a single 'crowded policy space' (Raab 1994) results in a high degree of institutional complexity and fragmentation. It is difficult, therefore, to monitor all key agencies even in the most elementary sense of developing and maintaining a reasonably informed overview, still less in terms of devising a more sophisticated supervisory framework (Benyon *et al.* 1993). The relationship between the various agencies is characterized by increased 'networking' between bodies with overlapping personnel, occupational backgrounds and objectives. This can lead to a self-corroborating world-view, a mutually reinforced 'internal security ideology' (Bigo 1994b) where professionals translate their occupational priorities into a policy perspective which emphasizes the needs of law enforcement above other social objectives and above concern for individual rights and freedoms.

The interaction of so many agencies in an expanding field of activity also leads to a degree of competition (Van Reenen 1989; Johnston 1992: 201–2). In the absence of a settled institutional structure, policing across borders comes to resemble an 'international commodity', with different organizations vying to provide a more attractive package. However, because it is an *internal market*, where providers and customers alike are either police organizations or the state and inter-state bureaucracies associated with them, this competitive environment tends to reinforce rather than reverse the homogenizing trend described above. Police organizations attempting to secure a niche in a market-place dominated by like-minded organizations will tend to present their product as one which meets security objectives more effectively than those of their rivals, rather than as one which pursues different objectives.

Competition produces rivalry within existing markets, and also a propensity to expand and colonize new markets. This helps to account for another aspect of the internal security ideology depicted by Bigo, namely its reach across an ever-widening spectrum of activities. As previously remarked, the scope of the JHA Title brings together issues as diverse as terrorism, drugs, organized crime, illegal immigration and asylum policy (Van Outrive 1992c: 19) as components of an indivisible 'security deficit' in the new borderless Europe; this has been achieved through the development of a common discursive and institutional framework, a single 'internal security field' (Bigo 1994b; see also chapter 5) in which the development of systems for collating and exchanging information about suspects across the range of issues plays an important part. The professional 'law and order' perspective could marginalize other viewpoints over core security matters and colonize broader areas of social policy; this trend runs against the idea of a system of accountability, genuinely responsive to a plurality of audiences and points of view.

Alternative Sources of Legitimacy

The political marginalization of the issue of police accountability would not, however, be possible, unless this were acceded to by a broad public. If accountability mechanisms are slow to develop, this is partly because international policing arrangements enjoy a degree of 'social legitimacy' (Weiler 1991: 2466–74) independently of the existence of these mechanisms. To explore this, a return to Baldwin's three forms of accountability is required. In his original argument (1987) each of the three forms—legislative, popular and due process—corresponds to a particular type of claim to legitimacy. Alongside these formal legal or constitutional sources of legitimacy, he identifies two other practical bases of legitimacy, namely expertise and institutional efficiency and effectiveness.

These practical tests help to give more authority to the developing institutions of international policing. Like many public service organizations, domestic police institutions seek to enhance their status and justify their decision-making autonomy by reference to a specialist 'knowledge mandate' (Halliday 1985). If policing is perceived as a matter of specialized technical skill, then its practitioners are more likely to be treated as respected professionals and less likely to be subjected to close scrutiny (Holdaway 1983; Brogden et al. 1988: 80–4). This claim can be made with greater and lesser degrees of persuasiveness (Baldwin 1987: 101). In many areas associated with developments in international crime and policing, it is particularly credible. In West European states, crimes of terrorism, drug-trafficking, money laundering, art theft, etc., have been tackled by specialist units, each claiming to possess their particular brand of esoteric knowledge, with their own necessarily confidential sources and techniques of criminal intelligence. Such claims, irrespective of whether they are defensible, are difficult to rebut and tend to have a self-justifying quality.

European policing institutions may also be well placed to attract public support, or at least to avoid criticism, on grounds of efficiency and effectiveness. In recent decades, police institutions in Western democracies have encountered increasing difficulty in defending their performance in terms of their traditional role of crime prevention and detection (Manning 1977; Punch 1985; Reiner 1991; Guyomarch 1991). The inexorable rise of recorded crime and a renewed ideological distrust of the public sector has made domestic police forces increasingly vulnerable to value-for-money scrutiny. The police attract considerable public scepticism, in common with a range of 'professionals', and the image of the police in many countries has suffered as a result of adverse public perception of their probity, as well as their effectiveness. One response to this has been to attempt to redefine the role of the police in more modest terms, as one party to a much wider social contract to set and maintain acceptable levels of public tranquillity rather than as the leading institution in the fight against crime (Reiner 1991; 1994a; see also chapter 5). However, this response has risks; a reduction in public expectations may ease the insistent pressure for tangible results, but it also threatens to relegate the police to a 'much lower pedestal' (Reiner 1991) in terms of occupational status and reputation, and diminishing their capacity to win resources from the public purse. The older image of the police as the primary custodians of law and order thus remains attractive to the police themselves, and continues to be emphasized in serious crime where a narrow audit of cost effectiveness makes the police most vulnerable to criticism.

The central problems which international policing aims at tackling (e.g. terrorism and drugs) are presented as a major, and essentially unquantifiable, threat to the social and political order. When these matters are woven together in law and order world-views to form a seamless 'internal security field', questions of efficiency become obscured by a powerful image of the police as the last line against social chaos (McLaughlin 1992; Dorn et al. 1992). A popular 'fear of crime', exploited by the mass media, has supported this image, encouraged the promotion of law-and-order policies to the top of political agendas, and weakened support for many traditional legal and operational restraints upon the police. Arguments in favour of technical expertise and against resort to quantifiable indices of efficiency and effectiveness in international policing thus achieve a form of ideological closure. They are effective because they successfully side-step questions about the underlying justification of the police.

In many domestic policing systems, the practical and formal grounds of legitimacy are linked in a way which necessitates some care being taken with the health of both. Domestic police forces require a steady flow of information from all sections of the public in order to exploit their expertise and achieve acceptable standards of effectiveness in crime-fighting. This information flow, however, depends on a high level of mutual trust between police and public, which is, at least partly, dependent upon public confidence that the police are properly answerable through constitutional mechanisms (Kinsey et al. 1986).

In the international system, on the other hand, this nexus between effectiveness, public co-operation and adequate accountability is much less well established (Den Boer 1994b: 181; Walker 1993a; 1993b). Sections of the public may be crucial informants for intelligence networks associated with supranational policing, but the public as a whole is not involved. The practical arguments which legitimize international police institutions tend to emphasize the need for decision-making autonomy in order to avoid compromising their efficiency, diluting their expertise, or sharing sensitive information: to the extent that such arguments are supported by the general public, the scope for strong accountability systems is further limited. Moreover, as the deviant groups targeted by international police co-operation are marginal to the experiences and sympathies of the majority of the general public, popular sentiment is less likely to be mobilized on behalf of those typically in conflict with the police in this area than in domestic policing. In sum, the social and political pressures for police accountability are currently less strong in the international domain than in the national domain.

Occupational Culture

Police officers of junior rank typically operate 'in regions of low visibility' (van Maanen 1983: 377) removed from direct supervisory oversight. As they are required to communicate rapidly and take decisions in different and unpredictable circumstances, they enjoy a high degree of practical discretion. A great deal of information is gathered at this level of policing about illegal activities and suspects. The task of harnessing the occupational culture of the rank and file and of different parts of the organization so as to achieve internal control and co-ordination, is one which all police organizations must confront. Accountability systems which seek to exert external influence over the workings of police organizations must be sensitive to internal difficulties if they are to be effective.

If these considerations are relevant to the operation of international policing systems, they may provide an additional reason for the prevalence of informalism, and the marginalization of the issue of accountability. Policy-makers may view pessimistically the prospects of formal control systems and may be discouraged from attempting to design these to a high specification. These attitudes are likely to remain unspoken, and any assessment of their contribution to informalism in the international domain is necessarily speculative. However, in light of the development of a more formal framework for Schengen, Europol and the JHA Title generally, these internal organizational difficulties will have to be taken directly into account in the future.

The special requirements of operational policing are taken into consideration in the design of provisions for data protection in and between police information systems. For example, the Council of Europe's Recommendation No. R(87)15 acknowledges that formal principles of protecting individual privacy rights have to be balanced against 'legitimate police activities' involving 'the classic and crucial tasks of the police', pointing towards 'adapting the principles to take account of particular requirements, notably in respect of the 'suppression of criminal offences' (Council of Europe 1988: 14). Both the Schengen Convention's and the draft Europol Convention's endorsement of the Recommendation, and their own data protection provisions, strike the balance closer to police requirements than to civil liberties (Raab 1994; Van Outrive 1992c;

Spencer 1990).[22] Police definitions of the purpose of data protection, arising out of cultural and operational needs for covertness and protection of the identity of informants, differ from those based on some views of individual rights.

How significant, therefore, are cultural impediments to accountability in the international domain? In general, the secrecy and solidarity of small units and working groups noted in numerous studies of police work (Skolnick 1975; Reiner 1992b) are likely to be important in international policing. First, the front-line activities associated with international policing in all Member States are dispersed across an unusually wide range of narrow specialist tasks organized into different police agencies or departments within agencies; in the case of the specialist border controls, they are often allocated to distinct organizational services. The different traditions, working practices and information networks of these different specialisms may lead to rivalry and disharmony. Secondly, the gulf in organizational status, experience and understanding between policy-making and monitoring on the one hand, and operational implementation on the other, may be more pronounced in international co-operative policing than in the area of purely domestic policing. The propensity of 'street cops' to resist or modify the designs of 'management cops' increases as a result (Reuss-Ianni and Ianni 1983). Thirdly, the solidarity of police officers is, *inter alia*, a territorial solidarity (Holdaway 1983), and depends upon a sense of doing the same work and sharing the same problems (Skolnick 1975: 52); therefore there is uncertainty on the extent to which operational units based in different states and operating in occupational environments largely unknown to one another can work together on a basis of mutual trust and respect. Even in a new centralized structure, such as EDU/Europol, where a system of liaison officers operates, a powerful legacy of distinctive national cultures and experiences among its new personnel has to be overcome to create cohesive working relationships.

Criticism often levelled against Interpol confirms this hypothesis. It has been alleged to be unduly slow and cumbersome, and an inadequate source and repository of information (Home Affairs Committee 1990: xxv–xxvii). According to a number of our respondents, such charges are in part due to a preference within

---

[22] *Statewatch* (1994), vol.4, No.3 May–June, p. 16. See also Arts. 12–24 of the German draft of the Europol Convention of Oct. 1994.

domestic policing systems for informal channels of communication, reflecting an impatience with and wariness of procedures which demand a detailed documentation record which may subsequently be subject to the critical scrutiny of senior officers, and even the judiciary. These complaints may also be explained by the unwillingness of domestic operational units to expedite inquiries by responding promptly to impersonal requests for assistance from abroad. This reflects the low priority given to the needs of any group outside an officer's operational frame of reference.

To achieve effective influence over an international police organization, therefore, accountability mechanisms must dovetail with a system of internal regulation which is sensitive to problems of control and co-ordination as they occur both within international organizations, and between these and the national organizations with which they communicate. The translation of the official mission of the organization into operational practice is difficult in the case of Interpol with its comparatively modest terms of reference. It will be all the more so in the case of a more ambitious venture such as Europol.

Future Prospects

None of the obstacles to the development of European police accountability, discussed in the previous sections, is likely to recede in the near future. Indeed, particularly in matters concerning occupational culture, the problems of co-operation will probably become more formidable as blueprints are gradually transformed into working institutions. The most fundamental difficulty, however, remains the sources of social legitimacy. The citizens of Europe have a passive role in the legitimation of European policing institutions: there is neither a strong sense on the part of professionals and policy-makers of the prudential value of accountability measures, nor a ground swell of popular opinion sufficiently organized to make effective demands in this area (Harlow 1992: 342)

Accountability guarantees are nonetheless important in the international domain. A concern for privacy in the face of increasing levels of surveillance (Flaherty 1989; Lyon 1994), and for the transparency of public institutions are grounded in values of human rights and democratic participation. They remain basic values regardless of the extent of public acquiescence in particular policing practices. Indeed, the extent to which individuals and minority rights are protected against abuses of police powers may vary according to the strength of majority sentiment supporting particular police institutions and practices. The problem of abuse of rights could become worse as exponents of the 'internal security ideology' tend to target clearly identifiable and relatively impotent minority groups, in particular asylum-seekers and sections of the immigrant population (Den Boer 1993a: 71). Accordingly, the relative lack of concerted public pressure for increased accountability at present does not detract from, but emphasizes the importance of developing an accountability framework which is vigilant in its protection against abuses of power.[23]

What are the prospects for improved systems of accountability? It is not possible here to address this question in detail, but some general points may be made. As international policing intrudes into mundane areas of crime and as the relative transparency of the newer arrangements encourages greater public understanding of their role, international policing activities may be de-mystified. Like domestic police institutions in the past, international policing institutions may have to come to terms with a more knowledgeable and critical audience, which will generate pressure for improved accountability. The demand for accountability may build on itself. Gray and Jenkins (1985: 138) argue that '[t]o be accountable is to be liable to present an account of, and to answer for, the execution of responsibilities to those entrusting those responsibilities'. Accountability involves the presentation and reception of an account according to certain codes. Therefore, it is predicated on a certain degree of openness and agreed meanings, and may serve to further de-mystify the activities upon which the account is constructed.

However, the tension between openness and the necessity for closure in policing remains, impeding the enhancement of accountability systems. The Committee on Civil Liberties and Internal Affairs of the European Parliament have proposed measures for improvement. As regards detailed questions of due process, for example, the appointment of a European Community Data

---

[23] The continuing absence of a powerful political lobby for enhanced accountability arrangements was demonstrated by the willingness of the Essen European Council in Dec. 1994 to extend the mandate of Europol's largely unaccountable precursor—the EDU—despite a lack of agreement over the accountability provisions in the draft Europol Convention. See *Statewatch*, vol. 4, No. 6, Nov.–Dec. 1994, 1; see also ch. 9 below.

Protection Officer and the extension of the jurisdiction of the new European Ombudsman were advocated. The Committee also proposed a constitutional reform which would integrate JHA matters within the mainstream of Community law, thus allowing judicial and parliamentary control of Europol (Robles Piquer 1993). However, constitutional reform is a slow and cumbersome business; the next stage is not due until 1996, with no guarantee even then that the JHA will be a priority within an increasingly volatile Euro-agenda.

The Committee recognized that, given the importance of exploiting opportunities whenever the political climate is favourable, an imaginative and flexible approach to the interpretation of the existing constitutional framework is required over and above a strategy of long-term constitutional reform. In an opinion subsequently endorsed by the full Parliament, it suggested that it might be possible to utilize the general powers of Community institutions granted in Article 235 of the EC Treaty to legislate on any matter concerning the attainment of the broad objectives of the Community, in order to establish Europol by means of a Community Regulation. By proceeding directly through Community legislation rather than through an international Convention, the normal procedures for the participation of the European Parliament, European Commission and national parliaments in the EC law-making process would apply, and the competence of the European Court of Justice to adjudicate would be guaranteed (Van Outrive 1992d: 10-13). A related recent proposal, which avoids the difficult issue of direct Community competence (see chapter 6), is an inter-institutional agreement in which the Parliament would be fully involved at every stage—drafting, approval and implementation—in various intergovernmental conventions, including the Europol Convention, being developed under Title VI.[24]

The other key macro-political problem, noted above, is the marginal status of policing matters in the institutions of a 'post-Hobbesian' EU, whose general legitimacy as a proto-federal institution is under attack from many quarters. The lack of pressure for robust measures of accountability at the European level is in part a function of the *limited* legitimacy of European political institutions generally. A frequent political response on the part of

---

[24] 'Participation by Parliament in international agreements in the fields of justice and home affairs', OJC, No. C 44/181, 14 Feb. 1994.

'anti-Europeans' is a 'double negation' in which distaste for European integration is expressed by a refusal to take seriously its institutions. It may require only a modest perceptual shift for significant anti-European forces to move from this attitude of unhealthy denial to one of healthily sceptical acceptance—from a position where the issue of accountability was artificially marginalized to one where it moved centre-stage.

Imaginative institutional design is one means by which an alteration of perspective could be brought about. An institutional scheme would have to remedy the democratic deficit at Community level without offending aspirations for continuing national control in an area traditionally reserved to the sovereign state. One way of reconciling these apparently conflicting objectives, suggested by the Committee on Civil Liberties and Internal Affairs, is to develop a system of *dual control*. The Committee, supported by the European Parliament, advocated new liaison arrangements between itself and Home Affairs supervisory committees in domestic parliaments, with the possible establishment of a joint secretariat (Robles Piquer 1993: 6).[25] Another suggestion is the linking of domestic official data protection agencies with machinery at the EU level in overseeing the processing of personal data—an arrangement envisaged in the draft directive on data protection and in the draft Europol Convention.

The attachment to the tradition of the Hobbesian state cannot be summarily legislated away. However, the measures suggested above have an important contribution to make; by treating the emerging European order as a shared, multi-layered framework of allegiances, rather than simply as a new version of a unified political authority ripe to replace the nation state (Weiler 1991: 2478–81; Walker 1994b), and by reflecting this novel complexity in particular proposals for the division of executive power and accountability, they demonstrate a more rounded understanding of the dynamics of European transformation and avoid needless confrontation with national sensitivities.

The other two major difficulties identified—the vested interests of various bureaucratic élites in European policing and the divisive occupational cultures of police work—alter the focus from the

---

[25] The improvement of co-operation between national parliaments and the European Parliament is itself a goal of the TEU; see Declaration on the Role of the National Parliaments in the EU.

wider social and political environment to the different levels *within* the law enforcement community. The capacity of police institutions to resist efforts at external influence and supervision is a central factor. The issues involved are difficult, but a consideration of certain basic principles of organization may suggest options for reform.

Fundamental organizational choices tend to revolve around a cluster of related variables which can be mapped onto a single continuum (Walker 1993b: 134–7). At one pole is a conception of international policing as a *highly integrated* set of arrangements. The emphasis here is upon an institutional framework with jurisdiction across the range of international crimes, bringing together policy and operational functions, and establishing a regime of central control. At the other pole is a conception of international policing as a *loosely structured* set of arrangements. The maintenance of organizational boundaries between different functional specialisms and strategic levels would be maintained, and the co-existence of regimes of equivalent status operating at different territorial levels would continue. Notwithstanding the advent of Europol, present arrangements are situated closer to the loosely structured pole.

In considering the objective of enhanced accountability, each ideal type has its merits and demerits. The highly integrated approach eliminates the dangers of a competition between different institutions vying to demonstrate the strength of their contribution to 'law and order'. It also has the advantage of providing a clear focus upon a single institution from which all lines of accountability flow, and of maximizing the prospects of reducing cultural discord between the different components of international policing. But to confer monopoly or dominant police power on a single institution carries disadvantages. Its scale of operations, range of legal powers, complexity of internal structure and vested professional interests may make it less susceptible to external control. The seductive professional and political attractions of the creation of an open-ended 'internal security field' (Bigo 1994b) may make it more difficult to prevent a monolithic organization colonizing new policy and operational domains. The loosely structured approach, on the other hand, has the advantage of establishing an ever-shifting balance of influence which prevents any single institution from consolidating an independent power base and developing mechanisms to insulate itself from external control. But, it has the disadvantage of encouraging a competitive rivalry within the internal market for policing, with potentially authoritarian consequences. Competing agencies also lack the resources and the motivation to confront problems of cultural co-ordination and control between law enforcement officers with different national backgrounds and expertise. Finally, it is a more fragmented, less settled and less transparent institutional framework on which to impose accountability systems.

From these balanced considerations, a hybrid *semi-structured* model of European co-operation emerges as the most effective method of promoting accountability. In this model, Europol would be the dominant international police organization in its domain, with a unified core concerned with policy-making and personnel functions. Around this core various services could be grouped, performing limited operational functions in matters such as information exchange, crime pattern analysis, co-ordination of national investigations, training, technological developments and so on, with some further sub-division into specialist units focusing on particular forms of crime. The loosely integrated 'dominant' organization would retain some control over co-ordination of staff and provide a relatively clear focus for accountability, but would be less likely than a centralized organization to insulate itself from external influences and develop entrenched interests and inflexible attitudes. In this model, Europol could develop in stages, gradually assuming new functions. This semi-structured solution has the added advantage of following the grain of present developments, as the Title VI arrangements have already absorbed Trevi's functions, and are ultimately destined to eclipse Schengen. An incremental adaptation to changing circumstances is the most likely way in which a fully-fledged European police agency will emerge.

Conclusion

If guarding the guardians is, indeed, 'one of the thorniest conundrums of statecraft', it poses even more difficult problems in the field of international relations. An effective framework of European police accountability must be achieved in the face of a general political culture ambivalent towards supranational regulation of law enforcement; despite the absence of an effective voice for those most vulnerable to the abuse of new powers of co-operation;

against the influence of professional bureaucracies jealous to reveal their position; and notwithstanding the difficulties of treating the disparate range of European police cultures and agencies within a single framework of control. Developments under the Schengen system and Title VI of the TEU have certainly opened up the possibility of a more substantial framework of police co-operation. Whether the extension of a European policing capacity will be matched by an enhancement of accountability arrangements remains to be seen.

9

The Future of European Police Co-operation

In this conclusion, we set out briefly the developments which we consider desirable if a more effective and legitimate system of policing the EU is to be achieved, and indicate some of the main factors which may facilitate or impede enhanced co-operation. A favourable political context, the commitment of political élites, and some criminal justice harmonization, approximation or mutual recognition are required in order for progress to be made towards the development of operational police powers at the European level, a common approach to international crime within European public policy, the improvement of the practice of co-operation, and enhanced systems of police accountability. Prospects in some of these areas are not good and there are potential pitfalls, even dangers, along the road to more integrated law enforcement arrangements. It is therefore possible to take a sceptical view and regard improved police co-operation as a low priority and even an undesirable objective.

A Favourable Political Context

The various elements that make up this context cannot be predicted with any certainty, unless and until clear progress towards enhanced co-operation is, in fact, made, but there are factors which would obviously be helpful. The key factors are; first, a stable membership of the EU because uncertainty over the size of the Union inhibits detailed planning about the form and intensity of co-operation. Secondly, institutional stability and a certain degree of predictability about the general structural development of the EU is essential; whether the EU strengthens the federal elements in its constitution, whether there is an acceptance of a multi-speed Europe, or whether the conservative view that the EU should be a predominantly intergovernmental organization, provides the spectrum of expectations in which police co-operation may take place. Clearly, the more integrationist the scenario, the more favourable to police co-operation, but it is also imperative that there is some level of agreement about the way ahead, however modestly or ambitiously this is viewed. The trajectory adopted will be influenced by a revival of, or a decline in, popular belief in the benefits of the EU to its citizens and Member States. General perceptions of the Union will determine whether there can be a 'legitimacy transfer' from the Member States to the EU which will allow the latter to be given executive police powers. These perceptions also influence more specific matters such as a willingness on the part of small states to be flexible on language policy so that one, two or three working languages could be used in police co-operation.

A favourable political context also has micro-level components relating specifically to policing matters. Given the general resilience of allegiance to the nation state in Western Europe, a belief that police co-operation can make progress without infringing state sovereignty is still necessary. Without this belief it would be impossible to gain a broad enough consent to new structures of co-operation. In addition, the European Union must be regarded as a reasonable territory for police co-operation, so that the problems of 'international crime' can be considered to be effectively confronted by co-operation within this configuration, rather than, for example, global co-operation with some regional structures (as in Interpol), or a special European police co-operation territory which included non-members as well as members of the EU. The decision to establish Europol suggests broad acceptance that the EU is, indeed, acceptable as a suitable geographical space for enforcement co-operation.

Political Will

Determined leadership by major Member States is the *sine qua non* of advances in this field. Structural fatalism, regarding closer police co-operation as dependent upon the outcome of objective factors, is misplaced and inadequate, because without deliberate and committed political action, bureaucratic inertia, divergent political interests, and the manoeuvres of political groupings antagonistic to closer co-operation, will lead to stalemate. Leadership implies both commitment on the part of key politicians and a high place on domestic political agendas of policing issues with European/ international implications. If political will is present much can be achieved; this view is shared by most of the professional law enforcement officers we spoke to in the course of our enquiry.

Political will is often expressed in terms of general aspirations to achieve certain ends. But the gap between rhetoric and practical concerns in fields such as civil liberties, data protection and criminal law procedures must be bridged if political will is to be translated into action. Without this bridge 'Euro-policing' risks being merely a rhetorical device used by politicians with other political priorities such as promoting a common immigration policy to further particular national or domestic interests (see chapter 5).

Criminal Justice Harmonization

This implies the development of a European Judicial Space (although the term has fallen into disuse). Harmonization of substantive and procedural criminal justice systems is difficult and not yet accepted as an objective. Rather, the major effort so far has been to seek to improve intergovernmental co-operative mechanisms, such as extradition and mutual assistance, so as to minimize the impediments which flow from essentially non-harmonized systems of criminal justice. Within the versatile framework of the third pillar, the successful negotiation and implementation of conventions on extradition, the regulation of the external frontier, the development of new criminal and customs information systems, and the establishment of Europol, will have the effect of enhancing intergovernmental co-operative mechanisms still further, in part by providing for a degree of harmonization of domestic procedural laws. A modest basis for harmonization is also created by other international treaty obligations. Some approximation of key concepts and practices is taking place as a result of the Schengen negotiations, and also as a result of the implementation of wider international agreements, notably the 1988 UN Drugs Convention and the 1990 Council of Europe Convention on money laundering and confiscation of proceeds. Within Community law, the doctrine of direct effect promises a more efficient harmonization of domestic laws, but although there have been important initiatives in money laundering, insider dealing, firearms, and, most recently, fraud against the Community, the highly restricted jurisdiction of

Community law in criminal or quasi-criminal matters remains a significant impediment (see chapter 6). Recognizing this limitation, Salisch and Speroni (1994) have proposed an extension of Community competence at the next intergovernmental conference in 1996 in order to oblige Member States to adopt a uniform conceptual and legislative framework for a range of offences in the EU, particularly with regard to membership of a criminal organization (which is not yet a criminal offence in some countries). The example of organized crime, moreover, also demonstrates how harmonization can be achieved by less formal means, through the emergence and voluntary adoption of a model of legislative 'best practice'. The approximation of the definitions of organized crime is already beginning to take shape as criminal intelligence services in the EU copy parts of each other's working definitions of organized crime (see chapter 1).

Operational Powers

During the drafting of the Europol Convention, there was a debate on whether its terms should leave open the possibility of adding operational powers of investigation, search and arrest to the remit of Europol. In theory, this could be achieved under the amendments clause of the German draft of the Convention (Article 40). However, despite a commitment in the political declaration attached to the TEU to conclude discussions of the extension of the criminal law enforcement jurisdiction of Europol before the end of 1994, no substantive resolution of the issue was possible within this deadline. A strong restatement of Germany's longstanding support for operational powers by the German Interior Minister, Manfred Kanther, at the Berlin meeting of JHA Ministers in September 1994, met with an unenthusiastic response, confirming that the majority of Member States remain opposed to such an initiative (see chapter 2).[1]

The absence of a federal structure in Europe, a common criminal justice system, and a supranational accountability mechanism,

---

[1] *Statewatch*. vol.4, No.5, Sept.–Oct. 1994, at p. 10. Despite a cautious approach to general operational powers, nine out of twelve members States (prior to the 1995 expansion) have accepted (in the Schengen and Benelux agreements) limited rights to operational cross-border policing by the forces of neighbouring countries. Even the UK has accepted very limited rights in the case of the Channel Tunnel. It is, however, a very big step to extend these precedents to cover common action through Europol.

makes operational powers for Europol extremely unlikely. However, even a Europol without operational powers may grow into a powerful institution, a prospect which may strengthen the argument against such powers. Europol may take on the SIRENE-function developed within Schengen, and it may play a role in the 'external security' sphere (countering threats of subversion from outside the EU). If the EU Member States favoured operational powers for Europol in the longer term, the development of Special Task Forces could be an attractive intermediate solution. These forces would be multi-national, operate across the internal boundaries of the EU, and last for the duration of a specific case or investigation. Members of the Task Forces would have executive powers only in their own countries and would have the status of observers and advisers when present on the territory of another Member State. A prerequisite for such a system is that there should be a close triangle of co-operation between the national prosecution authorities, law enforcement authorities and Europol.

A Common Approach to International Crime within European Public Policy

Since the 1970s there has been an attempt to foster a common approach within the Pompidou Group in the area of repression of the illegal use of drugs. As suggested in chapter 1, this has had limited success although some harmonization has taken place. Although the experience of other Member States (and other influential countries, particularly the United States) regularly informs national policy discussions, the process of developing common policies in this field is in its infancy. There are several ways forward.

One way is to develop a more systematic research capacity linked to policy. Thus, for example, the EU Member States could endeavour to make geographical maps of crime problem areas. These should not merely concentrate on the mapping of drug-trafficking routes (such as the Balkan route mapped by Interpol), but adopt a differentiated approach, with a concentration of multiple crime-phenomena (including urban crime, small border crime, cross-border crime, etc.). National attempts have, so far, not been encouraging. An example is the Aubert Report (1993) on the penetration of the mafia in France. This report drew maps of intensive mafia activity in France, but was quickly undermined by police disagreement with its contents. A systematic and rigorous approach to crime analysis through co-operation between law enforcement agencies could help to identify actual and potential cross-border problems.

The EU Member States could encourage European criminological studies (at present scarcely ever genuinely cross-national), with a view to harmonizing crime analysis, victimization studies, crime statistics, and related issues. Empirical criminological studies are at the moment predominantly national in character and are heavily concentrated in northern Europe. Comparisons between Member States are, as a result, notoriously difficult. Participation by Ministry of Justice officials or officials of EU institutions in European criminological research schemes would be crucial, in order to guarantee a dialogue between academics and policy-makers. One difficulty is that crime control issues have, in some countries, become highly political and governments may be unwilling to help sponsor genuinely independent research.

A Europe-wide strategy will inevitably be expressed in general terms and, when it is developed, its impact will be long-term. EU Member States should therefore co-ordinate crime strategies which are specifically aimed at certain regions within and on the periphery of the EU. There is scope for a dual strategy; a centralized approach through the mechanisms of the European Union and the Council of Europe, and for a decentralized approach, which can be effected through a series of bilateral and multilateral agreements and co-operative frameworks. Once regional and local transfrontier crime strategies have been seen to work, these will assist the development of more general European strategies in crime control. A balance is necessary between repressive and preventive crime strategies in a medium or long-term action programme. European co-operation in the crime control field should not be merely in the fields of police co-operation and repression as this would give substance to the arguments about the development of a security-dominated European 'police state'. Without contravening the principles of subsidiarity and sovereignty, the EU Member States could begin to fine-tune their criminal justice polices by co-ordinating social policies directed at the causes of crime.

Improvement of Cooperative Practice

In order to improve the practice of co-operation it is important to nurture an international police culture in which bilateral and multi-lateral co-operation in Europe is facilitated. The development of various exchange schemes (including study visits, short courses, sporting and social exchanges) and of police and customs foreign liaison officer networks are contributing to this end. A fairly rapid turnover of some of the personnel of the EDU, and, in due course, of Europol, will be desirable in order to give experience of this form of operational co-operation to as many police officers as possible.[2] There must be a parallel ambition to involve as many police officers as possible in local schemes of co-operation such as the joint police systems for the Channel Tunnel, and on the Franco-German and Franco-Spanish frontiers (Benyon *et al*. 1993: 204–18). 'Low-tech' schemes for face-to-face co-operation between officers, such as those developed for identifying criminals among tradition-ally nomadic populations, should also be encouraged and not dis-pensed with because of a belief in the efficacy of 'high-tech' methods.

A number of interesting and potentially useful proposals have also been made in the field of education and training. One is the development of a series of operational training courses and exchanges for police officers, similar to the Matthaeus programme for customs officers, as proposed by the Committee on Civil Liberties and Internal Affairs of the European Parliament (Salisch and Speroni 1994). This proposal revives in a different form the idea of a European police school or academy, earlier put forward by Piet Van Reenen (Van Reenen 1992). Intended for the system-atic training of officers engaged in transfrontier co-operation, such a police academy could also help to develop a common code of professional practice. Still more ambitiously, the proposal for a European police council (subsequently a European police

---

[2] Art. 5 of the German draft of the Europol Convention only commits signatory states to appointing one liaison officer to Europol HQ, although the Management Board may agree to increase this. As its more modest predecessor, the EDU, had a staff of 70 by the end of 1994, including not only liaison officers, but also analysts, planning and development officers, IT trainers etc., a relatively extensive turnover of national police officers can be anticipated in a fully fledged Europol. Nevertheless, it will be a number of years before there are significant numbers of officers in Member States with Europol experience.

programme) by Chief Constable Roger Birch (Home Affairs Committee 1990) was designed to give the police an independent voice at the European level and to help to spread best practice throughout the Member States. Of more immediate concern, the issue of common training facilities must be considered in Europol in order to facilitate co-operative working relationships between the officers seconded to Europol and the development of common concepts for international transactions. Increased language training, too, is a short and medium-term priority. So, too, is the production of glossaries of police terminology in different languages and more ambitious initiatives, such as Kent Constabulary's *Police Speak* project, which, *inter alia,* produced a preliminary lexicon of police terms for use by both English and French officers working in and around the Channel Tunnel. Overall, much remains to be done to educate police officers in co-operative techniques and attitudes, and a more systematic effort is required than has been made in the early years of Union-wide co-operation (Benyon *et al.* 1993: 110–15).

Improving co-operative practice also means designing systems of co-operation which are regarded as efficient. The third pillar of the TEU has done much to integrate various intergovernmental activities in the domain of police co-operation, international crime and immigration. A new Co-ordinating Committee has been created which acts as an intermediary between the Council of Ministers of Justice and Home Affairs and the steering groups. However, the current situation remains unsatisfactory for the following reasons.

First, a twin-track Europe exists as a consequence of the non-equivalence between the Schengen Agreements[3] and co-operation in the JHA framework. One consequence is the non-uniformity of the border control regime within the territory of the EU. In order to resolve this, the Schengen Agreement, or central parts of it, could be integrated in the third pillar of the Maastricht Treaty (Den Boer 1995b). A number of provisions in the Schengen Agreement facilitate this integration, such as the stipulation that only European Community Member States can become parties. Moreover, parts of the Schengen Agreement will be superseded by EU-wide agreements such as the Dublin Asylum Convention and the External Borders Convention (if and when ratified). The disadvantage of the strategy

---

[3] It was agreed in Bonn on 22 Dec. 1994 that it would be implemented by 26 March 1995 (Italy and Greece excluded).

of integration is that an intergovernmental body of rules has been developed by the five original Schengen signatories, without the influence of the more recent Schengen signatories (Italy, Spain, Portugal and Greece) or the potential Schengen signatories (Denmark, Ireland, the United Kingdom, Sweden, Finland and Austria), who cannot be assumed to be in sympathy with all parts of the Schengen scheme. For example, the Schengen Agreements provide for types of cross-border police co-operation which are not included under the JHA. Therefore, although merging of Schengen with JHA would resolve the problem of different border control regimes within the EU, the political obstacles to this remain formidable. The danger is that Schengen and JHA will remain as poorly co-ordinated systems.

Secondly, even if this problem is resolved, a properly integrated regime still poses certain efficiency problems. In its attempt to be comprehensive and to provide adequate links between political and administrative levels of decision-making, the third pillar has spawned a large and complex bureaucracy. This bureaucracy may suffer typical problems of delay, excessive formalism, buck-passing and a lack of transparency in the decision-making process (see chapters 2 and 8).

Thirdly, the 'formalization' of European police co-operation through inclusion in the third pillar of the TEU may decrease the input of professional and practical law enforcement expertise by putting most business in the hands of senior civil servants and officials. The first danger of this trend is that inappropriate criminal justice strategies (in the eyes of law enforcement professionals) may develop. The second danger is that, if disillusion spreads among police officers in the European Union about policies adopted, they may develop their own, unaccountable and informal networks of co-operation outside the JHA structure of the TEU.

Accountability Mechanisms

The issue of accountability, which is sometimes regarded by police officers, administrators, and politicians alike as a tiresome marginal matter, lies at the very core of the development of a balanced and efficient systems of police co-operation as well as progress towards genuine political union. Questions of accountability both to the general public and for policy actions which affect them directly (of particular relevance in the field of data protection) were analysed at length in chapter 8, and possible future scenarios were discussed. In the present context, we will confine ourselves to reinforcing and developing a key general point about the relationship between effectiveness and accountability.

Conventional wisdom in the JHA Council appears to recognize no significant relationship between effectiveness and accountability. The events surrounding the European Council meeting at Essen in December 1994 make this point with great clarity. The German Presidency was unable to fulfil its oft-proclaimed commitment to conclude negotiation of the Europol Convention. Accountability issues, including data protection, the role of the European Parliament and the jurisdiction of the European Court of Justice, provided the main stumbling-blocks. However, as a means of saving political face, and of demonstrating a continuing common commitment to progress in European police co-operation, the mandate of the EDU—intended as a temporary measure pending the establishment of Europol—was extended significantly to cover nuclear crime, illegal immigration networks, vehicle trafficking and associated money laundering activities.

The European Council Ministers seemed blind to the irony of their decision: that as consolation for a prize that could not be delivered because of disagreement over its accountability mechanism, they proposed to extend the scale of a measure which was even more deficient in accountability terms. Clearly, progress towards effective police co-operation was not to be thwarted just because optimal control systems were not yet in place.

This reveals a fundamental lack of awareness of the preconditions of effective police co-operation. Accountability arrangements are neither an irrelevance nor an impediment; rather, they are prerequisite to effective police co-operation. First, effective democratic accountability can help to overcome the 'organizational paradox' revealed in the previous section, whereby it appears that proper co-ordination and integration of JHA matters can only be purchased at the price of excessive bureaucracy. Effective mechanisms of oversight by representative bodies can help to ensure against insularity and complacency and to compensate for the opaqueness of internal decision-making processes. Secondly, as argued in chapter 8, satisfactory accountability arrangements help to secure the long-term popular legitimacy of policy systems; without public support and willingness to supply information, the effectiveness even of the specialized activities typical of international policing is likely to suffer. Thirdly, and of most immediate importance, a commitment to a robust supranational system of accountability might help to overcome the climate of mutual suspicion and caution which threatens to undermine the development of the JHA Chapter generally. In their post-Essen comments on the disappointing progress of the JHA Chapter in its first year of operation, both the outgoing European Commissioner, Padraig Flynn,[4] and the European Parliament,[5] drew attention to the stultifying effect of the continuing insistence of Member States on the use of intergovernmental co-operation practices, in particular unanimous decision-making. The preference for unanimity is at least partly applicable by reference to fear of a 'democratic deficit' at Union level. Only the veto, the Eurosceptics argue, stands between the Member States and the tyranny of the European Commission backed by a majoritarian Council. If, in the alternative, the European Parliament, legitimated by a distinctive democratic mandate, also had effective input to and overview of JHA decisions, the veto might no longer be insisted upon as a necessary constitutional long-stop, thus paving the way for more effective progress within the JHA Council along majoritarian lines.

The factors discussed under the various headings of this conclusion are all interconnected. The pattern of links between them is constantly shifting. A mixture of systemic pressures, chance and choice will determine whether federalization or fragmentation of law enforcement will be dominant in the 21st century. This mixture will also decide whether the balance of the common European policing effort will tip towards repression and authoritarianism or to an affirmation of democratic values.

[4] See *Agence Europe*, No. 6369, 2 Dec. 1994, at pp. 6 and 7.
[5] European Parliament Resolution on the Progress made during 1994 in the implementation of co-operation in the fields of justice and home affairs pursuant to Title VI of the Treaty on European Union, *European Parliament Proceedings*, 13 Dec. 1994.

References

AALBERTS, M. M. J. (1989). *Operationeel vreemdelingentoezicht in Nederland* (Arnhem).

AD HOC GROUP ON IMMIGRATION (1993). *Programme de travail du Groupe ad hoc 'Immigration' au cours de la Présidence belge*, SN 3675/93 WGI 1566, 1/7/93 (Brussels).

AHNFELT, E. and FROM, J. (1994). 'External Border Control and Police Cooperation in the European Union', ECPR Joint Sessions of Workshops, 17–22 April 1994, unpub. paper (Madrid).

ALBINI, J. L. (1986). 'Organised Crime in Great Britain and the Carribean', in R. J. Kelly (ed.), *Organised Crime: a Global Perspective*, (1986) Totowa, 95–112.

ALVAZZI DEL FRATE, A., ZVEKIC, U., and DIJK, J. M. VAN (eds.) (1993). *Understanding Crime. Experiences of Crime and Crime Control* (Rome).

ANDERSON, B. (1991). *Imagined Communities. An Enquiry into the Origins and Spread of Nationalism*, revised ed. (London).

ANDERSON, M. (1989). *Policing the World. Interpol and the Politics of International Police Cooperation* (Oxford).

—— (1991). *The French Police and European Police Cooperation*, Working Paper I, 'A System of European Police Cooperation after 1992' (Edinburgh).

—— (1993a). *Control of Organised Crime in the European Community*, Working Paper IX, 'A System of European Police Cooperation after 1992' (Edinburgh).

—— (1993b). 'La Coopération des Polices avec l'Europe de l'Est dans le Cadre de l'Union Européenne', *Cahiers de la Sécurité Intérieure*, 14, 2, 155–66.

—— (1994a). 'The Agenda for Police Cooperation', in M. Anderson and M. den Boer (eds.), (1994) 3–21.

—— (1994b), *Objectives and Instruments of Police Cooperation*, ECPR Joint Sessions of Workshops, unpub. paper (Madrid) 17–22.

—— and BOER, M. DEN (1992) (eds.). *European Police Co-operation*, Proceedings of a Seminar (Edinburgh).

—— and BOER, M. DEN (1994) (eds.). *Policing Across National Boundaries* (London).

AUBERT REPORT (1993). 'Rapport de la Commission d'Enquête sur les moyens de lutter contre les tentatives de pénétration de la mafia en France', *Journal Officiel*, Assemblée Nationale, 28 January, Document no. 3251.

BAAUW, P. (1991). 'Extradition and the (Additional) Schengen Agreement on the Abolition of Border Control', *Revue Internationale de Droit Pénal*, 62, 529–35.

O'BALLANCE, E. (1989). *Terrorism in the 1980s* (London).

BALDWIN, R. (1987). 'Why Police Accountability?', *British Journal of Criminology*, 32, 97–105.

BALDWIN-EDWARDS, M. and HEBENTON, B. (1994). 'Will the Schengen Information System be Europe's "Big Brother"?' in M. An¹erson. and M. den Boer (eds.), (1994) 136–57.

BARENTS, R. (1985). 'The System of Deposits in Community Agricultural Law: Efficiency v. Proportionality', *European Law Review*, 10, 239–49.

—— (1993). 'The Internal Market Unlimited: Some Observations on the Legal Basis of Community Legislation' *Common Market Law Review*, 30, 85–109.

BARTSCH, H.-J. (1991). 'The Western European Approach', *Revue Internationale de Droit Penal*, 62, 499–510.

BAYLEY, D. (1985). *Patterns of Policing* (New Brunswick).

BEAUMONT, P. and MOIR, G. (1994). *The European Communities (Amendment) Act 1993 with the Treaty of Rome (As Amended)—Text and Commentary* (London).

BECK, U. (1992). *The Risk Society* (London).

BENTHAM, K. (1992). 'A European Police Council', in M. Anderson and M. den Boer (eds.), (1992) 121–31.

BENYON, J., DAVIES, P. and WILLIS, P. (1990). *Police Cooperation in Europe: A Preliminary Report*. (Leicester).

BENYON, J., TURNBULL, L., WILLIS, A., WOODWARD, R. and BECK, A. (1993). *Police Cooperation in Europe: An Investigation* (Leicester).

BERKI, R. N. (1986). *Security and Society: Reflections on Law, Order and Politics* (London).

BIGO, D. (1994a). 'Les Controles aux frontières', Projet de Recherche (Paris).

—— (1994b). 'The European Internal Security Field: Stakes and Rivalries in a Newly Developing Area of Police Intervention', in M. Anderson and M. den Boer (eds.), (1994) 161–73.

—— (1994c). 'Terrorisme, drogue, immigration: les nouvelles figures de l'insécurité en Europe', unpub. paper.

—— and LEVEAU, R. (1992). *L'Europe de la Sécurité Intérieure*, Rapport de fin d'étude pour l'Institut des Hautes Etudes de la Sécurité Intérieure (Paris).

BIRCH, R. (1989). 'Policing Europe after 1992' Address to Royal Institute of International Affairs (London) 19 April, unpub. paper.

BITTNER, E. (1971). *The Functions of the Police in Modern Society* (Washington DC).

BLACK, D. (1991). *Triad Takeover* (London).

BOER, M. DEN (1991a). *The Police in the Netherlands and European Co–operation*, Working Paper IV, 'A System of European Police Co–operation after 1992' (Edinburgh).

—— (1991b). *Schengen: Intergovernmental Scenario for European Police Cooperation*, Working Paper V, 'A System of European Police Cooperation after 1992', (Edinburgh).

—— (1992). *Police Co-operation after Maastricht*, Research Paper No 2/92, European Community Research Unit (Hull).

—— (1993a). *Immigration, Internal Security and Policing in Europe*, Working Paper VIII, 'A System of European Police Co-operation after 1992' (Edinburgh).

—— (1993b). 'Police Cooperation and Regulatory Frameworks', Third Biennial International Conference ECSA, unpub. paper (Washington, DC).

—— (1994a). 'Europe and the Art of International Police Cooperation: Free Fall or Measured Scenario?', in D. O'Keeffe, and P. Twomey. (eds.), (1994) 279–91.

—— (1994b). 'The Quest for European Policing: Rhetoric and Justification in a Disorderly Debate', in M. Anderson and M. den Boer (eds.), (1994)174–96.

—— (1994c). 'Rhetorics of Crime and Ethnicity in the Construction of Europe', ECPR Joint Sessions, unpub. paper (Madrid).

—— (1995a). 'Moving between Bogus and Bonafide: The Policing of Inclusion and Exclusion in Europe', in R. Miles and D. Thränhardt (eds.), (1995) *Migration and European Integration: The Dynamics of Inclusion and Exclusion* (London), 92–111.

—— (1995b). 'Police Cooperation in the TEU: Tiger in a Trojan Horse?', *Common Market Law Review*, 32.

—— and Walker, N. (1993). 'European Policing after 1992', *Journal of Common Market Studies*, 31, 1, 3–28.

BÖGL, G. (1994). 'Grenzüberschreitende organisierte Kriminalität zwischen Österreich und ehemaligen Ostblockländern', Transpol (ed.), *Internationalisering door Grenzeloze Samenwerking* (Lelystad), 21–32.

BOURDIEU, P. (1992. *Language and Symbolic Power*, ed. and introd. by J. B. Thompson (Cambridge).

BOVENKERK, F. (1992). *Hedendaags Kwaad, Criminologische Opstellen* (Amsterdam).

BRAMMERTZ, S., VREESE, S. and THYS, J. (1993). *Collaboration Policière Transfrontalière* (Bruxelles).

BRESLER, F. (1992). *Interpol* (Weert).

BRION, F., VERHEYEN, L. and SPIESSENS, G. (1994). *Études de l'Immigration. L'Inégalité Pénale; Immigration, criminalité et système d'administration de la justice pénale* (Louvain-la-Neuve).

BRODEUR, J. P. (1983). 'High Policing and Low Policing: Remarks about the Policing of Political Activities', *Social Problems*, 30, 507–20.

BROGDEN, M. (1990). 'The Origins of the South African Police— Institutional versus Structural Approaches', *Acta Juridica*. 6, 1–20.

——, JEFFERSON, T. and WALKLATE, S. (1988). *Introducing Policework*. (London).

BRYANT, C. (1991). 'Europe and the European Community', *Sociology*, 25, 189–207.

BULL, H. (1977). *The Anarchical Society* (London).

BULLINGTON, B. (1993). 'All about Eve: The Many Faces of US Drugs Policy', in F. Pearce, M. Woodiwiss (eds.), (1993) *Global Crime Connections: Dynamics and Control* (Basingstoke), 32–71.

BULMER, S. J. (1993). 'Community Governance and Regulatory Régimes', Third Biennial International Conference ECSA (Washington, DC), unpub. paper.

BUNYAN, T. (1991). 'Towards an Authoritarian European State', *Race and Class*, 32, 3, 19–27.

BUSCH, H. (1991). 'Die Debatte um organisierte Kriminalität in der BRD', *Bürgerrechte und Polizei*, 39, 2, 6–16.

—— and Funk, A. (1995). 'Undercover Tactics as an Element of Preventive Crime Fighting in the Federal Republic of Germany', in C. Fijnaut, and G. Marx, (eds.), *Undercover: Police Surveillance in Comparative Perspective* (Deventer/Boston).

BUTT-PHILIP, A. (1989). *European Border Controls: Who Needs Them?*, Discussion Paper 19, RIIA (London).

—— (1991). 'Border Controls: Who Needs Them?', *Public Policy and Administration*, 6, 2, 35–54.

BUZAN, B. (1991). *People, States and Fear. An Agenda for International Security Studies in the Post–Cold War Era* (New York), 2nd ed.

—— (1993). 'Introduction: The changing security agenda in Europe', in O. Waever, B. Buzan, M. Kelstrup, and P. Lemaitre (eds.), (1993) *Identity. Migration and the New Security Agenda in Europe* (London), 1–14.

CALVI, F. (1993). *Het Europa van de peetvaders: de mafia verovert een continent* (Leuven/Amsterdam).

CARLSON, S. and ZAGARIS, B. (1991). 'International Cooperation in Criminal Matters: Western Europe's International Approach to International Crime', *Nova Law Review*, 15, 551–79.

CAMERON-WALLER, S. (1994) 'Interpol's Point of View', in A. Pauly (ed.), (1994) *Schengen en panne* (Maastricht), 101–110.

CASTLES, S., and Miller, M. J. (1993). *The Age of Migration. International Population Movements in the Modern World*, (London).

CERVELLO, C. (1990). 'Analyse comparée des législations pénales des pays membres du groupe Pompidou en matière de lutte contre l'usage et le trafic de stupéfiants', *Revue science criminelle*, 3, 538–47.

CHOO, A. (1994). 'Ex Parte Bennett: The Demise of the Male Captus Bene Detentus Doctrine in England?', *Criminal Law Forum*, 5, 165–79.

CHOISEUL-PRASLIN, C. M. (1991). *La drogue* (Paris).

CHRISTODOULIDIS, E., and Veitch, T. S. (1994). 'Terrorism and Systems Terror', *Economy and Society*, 23, 459–83.

CLARK, J. A. and SANCTUARY, C. J. (1992). 'Anti-drug smuggling operational research in HM. Customs and Excise', *Public Administration*, 70, 4, 577–89.

CLARK, R. (1988). 'Offences of International Concern: Multilateral State Treaty Practice in the Forty Years Since Nuremburg', *Nordic Journal of International Law*, 57, 49–119.

—— (1993). 'United Nations Model Treaties on Cooperation in Criminal Matters', in *Action Against Transnational Criminality: Papers from the 1992 Oxford Conference on International and White Collar Crime* (London), 141–146.

CLARKE, M. (1993). 'EEC Fraud: A Suitable Case for Treatment', in F. Pearce and M. Woodiwiss (eds), *Global Crime Connections* (London), 162–86.

CLOSA, C. (1992). 'The Concept of Citizenship in the Treaty on European Union', *Common Market Law Review*, 29, 1137–69.

CLUTTERBUCK, R. (1990). *Terrorism, Drugs and Crime in Europe after 1992* (London).

COHEN, H. (1985). 'Authority: The Limits of Discretion' in F. A. Elliston and M. Feldberg (eds.), *Moral Issues in Police Work*, (New Jersey), 27–42.

COLLIER, A. (1992). 'The Problems of Measuring Cross-Frontier Crime', 1992 and Cross Frontier Crime Conference, unpub. paper (Southampton).

COLLINSON, S. (1993). *Beyond Borders: West European Migration Policy towards the 21st Century* (London).

COMMISSION OF THE EUROPEAN COMMUNITIES (1988). *Communication of the Commission to the Council on the abolition of controls of persons at intra-Community borders*. COM (88) 640, (Brussels) 7 December.

—— (1992a), *Amended Proposal for a Council Directive on the Protection of Individuals with Regard to the Processing of Personal Data and on the Free Movement of Such Data* COM (92) 422 final—SYN 287 (Brussels).

—— (1992b). *XXIst Report on Competition Policy—1991* (Brussels).

—— (1993). *Summary Report of the Study on the Systems of Administrative and Criminal Penalties of the Member States and on the General Principles Applicable to Community Penalties* (Commission Staff Working Paper—incorporating Delmas-Marty Report), SEC (93) 1172 (Brussels), 16 July.

—— (1994a). *Communication from the Commission to the Council and the European Parliament on Immigration and Asylum Policies*, COM (94) 23 final (Brussels), 23 February.

—— (1994b). *The Community Internal Market—1993 Report*, COM (94) 55 final (Brussels), 14 March.

—— (1994c). *Proposal for a Council Regulation (EC, Euratom) on protection of the Community's financial interests* (Proposal for a Council of the European Union Act establishing a Convention for the protection of the Communities' financial interests), COM (94) 214 final (Brussels), 15 June.

—— (1994d), *Protecting the Financial Interests of the Community: The Fight against Fraud*, The Commission's Anti-Fraud Strategy Work Programme for 1994 (Brussels).

CONNOR, W. (1969). 'Myths of Hemispheric, Continental, Regional, and State Unity', *Political Science Quarterly*, 84, 4, 555–82.

COONEY REPORT (1992). *Report on the Spread of Organized Crime linked to Drugs Trafficking in the Member States of the European Community*, European Parliament Session Documents, A3–0358/91, 23 April.

COPPEL, J. and O'NEILL, A. (1992). 'The European Court of Justice: taking rights seriously?', *Legal Studies*, 12, 227–45.

CORSTENS, G. J. M. (1994). 'Inbreken in de rechtsstaat', *Nederlands Juristenblad*, 15 April, 15, 497–98.

Council of Europe (1969). *Explanatory Report of the European Convention on Mutual Assistance in Criminal Matters*.

—— (1975). *Explanatory Report on the Additional Protocol to the European Convention on Extradition*.

—— (1978a) *Explanatory Report on the Second Additional Protocol to the European Convention on Extradition*.

—— (1978b). *Explanatory Report on the Additional Protocol to the European Convention on Mutual Assistance in Criminal Matters*.

—— (1979). *Explanatory Report on the European Convention on the Suppression of Terrorism*.

—— (1980). European Committee on Crime Problems, *Report on Decriminalisation* (Strasbourg).

—— (1983). *Explanatory Report on the Convention on the Transfer of Sentenced Persons*.

—— (1985a). *Explanatory Report on the European Convention on Extradition*.

—— (1985b). *Explanatory Report on the European Convention on the Transfer of Proceedings in Criminal Matters*.

—— (1988). *Regulating the Use of Personal Data in the Police Sector* (Strasbourg).

—— (1989). *Explanatory Report on the Convention on Insider Trading and its Protocol*.

—— (1991). *Explanatory Report on the Convention on Laundering, Search, Seizure and Confiscation of the Proceeds from Crime.*

CREMONA, M. (1994). 'The Common Foreign and Security Policy of the European Union and the External Relations Powers of the European Community', in D. O'Keeffe and P. Twomey, (eds.), (1994) 247–58.

CRUZ, A. (1990). *An Insight into Schengen, Trevi and other European Intergovernmental Bodies*, CCME Briefing papers No. 1 (2nd. ed.) (Brussels).

CULLEN, P. (1993). 'Money Laundering: The European Community Directive', in H. MacQueen (ed.), *Money Laundering*, Hume Papers on Public Policy, 1, 2 (Edinburgh).

DATA PROTECTION REGISTRAR (1989). *Fifth Report of the Data Protection Registrar*, June 1989, HC 472, Session 1988–9 (London).

—— (1991). *Seventh Report of the Data Protection Registrar*, June 1991, HC 553, Session 1990–91 (London).

—— (1994). *Tenth Report of the Data Protection Registrar*, June 1994, HC 453, Session 1993–4.

DEHOUSSE, R. (1994). 'From Community to Union', in R. Dehousse (ed.), *Europe after Maastricht An Ever Closer Union?* (Munich).

—— and Weiler, J. H. H. (1990) 'The Legal Dimension' in W. Wallace (ed), *The Dynamics of Political Integration*, (London), 242–60.

DELANY, H. and Hogan, G. (1993). 'Anglo–Irish Extradition Viewed from an Irish Perspective', *Public Law*, 93–120.

DELMAS–MARTY, M. (1993). *Comparative Study of the Laws, Regulations and Administrative Provisions of the Member States Applicable to Fraud Against the Community Budget: Final Report*, Commission of the European Communities (Brussels), unpub. paper.

DIEDERICHS, O. (1991a). 'Verfassungsschutz und Organisierte Kriminalität', *Bürgerrechte und Polizei*, 39, 2, 68–71.

—— (1991b). 'Zeugenschutz', *Bürgerrechte und Polizei*, 39, 2, 40–1.

DIJK, J. M. (1993). 'More than a Matter of Security. Trends in Crime Prevention in Europe', in F. Heidensohn and M. Farrell (1993) (eds.), 27–42.

——, and MAYHEW, P. (1993). 'Criminal Victimisation in the Industrialised World: Key Findings of the 1989 and 1992 International Crime Surveys', in A. Alvazzi del Frate, U. Zvekic and J. M. van Dijk (eds.), (1993) 1–49.

DINE, J. (1993). 'European Community Criminal Law?', *Criminal Law Review*, 246–54.

DIVISIE CENTRALE RECHERCHE INFORMATIE (1994). *Jaarbericht 1993.*

DOORN, J. VAN (1993). 'Drug trafficking networks in Europe', *European Journal on Criminal Policy and Research*, 1, 2, 96–104.

DORN, N. (1993). 'Subsidiarity, Police Cooperation and Drug Enforcement; some structures of policy–making in the EC', *European Journal on Criminal Policy and Research* vol.1, no. 2, 30–47.

DORN, N., MURJI, S. and SOUTH, N. (1992). *Traffickers: Drug Markets and Law Enforcement* (London).

—— and SOUTH, N. (1993). 'Drugs, crime and law enforcement. Some issues for Europe', in F. Heidensohn and M. Farrell (eds.), (1993) 72–83.

DOWRICK, F. (1987). 'Council of Europe Juristic Activity 1974–86', *International and Comparative Law Quarterly*, vol. 36, 633–47.

DRIESSEN, F. M. H. M. and Jansen, H. F. A. (1991). *Drugshandel na 1992*, Utrecht.

DRÜKE, L. (1994) 'The Position of the UNHCR', Second Expert Meeting on Third Pillar of the Union Treaty, Collège d'Europe, 19/20 September 1994, unpub. paper (Bruges).

DUFF, A., PINDER, J. and PRYCE, R. (1994) (eds.). *Maastricht and Beyond* (London).

DUKE, W. (1970). 'Principles Underlying the European Convention on Extradition', *Legal Aspects of Extradition Among European States* (Strasbourg), 29–48.

DUMORTIER, J. (1992). 'Het Schengen Informatie Systeem en de bescherming van persoonsgegevens', in C. Fijnaut, J. Stuyck and P. Wytinck (eds.), (1992) *Schengen: Proeftuin voor de Europese Gemeenschap?* (Antwerpen), 119–73.

DUNLEAVY, P. (1989) 'The Architecture of the British Central State', *Public Administration*, 67, 249–76; 391–418.

DUSSAIX, R. (1971). 'Some Problems Arising from the Practical Application, from the Judicial Point of View, of the European Convention on Mutual Assistance in Criminal Matters', in European Committee on Crime Problems, *Problems Arising from the Practical Application of the European Convention on Mutual Assistance in Criminal Matters* (Strasbourg), 37–56.

DUYNE, P. C. VAN (1991). 'Crime Enterprises and the Legitimate Industry in The Netherlands', in C. Fijnaut and J. Jacobs (eds.), (1992) 55–71.

—— (1993). 'Implications of cross-border crime risks in an open Europe', *Crime, Law and Social Change*, 20, 99–111.

EDWARD, D. (1990). 'Constitutional Rules of Community Law in EEC Competition Cases', in B. Hawk (ed.), *Annual Proceedings of the Fordham Comporate Law Institute* (New York).

EMSLEY, C (1993). 'Peasants, gendarmes and state formation', in M. Fulbrook (ed.), (1993) *National Histories and European History* (London).

ERICSON, R. (1994). 'The Division of Expert Knowledge in Policing and Security', *British Journal of Sociology*, 45, 2, 149–75.

EUROPEAN PARLIAMENT (1993). Resolution on free movement of persons pursuant to Article 8a of the EEC Treaty, *Official Journal of the European Communities*, C 255, 20 September, 183–5.

FAIRCHILD, E. (1988). *German Police* (Illinois).

FALK MOORE, S. (1978). *Law as Process: An Anthropological Approach.* (London).

FERNHOUT, R. (1993). 'The United States of Europe have commenced. But for whom?', *Netherlands Quarterly of Human Rights*, 3, 249–65.

FIJNAUT, C. (1979). *Opdat de macht een toevlucht zij? Een historische studie van het politieapparaat als een politieke instelling*, Antwerpen, 2 vols.

—— (1991). 'Police cooperation within Western Europe', in F. Heidensohn and M. Farrell, (eds.), (1993) 103–21.

—— (1993a) 'The 'Communitization' of Police Cooperation in Western Europe', in H. G. Schermers, *et al.* (eds.), (1993) *Free Movement of Persons in Europe* (Dordrecht/The Hague), 75–92.

—— (1993b). 'The Schengen Treaties and European Police Co-operation', *European Journal of Crime, Criminal Law and Criminal Justice*, 1, 1, 37–56.

——, and HERMANS, R. J. (eds.) (1987). *Police Cooperation in the European Community* (Lochem).

—— and JACOBS, J. (eds.), (1991) *Organized Crime and its Containment. A Transatlantic Initiative* (Deventer/Boston).

—— and Marx, G. T. (eds.), (1995) *Undercover: Police Surveillance in a Comparative Perspective*, Deventer/Boston.

—— PETERS, T. and WALGRAVE L. (1990). 'Politie, gevangeniswezen en jeugdrecht in België', in *Justitiële Verkenningen*, 16, nr. 9, 74–94.

FINNIE, W. (1990). 'Old Wine in New Bottles? The Evolution of Anti–Terrorist Legislation', *Judicial Review*, 35, 1–22.

FLAHERTY, D. (1989). *Protecting Privacy in Surveillance Societies* (Chapel Hill, North Carolina).

Fode, H. (1993a). 'Cooperation in Law Enforcement, Criminal Justice and Legislation in Europe. Nordic Experience', in H. G. Schermers, *et al.* (eds.), (1993) 61–9.

—— (1993b). *Presentation on Europol.* Paper presented at the regional European Interpol Conference, 31 March–2 April, (Bern), unpub. paper.

FORD, G. (1991). *Report on the Findings of the Inquiry*, European Parliament, Committee of Inquiry on Racism and Xenophobia (Brussels–Luxembourg).

FUNK, A. (1994) 'Control Myths: the Eastern Border of the Federal Republic of Germany before and after 1989', ECPR Joint Sessions (Madrid), unpub. paper.

GALLIE, W. B. (1956). 'Essentially Contested Concepts', *Proceedings of the Aristotelian Society*, 56.

GAMBETTA, D. (1993). *The Sicilian Mafia. The Business of Private Protection* (Cambridge, Mass./London, England).

GEARTY, C. A. (1983). 'The European Court of Human Rights and the

Protection of Civil Liberties: An Overview', *Cambridge Law Journal*, 52, 89–127.

GEIGER, R. (1986). 'Legal Assistance Between States in Criminal Matters', *Encyclopedia of Public International Law*, 9 (Oxford), 248–55.

GELLNER, E. (1993). *Nations and Nationalism*, Oxford.

GEYSELS, F. (1990). 'Benelux, the Forerunner of the European Community in the Field of the Free Movement of Persons Across Internal Frontiers?', *Police Journal*, 103–20.

GIDDENS, A. (1987a). 'Nation–States and Violence' in Giddens (1987b), 166–182.

—— (1987b). *Social Theory and Modern Sociology* (Cambridge).

—— (1990). *The Consequences of Modernity* (Cambridge).

—— (1991). *Modernity and Self–Identity: Self and Society in the Late Modern Age* (Cambridge).

GILBERT, G. (1985). 'Terrorism and the Political Offence Exception Reappraised, *International and Comparative Law Quarterly*, 34, 695–723.

—— (1991). *Aspects of Extradition Law* (London).

—— (1992). 'Crimes Sans Frontières: Jurisdictional Problems in English Law', *British Year Book of International Law*, 415–42.

GILMORE, W. C. (1990). 'International Action Against Drug Trafficking: Trends in United Kingdom Law and Practice', *International Lawyer*, vol. 24, 365–92.

—— (1991). *Going after the Money: Money Laundering, The Confiscation of the Assets of Crime and International Cooperation*, Working Paper VI, 'A System of European Police Cooperation' (Edinburgh).

—— (1992a). *Combatting International Drugs Trafficking: The 1988 United Nations Convention Against Illicit Traffic in Narcotic Drugs and Psychotropic Substances* (London).

—— (1992b). 'Extradition and the Political Offence Exception: Reflections on United Kingdom Law and Practice', *Commonwealth Law Bulletin*, vol. 18, 701–19.

—— (ed.), (1992c). *International Efforts to Combat Money Laundering*. Cambridge International Documents Series, 4 (Cambridge).

—— (1992d). 'Introduction', in Gilmore, W.C. (1992c).

—— (ed.), (1993a). *Action Against Transnational Criminality: Papers from the 1992 Oxford Conference on International and White Collar Crime*, Vol. II (London), 89–96.

—— (1993b). *Extradition and the Europe of the Twelve*, Working Paper XII, 'A System of European Police Co-operation after 1992', (Edinburgh).

—— (1993c). 'Money Laundering: The International Aspect', *Money Laundering*, Hume Papers on Public Policy, 1, 2, 1–11.

—— (1993d). 'Police Co-operation and the European Communities:

Current Trends and Recent Developments', *Commonwealth Law Bulletin*, 19, 1960–1975.

—— (1993e). 'State–Sponsored Abduction', Paper LMM (93) 12, Meeting of Commonwealth Law Ministers, 15–19 November 1993 (Mauritius), unpub. paper.

—— (1994). *Mutual Assistance in Criminal and Business Regulatory Matters* (Cambridge).

GILL, P. (1994). *Policing Politics: Security Intelligence and the Liberal Democratic State* (London).

GIOT–MIKKELSEN, M. (1993). 'European Police Cooperation—The Challenge of the 1990s', in W. C. Gilmore, (ed.), (1993a) 84–96.

GLEIZAL, J-J, GATTI–DOMENACH, J and JOURNES, C. (1993). *La Police. Le cas des démocraties occidentales* (Paris).

GOLD, M. and LEVI, M. (1994). *Money–Laundering in the UK: An appraisal of suspicion–based reporting* (London).

GOLDSMITH, A. (1990). 'Taking Police Culture Seriously: Police Discretion and the Limits of the Law', *Policing and Society*, 1, 91–114.

Goldsmith, A. (ed.), (1991) *Complaints Against the Police: The Trend to External Review*. (Oxford).

GOLDSTOCK, R. (1991). 'Organized Crime and Anti-Organized Crime Efforts in the United States: an Overview', in C. Fijnaut and J. Jacobs (eds.), (1991) 7–14.

GORDON, G. H. (1978). *The Criminal Law of Scotland*, 2nd. ed. (Edinburgh).

GORDON, P. (1985) *Policing Immigration. Britain's Internal Controls* (London/Sydney).

GRANGE, K. (1994). 'The Impact of Data Protection upon European Police Information Flows and the Specific Implications for Immigration and Asylum', ECPR Joint Sessions (Madrid), unpub. paper.

GRAY, A. and JENKINS, W. (1985). *Administrative Politics in British Government* (Brighton).

GREEN, N., HARTLEY, T. C., and USHER, J. A. (1991). *The Legal Foundations of the Single European Market* (Oxford).

GREGORY, F. (1994). 'Unprecedented partnerships in crime control: law enforcement issues and linkages between Eastern and Western Europe since 1989', in M. Anderson and M. den Boer (eds.), (1994) 85–105.

—— and COLLIER, A. (1992) 'Cross Frontier Crime and International Crime—Problems, Achievements and Prospects with reference to European Police Co–operation', in M. Anderson and M. den Boer (eds.), (1992) 71–92.

GYOMARCH, A. (1991) 'Problems of Law and Order in France in the 1980s: Politics and Professionalism', *Policing and Society*, vol. 1, 319–32.

HAAS, E. B. (1971) 'The Study of Regional Integration: Reflections on the

Joy and Anguish of Pretheorizing' in N. L. Lindberg and S. Scheingold (eds.), *Regional Integration: Theory and Research*. (Cambridge, Mass.).

HALL, J. and IKENBERRY, G. J. (1989). *The State* (Milton Keynes).

HALL, S. *et al.* (1978). *Policing the Crisis* (London).

HALLIDAY, T. C. (1985). 'Knowledge Mandates: Collective Influence by Scientific, Normative and Syncretic Professions', *British Journal of Sociology*, 36, 421–47.

HAM, P. VAN (1993). *The EC, Eastern Europe and European Unity. Discord, Collaboration and Integration since 1947* (London).

HARLOW, C. (1992). 'A Community of Interests? Making the Most of European Law', *Modern Law Review*, 55, 331–50.

HARMSEN, R. (1994). 'A European Union of Variable Geometry: Problems and Perspectives', *Northern Ireland Legal Quarterly*, 45, 109–33.

HARRIS, G. (1994) *The Dark side of Europe: the Extreme Right Today* (Edinburgh).

HARRISON, A. (1992) 'The Potential of Interpol as the Main Communications and Liaison Function for European Police Co-operation with Special Reference to Fraud', in M. Anderson and M. den Boer (eds.), (1992) 35–40.

HARTLEY, T. C. (1988). *The Foundations of European Community Law* 2nd ed., (Oxford).

HAWKINS, K. (1984) *Environment and Enforcement* (Oxford).

HEIDENSOHN, F. (1993). 'Introduction. Convergence, Diversity and Change', in F. Heidensohn and M. Farrell. (eds.), (1993) 3–13.

—— and FARRELL, M (eds.), (1993) *Crime in Europe* (2nd ed.) (London).

HEISLER, M. O., and LAYTON–HENRY, Z. (1993). 'Migration and the links between social and societal security', in O. Waever, B. Buzan, M. Kelstrup, and P. Lemaitre (eds.) (1993), *Identity, Migration and the New Security Agenda in Europe* (London), 148–66.

HELD, D. (1989a). *Political Theory and the Modern State*. (Milton Keynes).

—— (1989b). 'Sovereignty, National Politics and the Global System' in Held (1989a), 214–42.

HELSINKI INSTITUTE FOR CRIME PREVENTION AND CONTROL (1985). *Criminal Justice Systems in Europe* (Helsinki).

HERMAN, E. S., and Chomsky, N. (1988). *Manufacturing Consent. The Political Economy of the Mass Media* (New York).

—— and O'SULLIVAN, G. (1991). '"Terrorism" as Ideology and Cultural Industry', in A. George, (ed.), (1991) *Western State Terrorism* (Cambridge), 39–75.

HESSE, K. (1993). *Grundzüge des Verfassungsrechts der Bundesrepublik Deutschland*, 19th revised ed. (Heidelberg).

HIX, S. (1994). 'The Study of the European Community: The Challenge to Comparative Politics', *West European Politics*, 17, 1–30.

HM GOVERNMENT (1985). 'Extradition', Cmnd. 9421 (London).
—— (1992). 'Developments in the European Community: July to December', Cmnd. 1857 (London).
—— (1993). *Scrutiny of the Intergovernmental Pillars of the European Union: Observations by the Secretary of State for Foreign and Commonwealth Affairs and the Secretary of State for Home Affairs*, Cmmd. 2471 (London).
HOBBS, D. (1990) *Doing the Business* (Oxford).
—— (1994). 'Professional and Organized Crime in Britain', in M. Maguire, R. Morgan and R. Reiner (eds.), (1994) *The Oxford Handbook of Criminology* (Oxford), 441–68.
HOBSBAWM, E. J. (1991). *Nations and Nationalism since 1780* 2nd ed., (Cambridge).
HOFFMAN, S. (1966). 'The Fate of the Nation–State and the case of Western Europe', *Daedalus*. 85, 872–77.
—— (1993). 'Goodbye to a United Europe?', *New York Review of Books*, 27 May, 40, 10, 27–31.
HOFSTEDE, G., TWUYVER, M. VAN, KAPP, B. *et al.* (1993). *Grensover-schrijdende politiesamenwerking tussen België, Duitsland en Nederland binnen de Euregio Maasrijn* (Maastricht).
HOLDAWAY, S. (1983). *Inside the British Police* (Oxford).
HOME AFFAIRS COMMITTEE, HOUSE OF COMMONS (1990). *Practical Police Cooperation in the European Community*, 7th Report, 1989–90, HC 363–1 (London).
—— (1992). *Migration Control at External Borders of the European Community*, Session 1991–92, Minutes of Evidence, No. 215 (London).
—— (1993). *Intergovernmental Co-operation in the Fields of Justice and Home Affairs*, Minutes of Evidence, Wednesday 15 December, H.C. 121–i (London).
HOME AFFAIRS COMMITTEE (1994). *Organised Crime*, Session 1994–5; House of Commons Paper 18–II, Minutes of Evidence and Memorandum (London).
HOME OFFICE (1982). *A Review of the Law and Practice of Extradition in the United Kingdom: Report of an Interdepartmental Working Party* (London).
—— (1993). *Extradition: A Guide to Procedures of EC Member States (Incorporating Contact Points)* (London).
HONDIUS, F. (1993). 'Mutual Assistance between Business Regulatory Bodies–Treaty Aspects', in Gilmore, W. C. (ed.) (1993a), 20–6.
HOOGENBOOM, A. B. (1991). ' "Grey Policing": A Theoretical Framework', *Policing and Society*, 2, 17–30.
—— (1994). *Het Politiecomplex. Over de samenwerking tussen politie, bij-zondere opsporingsdiensten en particuliere recherche* (Arnhem).

HOPKINS, A. (1994). 'Compliance with what? The Fundamental Regulatory Question', *British Journal of Criminology*, 34, 4, 431–43.

HOPT, K. J. (1990). 'The European Insider Dealing Directive', *Common Market Law Review*, 27, 51–82.

HOUSE OF LORDS (1989). '1992: Border Control of People', Select Committee in the European Communities, 22nd Report, 1988–89 (London).

—— (1990). *Money Laundering*, Report from the Select Committee on The European Communities, Session 1990–91, First Report (with evidence) (London).

—— (1993a). *Enforcement of Community Competition Rules*. Select Committee on the European Communities, Session 1993–94, 1st report (London).

—— (1993b). *Scrutiny of the Intergovernmental Pillars of the European Union*, Select Committee on the European Communities, Session 1992–93, 28th Report, HL Paper 124.

HUBERTS, L. (ed.), (1992). *Bestuurlijke fraude en corruptie in Nederland* (Amsterdam).

IHESI (1992). *Polices d'Europe*, avec la collaboration de J. M. Erbes, J.-C. Monet, A. Funk, etc. (Paris).

JENNINGS, R. and WATTS, A. (eds.), (1992). *Oppenheim's International Law*, 9th ed. (London).

JENSEN, R. B. (1981). 'The International Anarchist Conference of 1898 and the Origins of Interpol', *Journal of Contemporary History*, 16, 323–47.

JESSOP, B. (1990). *State Theory: Putting Capitalist States in their Place* (Cambridge).

JOHNSTON, L. (1992) *The Rebirth of Private Policing* (London/New York).

JOURNES, C. (1993). 'The Structure of the French Police System. Is the French Police a National Force?', *International Journal of the Sociology of Law*, vol. 21, 281–87.

JOUTSEN, M. (1993). 'Organised Crime in Eastern Europe', *Criminal Justice International*, 2, 9, 11–18.

KAISER, G. (1990). 'Criminaliteitsbeleid in een herenigd Duitsland', *Justitiële Verkenningen*, 16, 9, 18–37.

KAPLAN, D. and DUBRO, A. (1990). *Yakusa: la Mafia japonnaise* (Paris).

KARLE, B. (1970). Some Problems Concerning the Application of the European Convention on Extradition, in *Legal Aspects of Extradition Among European States* (Strasbourg), 51–68.

KEITH, M. (1993). *Race, Riots and Policing. Lore and Disorder in a Multi-racist Society* (London).

KENDALL, R. (1992). 'Interpol Today', *Policing*, 8, 279–85.

KEOHANE, R. O. (1993). 'Goodbye to a United Europe?', *New York Review of Books*, 27 May, 40, 10, 27–31.

KEOHANE, R. O. and HOFFMAN, S. (1991a) 'Institutional Change in Europe in the 1980s', in R. O. Keohane and S. Hoffman (eds.) (1991b).
—— (1991b). *The New European Community* (San Francisco).
KERSE, C. (1994). *EEC Antitrust Procedure*, 3rd ed. (London).
KEYSER–RINGNALDA, F. (1994). *Boef en buit. De ontneming van wederrechtelijk verkregen vermogen* (Arnhem).
KILLIAS, M. (1993). 'Will open borders result in more crime? A criminological statement', *European Journal on Criminal Policy and Research*, vol. 1, no. 3, 7–9.
KING, M. (1994). 'Conceptualizing "Fortress Europe": a consideration of the process of inclusion and exclusion', ECPR Joint Sessions (Madrid), unpub. paper.
KINSEY, R., Lea, J. and Young, J. (1986). *Losing The Fight Against Crime* (Oxford).
KLERKS, P. (1993a). 'Police forces in the EC and EFTA countries', in T. Bunyan (ed.), (1993) *Statewatching the New Europe: a handbook on the European state* (Nottingham), 41–5.
—— (1993b). 'Security services in the EC and EFTA countries', in T. Bunyan (ed.), (1993) *Statewatching the New Europe: a handbook on the European state* (Nottingham), 66–68.
KLOCKARS, C. J. (1985). *The Idea of Police* (Beverley Hills).
KORF, D. J. (1990). 'Jatten alle junkies? Criminaliteit en drugsgebruik in Nederland', *Tijdschrift voor Criminologie*, 2, 105–23.
KRIZ, G. (1992). 'International Co-operation to Combat Money Laundering: The Nature and Role of Mutual Legal Assistance Treaties', *Commonwealth Law Bulletin*, vol. 18, 723–34.
KÜHNE, H–H (1991). *Kriminalitätsbekämpfung durch innereuropäische Grenzkontrollen* (Berlin).
LACAZE, J. (Rapporteur), (1994). *Report of the Committee on Foreign Affairs and Security on terrorism and its effects on security in Europe*, European Parliament Session Documents, 2 February, A3–0058/94 (Brussels).
LANE, R. (1993). 'New Competences under the Maastricht Treaty', *Common Market Law Review*, 30, 939–79.
LANGFELDT, M. (1991). 'Agreements of the Federal Republic of Germany to Supplement the European Convention on Extradition of 13 December 1957 and to Facilitate its Application', *Revue Internationale de Droit Penal*, vol. 62, 523–28.
LATTER, R. (1991). 'Crime and the European Community after 1992', Wilton Park Papers No. 31 (London).
LAVOIE, C. (1992). 'The Investigative Powers of the Commission with Respect to Business Secrets under Community Competition Rules', *European Law Review*, 12, 20–40.

LENSING, H. (1993). 'The Federalization of Europe: Towards a Federal System of Criminal Justice', *European Journal of Crime, Criminal Law and Criminal Justice*, 1, 3, 212–29.

LEROY, B. (1991). *The Community of Twelve and the Drug Demand — Comparative Study of Legislations and Judicial Practice*, Doc CEC/LUX/V/E/1/28/91 (Brussels).

LEVI, M. (1991). 'Pecunia non olet: Cleansing the money-lenders from the Temple', *Crime, Law and Social Change*, 16, 217–302.

—— (1993a). 'Developments in business crime control in Europe', in Heidensohn, F. and Farrell, M. (1993) (eds.), 172–87.

—— (1993b), 'The Extent of Cross-Border Crime in Europe: the view from Britain', in *European Journal of Criminal Policy and Research*, vols. 1–3, 57–76.

—— and MAGUIRE, M. (1992) 'Crime and Cross–Border Policing in Europe', in J. Bailey (ed.), *Social Europe* (London and New York), 165–89.

LINDBERG, L. N. (1963). *The Political Dynamics of European Integration* (Stanford).

LLOYD, I. (1994). 'Data Protection: Brussels Takes Over?', *Scots Law Times*, 83–7.

LOUIS, J.-V. (1990). *The Community Legal Order*, 2nd ed. (Luxembourg).

LOWE, A. and YOUNG, J. (1978). 'Suppressing Terrorism under the European Convention: A British Perspective', *Netherlands International Law Review*, vol. 25, 305–33.

LÜDERSSEN, L. (1985). 'V–Leute — Die Falle im Rechtsstaat' (Frankfurt am Main).

LYON, D. (1991). 'British Identity Cards: the Unpalatable Logic of European membership?' *The Political Quarterly*, 62, 3, 377–85.

—— (1994). *The Electronic Eye. The Rise of the Surveillance Society* (Cambridge).

MAANEN, J. VAN (1983). 'The Boss: First–Line Supervision in the American Police Agency', in M. Punch (ed.), (1983), *Control in the Police Organisation*, (Cambridge, Mass.), 275–317.

McCLEAN, D. (1992). *International Judicial Assistance* (Oxford).

MacCORMICK, N. (1993) 'Beyond the Sovereign State', *The Modern Law Review*, 56, 1–18.

McGAW, D. (1991). 'Governing Metaphors: the War on Drugs', *The American Journal of Semiotics*, vol. 8, No. 3, 53–74.

MACKAY, LORD J. (1992). *Diversity in Unity — European Laws*, Text of 1992 Churchill Memorial Lecture, unpub. paper.

McLAUGHLIN, E. (1992). 'The Democratic Deficit: European Union and the Accountability of the British Police', *British Journal of Criminology*, 32, 473–87.

McMahon (1994). '12, 16, 20 or 24? The future shape of the European Union', *Northern Ireland Legal Quarterly*, 45, 134–51.

Maguire, M. (1994). 'Crime Statistics, Patterns and Trends', in M. Maguire, R. Morgan, and R. Reiner (eds.), *The Oxford Handbook of Criminology* (Oxford), 233–91.

Majone, G. (1993). 'The European Community between Social Policy and Social Regulation', *Journal of Common Market Studies* 31, 154–70.

Mandela, N. (1994). *Long Walk to Freedom* (London).

Manning, P. C. (1977). *Police Work: The Social Organisation of Policing* (Cambridge, Mass.).

Marenin, O. (1982). 'Parking Tickets and Class Repression: The Concept of Policing in Critical Theories of Criminal Justice', *Contemporary Crises*, 6, 241–66.

Marshall, T. H. (1950). *Citizenship and Social Class and other Essays* (Cambridge).

Martin, J. M., and Romano, A. T. (1992). *Multinational Crime. Terrorism, Espionage, Drug and Arms Trafficking* (London).

Martiniello, M. (1995). 'European Citizenship, European Identity and Migrants: towards the post–national state?', R. Miles and D. Thränhardt (eds.), (1995) *Migration and European Integration: The Dynamics of Inclusion and Exclusion*, (London), 37–52.

Matka, E. (1990). 'Uses and Abuses of Crime Statistics', *Crime and Justice Bulletin*, November, no. 11, 1–8.

Mawby, R. I. (1990). *Comparative Policing Issues. The British and American System in International Perspective* (London).

Meehan, E. (1993), 'Citizenship and the European Community', *The Political Quarterly*, 64, 172–86.

Meijer, R. F. (1994). Internationale statistische samenwerking nog in kinderschoenen, *Juist*, January, 10–11.

Meyer, J (1990). The Vicarious Administration of Justice: An Overlooked Basis of Jurisdiction, *Harvard International Law Journal*, vol. 31, 108–16.

Miers, D. R. and Page, A. C. (1990). *Legislation*, 2nd ed. (London).

Miles, R. (1993). 'Community Policing', *Computing*, 4 February.

Millar, D. (1992) 'Citizenship and European Union', ECPR Joint Sessions, (Limerick), unpub. paper.

Milward, A. S. (1992). *The European Rescue of the Nation-State* (Berkeley, Cal.)

Minc, A. (1993). *Le nouveau moyen age* (Paris).

Ministerie van Justitie, Ministerie van Binnenlandse Zaken (1992). *De georganiseerde criminaliteit in Nederland. Dreigingsbeeld en plan van aanpak* (Den Haag).

Monet, J.–C. (1993). *Polices et sociétés en Europe* (Paris).

MORAVCSIK, A. (1993). 'Preferences and Power in the European Community: A Liberal Intergovernmentalist Approach', *Journal of Common Market Studies*, 31, 472–524.

MÜLLER–GRAFF, P.-C. (1994). 'The Legal Bases of the Third Pillar and its Position in the Framework of the Union Treaty', *Common Market Law Review*, 31, 493–510.

MULLER–RAPPARD, E. (1989). 'The European System', in M. C. Bassiouni (ed.), (1989) *International Criminal Law*, vol. II (New York) 95–119.

NADELMANN, E. (1990). 'Global Prohibition Regimes: The Evolution of Norms in International Society', *International Organization*, vol. 44, 479–526.

—— (1993). *Cops Across Borders. The Internationalization of U.S. Criminal Law Enforcement* (Pennsylvania).

—— (1995). *Criminalization and Crime Control in International Society*, (Princeton).

NATIONAL CRIMINAL INTELLIGENCE SERVICE (1994). *Annual Report 1993/4.* (London).

NAYER, A. (1994). 'Foreigners, Immigrants, Refugees and Proximity Control in Belgium', ECPR Joint Sessions (Madrid), unpub. paper.

NEUWAHL, N. (1994). 'Foreign and Security Policy and the Implementation of the Requirement of "Consistency" under the Treaty on European Union', in O'Keeffe, D. and Twomey, P. (eds.), (1994) 227–46.

NEWBURN, T. and MORGAN, R. (1994). 'A New Agenda for the Old Bill', *Policing*, Autumn, 10, 3, 143–50.

NILSSON, H. (1991). 'The Council of Europe Laundering Convention: A Recent Example of a Developing International Criminal Law', *Criminal Law Forum*, vol. 2, 419–41.

NORMAN, P. (1992). *Computerized Information Systems for Policing the Borders of the European Community*, Liberty Working Paper (London).

NORTHERN IRELAND OFFICE (1993). 'Tackling Terrorist Finance', in Gilmore, W. C. (ed.), (1993) 19–22.

NUGENT, N. (1992). 'The Deepening and Widening of the European Community: Recent Evolution, Maastricht, and Beyond', *Journal of Common Market Studies*, 30, 312–28.

NUTTALL, S. (1992) *European Political Co-operation* (Oxford).

OGATA, S. (1993). 'Refugees and asylum–seekers: a challenge to European immigration–policy', *Towards a European Immigration Policy*, The Philip Morris Institute for Public Policy Research, October, 10–20 (Brussels).

O'KEEFFE, D. (1991). 'The Schengen Convention: A Suitable Model for European Integration?', *Yearbook of European Law*, vol. II, 185–219.

—— (1994). 'Non–accession to the Schengen Convention: the Cases of the

United Kingdom and Ireland', in A. Pauly (ed.), *Schengen en panne*, (Maastricht), 145–53.

—— and TWOMEY, P. (eds.),(1994), *Legal Issues of the Maastricht Treaty* (London).

d'OLIVEIRA, H. U. JESSURUN (1993). 'Fortress Europe and (extra–communitarian) Refugees: co–operation in sealing off the external borders, H. G. Schermers, *et al.* (eds.), (1993) 166–82.

OSTROM, E., PARKS, R., and WHITAKER, G. P. (1978). *Patterns of Metropolitan Policing* (Cambridge, Mass.).

OVERBEECK, W. B. J. VAN (1994). 'The Right to Remain Silent in Competition Investigations: the Funke Decision of the Court of Human Rights Makes Revision of the ECJ's Case Law Necessary', *European Competition Law Review*, 3, 127–33.

OUTRIVE, L. VAN (1992a). *Europol*, Committee on Civil Liberties and Internal Affairs, European Parliament (Strasbourg).

—— (1992b). *Police Co–operation*, Committee on Civil Liberties and Internal Affairs, European Parliament (Strasbourg).

—— (1992c). *The Entry into Force of the Schengen Agreements*, Committee on Civil Liberties and Internal Affairs, European Parliament (Strasbourg).

—— (1992d). *The Setting Up of Europol*, Committee on Civil Liberties and Internal Affairs, European Parliament (Strasbourg).

PAASCH, E. (1987). 'Der liberale Nachbar liefert auch Probleme: Niedersachsens Kampf gegen internationale Drogenströme', *Kriminalistik*, vol. 41, 8/9, 481–83.

PARIDAENS, D. (1991). 'The Extradition of Nationals According to Dutch Law', *Revue Internationale de Droit Penal*, vol. 62, 515–21.

PASSAS, N. and NELKEN, D. (1993). 'The thin line between legitimate and criminal enterprises: Subsidy Frauds in the European Community', *Crime, Law and Social Change*, 19, 223–43.

PAULY, A. (ed.), (1994). *Schengen en panne* (Maastricht).

PEARCE, F. (1976). *Crimes of the Powerful: Marxism. Crime and Deviance* (London).

—— and TOMBS, S. (1993). 'US Capital versus the Third World: Union Carbide and Bophal', in F. Pearce and M. Woodiwiss (eds.), (1993) *Global Crime Connections: Dynamics and Control* (Basingstoke), 187–211.

PEEK, J. H. A. M. (1990). 'Schengen: wegwijzer naar een gewijzigd Europa', in G. N. M. Blonk, C. Fijnaut and E. de Kerf, (eds.), (1990) *Grensverleggende Recherche*, (Lochem), 111–29.

—— (1994). 'Police Cooperation', Second Expert Meeting on Third Pillar of the Union Treaty, Collège d'Europe, 19/20 September 1994, (Bruges), unpub. paper.

PIJL, D. (1991). 'Organized Crime and Police Corruption in The Netherlands', in C. Fijnaut, and J. Jacobs (eds.), (1991) 101–17.

PITSCHAS, R. (1993). 'Innere Sicherheit und Internationale Verbrechens-bekämpfung als Verantwortung des demokratischen Verfassungsstaates', *Juristen Zeitung*, vol. 48, issue 18, 857–66.

PITTS, J. (1993). 'Thereotyping: Anti–racism, Criminology and Black Young People', in D. Cook and B. Hudson (eds.), (1993) *Racism and Criminology* (London/Thousand Oaks/New Delhi), 96–117.

POGGI, G. (1978). *The Development of the Modern State* (Stanford).

POGGI, G. (1990). *The State: Its Nature. Development and Prospects* (Cambridge).

POMPIDOU GROUP (Co–operation Group to Combat Drug Abuse and Illicit Trafficking in Drugs), Council of Europe (1994). *Multi–city study: Drug misuse trends in thirteen European cities* (Strasbourg).

POSNER, H. L. (1988). *Warlords of Crime. The Chinese Secret Societies: the New Mafia* (London).

PRIEß, H.–J. and SPITZER, H. (1994). 'Die Betrugsbekämpfung in der Europäischen Gemeinschaft', *Europäische Zeitschrift für Wirtschaftsrecht*, Heft 10, 297–304.

PROJECT TEAM EUROPOL (1993). *The Position of Europol within the Framework of European Cooperation. Member State Institutions, European Information Systems, International Organizations and Agencies.*

PUNCH, M. (1979). 'The Secret Social Service', in S. Holdaway (ed.), (1979) *The British Police* (London).

—— (1985). *Conduct Unbecoming*, (London).

—— (1989). 'Researching Police Deviance: a personal encounter with the limitations and liability of field–work', *British Journal of Sociology*, 40, 177–204.

RAAB, C. D. (1994). 'Police cooperation: the prospects for privacy', in M. Anderson and M. den Boer (eds.), (1994) 121–36.

—— and BENNETT, C. (1994). 'Protecting privacy across borders: European policies and prospects', *Public Administration*, 72, 95–112.

RAMM, R. A. C. (1990). 'The Yardies: England's Emerging Crime Problem', *FBI Law Enforcement Bulletin*, 6, 59, 1–4.

RAWLS, J. (1987). 'The Idea of an Overlapping Consensus', *Oxford Journal of Legal Studies*, 9, 1–25.

RAWORTH, P. (1994). 'A Timid Step Forwards: Maastricht and the Democratization of the European Community', *European Law Review*, 16–33.

REENEN, P. VAN (1989). 'Policing Europe after 1992: Cooperation and Competition', *European Affairs*, vol. 3, No. 2, 45–53.

—— (1992), 'Today's Training: A European Police Institute', in M. Anderson and M. den Boer, (eds.), *European Police Co–operation* Proceedings of a Seminar (Edinburgh), 131–45.

REINER, R. (1991). 'A Much Lower Pedestal', *Policing*, vol. 7, 225–38.

—— (1992a) 'Fin de Siècle Blues: The Police Face The Millennium', *The Political Quarterly* 63, 37–49.

—— (1992b). *The Politics of the Police*, 2nd ed. (Brighton).

—— (1993). 'Police Accountability: Principles, Patterns and Practices', in R. Reiner and S. Spencer (eds.), *Accountable Politics: Effectiveness, Empowerment and Equity* (London), 1–23.

—— (1994a) 'Policing and the Police' in M. Maguire, R. Morgan, and R. Reiner, (eds.), *The Oxford Handbook of Criminology* (Oxford), 705–72.

—— (1994b), 'What should the Police be Doing?', *Policing*, Autumn, 10, 3, 151–57.

REINKE, S. (1992). 'The EC Commission's Anti–Fraud Activity', in M. Anderson and M. den Boer (eds.), (1992) 13–30.

RÉPUBLIQUE FRANÇAISE–SÉNAT (1994). Deuxième Session Extraordinaire de 1993–1994, No. 262. Annexe au procès verbal de la séance du 25 janvier 1994. Rapport d'information fait au nom de la mission commune d'information chargée d'examiner la mise en place et le fonctionnement de la Convention d'Application de l'Accord du 14 juin 1985.

REUSS–IANNI, E. and IANNI, F. (1983). 'Street Cops and Management Cops: The Two Cultures of Policing', in M. Punch (ed.), (1983) *Control in the Police Organisation* (Cambridge, Mass.), 251–74.

'REVIEW SYMPOSIUM', in Reiner (1992a), 26, 94–105.

RILEY, L. (1991), Counterterrorism in Western Europe: Mechanisms for International Cooperation, MA Thesis, University of Essex (Essex).

RILEY, L. (1993). *Counterterrorism in Western Europe: Mechanisms for International Cooperation*, Working Paper X, 'A System of European Police Cooperation after 1992' (Edinburgh).

ROACH, J. and THOMANECK, J. (eds.), (1985). *Police and Public Order in Europe* (London).

ROBERT, P. and OUTRIVE, L. VAN (eds.), (1993). *Crime et justice en Europe* (Paris).

ROBERTSON, K. (1994). 'Practical police cooperation in Europe: the intelligence dimension', in M. Anderson, and M. den Boer (eds.), (1994) 106–20.

ROBERTSON, R. (1992). *Globalization: social theory and global culture* (London).

ROBLES PIQUER, C. (1993). *Cooperation in the field of justice and internal affairs under the Treaty on European Union (Title VI and other provisions)*. Committee on Civil Liberties and Internal Affairs of the European Parliament (Brussels).

ROSENTHAL, U. and CACHET, A. (1992), 'De bedrieglijke eenvoud van het (mede)beheer', in *Magistraat met Beleid* (Arnhem), 129–43.

RUYVER, B. DE (Promotor) (1992) and Onderzoeksgroep Drugbeleid,

Strafrechtelijk Beleid en Internationale Criminaliteit (1992). *Kansar-moede, druggebruik, criminaliteit* (Ghent).

—— BRUGGEMAN, W. and ZANDERS, P. (1993). 'Cross–border crime in Belgium', *European Journal on Criminal Policy and Research*, vol. 1–3, 87–100.

SALISCH, H. and SPERONI, F. (1994). *Report of the Committee on Civil Liberties and Internal Affairs on criminal activities in Europe*, A3–0033/94, (Brussels).

SALTMARSH, G. (1993). 'Organised/Enterprise Crime', *Organised Crime Conference: A Threat Assessment*, 24–26 May, (Hampshire).

SAVONA, E. U. and DEFEO, M. A. (1994). 'Money Trails: International Money Laundering Trends and Prevention/Control Policies', International Conference on Preventing and Controlling Money Laundering and the Use of the Proceeds of Crime: a Global Approach, Italy, 18–20 June 1994, unpub. paper.

SCANDONE, G. and ATZORI, P. (1990). *Le polizie d'Europa* (Roma).

SCHERMERS, H. G. (1990). 'The Scales in Balance: National Constitutional Court v. Court of Justice', *Common Market Law Review*, 27, 97–105.

—— (1992). Memorandum submitted as evidence to House of Lords 'Human Rights Re–examined', Minutes of Evidence, Select Committee on the European Communities, Session 1992–93, 3rd Report (London), 54–6.

—— *et al.* (eds.), (1993). *Free Movement of Persons in Europe. Legal Problems and Experiences* (Dordrecht/The Hague).

SCHLESINGER, P. and TUMBER, H. (1994). *Reporting Crime. The Media Politics of Criminal Justice* (Oxford).

SCHMITTER, P. C. (1990). 'The European Community as an Emergent and Novel Form of Political Domination', draft article in progress.

SCHULTZ, H. (1970). 'The Principles of the Traditional Law of Extradition', in Council of Europe, *Legal Aspects of Extradition Among European States* (Strasbourg), 9–23.

SCHUTTE, J. (1991). 'The European Market of 1993: Test for a Regional Model of Supranational Criminal Justice or of Interregional Cooperation in Criminal Law', *Criminal Law Forum*. 3, 1, 55–83.

SEVENSTER, H. (1992). 'Criminal Law and EC Law', *Common Market Law Review*, 29, 29–70.

SHARPSTON, E. (1993). 'Interim and Substantive Relief in Claims under Community Law', *Current EC Legal Developments Series* (London).

SHEARING, C. (1981). 'Subterranean Processes in the Maintenance of Power', *Canadian Review of Sociology and Anthropology*, 18, 283–98.

SHEPTYCKI, J. W. E. (1994). 'Technical Devils and Bureaucratic Antics on the Edge of the Fourth Estate: The Makings of a Post modern State', unpub. paper.

SHILS, E. (1982). *The Constitution of Society* (Chicago).

SKOLNICK, J. (1975). *Justice Without Trial: Law Enforcement in Democratic Society*. 2nd ed. (Berkeley).

SMITH, A. D. (1986). *The Ethnic Origin of Nations* (Oxford).

—— (1991). *National Identity* (London).

SOAFER, A. (1985). 'The Political Offence Exception and Terrorism', US Department of State (Washington, DC).

SOLOMOS, J. (1993). 'Constructions of Black Criminality: Racialisation and Criminalisation in Perspective', D. Cook,. and B. Hudson (eds.), (1993) *Racism and Criminology* (London/Thousand Oaks/New Delhi), 118–35.

SOUTH, N. (1994). 'Drugs: Control, Crime and Criminological Studies', in M. Maguire, R. Morgan and R. Reiner (eds.), *The Oxford Handbook of Criminology* (Oxford), 393–440.

SPARKS, R. (1992). *Television and the Drama of Crime: Moral Tales and the Place of Crime in Public Life* (Buckingham).

SPENCER, M. (1990). *1992 and All That. Civil Liberties in the Balance* (London).

STEIN, T. (1985). 'Extradition', *Encyclopedia of Public International Law*, vol. 8, (Oxford), 222–29.

STORBECK, J. (1994a). 'Europol bis 1996', in Transpol (ed.), (1994) *Internationalisering door Grenzeloze Samenwerking* (Lelystad), 77–84.

—— (1994b), 'Europol: Rückblick-Einblick-Ausblick', *Delikt en Delinkwent*, vol. 24, 452–63.

STREECK, W. and SCHMITTER P. C. (1991). 'From National Corporatism to Transnational Pluralism: Organized Interests in the Single European Market', *Politics & Society*, 19, 133–64.

TASCHNER, H. C. (1990). *Schengen oder die Abschaffung der Personenkontrollen an den Binnengrenzen der EG*, Vorträge, Reden und Berichte aus dem Europa Institut, Saarbrücken, No. 227 (Prof. dr. Georg Ress (ed.).

TAYLOR, I. (1992). 'The International Drug Trade and Money Laundering: Border Controls and Other Issues', *European Sociological Review*, 8, 181–93.

—— (1994). 'The Political Economy of Crime', in M. Maguire, R. Morgan, and R. Reiner, (eds.), *Oxford Handbook of Criminology* (Oxford), 469–510.

TAYLOR, J., WALTON, P. and YOUNG, J. (1974). *Critical Criminology* (London).

TIEDEMANN, K. (1993). 'Europäisches Gemeinschaftsrecht und Strafrecht', *Neue Juristische Wochenschrift*, 23–31.

TILLY, C. (1990). *Coercion, Capital and European States* (Cambridge).

TIMMERMANS, C. W. E. (1993). 'Free Movement of Persons and the Divisions of Powers between the Community and Member States—Why do it the Intergovernmental Way?, in H. G. Schermers *et al.* (eds.), (1993) 352–68.

TREVI (1991). *The Development of Europol*, Report from the Trevi Ministers to the European Council in Maastricht.

TSIMAS, K. (Rapporteur), (1992). *Draft Report on the abolition of controls at internal borders and free movement of persons within the EC*, Committee on Civil Liberties and Internal Affairs of the European Parliament.

TWOMEY, P. (1994). 'The European Union: three Pillars without a Human Rights Foundation', in D. O'Keeffe and P. Twomey (eds.), (1994) 121–32.

VAGG, J. (1992). 'The Borders of Crime: Hong Kong—China Cross–Border Criminal Activity', *British Journal of Criminology*, 310–28.

VERCHER, A. (1992). *Terrorism in Europe. A Comparative Legal Analysis* (Oxford).

VERGNOLLE, J.-L. (1992). 'The Matthaeus Programme', in M. Anderson. and M. den Boer (eds.), (1992) 171–74.

VERVAELE, J. A. E. (1992). *Fraud against the Community—the Need for European Fraud Legislation* (Deventer).

VIOLANTE, L. (1993). 'Round Table — Citizens and Criminal Justice', in A. Alvazzi del Frate, *et al.* (eds.), (1993) 415–16.

WADE, E. C. S., and BRADLEY, A. W. (1993). *Constitutional and Administrative Law*, 11th ed. (ed. by A. W. Bradley, and K. D. Ewing with T. St J. N. Bates) (London/New York).

WADHAM, J. (1994). 'The Intelligence Services Act 1994'. *The Modern Law Review*, vol. 57, 916–27.

WAEVER, O. (1993). 'Societal Security: the concept' in Waever, O. *et al.* (eds.), (1993) 17–40.

—— BUZAN, B., KELSTRUP, M. and LEMAITRE, P. (eds.), (1993). *Identity. Migration and the New Security Agenda in Europe* (London).

—— and KELSTRUP, M. (1993). 'Europe and its nations: political and cultural identities' in WAEVER, O. *et al.* (eds.), (1993) 40–92.

WALKER, N (1991). *The United Kingdom Police and European Co-operation*, Working Paper III, 'A System of European Police Co-operation after 1992' (Edinburgh).

—— (1992). 'The Dynamics of European Police Cooperation: The UK perspective', *Commonwealth Law Bulletin*, 18, 1509–22.

—— (1993a), 'The Accountability of European Police Institutions', *European Journal on Criminal Policy and Research*, vol. 1, no. 4, 34–52.

—— (1993b), 'The International Dimension', in R. Reiner and S. Spencer (eds.), (1993) *Accountable Policing : Effectiveness Empowerment and Equity* (London), 113–71.

—— (1994a), 'European Integration and European Policing: A Complex Relationship' in M. Anderson and M. den Boer (eds), 22–45.

—— (1994b). 'Reshaping the British Police: the International Angle', *Strategic Government*, vol. 2, No. 1, 25–34.

—— (1995). 'Policing the European Union: The Politics of Transition', in O. Marenin (ed.), *Policing Change, Changing Police* (New York).

WALKER, S. (1992). *The Police in America: An Introduction* 2nd ed. (New York).

WARBRICK, C. and Sullivan, G. R. (1994). 'Criminal Jurisdiction', *International and Comparative Law Quarterly*, vol. 43, 460–66.

WARDLAW, G. (1989). *Political Terrorism: Theory, Tactics and Counter-Measures*, 2nd. ed. (Cambridge).

WEATHERILL, S. (1994). 'Beyond Preemption? Shared Competence and Constitutional Change in the European Community', in D. O'Keeffe and P. Twomey (eds.) 13–33.

—— and BEAUMONT, P. (1993). *EC Law* (London).

WEBER, M. (1948). 'Politics as a Vocation', in *Essays from Max Weber*, (London).

WEILER, J. H. H. (1991). 'The Transformation of Europe', *Yale Law Journal* 100, 2403–83.

WEL, J. VAN DER, and BRUGGEMAN, W. (1993). *Europese Politiële Samenwerking. Internationale Gremia* (Brussels).

WERDMÖLDER, H. and MEEL, P. (1993). 'Jeugdige allochtonen en criminaliteit. Een vergelijkend onderzoek onder Marokkaanse, Turkse, Surinaamse en Antilliaanse jongens', *Tijdschrift voor criminologie*, 3, 35, 252–76.

WERKGROEP VOORONDERZOEK OPSPORINGSMETHODEN (1994). *Opsporing Gezocht*, Tweede Kamer der Staten–Generaal, Vergaderjaar 1994–95, 23 945, nr. 1 ('s–Gravenhage).

WEßLAU, E. (1991). 'Zum Entwurf eines Gesetzes zur Bekämpfung der organisierten Kriminalität', *Bürgerrechte und Polizei*, 39, 2, 42–8.

WILSON, J. Q. and KELLING, G. (1982). 'Broken Windows', *Atlantic Monthly*, March, 29–38.

WILKINSON, P. (1974). *Political Terrorism* (London).

WILKITZKI, P. (1991). 'Defences, Exceptions and Exemptions in the Extradition Law and Practice and the Criminal Policy of the Federal Republic of Germany (Excluding the "Political Offence" Defence), *Revue Internationale de Droit Penal*, vol. 62, 281–89.

—— (1992). 'Development of an Effective International Crime and Justice Programme — A European View', in A. Eser, and O. Lagodny, (eds.), (1992) *Principles and Procedures for a New Transnational Criminal Law* (Freiburg), 267–91.

WOODWARD, R. (1993). 'The Establishment of Europol: A Critique', *European Journal on Criminal Policy and Research* vol. 1, No. 4, 7–33.

WYNGAERT, C. VAN DEN (1980). *The Political Offence Exception to Extradition* (London).

WYNGAERT, C. VAN DEN (1990), 'Applying the European Convention on Human Rights to Extradition: Opening Pandora's Box?', *International and Comparative Law Quarterly*, 39, 757–79.

—— (1991). 'The Political Offence Exception to Extradition: How to Plug the 'Terrorist Loophole' Without Departing from Fundamental Human Rights', *Revue Internationale de Droit Penal*, 62, 291–310.

YOUNG, J. (1984). 'The Political Offence Exception in the Extradition Law of the United Kingdom', *Legal Studies*, vol. 4, 211–23.

ZACHERT, H.-L. (1992a). 'Migratie en Criminaliteit', *Politeia*, 21 December, 14–18.

—— (1992b). 'Der neue kriminalgeographische Raum in Folge der Öffnung des Binnenmarktes' *Politische Studien*, vol. 43, issue 326, 25–36.

ZANDERS, P. (1994). 'Europese Politiesamenwerking in een historisch perspektief', in Transpol (ed.), *Internationalisering door grenzeloze samenwerking* (Lelystad), 7–20.

ZIEGENAUS, H. (1992). 'Sicherheitsdefizite der Grenzöffnung—Kompensationsmöglichkeiten', *Politische Studien*, vol. 43, issue 326, 37–44.

Cases Cited

European Court of Justice:

Case 8/56 Acciaierie Laminatoi Magliano Alpi (ALMA) *v*. High Authority of the European Coal and Steel Community (ECSC) [1957 and 1958] ECR 95.

Case 1/63 Macchiorlati Dalmas & Figli *v*. High Authority of the ECSC [1963] ECR 303.

Cases 41, 44 and 45/69 ACF Chemiefarma and others *v*. Commission [1970] European Court Reports (ECR) 661.

Case 11/70 Internationale Handelsgesellschaft mbH *v*. Einfuhr- und Vorratsstelle für Getreide und Futtermittel [1970] ECR 1125.

Cases 209–15, 218/78 Van Landewyck *v*. Commission [1980] ECR 3125.

Case 117/83 Karl Könecke GmbH *v*. BALM [1984] ECR 3291.

Cases C-89 etc. / 85 A. Ahlström Osakeyhtiö e.a. *v*. Commission [1993] ECR I–1307 [1993] 4 *CMLR* 407.

Case 137/85 Maizena GmbH *v*. BALM [1987] ECR 4587.

Case 281, 283–5, 287/85 Germany and others *v*. Commission [1987] ECR 3203.

Case 288/85 Hauptzollamt Hamburg–Jonas *v*. Plange Kraftfutterwerke GmbH [1987] ECR 611.

Case 186/87 Ian William Cowan *v*. Trésor Public [1989] ECR 195.

Case 321/87 Commission *v*. Belgium [1989] ECR 997.

Case 374/87 ORKEM *v*. Commission [1989] ECR 3283.

Case 68/88 Commission *v*. Greece [1989] ECR 2965.

Case C–265/88 Criminal Proceedings against Lothar Messner [1989] ECR 4209.

Case C–326/88 Anklagemyndighede *v*. Hansen & Son I/S [1990] ECR I–2911.

Case T–1/89 Rhone–Poulenc *v*. Commission [1991] ECR II – 867.

Case C–213/89 The Queen *v*. Secretary of State for Transport, ex parte Factortame Ltd. et al, [1990] ECR I–2433.

Case C–300/89 Commission *v*. Council [1991] ECR I–2867.

Cases C–6/90 and 9/90 Andrea Francovich and another *v*. Italy [1991] ECR I–5357.

Case T–24/90 Automec Srl *v*. EC Commission [1992] 5 *CMLR* 431.

Case C–159/90 Society for the Protection of the Unborn Child Ireland Ltd. *v*. Grogan [1991] ECR I–4685; [1991] 3 *CMLR* 849.

Case C–240/90 Germany *v.* Commission [1992] ECR I–5383.

Case C–271/91 Marshall *v.* Southampton and South West Hampshire Area Health Authority [1993] ECR I–4367 [1993] 3 *CMLR* 293.

Case C–445/93 European Parliament *v.* Commission, OJ. C 1, 4.1.94, pp. 12–13.

Other Cases

Chappell *v.* United Kingdom 1990 12 *EHRR* 1.

R. *v.* Home Secretary *ex parte* Brind [1991] Appeal Cases 696 (House of Lords).

Société Stenuit *v.* France (decision of European Commission of 30 May 1991; case withdrawn from Court of Human Rights) [1992] 14 *EHRR* 509.

Funke *v.* France 1993 16 *EHRR* 297.

Decision of the German Federal Constitutional Court (*Bundesverfassungsgericht*) of 12 October 1993, 2 BvR 2134/92 and 2 BvR 2159/92, BVerfGE 89, 155; *NJW* 1993, 3047; reported in English as Manfred Brunner and others *v.* The European Union Treaty, [1994] 1 *CMLR* 57.

Legislation Cited

Council Regulation 17, First Regulation implementing Articles 85 and 86 of the EEC Treaty, O.J. Special Edition 1962, No. 204/62, page 87.

Council Directive 89/592/EEC of 13 November 1989 co–ordinating regulations on insider dealing, O.J. L 334, 18.11.89, page 30.

Council Directive 91/308/EEC of 10 June 1991 on the prevention of the use of the financial system for the purpose of money laundering, O.J. L.166, 28.6.91, page 77.

Council Directive 91/477/EEC of 18 June 1991 on control of the acquisition and possession of weapons, O.J. L 256, 13.9.91, p. 51.

Council Regulation (EEC) 3677/90 of 13 December 1990 laying down measures to be taken to discourage the diversion of certain substances to the illicit maufacture of narcotic drugs and psychotropic substances, O.J. L 357, 20.12.90, p. 1.

Council Directive 93/7/EEC of 15 March 1993 on the return of cultural objects unlawfully removed from the territory of a Member State, O.J. L 74, 27.3.93, p. 74.

Proposal for a Council Regulation (EC, Euratom) on protection of the Community's financial interests and Proposal for Council of the European Union Act establishing a Convention of the Communities' financial interests, COM (94) 214 final, Brussels, 15.6.1994, 94/0146 (CNS).

Index

Lightning Source UK Ltd.
Milton Keynes UK
UKOW051353200213

206541UK00007B/53/A